Themes for Inclusive Classrooms: Lesson Plans for Every Learner

Laverne Warner, Sharon Lynch, Diana Kay Nabors, and Cynthia G. Simpson

Dedication

To our colleagues in the Department of Language, Literacy, and Special
Populations at Sam Houston State University in Huntsville, TX

Additional Gryphon House Books by the authors:

Inclusive Lesson Plans Throughout the Year by Laverne Warner, Sharon Lynch,
    Cynthia G. Simpson, and Diana Kay Nabors
Preschool Classroom Management by Laverne Warner and Sharon Lynch

EARLY CHILDHOOD

Themes for
INCLUSIVE
Classrooms
Lesson Plans for
Every Learner

Laverne Warner

Sharon Lynch

Diana Kay Nabors

Cynthia G. Simpson

Illustrated by
Deborah C. Johnson

Bulk purchase

Gryphon House books are available for special premiums and sales promotions as well as for fund-raising use. Special editions or book excerpts also can be created to specification. For details, contact the Director of Marketing at Gryphon House.

Disclaimer

Gryphon House, Inc. and the authors cannot be held responsible for damage, mishap, or injury incurred during the use of or because of activities in this book. Appropriate and reasonable caution and adult supervision of children involved in activities and corresponding to the age and capability of each child involved is recommended at all times. Do not leave children unattended at any time. Observe safety and caution at all times.

Every effort has been made to locate copyright and permission information.

Themes for Inclusive Classrooms: Lesson Plans for Every Learner

Laverne Warner, Sharon Lynch, Diana Kay Nabors, Cynthia G. Simpson

Illustrations: Deborah C. Johnson

© 2008 Laverne Warner, Sharon Lynch, Diana Kay Nabors, and Cynthia G. Simpson
Printed in the United States of America.

Published by Gryphon House, Inc.
10726 Tucker Street, Beltsville, MD 20705
301.595.9500; 301.595.0051 (fax); 800.638.0928 (toll-free)

Visit us on the web at www.ghbooks.com

Library of Congress Cataloging-in-Publication Data
Themes for inclusive classrooms : lesson plans for every learner / Laverne Warner ... [et al.].
      p. cm.
   ISBN 978-0-87659-004-1
 1. Inclusive education--United States. 2. Children with disabilities--Education (Early childhood)--United States. 3. Lesson planning--United States. I. Warner, Laverne, 1941-
   LC1201.T468 2008
   371.9'043--dc22

                        2007047334

Gryphon House is a member of the Green Press Initiative, a nonprofit program dedicated to supporting publishers in their efforts to reduce their use of fiber-sourced forests. This book is printed on paper using 30% post-consumer waste. For further information, visit www.greenpressinitiative.org.

Table of Contents

Introduction

Good teachers plan. Just as architects use blueprints, doctors and dentists use x-rays and pilots use flight plans, effective teachers organize for instruction. They think about what they want to teach, how they want to teach it, and when they will teach it. Implementing effective instruction requires forethought, time, and knowledge of children.

Themes for Inclusive Classrooms: Lesson Plans for Every Learner is designed for both veteran and novice teachers who have a classroom with a child (or children) with special needs, or who have a classroom of typically developing children. This book will help new teachers develop plans and provide veteran teachers with new ideas and approaches to add spark their classroom teaching.

What Is Lesson Planning?

What does lesson planning mean? Basically, six components are essential for each lesson plan.

1. Objective(s) (what you want to teach)
2. Materials needed for the lesson
3. The lesson activity (or activities)
4. Review of the content (sometimes referred to as closure)
5. Assessment strategy (to determine what children learned from the lesson)
6. Curriculum extensions (multiple extensions of a lesson that connect the concept to other curricular areas)

Planning ensures that each component is included in the lesson. Writing objectives for every lesson shows teachers' understanding that good planning yields results. When a lesson is well planned with a specific objective (or objectives) in mind, then teacher are better able to demonstrate observable outcomes. In addition, if lessons aren't going well, teachers can notice the problems and adjust accordingly. They might modify the activity, spontaneously choose another activity, or they might abandon the lesson, choosing to teach it at a later date. Planning follow-up activities in various centers is also easier if the learning objective(s) is clear.

Assessment strategies are a direct effort to determine children's knowledge and skill acquisition. In an era of accountability, all interested parties, including teachers and parents, want to know what children are learning.

Lesson plans are the foundation that keeps the day running smoothly from beginning to end. Teachers find planning helps keep children on task and motivated to learn. Once a concept has been introduced, teachers can determine whether children have acquired the knowledge and plan for additional exposure to the concept if necessary. Teachers are better able to communicate to parents the content children have received and provide feedback to them about whether children are learning the information.

Teachers also discover that planning ahead makes it more possible to meet the needs of all children. This book recognizes that all children learn in a variety of ways. No one lesson fits all children. If a child has autism, for example, modifications are needed to meet her or his needs. If teachers plan ahead, they can include lesson adaptations for every child in the group. *Themes for Inclusive Classrooms: Lesson Plans for Every Learner* provides recommended modifications and accommodations that help teachers plan for all the children in the classroom.

Good teachers plan; great teachers plan and reflect. After the lesson is taught, they ask themselves, "What went well? How can I improve this lesson? Did I meet Oralio's needs today? And Taylor's? What will I do differently next time I use this lesson?" If plans aren't working, then teachers need to develop alternative strategies to meet the needs of the children they serve.

Themes for Inclusive Classrooms: Lesson Plans for Every Learner will be one of the resources teachers use to prepare lessons for their preschool classrooms. No one resource is ever completely adequate for any classroom, but we are hopeful that what you find in this book will improve the quality of teaching in your classroom.

Lesson Planning for Inclusive Early Childhood Classrooms

Planning for Children's Needs

The phrase "developmentally appropriate practice" means that the teaching strategies used and classroom activities planned for young children match their developmental needs and characteristics. Children should have experiences that allow them to feel competent as learners, and, at the same time, that are challenging enough to ensure that they are learning.

Planning to meet children's needs means that you, as the teacher or caregiver, know your children. If you are working in a kindergarten setting, you know that most five-year-olds are curious, active, social, spontaneous, and egocentric. When you plan for kindergartners, organize activities that will keep them busy, spark their creative and cognitive minds, and provide social experiences. Beyond that, you need to know individual children. For example, Martin is five, but he may be shy, reserved, quiet, intelligent, and methodic in his approach to learning, quite unlike his peers. As Martin's teacher, you plan activities to entice him and enhance his capacity for learning. When you plan for children, look at all aspects of children's development, taking into account individual differences.

Planning for children's needs also means focusing on all developmental domains, including physical (movement and physical activity), social and emotional (interactions with others), intellectual or cognitive (being challenged to learn), and creative (self-expression).

As you plan for children's learning, consider all aspects of children's development, including:
+ providing activities that promote success in the classroom,
+ encouraging important social and emotional skills essential to lifelong physical and mental health,
+ developing age-appropriate expressive experiences, and
+ allowing exploration and discovery to ensure that learning is meaningful and relevant.

Create diverse lesson plans that meet many of the children's needs, interests, and abilities. While listening to a book may not hold the interests of all of the children, reading about alligators (or any other animal that the children are interested in), then crawling like alligators, snapping mouths like alligators, and pretending to sleep or swim like alligators keeps the lesson alive and the children engaged. As an observant teacher, you know what children need and you plan accordingly.

Best Practices in Inclusive Early Childhood Classrooms

The principles that guide best practices include:
+ developing topics of study that are relevant to the children you teach;
+ allowing children choices as much as possible;
+ limiting large-group experiences;
+ providing activities that meet children's developmental needs;
+ using centers and center play for child-directed play and instructional purposes;
+ developing hands-on activities that allow children to work directly with objects and materials in their environment;
+ utilizing individualized instruction as often as possible; and
+ planning activities that offer multi-level challenges for children.

The guidelines suggest that every classroom varies in its approach to what constitutes "best practices." A teacher's class in urban Detroit is likely to be different in cultural makeup from a class of children in Del Rio, Texas. Appropriate classroom strategies begin with the children in the classroom and match the guidelines in diverse ways. Strategies for use in a classroom are detailed below.

Center Choices
Children need opportunities for making choices every day. Decision-making skills are developed as children decide which center to visit. Learning to select activities and staying with a choice offer important lessons.

Instructional Centers
While centers provide opportunities for child-directed play, some may be designed for specific instructional purposes. For example, a Writing Center allows children to explore and experiment with print. A Literacy Center shows how print is formed. Asking children to dictate their stories as you (or other helpers in the classroom) write them stresses the importance of being able to use and read print.

Discovery Centers
Set up special tables in the classroom to display materials relating to a topic of study that attract children to topics they might otherwise overlook. For example, placing an Ant Farm and books about ants on a special table allows children to

observe and find out about ants on their own; hence, the name Discovery Center!

Group (or Circle) Times
Limit large group time. Presenting lessons early in the morning when children are fresh allows them to absorb information more easily. Keeping activities within lessons short (about 20 minutes) and to the point helps children gain maximum knowledge in a minimum of time. Overall, lessons should take no longer than 20–30 minutes. Vary activities within the lesson to accommodate children's needs across developmental domains.

Hands-On Experiences
Focus on hands-on activities that allow children to safely touch, taste, smell, and look closely at objects that are topics of classroom discussion. For example, if earthworms are the topic, try to bring earthworms to class. If feather pillows are a topic of discussion, bring in feather pillows for children to touch and smell. Cutting open and tasting a watermelon is far more engaging for children than simply looking at a picture of a watermelon. Hands-on experiences offer powerful learning opportunities.

Projects
Projects typically require several days or even weeks to complete; they accompany and relate to a topic and to children's interests. Examples include building a fire truck during a transportation theme, constructing a farm in the sandbox when learning about farm animals, making pretend musical instruments when talking about music and musicians, or acting out nursery rhymes.

Word Walls
Word Walls are permanent collections of words that are meaningful to children. Word Walls may be on chalkboards, on charts, or on large pieces of paper. As themes are introduced to children, write down words that accompany the themes to help children understand that print has meaning and that print is predictable (the words are pronounced the same way each time one sees them. Pairing pictures with words on the Word Wall helps children to associate print with concepts.

Big Books
Big books are oversized children's books that are designed for use with groups of children. The pages and pictures are large, and the print is large. When you use big books, run your hands under the print to help children see specific words and understand that print has meaning.

Individualized Instruction

Working one-on-one with children in various centers is the best way to approach and support their learning. Individualized instruction is as simple as helping a child put a puzzle together or sitting nearby and responding to children's questions on how to make certain alphabet letters. In inclusive classrooms, the need for individualized instruction is critical.

Planning the Classroom Environment

The classroom environment is the child's home away from home as well as the learning environment. The classroom must be warm and inviting and packed with learning opportunities for the children as they learn new concepts and practice developing ones. Set up classrooms that:

✦ are visually appealing,
✦ offer choices to all children,
✦ have logically arranged centers, and
✦ are safe places to learn.

Visual Appeal

Every classroom should offer an appealing work environment for you and an enticing learning environment for children. Rugs and mats add warmth to tile floors. Use natural light from windows as much as possible and reduce the overhead lights (often fluorescent lighting). The warm, full spectrum of natural classroom light and colors within the classroom will add a warm healthy glow to your classroom. Add decorations, including children's work and charts, around the classroom for display and to reinforce skills. Remember to place these displays at the children's eye level. You may need to change the light bulbs in your classroom if the glare interferes with children's learning.

Walk around your classroom on your knees to see what the children see. You may be surprised that they have a different view of the room. You also want the room to be pleasant to other adults that enter the room. When you put up material for adults, hang it at a level appropriate for them. Hanging things from the ceiling can be eye-appealing to children as they scan the total environment, but it is out of their line of sight as they work in the classroom. Hang appropriate items from the ceiling, such as an art project of birds; rules, directions, or reinforcement items are not appropriate to hang from the ceiling.

Offer a Choice to All Children

In planning the layout of the classroom it is important to designate places for large group activities, small group activities, and individual activities. The area for large group gatherings may include a cart or shelf. This is where you can keep your daily and weekly plans, folders for observational notes, and materials for that day's group lesson. The children will sit on the floor in this large group area, so displays and charts should be at their seated eye level. The space should be large enough for each child in the group to stand or sit without touching or bumping other children. A child's "bubble space" is the size of a small, invisible bubble that surrounds the child when seated cross-legged on the floor and making an "elbows in" circle around his or her body. When playing movement games this "bubble space" expands to the size of full arm circles around the child's body. To create a large enough space in the classroom for large group times, visualize the number of children and their "bubble space" areas. Keep this large group area free of tables, chairs, open shelves, and anything else that may hinder children from participating in group activities.

Small group areas can be situated within activity centers or in portions of the large group area. Organize activity centers so that the children will have a choice of activities. The total number of places in the activity centers should be at least one and one-half times the number of children in the classroom. For example, if there are 16 children in your class, plan to have 24 possible places for children to select. Each center should have a posted number of how many participants are allowed in that center, determined by the type of activity. For example, the space in the block area may allow for four to six children, where the Listening Center may only allow for two to four children. Arrange all materials in activity centers so they are easily accessible to all of the children, including children who are limited in physical abilities by either range of motion or size. Include all necessary materials in that center so the children do not need to leave the center to get what they need. Shelves and trays allow for easy access, neat organization, and simple cleanup of the materials.

Children need time to learn with others and also time to learn alone. Many children can work together in an activity center, but some children may wish to have a space away from others to work on a project, read a book, or just think. It is important to plan for individual space for children. To meet the needs of the children in your classroom, you may need to set up both a quiet area with pillows to comfort the child and a table/chair area where a child can work on a difficult problem or puzzle. Not only is it important to provide for individual learning areas, it is also important to provide an individual "home base" area for each child, a place where each child has his or her own space, whether a particular seat or rug on the floor or a cubby and a hook for his or her exclusive use. This gives each child ownership of a small place in the classroom, a physical spot that represents their belongingness in the class.

Arrangement of Centers

When children are fully engaged in play, some centers are louder than others. It is wise to separate the noisier centers, such as Home Living and Blocks, from the quieter centers, such as the Listening Center, which could be interrupted by the activity noise coming from the Block Center. Create a wave of sound in the classroom by placing noisier centers next to mid-activity noise centers, which, in turn, are next to quiet centers. Then continue around the room with mid-activity noise centers, and then back to noisier centers. Locate messy centers that need water for cleanup near a classroom sink. Centers that need electricity, such as the Listening Center, should be near a wall electrical outlet to avoid stretching electrical cords across the room. During the course of the year, there will be changes to your centers. Add or remove materials from various centers as children grow in knowledge and experience. Some centers are specific to a particular topic or theme and are only set up in the classroom during the time of study.

Planning your classroom environment provides you and the children with an inviting place for learning. As you plan your classroom, lay out the centers on paper prior to moving furniture. Don't be surprised if you need to shift some centers around once you have seen the centers come alive with children and learning opportunities.

Safety

Safety is always an important consideration in the early childhood classroom. In order to ensure a safe classroom, examine class materials and furniture every day. Remove any broken materials until they are repaired or replaced. Teaching children how to use materials properly in activity centers will reduce the likelihood of broken materials and help to ensure that no harm will come to them. But accidents do happen. Observation and monitoring keep children safe.

Maintaining visual contact with children is a must for assuring their safety, assessing their learning, and using inquiry to develop their learning. Low shelving and dividers between activity centers allow you to monitor all areas of the classroom wherever you are located.

Traffic flow in the classroom is another important consideration. Wide open spaces invite large, active movements; smaller areas invite a more careful and planned movement. Placing the large group area on one side or corner of a classroom reduces the likelihood that children will run, hop, and dance their way to another center. Areas between activity centers must be free of items that may be accidentally stepped on or tripped over. This includes the arms, legs, and hands of other children. In each activity center, it is best to have the children engage in activities in a way that their bodies and the materials they are using do not spill over into traffic areas. Define activity areas by placing colored tape on the floor or rugs in the activity center.

Including All Children: Modifications and Accommodations

Every child with a disability has the right to accommodations and modifications in order to succeed. For children with disabilities to be successful both socially and academically, they may require specific accommodations to lessons and instruction, as well as specific adaptations to the physical environment.

The Individuals with Disabilities Education Act (IDEA) identifies and defines disabilities that establish eligibility for special education services. The law states that children with disabilities should be served in the environment that is most like that of their non-disabled peers (least restrictive environment). This environment is often referred to as an inclusive setting.

For effective inclusion, you must be flexible, adaptable, and supportive of all children. You must be willing to make adaptations to the structure of the classroom and in the delivery of instruction to meet the challenge of including children with disabilities into the setting with non-disabled peers (SPeNCE, 2001). This section provides general guidelines and specific examples of instructional modifications and classroom accommodations.

General Characteristics of Children With Specific Disabilities

Children with specific disabilities are often lumped into one "disability category" without consideration of the type of disability that child may have. Children with special needs who are more commonly placed in inclusive early childhood classrooms are often placed in a broad category of "higher-incidence" disabilities. Such disabilities include speech and language impairments, specific learning disabilities, emotional disturbance, and mental retardation. The degree of severity of each disability may vary from mild to more severe in nature. Children with low-incidence disabilities such as visual impairments, hearing impairments, orthopedic impairments, autism, other health impairments, and severe multiple impairments are not seen as often in child care settings. However, in recent years, the number of children with lower-incidence disabilities in early childhood classrooms has been rising.

Although 13 disabilities are addressed in IDEA 2004, the following disability categories are more closely linked to the structure of this book. Although **Learning Disabilities** is a category identified in IDEA, we decided not to address Learning Disabilities in the accommodation sections of each lesson plan. For preschoolers, learning disabilities when diagnosed, fall typically in the areas of listening comprehension and oral expression. The accommodations for speech and language impairments for each chapter address each of these areas.

In recent years, the number of children diagnosed with **Autism** has increased, and, thus, more children with autism are being enrolled in early childhood classrooms. Autism is classified as a developmental disability, generally becoming evident before the age of three. Children with autism typically have difficulty in communication and social interactions. They frequently demonstrate repetitive motor behaviors such as rocking or hand weaving.

Children with **Speech and Language Disorders** are commonly cared for in inclusive classrooms. Children with such impairments tend to have problems in communication and possibly in oral motor functions. Children with speech and language disorders may have impairments related specifically to the proper enunciation of specific sounds (articulation disorders) or language impairments that involve syntax or semantic errors in speech. Language disorders may also involve delayed language or limited vocabulary.

A **Hearing Impairment,** as referred to in this book, is an impairment in hearing that negatively affects a child's educational performance. This impairment would not be so severe that a child could not hear speech and environmental sounds in the classroom when wearing a hearing aid. If the child cannot hear speech or environmental sounds, even with the help of a hearing aid, then the child would be identified as deaf.

Another sensory impairment addressed within the accommodation section of the lesson plans is **Visual Impairment.** Children with visual impairments are identified as those children who, even with correction (such as glasses or contacts), experience limited vision that adversely affects their educational experience.

The National Dissemination Center for Children with Disabilities (NICHCY) defines **Mental Retardation** as a term used "when a person has certain limitations in mental functioning and in skills such as communicating, taking care of him or herself, and social skills. These limitations will cause a child to learn and develop more slowly than a typical child. Children with mental retardation may take longer to learn to speak, walk, and take care of their personal needs such as dressing or eating." Mental retardation may or may not coexist with other specific disabilities such as speech and language impairment, a hearing impairment or other health impairments. Within the context of this book, we use the term **Cognitive and/or Developmental Delays** rather than mental retardation because many early education programs do not diagnose mental retardation at young ages.

Emotional Disturbance is another disability identified under IDEA. Children identified with an emotional disturbance show one of the following problems for an extended period of time:
+ difficulty learning that is not due to lack of intelligence, problems with vision or hearing, or health problems;
+ difficulty getting along with peers or teachers;
+ inappropriate types of behavior or feelings under normal circumstances;
+ an overall mood of unhappiness or depression that is not due to temporary problems in the home or in development; and
+ a tendency to develop physical symptoms (for example, stomachaches or headaches) or fears associated with personal or school problems.

To be diagnosed as emotionally disturbed, the child shows symptoms far beyond typical childhood behavior when experiencing a traumatic life event.

Emotional disturbance is usually not the result of a single cause. It is often associated with a variety of factors, such as problems in the home, difficulty in school with developmental skills such as language and later academic skills, a family history of emotional problems, and environmental stressors. A psychologist diagnoses this disability. Although emotional disturbance is occasionally diagnosed in preschoolers, it is identified most often in the upper elementary and middle school years.

Other Health Impairments refer to significant limitations in strength, vitality, or alertness that affect a child's learning. This disability can be the result of asthma, heart problems, diabetes, or other health issues, and includes children diagnosed with **Attention Deficit Hyperactivity Disorder (ADHD).** ADHD is diagnosed by a physician or psychologist, and includes children with serious problems with overactivity or attention, or both.

Children with **Orthopedic Impairments** have physical disabilities such as a loss of limb, cerebral palsy, or amputation that negatively affects their educational experience. Many children with specific Orthopedic Impairments use wheelchairs or other assistive devices for mobility.

The last specific disability is **Multiple Disabilities.** A child with a multiple disabilities possesses a combination of specific disabilities; for example, an orthopedic disability and developmental delays.

For additional information, the National Dissemination Center for Children with Disabilities—a leading source of information and resources for parents, caregivers, educators, and other professionals in the field of special education—provides a complete resource list and fact sheet on each of the above mentioned disabilities. Fact sheets, parent resources, and teaching tips are available on its website (www.nichcy.org/resources).

Accommodations or Modifications

Accommodations or modifications for children with special needs usually focus on three primary areas: the curriculum, the method or delivery of instruction, and the physical environment. Within these areas, eight areas where modifications are most frequently made in the classroom are as follows:

+ environmental support—altering the physical environment to increase participation,
+ materials adaptation—modifying materials to promote independence,
+ activity simplification—breaking down a complicated task into smaller parts or steps,
+ child preferences—capitalizing on a child's favorite activity,
+ special equipment—using adaptive devices to facilitate participation,
+ adult support—employing direct adult intervention to support the child's efforts,
+ peer support—having classmates help children learn by modeling and assistance, and

✦ invisible support—arranging naturally occurring events to assist inclusion (Sandall et al, in press).

The terms *modifying* and *accommodating* are two separate concepts. To accommodate instruction, you might provide a new way for a child to access information, or change how the child demonstrates mastery of a skill. Accommodating instruction, however, does not mean providing a substantial change in the level, content, or assessment criteria. This accommodation could be thought of as a support to enable the child to utilize the same learning material as the other children. For example, an accommodation for a child with a language impairment might entail assessing her learning by having her choose a picture to represent a concept (such as which ball is blue), rather than telling you verbally. The child is still expected to learn the concept, although she is not required to tell you. Instead of telling you that one ball is blue, she would point to the picture of a blue ball when shown pictures of balls that are different colors.

A *modification* would entail changing the criteria on an assessment task. For instance, instead of assessing a child's ability to recite numbers 1–10, the child might be expected to recite the numbers 1–5. A modification would be a change in what a child is expected to learn.

Deciding which accommodations or modifications to use will depend on the instructional objective and the individual needs of the child. In public school settings, the Individual Education Plan (IEP) team determines which accommodations and adaptations are appropriate based on a variety of data. Examples of accommodations and modifications to the classroom environment, curriculum content, and method of instruction and assessment can be found in Tables 1–3.

Accommodations and modifications are types of adaptations that are made to the environment, curriculum, instruction, or assessment practices in order for children with disabilities to be successful learners and to participate actively with other children in the classroom and in whole-school activities (Peak Parent Center, 2003). However, these adaptations alone cannot ensure the success of children with disabilities in inclusive settings. You must provide a variety of measures, including promoting interaction among children with and without disabilities. Also important is the evaluation of your own beliefs and attitudes toward inclusion (SPeNCE, 2001). Successful inclusion is guided by your willingness to accept change and provide accommodations within the daily routine.

Table 1

Examples of Accommodations/ Modifications to the Classroom Environment

Altering seating arrangements to meet the needs of the child, such as near the teacher or a peer buddy, near a quiet space, and so on	All identified disabilities
Rearranging the layout of classroom furniture to meet children's needs	All identified disabilities
Providing space for movement within the classroom setting	Orthopedic Impairment
Limiting clutter on walls as a means to reduce distractions	Autism, Other Health Impairment (ADHD)
Designating quiet areas in the room	Autism, Emotional Disturbance
Providing carpet squares for young children to sit on	Autism
Adapting writing utensils/building up pencils/pens/paintbrushes	Orthopedic Impairment
Providing soft music or "white noise"	All identified disabilities, except Autism, if used for sensory stimulation
Reducing noise level in room	Visual Impairment, Hearing Impairment
Changing amount of lighting/brightening or dimming	Visual Impairment, Autism
Adapting furniture, such as lowering chairs, securing desks	Orthopedic Impairment
Creating slant boards throughout room for writing support and painting	Orthopedic Impairment
Using pegs to adapt handles on puzzles, doors, shelving, coat racks, and backpack areas	Orthopedic Impairment, Cognitive and/or Developmental Delay

Table 2

Examples of Accommodations/ Modifications to Curriculum Content

Using real objects instead of pictures for math-based activities involving counting aloud or with fingers	Cognitive and/or Developmental Delay
Reducing number of steps involved in completing a specific task	Cognitive and/or Developmental Delay
Accepting answers of general concepts vs. specific concepts	Autism, Cognitive and/or Developmental Delay
Assigning child a peer buddy for activity support	Cognitive and/or Developmental Delay, Emotional Disturbance

Table 3

Examples of Accommodations/ Modifications to the Mode of Instruction and Evaluation

Providing one-to-one instruction	All identified disabilities
Avoiding speaking with your back to the child	Hearing Impairments
Providing daily structure	Autism, Emotional Disturbance, Cognitive and/or Developmental Delay
Using short sentences and simple directions	Cognitive and/or Developmental Delay, Autism
Modifying pace of instruction	Cognitive and/or Developmental Delay
Prefacing activity with introduction/ sequence of events	Visual Impairments
Varying method of instruction, such as small groups, large group and independent activities	Cognitive and/or Developmental Delay
Providing more frequent questioning and feedback	Autism, Cognitive and/or Developmental Delay
Providing sample of end product	Cognitive and/or Developmental Delay, Autism
Incorporating sign language into daily activities, such as Circle Time, small group activities, and large group instruction	Hearing Impairments

Table 3

Examples of Accommodations/ Modifications to the Mode of Instruction and Evaluation (continued)

Providing more frequent opportunities for language usage	Speech and Language Impairment
Encouraging and reinforcing positive behavior	All identified disabilities with emphasis on Emotional Disturbance
Increasing size of font on visual presentations (utilization of Big Books)	Visual Impairments
Extending "wait time" for child's responses	Autism, Cognitive and/or Developmental Delay, Speech and Language Impairment
Allowing additional time to complete tasks and activities	Cognitive and/or Developmental Delay, Emotional Disturbance
Incorporating switches or other assistive technology devices	Orthopedic Impairments, Multiple Disabilities
Adapting evaluation to include portfolios or video/audio recordings	Visual Impairments
Using activity and self-monitoring checklists with pictorial representation	Autism, Cognitive and/or Developmental Delay
Providing opportunities to redirect child's behavior as needed, with constant feedback	Emotional Disturbance, Cognitive and/or Developmental Delay
Supporting activities with sensory materials	Visual Impairments
Using bookstands to hold materials in place	Orthopedic Impairments
Using real objects instead of pictures whenever possible	All children benefit from this form of instruction including children with and without disabilities

Following are some general modifications/accommodations for each category of children with special needs. For example:

General Modifications/Accommodations to Consider When Teaching Children with Autism:
+ During the lesson, use pictures, objects, signs, and gestures to provide visual support for the child.
+ Refer to pictures and objects as you present the lesson.

General Modifications/Accommodations to Consider When Teaching Children with Speech or Language Impairments:
+ Provide a carrier phrase if the child does not respond to a question. An example of a carrier phrase is to show a child a toy plane or a picture of a plan and say, "When we go on an airplane it ____." If the child responds "flies," then expand the response by saying, "It flies in the sky." If the child does not respond, then supply the word "flies" and ask the child to repeat it.
+ When brainstorming, let other children's responses serve as a model of the type of response needed.

General Modifications/Accommodations to Consider When Teaching Children with Hearing Impairments:
+ Seat the child across from you where he can see your lips and face.
+ Repeat key concepts and check for understanding periodically.
+ Use pictures and objects to refer to throughout the lesson.

General Modifications/Accommodations to Consider When Teaching Children with Visual Impairments:
+ Verbally describe books and pictures.
+ Describe pictures as you present them.
+ When showing objects, let the child feel and touch them.

General Modifications/Accommodations to Consider When Teaching Children with Cognitive and/or Developmental Disabilities:
+ Use short sentences and simple vocabulary.
+ Repeat key concepts from the lesson and review them daily after completing the lesson.

General Modifications/Accommodations to Consider When Teaching Children with Emotional Disturbance:
+ Seat the child next to you during the lesson.

General Modifications/Accommodations to Consider When Teaching Children with Other Health Impairments/Attention Deficit Hyperactivity Disorder:
+ Make sure that you have the child's attention before you speak.
+ Establish a consistent signal to get the child's attention.

General Modifications/Accommodations to Consider When Teaching Children with Orthopedic Impairments:

✦ Help the child do the motions in the song.

Writing Instructional Objectives

In this age of accountability, instructional objectives are an important aspect of educational programs. Writing instructional objectives helps you use your time, and the children's time, wisely.

Use these steps for developing instructional objectives:
1. Decide exactly what you want to teach.
2. Write what you want to teach in observable and measurable terms.
3. Divide the skills that you want to teach into several smaller parts, if needed.

What to Teach
Effective educational programs begin with effective curriculum development. If your center or school has an adopted curriculum, it may have a list of overall goals targeted for young children. While the goals listed in the curriculum are appropriate for the children, they often are broad rather than specific. Instructional objectives should help you determine what you want to teach as well as the concepts children should learn. For example, the curriculum may have as a goal, "The child will develop an awareness of shapes." This age-appropriate and valid aim requires work before it takes the form of an instructional objective. You must decide exactly what you want to teach in relationship to the goal. Which shapes do you want children to recognize? How will they show you that they recognize the shapes? Do you expect them to name each shape? How will they describe the shapes? Consider questions such as these when you determine instructional objectives.

Stating the Objective Behaviorally
When you state the objective behaviorally, describe a behavior or action that is observable and measurable. For example, if you expect children to recognize shapes, they must do this through some specific action, such as pointing to named shapes (circle, square, triangle), naming shapes (circle, square, triangle), or verbally describing shapes (the round one, the one with three sides). If you expect children to know letters of the alphabet, they must demonstrate this knowledge in a manner such as pointing to named letters or naming the letters presented.

Some words are associated with visible and measurable objectives, while other words are vague and non-explicit. The chart on the next page gives examples of clear versus vague vocabulary.

Vague	Clear
Knows colors	Points to named primary colors
Recognizes shapes	Names circle, square, triangle
Appreciates	Tells three good things about…
Participates	Sings songs with the group; follows directions given in a group; uses three-word sentences related to ongoing activity
Attends to	Looks at speaker during group activity
Learns	Verbally answers three questions about…; tells three characteristics of…
Enjoys	Demonstrates positive facial expression

Instructional Objective to Activities

When you teach, you start from the instructional objective and then use developmentally appropriate activities to teach the specific objective. For example, you can start from the objective "The child will use a complete sentence to describe one characteristic of a shape (circle, square, triangle)." The activity could be an art activity where children decorate masks with various pre-cut shapes. When the children share their masks with the class, they can describe the masks. You can scaffold the children's descriptions so the children describe the shapes they used on their masks.

Another example is illustrated in the table below that shows how one developmentally appropriate skill can be addressed during several ongoing activities. When you know the concepts and skills that you want to teach, you can weave them throughout your daily schedule.

One Objective	Many Activities
The child will verbally use the terms "big" and "little" to describe sizes.	Chooses car (big/little) to play with during centers
	Describes turtles as big/little during a unit on turtles
	Chooses the ball (big/little) to play with during outdoor play
	Chooses the mat (big/little) to sit on during Circle Time

Activity to Instructional Objectives

Even if you have a wealth of knowledge of activities that children enjoy, you may not have analyzed the activities for suitability in exploring the skills incorporated within the activity. When you analyze the activity, you will find many learning opportunities for addressing instructional objectives related to the school curriculum.

The table below shows how one activity involves many skills. When you plan your daily schedule and are aware of concepts and skills that need to be addressed, you can maximize the children's opportunities to learn.

One Activity	Many Objectives
Painting on an easel	The child will name primary colors (select paint color of choice).
	The child will use the words big/little to describe objects (choose a paintbrush).
	The child will use pincer grasp to pick up objects.
	The child will paint/draw/color, keeping within the boundaries of the page.

Things to Remember

The following guidelines should help you in developing instructional objectives:

+ Instructional objectives should be observable and measurable.
+ Instructional objectives can be broken down into smaller units, as needed.
+ Instructional objectives can use a variety of activities to teach skills.
+ Activities can be analyzed to determine the skills that they incorporate.
+ In the age of accountability, it is vital to understand what you are teaching.

Planning for Curriculum Connections

Planned lessons may highlight a single curriculum area such as science or math and still cover additional curricular areas. During the planning phase, assess what you know about the children and their knowledge base. This will include assessing what the children have previously learned or experienced about the topic at hand, what the children want to know about the topic, and what additional knowledge is important for the children to experience. This three-tiered process will help you make the activity relevant and purposeful. Connection to other curricular areas will allow the children to practice the new concept and to view it in other ways.

For instance, the child who sees a few raindrops on a window may know that these droplets can be measured and counted. He can count the droplets. He can reproduce the location of the drops on a piece of paper. The child may even describe the droplets using size and positional relationships: "The big one is above the two little ones." The observation, recording, and discussion demonstrate the child's ability to use the scientific process to organize and make meaning in his or her environment.

In a well-planned classroom, you can add to the experiences of the raindrop with an oral language discussion about raindrops or by singing a song, such as "Pitter, Patter." The Literacy Center may offer books about rain, water, and storms. In the Science Center, there may be eyedroppers, colored water, jar lids, and measuring beakers. In the Art Center, colored water, straws, and art paper will allow children to create designs with water droplets. These fun, varied activities bring a single educational topic into many different curricular areas.

A well designed classroom will allow for multiple extensions of a lesson, providing various forms that illustrate meaningful connections between the concept and the curricular areas. Content areas such as Math, Science, Language and Literacy, Social Studies, Art, Music, and Dramatic Play often include learning that overlaps areas. For example, even though counting from 1–10 is a math concept, blending this exercise with manipulative ladybugs adds the science-based component of observation. Children can count the dots on the back of a ladybug using one-to-one correspondence. They can read a story about the protective coloration of the ladybug (Science and Literacy). This can be infused with songs about ladybugs and physical movement activities as children observe and catch ladybugs on the playground (Music, Movement, and Outdoors).

Teaching through the unit themes in this book allows children to learn concepts in various curricular areas. Each unit addresses a variety of curricular areas using different approaches to meet children's developmental domains of learning.

Assessment and Evaluation of Young Children

The National Association for the Education of Young Children (NAEYC) promotes and provides resources on developmentally appropriate practices— including assessment of young children—to teachers. Understanding that young children are in a rapid period of growth and development and are easily distracted makes it clear that assessment of young children can pose unique problems (Katz, 1997), including short attention spans, inability to establish rapport with unfamiliar adults, separation from parents or primary caregivers, inconsistency in responses, insufficient expressive language, heightened stress during the assessment process, and lack of sensitivity towards cultural differences. Such factors suggest that traditional standardized assessment practices acceptable for older children may hold little value in the assessment of young children.

Recognizing the problems associated with assessing young children and acting proactively, many teachers and caregivers have turned toward alternative means in assessing young children. Portfolio assessment is one form of alternative assessment emerging in the field of education. Regardless of which type of assessment process you choose to implement in your classroom, you should use ongoing assessment, multiple methods of assessment, and common sense when examining results of the assessment data obtained from young children.

Purpose of Assessment

As you select the type of assessment processes to use in your classroom, first examine the main purposes for which the assessment data will be used, which may include:

✦ for instructional planning,
✦ to ensure teaching effectiveness,
✦ to communicate and provide feedback to families,
✦ to establish eligibility for special education services,
✦ to guide curriculum and instruction decisions,
✦ for placement or promotion purposes, and
✦ to monitor the progress of a child in meeting standards or guidelines.

Principles and Guidelines in Assessing Young Children

After determining the need for assessment and the purpose of the assessment results, begin to set up the assessment process of your choice. Adhere to general principles and guidelines to assure that the assessment process is valid and reliable. Bates and Barratt (2000) offer six general principles for screening and assessment.

1. Assessment should be conducted only if such assessment will benefit the child.
2. Assessment should be reliable, valid, fair, and tailored to a specific purpose.
3. Method and content of data collection should be age-appropriate.
4. Assessment should be linguistically appropriate.
5. Parents should be a valued as a source of information.
6. Policies should recognize that the relationship of results obtained by the assessment of young children to later performance increases with the child's age.

In conducting any assessment, it is your responsibility to remain fair and impartial. This can be achieved by being as objective as possible, avoiding labeling or categorizing children, accurately collecting and recording information, and taking time to reflect on assessment procedures and instructional practices.

Authentic Assessment

The use of authentic assessment with young children has increased in the past decade with the recognition that the formal, standardized assessment measures used for older children often fail to evaluate accurately what learning has taken place with young children. Authentic assessment can provide reliable and usable information. To evaluate what a person has learned, the assessment used should provide a collective picture of an individual child's strengths and weaknesses. Authentic assessment processes used with young children present them with real-world situations and challenges that require them to apply their knowledge and skills in responding to tasks in meaningful, real-life contexts.

Portfolio Assessment

The use of portfolios has increased as teachers have become more involved in designing curriculum and assessing children. Portfolio assessment is defined as a purposeful collection of children's work samples that displays progress of predetermined outcomes and achievements in one or more developmental domains. Together with the child, you systematically collect the work sampling over time. This "snapshot" of a child's classroom-based performance can be integrated into existing curriculum, allowing the portfolio to be seen as a supplement to curriculum rather than a separate assessment measurement.

"Collect, Select, and Reflect" has been loosely used as a starting point for entering into the portfolio process. As the statement implies, you and the children begin to collect children's work samples throughout the year. The materials selected should align with the purpose of the assessment process.

Sample Items for Children's Portfolios

Paintings	Drawings
Writing Samples	Photographs/Videos/Audio tapes
Dictated Stories	Checklists
Children's Journals	Parent Comments/Interviews
Children's Reflections	Anecdotal Records
Teacher Comments	Documentation of Peer Interactions

Strong samples of work provide an accurate, "authentic" picture of the needs of the individual child and can provide a mechanism to evaluate how the curriculum used will meet (or has met) those needs. This holds true especially when assessing children with identified or possible disabilities.

Once the collection process is underway, you and the child should collaboratively select items to place into the portfolio (a container that can be placed within reach of the children and can hold an ample amount of materials). These items must match the purpose of the assessment. For instance, if the purpose of assessment is evaluating the effectiveness of the literacy program, writing samples and dictated stories are valuable selection pieces. During a conference with the child, offer feedback on the progress he or she is making. The child can self-reflect on the pieces while you write down that child's reflection for future evaluation. Take time to share your reflections of the selected pieces by identifying children's strengths, interests, and needs. Such information can help you to evaluate the design of the curriculum and to determine what you need to do to meet the needs of the children in your classroom.

Understanding and Assessing the Progress of a Child with a Disability

Every child who enters the classroom brings with him or her a wealth of prior knowledge and experiences as well as differing abilities. Evaluating the progress of children is as valid for a child with a disability as it is for a child without a disability. The use of portfolio assessments will strengthen the documentation needed to identify the child as needing additional support or to document the progress in which the child is progressing towards his or her Individual Education Plan (IEP) or Individual Family Service Plan (IFSP). Researchers have found that information gathered in portfolios leads to more specific and helpful recommendations in improving instructional programs in comparison to norm-referenced assessment data results (Rueda & Garcia, 1997).

Children with disabilities are typically given standardized assessment measures to determine progress and establish eligibility. This limited approach often overlooks the fact that children with disabilities, as well as all young children, tire easily, become easily distracted, and are frequently inconsistent in responses. This is especially evident when assessing a child with sensory impairments. To avoid inaccurate assessment results, use a wide range of assessment techniques and verify assessment results with multiple sources.

Portfolio assessment, as well as other authentic assessment practices, provides ongoing assessment materials to assist in placement and instructional decisions. The portfolio also demonstrates the strengths and progress the child is making. Parents of children have the opportunity to see aspects of their child's life that take place at school. Social and emotional development, cognitive development, physical development, and self-help skills can be accurately and materially represented in the portfolio.

Assessment and evaluation of young children is not without controversy in the field of early childhood education, but it is a vital tool. Identifying and utilizing non-traditional forms of assessment such as portfolio assessment enables you to obtain information about the children in your classroom. This information strengthens curriculum, meets the academic needs of children, and provides children with ownership over the learning and evaluation process.

How to Use This Book

We hope you find *Themes for Inclusive Classrooms: Lesson Plans for Every Learner* useful in your classroom. Children will enjoy and benefit from the learner-centered experiences in the lesson plans, and the accompanying accommodations and modifications. The following are tips for successfully incorporating the lesson plans in this book as you plan for children's learning:

1. Because you know your children better than we do, use these lesson plans as guides for your classroom. Using your own questions, choosing your own activities from the suggestions in this book, and adapting specific ideas to your children's needs is the best plan of action. Our hope is that you will find our ideas useful for developing optimal learning experiences for your children.

2. As you begin any lesson, familiarize yourself with the plan prior to starting activities. Putting your nose in this book while working with children will not facilitate their learning. They may become bored or disinterested if you are not sharing information with them confidently. Make eye contact with your group, and you will find that activities generate spontaneity and enjoyment for the children.

3. Use our lessons in relationship to what you know about your children. Not all recommendations in our plans will be appropriate for every group of young children. If your children do not sit still for any length of time, you may need to divide the lessons into two or three sessions to introduce concepts to smaller groups of children. Continuing to follow a lesson plan when children are obviously not interested causes stress for everyone.

4. Not all lessons are relevant for your children. A study of seashore life may not be appropriate in Oklahoma, for example. If this is the case, skip the lesson or develop one of your own that you know will help your children feel successful.

5. Throughout the book, we have suggested time frames for each of the lessons. These are approximations; children's responses to lessons will determine the time needed to teach the lesson. Some topics will create interest and passionate discussions among children, while others will be less attractive to them. Be willing to adapt to their needs.

6. Occasionally lessons may need to be abandoned, for instance, when children do not respond as you had hoped. If this happens, prepare the lesson again another day, or consider finding another approach to sharing the lesson concepts with the children.

7. On other occasions, responses from children will change the direction of the lesson plan. This is called a "teachable moment," and following the children's lead will yield more learning on their part. As you are reading a book, for example, children might become excited about the spider they see on a page, and you will spend time discussing the habits of spiders rather than continuing to read the book. As Bev Bos suggested, "Life is a conversation," and allowing children an opportunity to talk about what they want to talk about is important to their cognitive development. Take advantage of "teachable moments." They are the heart of teaching children.

8. While modifications and accommodations are essential for children who have special needs, many modifications and accommodations in this book will be helpful for typically developing children.

9. Because we wanted each lesson to include modifications and accommodations for children in all categories of special needs, there is some repetition of ideas in the modifications and accommodations in this book. The repetition is there because the ideas are ones that meet the needs of the learners.

10. If the modifications and accommodations listed in a specific lesson plan do not meet the needs of the child in your class, review the modifications and accommodations in other lessons to find one that might work better for the child in your class.

11. Throughout this book, we have suggested children's books for some of the lessons. If you do not have a particular book, substitute with another appropriate title. Teaching children always demands flexibility on the part of the teacher.

12. Most importantly, demonstrate your enjoyment of learning when you are working with children. If you do not enjoy learning, then children will not understand that learning is worthwhile. Your attitude is key in the development of learning in children.

Lesson Components Defined

Use the following information about each of the elements in the lesson plans in this book, to plan for teaching and interacting with children.

Title
The title describes the content of the lesson as it relates to the unit theme.

Objectives
Objectives are designed to show teachers what children will learn as a result of the lesson.

Time
Time frames will vary based on children's interest levels and their ability to stay focused on lesson content.

Materials
A list of materials needed to teach each lesson accompanies the plan.

Preparation
This describes anything that needs to be done prior to beginning the lesson.

Lesson
Each lesson will have an activity or activities to teach the defined objectives while the children are gathered in a group time, often referred to as Group or Circle Time. Use the activities as written, add your own activities, or delete activities you think are inappropriate for the children in your class. Lessons include questions and suggestions for comments as the lesson is presented.

Review
Reviewing the content at the end of the lesson is often called a closure. The purpose of closures is to help children remember the content of the lesson.

Assessment Strategies
The assessment strategies in the lesson plans are to help you find out what the children learned by participating in the lesson. With young children, assessment is almost always done on an individual basis.

Accommodations/Modifications
This component is the backbone of this book. Knowing how to modify lessons for individual learners in the classroom helps teachers reach all children.

Curriculum Connections
Curriculum connections are activities that reinforce and extend the learning of the original lesson. Connecting the content in various centers or with follow-up activities ensures that children are developing concepts that enhance their learning.

References

Bates, L. & Barratt, M. Ph.D. November, 2000. Institute for Children, Youth, & Families, 27 Kellogg Center, Michigan State University, East Lansing, MI 48824, with Consortium for Applied Research on Child Abuse & Neglect (ARCAN) and Michigan Children's Trust Fund. http://www.icyf.msu.edu/publicats/z5dissem/assess-p.html

Katz, L.G. 1997. *A developmental approach to assessment of young children.* ERIC Clearinghouse on elementary and Early Childhood Education. Champaign, IL: ERIC Digest. ED407172.

Mastropieri, M. & Scruggs, T. 2004. *The inclusive classroom: Strategies for effective instruction.* Upper Saddle River, NJ: Prentice Hall.

Peak Parent Center: Accommodations and Modifications Fact Sheet (2003) Retrieved on April 20, 2004, from http://www.peakparent.org/pdf/fact_sheets/accommodations.pdf

Prater, M. 2000. She will succeed: Strategies for successful inclusive classrooms. *Teaching Exceptional Children.* Vol. 35, no.5, 58–64.

Rueda, R. & Garcia, E. 1997. Do portfolios make a difference for diverse students? The influence of type of data on making instructional decisions. *Learning Disabilities Research and Practice,* 12(2), 114–122.

Sandall, S. R., Joseph, G., Chou, H., Schwartz, I.S., Horn, E., Lieber, J., Odom, S.L., & Wolery, R. (in press). Talking to practitioners: Focus group report on curriculum modifications in inclusive preschool classrooms. *Journal of Early Intervention.*

SPeNCE Fact Sheet: Study of Personnel needs in Special Education. (2001). Retrieved April 23, 2004, from http://www.spense.org/Results.html

LESSON PLANNING

CHAPTER 2 Transportation

As you begin the study of transportation, visit car dealerships, motorcycle dealerships, and boat dealerships to pick up brochures about various modes of transportation to place on a special interest table. Locate magazines that have pictures of cars, trucks, SUVs, and so on, such as *Car and Driver, Road and Track*, and *Motor Trend*. Asking parents who are car or boating enthusiasts to donate magazines about cars or boats will help you make a connection with the families. Magazines about flying are also available, but they might be more difficult to find.

Invite children to cut out pictures from the magazines described in the paragraph above or have them draw their own pictures. You might want to help children prepare several large murals on which to place their drawings or pictures. Have them paint one large mural with gray tempera paint and help them position a line down the middle to represent a street or highway. Invite the children to paint white clouds on blue paper to represent the sky, and use another large piece of blue paper to represent water (or ocean).

This unit of study will take several weeks, so plan for children to create each mural at the appropriate time as an introductory lesson to each new subtopic (land, air, and water transportation).

Consider setting up a special collection of books about transportation. Paul Strickland has a number of books about vehicles, including *Cars, All About Trucks, Trains, Planes, Big Dig, All About Tractors, Special Engines, Big Dig,* and *Diggers.* Richard Scarry also has a number of books devoted to the transportation theme: *Cars and Trucks from A to Z, Cars and Trucks and Things That Go, A Day at the Fire Station,* and *A Day at the Airport.* Other choices include *Dig!* by Andrea Zimmerman and David Clemesha and *Hard Working Wheels* by Chum McLeod.

This is a theme that you can adjust to the interests of the children in your class if you listen carefully to what they know about transportation. Some children and their families attend NASCAR races, for example, and you'll want to plan lessons that cater to this specific interest.

Introduction to Transportation

Time
25 minutes

Materials
variety of transportation toys representing land, air, and water transportation (including transportation items from the playground, such as wagons, tricycles, and other wheel toys)

pictures of types of transportation (for land, air, and water travel)

Cars and Trucks and *Things That Go* by Richard Scarry

Objectives

Children will:
1. Name at least one form of transportation.
2. Identify that people travel on land, in the air, and on water.

Lesson

✦ Begin the lesson by asking children how they traveled to school that day.

✦ After they have identified their means of travel, explain that they will be learning about transportation for several weeks. Mention that transportation is how people travel from one place to another.

✦ Show the children a variety of transportation toys such as boats, cars, trucks, trains, and planes, and ask them to tell how people travel for each selection.

✦ Explain that travel can occur in three places: on land, in the air, or on water.

✦ Show the transportation pictures and ask children to identify where each type of transportation would take place. Sort the pictures into three stacks (land, air, and water) as this activity progresses.

✦ Tell the children that walking is one of the simplest forms of transportation. Say, "When we walk across the classroom, we are traveling from one place in the classroom to another."

✦ Ask the children to name other places where they might walk.

✦ Show the book, *Cars and Trucks* and *Things That Go* to introduce children to the concept that various types of transportation exist.

✦ Invite the children to paint a large "street" mural to use in the classroom during Center Time.

Modifications/Accommodations

Autism: Since vehicles have motors that make interesting noises, this type of sensory experience is appealing to many young children, but especially those with autism who have unusual responses to sensory stimulation. Many children with autism have a high interest in transportation. Build on this interest by inviting the child to talk about the transportation toys you observe him playing with during centers or free time. During the lesson, use pictures, objects, signs, and gestures to provide visual support for the child. Some gestures that you can use are airplane (fingers together, one hand flying in the sky for airplane), boat (cup hands and move in an S pattern), truck (pull the horn twice and "beep"), and car (pretend to drive with both hands).

Review
Ask the children to identify different types of transportation.

Assessment Strategy
On an individual basis, ask each child to name three ways people travel.

Speech or Language Impairments: Provide a carrier phrase if the child does not respond to a question. For example, when showing a plane, say, "When we go on an airplane it ____." If the child responds "flies," then expand the response by saying, "It flies in the sky." If the child does not respond, then supply the word "flies" and have the child repeat it. Then provide the carrier phrase to elicit the response from the child. For the assessment, allow the child to select "the one that goes in the water," "the one that flies in the sky," and so on.

Hearing Impairments: Seat the child across from you where he can see your lips and face. Repeat key concepts and check for understanding periodically. Use pictures and objects to refer to throughout the lesson.

Visual Impairments: Verbally describe books and pictures of different types of transportation. Provide physical assistance when the child helps paint the large "street" mural.

Cognitive and/or Developmental Disabilities: Use short sentences and simple vocabulary as you show the types of transportation. Show toy representations of cars, boats, trucks, and airplanes throughout the lesson. Repeat key concepts and review them daily after completing the lesson.

Emotional Disturbance: Seat the child next to you during the lesson. Have the child help you by turning pages in Cars and Trucks and Things That Go. Affirm him for helping. Be sure to use "proximity control" while the child works on the mural by standing nearby as he works on the mural.

Other Health Impairments/Attention Deficit Hyperactivity Disorder: Incorporate movement into the lesson by pretending to drive each of the forms of transportation. Use a signal, such as raising one finger, to gain the child's attention before you speak.

Orthopedic Impairments: Help the child paint the classroom mural. Provide a stamp pad and stamps of cars or other forms of transportation to enable the child to be more independent in this activity.

Curriculum Connections

✦ **Art**: Invite the children to create a street or highway mural on a large piece of butcher paper using gray paint. Set up a schedule for small groups of children to work at a time. Recognize that some children will not want to paint and accept their decision to skip this activity.

✦ **Math**: Use a graph to show how each child comes to school every day. Place picture cues at the top of each column so the children can do this activity independently by writing their name (or marking an X) in the appropriate column.

✦ **Outdoors**: Add a new wheel toy to the playground collection. Or, bring in a spare tire for children to roll around the playground.

Walking

Time
15 minutes

Materials
pair of walking shoes
Spot's First Walk by Eric Hill
   (optional)

Objectives

Children will:
1. Explain that walking is the most basic way that people travel.
2. Demonstrate different ways to walk.

Lesson

✦ Remind the children that they are learning about transportation.
✦ Explain that the most basic way to travel from one place to another is to walk, and that before cars were invented, walking was the most popular form of travel.
✦ Ask the children to name places where they walk to and times when they walk.
✦ Show the children the walking shoes and explain that they make walking feel easier.
✦ Briefly describe devices (crutches or braces) that some people use when they have difficulty walking.
✦ Ask the children to walk around the room or playground with you. Demonstrate how to "walk in place."
✦ Discuss movable sidewalks (often seen in airports), escalators, and elevators. Explain that these machines make traveling on foot easier. Invite the children to tell about any experiences they have had with these special devices.
✦ If you wish (and if time permits), read *Spot's First Walk* to the children.

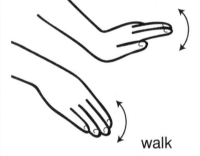

walk

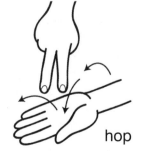

hop

Modifications/Accommodations

Autism: Use pictures, objects, and gestures throughout the lesson. Distinguish actions that we use to move from one place to another: walking, running, rolling, hopping, or jumping. Show the actions and the basic sign for each. Basic signs can be found on the websites listed in Chapter 1 in the section where sign language is discussed. Talk about walking as the easier way to go from one place to another because it is not as tiring as running, rolling, hopping, or jumping.

Speech or Language Impairments: When asking the child to tell about experiences with elevators, escalators, or moving sidewalks, show pictures of each of them.

Hearing Impairments: Seat the child where she can see your lips and face. Repeat key concepts and check for understanding periodically. Use pictures and objects as you present the lesson. If the child uses sign language, demonstrate the signs for the actions of *walking and hopping*. Demonstrate the actions after each sign. If the child signs well, have the child demonstrate the sign and the children demonstrate the action.

Review

Ask children to demonstrate walking.

Assessment Strategy

Ask children individually to describe a walk they remember taking.

Visual Impairments: Describe the pictures as you read *Spot's First Walk.* Let the child hold and feel the walking shoes as you present them during the lesson. Describe and physically demonstrate walking in place.

Cognitive and/or Developmental Disabilities: Use simple vocabulary and sentences, repeat key concepts, and use pictures, gestures, and signs.

Emotional Disturbance: Seat the child next to you during the lesson. Let her help by turning the pages in the book from time to time as you read *Spot's First Walk.* Affirm the child for helping and participating. When talking about the use of crutches and braces, emphasize being a good helper when people use these devices. Discuss why it is important to be patient with our friends who may not be able to move quickly.

Other Health Impairments/Attention Deficit Hyperactivity Disorder: Establish a consistent signal to get the child's attention. Make sure you have the child's attention before you speak. Check for understanding periodically during the story *Spot's First Walk.*

Orthopedic Impairments: Invite the child to tell about using a walker, crutches, wheelchair, or other adaptive equipment to go from one place to another. Assist the child as needed to take the class walk.

Curriculum Connections

✦ **Art:** Invite the children to tear or cut out pictures of people's legs from magazines and glue them on the street mural started in the introductory lesson.

✦ **Connecting with Home:** Inform parents about the lesson on walking and ask them to walk with their children in their neighborhoods or any other place where they like to walk.

✦ **Dramatic Play:** Add a pair of child-sized crutches to the Dramatic Play Center.

✦ **Transitions:** When children are waiting in line to go home at the end of the day or any other time during the day when they have to wait, ask them to "walk in place" as a way to remember to lesson.

Cars

Time
25 minutes

Materials
toy cars
picture of a taxi
car brochures
My Car by Byron Barton
"Taxis," a poem by Rachel
 Field in the *Arbuthnot
 Anthology of Children's
 Literature*

Objectives

Children will:
1. Identify the car as a type of transportation.
2. Describe an experience they have had while riding in a car.

Lesson

+ Hold up a toy car (or a car brochure) and tell children that cars are one of the most popular ways people travel.
+ Ask them to describe the cars they ride in on a regular basis.
+ Read *My Car* to the children (or another suitable selection).
+ Show a picture of a taxi and explain that taxis are used to transport people from one place to another for money (a fare).
+ If available, share the first verse of "Taxis" by Rachel Field.
+ Talk about streets and highways. If there is an interstate highway nearby, name it for the children.
+ Say, "Things that move, including cars, need some type of fuel. Cars need gas." Ask children to talk about trips to neighborhood gas stations.

Modifications/Accommodations

Autism: Label the parts of the car on a picture and name each part. Then ask the child to name the parts of the car. If the child does respond, have him repeat the names of the parts after you. Use pictures as well as a toy car and taxi to refer to during the lesson, review, and discussion.

Speech or Language Impairments: Review the names of the parts of the car and then ask the child their names. Provide the first sound of the car part as a cue for the name if the child does not name the part. When asking questions, provide a carrier phrase if the child does not answer. For example, during the review you can begin a response with "When we drive a car, we use a ____ (pantomime steering wheel)."

Hearing Impairments: Seat the child across from you so he can see your lips and face. Repeat words as needed, checking for understanding periodically during the lesson. Refer to the picture or object (car, car parts) as the children name them.

Visual Impairments: Describe the pictures in the book as you read it. When asking the child to name parts of the car during the review, let him hold and feel the car. Ask him to find the parts of the car on the toy car by touching them.

Review

Ask children to name as many different parts of a car as they can remember from the lesson discussion.

Assessment Strategy

Show a toy car to each child and ask him to tell about an experience riding in a car.

Cognitive and/or Developmental Disabilities: Use simple, short phrases and explanations during the lesson. If the child does not respond to questions, use a carrier phrase (see the accommodation for speech or language impairments), completing the phrase if needed. Then have the child repeat after you. Use gestures and signs freely. For the assessment, have the child locate the type of transportation that he rides to the store in by pointing to a picture (show a car and another form of transportation). In the assessment also ask what and where questions to lead the child to tell you about an experience riding in a car.

Emotional Disturbance: Seat the child near you and provide very close supervision and monitoring throughout the lesson. When the children hold the toy car and tell about an experience riding in a car for the assessment, emphasize handing the car to the next child on the count of three (1, 2, 3, now it's time to hand the car to _____). Do this with each child in the circle if you have children in the classroom who have difficulty giving up the object they are holding. Affirm each child for sharing with friends.

Other Health Impairments/Attention Deficit Hyperactivity Disorder: Before the review, let the children stretch and then sit down. As each child takes turns naming the parts of the car, have the child stand and look at a large toy car as he names parts.

Orthopedic Impairments: Assist the child with feeling and touching the objects you present throughout the lesson.

Curriculum Connections

✦ **Art:** Provide a pan of paint (any color), plastic cars, and large pieces of paper in the Art Center. Children dip the cars in the paint and then "drive" the cars on a piece of paper to make an interesting tire design. Allow the paint to dry and display the tire designs on a classroom bulletin board.

✦ **More Art:** Ask children to cut out (or tear) pictures of cars from magazines and paste them on the street mural (see introductory lesson on pages 40-41).

✦ **Connecting with Home:** Encourage parents to talk to their children about the parts of the cars they use—the dashboard, the speedometer, the turn signal, the seats, the wheels, gas tank, and so on.

✦ **Dramatic Play:** Place a steering wheel in the Block Center to promote dramatic play. Encourage children to experiment with ways to anchor the steering wheel by leaning it against a stack of blocks. Old steering wheels may be purchased at a local junkyard.

LAND TRANSPORTATION

Trucks, Minivans, and SUVs

Time
20 minutes

Materials
pictures of trucks, minivans, and SUVs
dealership brochures showing trucks, minivans, and SUVs
plastic toy car
flip chart and marker (optional)

Objectives

Children will:
1. Identify a truck, minivan, or SUV by name.
2. Name one characteristic of larger vehicles that is different from a car.

Lesson

✦ Begin the lesson by showing the children a toy car and asking them to identify it from what they learned in a previous lesson.

✦ Show them the brochures and pictures and say, "Many people own larger vehicles such as pickup trucks, minivans or SUVs."

✦ Explain that they will be talking about larger vehicles in today's lesson. Ask, "Have any of you ever ridden in a truck, a minivan, or an SUV?"

✦ Talk about the ways larger vehicles differ from cars (they have more room and more storage space in them, they often have sliding doors, they usually have running boards, which is a step that allows passengers to step up to get into the vehicle, and seats may fold down or fold out of sight).

✦ Brainstorm reasons why someone might want to buy larger types of transportation. Record this information on a classroom chart.

✦ End the lesson with the following rhyme:

Let's Go Riding by Laverne Warner
Let's go riding in the truck, truck.
Let's go riding in the truck, truck.
Let's go riding in the truck, truck,
Everyone, come along!

Modifications/Accommodations

Autism: While talking about the distinguishing features of each of these vehicles (trucks, minivans, and SUVs), point out the distinguishing features on toy vehicles or in pictures. Use pictures and toy vehicles throughout the lesson to provide a visual reference.

Speech or Language Impairments:, When brainstorming, let other children's responses serve as a model of the type of response needed. Provide a carrier phrase, if necessary. To build vocabulary, the above accommodations for children with autism also are helpful for the child with speech or language problems.

Hearing Impairments: Seat the child where she can see your lips. Use pictures and objects throughout the lesson. Repeat key vocabulary and concepts, checking periodically for understanding. If the child uses sign language, invite her to share signs for these vehicles with the class.

Review

Ask the children to tell review the characteristics that differentiate cars from trucks, minivans, or SUVs.

Assessment Strategy

Show children the same pictures of trucks, minivans, and SUVs that you used during the lesson and ask them to identify each one.

Visual Impairments: Let the child hold and feel toy vehicles during the lesson. Use the toys rather than pictures for the assessment activity. When showing pictures to the group, describe them.

Cognitive and/or Developmental Disabilities: Use simple vocabulary and short sentences in your explanations and during the lesson. Repeat key vocabulary. Collect realistic pictures of minivans, trucks, and SUVs and sort them into piles as part of the lesson. Help the child to do this with assistance. After the lesson, review this activity daily to reinforce vocabulary concepts.

Emotional Disturbance: Seat the child next to you during the lesson. Enlist the child's help in putting materials into a "finished box" as you finish using them. A "finished box" is any box that you choose to place materials in as you finish with them. Label the box as the "finished box" and use it frequently during lessons.

Other Health Impairments/Attention Deficit Hyperactivity Disorder: Incorporate movement into the lesson by pretending to drive trucks, minivans, or SUVs thorough pantomime. Have the children describe what they are doing as they pretend to drive. For the child with ADHD, make sure that you have her attention before you speak.

Orthopedic Impairments: For the assessment, show the child groups of two to three pictures and ask him to look at the _____. Separate the pictures with at least ten inches between so that you can see where the child is looking. This technique is also known as "eye pointing."

Curriculum Connections

+ **Art:** Ask children to find pictures of trucks, minivans, or SUVs in magazines to cut out (or tear) to place on the street mural (see introductory lesson on page 41).
+ **Connecting with Home:** Ask a parent who owns a minivan or SUV to bring it to school one day so children can take a closer look at it. Give them an opportunity to climb in and out of it.
+ **Writing:** Prepare cardboard cutouts of cars, trucks, minivans, and SUVs to place in the Writing Center. Ask individual children to identify specific patterns with their eyes closed. These cutouts can be put into the Art Center as well, if children want to trace them and cut them out.

Buses

Time
20 minutes

Materials
pictures of buses
The Big Red Bus by Judy
    Hindley or any version of
    The Wheels on the Bus
plastic toy cars, trucks, and
    buses

Objectives

Children will:
1. Identify the bus as a mode of public transportation.
2. Identify a picture of a bus.
3. Sing "The Wheels on the Bus."

Lesson

✦   Ask children if any of them have ever ridden on a bus. Give them an opportunity to share their experiences.
✦   Ask if they know how city buses and school buses are alike and different.
✦   Introduce the concept of public transportation to the children. Talk about other types of public transportation (taxis, trains, or subways).
✦   Point out to children that buses are very large in comparison to other types of family transportation and show the plastic toys.
✦   Read *The Big Red Bus* or *The Wheels on the Bus* to children (or a similar selection about buses).
✦   If children know "The Wheels on the Bus," sing the song with them to end the lesson.

Modifications/Accommodations

Autism: Refer to pictures and objects as you present the lesson. "Why" questions are very difficult for children with Autism because they are more abstract than "who, what, when, and where" questions. For the review ask the child who drives a bus, or where you can go on a bus.

Review

Ask children to tell why the bus is considered a mode of public transportation.

Assessment Strategy

Show pictures of various types of transportation vehicles and ask individual children to identify the bus.

Speech or Language Impairments: When asking about the similarities and differences between city buses and school buses, repeat the responses and write them on a chart. For the review, help the child by saying, "A bus is a type of public transportation because ____."

Hearing Impairments: Seat the child across from you where he can see your lips and face. Repeat your phrases and check for understanding. As you read *The Big Red Bus*, point out the pictures and repeat their names.

Visual Impairments: When you read the story *The Big Red Bus*, describe the pictures. For the assessment, use objects rather than pictures.

Cognitive and/or Developmental Disabilities: For the review, ask the child to identify which is a form of public transportation: a bus, car, or bicycle. Use small toy objects rather than pictures for the review and the assessment. Use simple language and vocabulary throughout.

Emotional Disturbance: Seat the child close to you and supervise him closely during the lesson. Encourage his participation using hand motions with the song "Wheels on the Bus," if the child does not sing along with you. When he does sign note this by positive facial expressions and eye contact.

Other Health Impairments/Attention Deficit Hyperactivity Disorder: Establish a consistent signal (like a raised finger or a similar gesture) to get the child's attention. Make sure that you have the child's attention before speaking. Take a stretch break after reading the story.

Orthopedic Impairments: During the assessment, allow the child to look at the bus for a response. During the song "Wheels on the Bus" help the child to perform the motions to the song.

Curriculum Connections

✦ **Art:** Ask children to find pictures of buses in magazines to cut out (or tear) to glue onto the street mural (see introductory lesson on page 41).

✦ **Dramatic Play:** Place a large refrigerator box in a prominent spot near the Art Center so children can construct a bus. Ask the children who ride buses on a regular basis to observe the components of the bus they ride that could be added to the classroom bus. Take pictures of the project as the children work on it to share as a record of their work. This activity will take several days to complete, and the children will enjoy playing with the bus when it is finished.

✦ **Field Trip:** If you discover that many of the children have had little or no experience with buses, plan a field trip on a bus. Or encourage parents to take their child for a ride on a bus if a field trip is not a practical idea for your classroom.

Trikes and Bikes

Time
15 minutes

Materials
a tricycle
pictures of other single-driver
    modes of transportation
    (bicycles, motorcycles,
    scooters, playground
    wheel toys, and so on)
bike safety helmet

Objectives

Children will:
1. Distinguish that bicycles have two wheels and tricycles have three wheels
2. Tell why riders on trikes and bikes should wear helmets.

Lesson

✦ Tell the children that they are going to talk about vehicles that have fewer than four wheels.
✦ Show the tricycle and ask children to identify it. Ask, "What makes the tricycle unique?" (it has three wheels, only one person can ride it at a time, and so on)
✦ Ask children if they know other types of transportation that can be ridden by only one person at a time (bicycle, tricycles, and many playground wheel toys).
✦ As children name the types, show the corresponding picture.
✦ Hold up the safety helmet and ask children why bike riders need to wear one.
✦ Explain that people who ride bikes and motorcycles on the street need to take extra precaution for safety reasons. Say, "All bike riders have to obey traffic signs and signals, just like car and truck drivers."

Modifications/Accommodations

Autism: Show the child pictures of the bicycle and tricycle. Demonstrate how they are the same (point to each seat and say, "seat"; point to each set of handlebars and name them; and so on). Count the number of wheels on each to show how they are different. During the lesson, refer to pictures and objects frequently.

Speech or Language Impairments: Provide a carrier phrase if the child does not respond to questions. For example, "A vehicle that has three wheels is ____." If they do not respond, hold up a picture and have them complete the sentence.

Hearing Impairments: Use pictures and objects to refer to throughout the lesson. Repeat phrases frequently and check for understanding. Seat

Review

Review the names of the vehicles talked about in the lesson and ask children to tell how many wheels each has.

Assessment Strategy

Show a collection of transportation pictures and ask individual children to find a trike or a bike from the set.

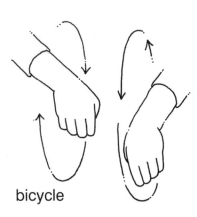

bicycle

the child across from you so she can see your face and mouth. Use sign for *bicycle* if the child uses sign language. As you show the pictures of the bikes, trikes, and riding toys, make sure that the child can see them clearly.

Visual Impairments: Describe pictures as you present them. When showing objects, let the child feel and touch them.

Cognitive and/or Developmental Disabilities: Use simple vocabulary and language as you present concepts. During the lesson count the number of wheels on each vehicle and show a number card to represent each number. Have the child count the wheels with you.

Emotional Disturbance: When talking about safety, wearing helmets, and obeying traffic signs, emphasize the fact that we do not want to be hurt or to hurt anyone else. Seat the child next to you and provide close supervision during the lesson.

Other Health Impairments/Attention Deficit Hyperactivity Disorder: Include movement in the lesson as you talk about various vehicles. Have the children demonstrate how to ride each of them.

Orthopedic Impairments: For the assessment, let the child respond by looking at the tricycle or bicycle. Show only two or three pictures at a time when asking the child to show you the bike or trike.

Curriculum Connections

✦ **Art:** Encourage children to cut out bike or trike pictures from magazines to add to the ongoing transportation mural.

✦ **Outdoors:** Prepare a special "trike track" for children to use during playtime.

✦ **Special Visitor:** Ask a parent who owns a motorcycle to bring it to school one day for children to observe in a close way. Be sure the parent brings along his or her safety helmet.

Wagons

Time
20 minutes

Materials
wagon (from the playground)
My Treasure Hunt by Susan Simon

Preparation
Place the wagon in the Circle Time area prior to beginning the lesson.

Objectives

Children will:
1. Identify that wagons can carry cargo (or freight).
2. Describe what wagons look like.

Lesson

✦ As children gather for the lesson, ask what they see in the Circle Time area.
✦ Ask children how many of them have wagons at home.
✦ Allow children an opportunity to tell experiences they have had with their wagons (and with the wagons at school).
✦ Ask, "Do wagons carry cargo (or freight) like trucks do? What types of cargo (or freight) do you put in your wagons?" Explain to the children what the words *cargo* and *freight* mean.
✦ Lead children to understand that wagons (even small ones) help make our lives easier because they carry loads for us.
✦ Read *My Treasure Hunt* to the children (or another suitable selection about wagons).
✦ When talking about wagons, show several pictures of different types on wagons. Name each wagon and have the child tell you about its color and other distinguishing features. Play a game with the pictures and have the children tell when they see a wagon as you turn each picture card over.

Modifications/Accommodations

Autism: When talking about wagons, show several pictures of different types on wagons. Name each wagon and have the child tell you about its color and other distinguishing features. Play a game with the pictures and have the children tell when they see a wagon as you turn each picture card over.

Speech or Language Impairments: Provide a carrier phrase if the child does not respond during the review. For example, begin the sentence with, "In my wagon I can carry _____." If the child still does not answer, complete the sentence and have him repeat it. Then ask the question with the carrier phrase and wait for the child to respond. Finally, ask the question and wait for the child to respond independently.

Hearing Impairments: Seat the child across from you where he can see your face and mouth. Use gestures frequently. Repeat your words often, checking for understanding. During the story *My Treasure Hunt*, point out the pictures and name them.

Visual Impairments: Describe the pictures in the story. For the assessment, have objects rather than pictures and ask the child to find the wagon.

Review

To summarize the lesson, ask the children what cargo or freight they carry in their wagons.

Assessment Strategy

Add pictures of wagons to the transportation collection and ask individual children to pick out a wagon from the rest of the vehicles in the collection.

Cognitive and/or Developmental Disabilities: During the lesson use simplified vocabulary and language, repeating phrases often Use objects during the lesson to make it more concrete, such as the wagon itself and the cargo or objects to be carried. Count the number of wheels on the wagon and point out its distinguishing characteristics (handle, wheels, bed of the wagon).

Emotional Disturbance: Seat the child next to you during the lesson. Enlist the child's help by having him turn the pages during the story from time to time. Emphasize being careful when pulling a wagon so that the wagon does not turn it over. Demonstrate the safe way to make a turn when pulling a wagon. This is a good skill for all children, but safety is particularly important to emphasize with this child.

Other Health Impairments/Attention Deficit Hyperactivity Disorder: Incorporate movement into the lesson by having the children show (through pantomime) how to pull and push a wagon. Then have them show how to push and pull a heavy load and a light load.

Orthopedic Impairments: For the assessment, allow the child to respond by looking at the picture of the wagon from a group of two pictures.

Curriculum Connections

+ **Art:** Provide small boxes (matchbox size) and red paint for children to design their own pretend wagons.
+ **Outdoors:** Develop a treasure hunt to use during outdoor play. Provide children with picture cards indicating that they must pick up items on the playground and deliver them to another spot using a wagon. For example:
  + pick up three blocks and take them to the water table
  + take a cup of water from the water table to a bucket near the swing set
  + find a small truck and take it to the teacher

  If you wish, provide the participants with a "treasure" when they have completed the hunt, such as a small eraser or fruit treat. Pair children, who might have difficulty with this task, with children who can give them assistance.
+ **Science:** With small groups of children, talk about scientific principles as they relate to wagons, such as wheels being round, how wagons are shaped so that cargo can be moved from one spot to another, a wagon's fuel source (human energy), and how humans develop energy (good nutrition).

Trains

Time
25 minutes

Materials
pictures of train and specific train cars
Trains by Gail Gibbons
train set (if possible)

Preparation
If a train set is available, display it in the Circle Time area prior to children coming to the lesson. As children arrive, allow them to observe it for a few minutes before beginning the lesson.

Objectives

Children will:
1. Identify trains as a type of transportation.
2. Name one type of train car.

Lesson

✦ Begin by asking how many children have ever ridden on a train.
✦ Say, "Let's talk about all of the cars on the train." Explain that each segment of the train is called a "car."
✦ Introduce the individual cars to the children: the engine, the tank car, the flatbed car, the passenger car, the refrigerated car, cattle car, and the caboose. Talk about what each car carries (you can use the words *cargo* and *freight* again to reinforce their meaning).
✦ Tell the children that the engineer is the person who drives the train.
✦ Also, explain that trains ride on tracks.
✦ Read *Trains* to the children (or another selection about trains that is available).
✦ Ask children to stand in a circle and show them how to attach their hands to the child in front of them. Ask them to shuffle their feet to move forward and chant "choo choo" as they pretend to be a train in motion. Demonstrate how their arms can move back and forth just as if they were the wheels of a train.

Modifications/Accommodations

Autism: Trains often are an area of high interest for children with autism and they sometimes know many things about trains. Build on the child's interest by letting the child take the lead in answering questions and telling what she knows about trains. Use pictures and objects throughout the lesson to provide a visual reference for this child.

Review

Ask children to name individual train cars as you give them clues about the car:

✦ This car carries fuel or oil.
✦ This car carries food that needs to be kept cold.
✦ This car carries people who ride on the train.
✦ This car is the last car on the train.
✦ The engineer rides in this car.

Assessment Strategy

Have individual pictures of various train cars and ask small groups of children to identify the names of the cars.

Speech or Language Impairments: During the review, display pictures or the toy train to provide a visual reference for the child so that she can better participate. During the review limit the choices by showing two or three cars and then giving the clues.

Hearing Impairments: Seat the child across from you where she can see your mouth and face. Repeat key vocabulary and concepts during the lesson, checking periodically for understanding. When introducing each car during the lesson, hold up each car so that the child can see it clearly.

Visual Impairments: Describe the pictures in the book and other pictures as you present them during the lesson. Let the child feel and touch the cars of the toy train. Use the toy train cars during the assessment activity.

Cognitive and/or Developmental Disabilities: Use simple vocabulary and language throughout the lesson. Use real objects to tell about the train cars. Limit choices (as in Speech or Language Impairments above) during the review.

Emotional Disturbance: Seat the child near you during the lesson. Allow the child to turn the pages in the book from time to time to maintain interest and participation. Before making the choo-choo in the circle, remind the children about being kind to our friends and how to make a circle.

Other Health Impairments/Attention Deficit Hyperactivity Disorder: Establish a clear signal to get the child's attention, such as a raised finger. Make sure you have the child's attention before speaking. Stand next to the child as you make the choo-choo, or have the children make the choo-choo and monitor the child closely.

Orthopedic Impairments: During the assessment activity, allow the child to respond by looking at the train cars to identify them. Show only two or three cars to choose from at a time.

Curriculum Connections

✦ **Art:** Provide shoeboxes, paint, paintbrushes, markers, and other art supplies for children to use to create train cars. Put the train cars together and display in the classroom.
✦ **Dramatic Play:** Place a non-motorized train set in the Manipulatives Center or on the Discovery Table to encourage the children's dramatic play.
✦ **Language and Literacy:** Read the poem "The Baby Goes to Boston" in the *Arbuthnot Anthology* about a train and encourage the children to chant the rhyming words.
✦ **Social Studies:** Place the train set on a special table in the classroom so children can observe its movement and talk about what trains do, what they transport, and so on.

Big Trucks

Time
20 minutes

Materials
pictures of big trucks
plastic big truck toy (if
    possible)
Richard Scarry's *Cars and
    Trucks and Things That
    Go*

Objectives

Children will:
1. Identify an 18-wheeler as a "big truck."
2. Learn what the word *cargo* means.

Lesson

✦ Begin by holding up Richard Scarry's *Cars and Trucks and Things That Go* and telling children that they will be talking about big trucks today.

✦ Look at a few pertinent pages in the book that pertain to the lesson topic.

✦ Ask several questions about the study:
   ✦ Why do you think these are called big trucks?
   ✦ Where have you seen trucks that are this big?
   ✦ What do you think big trucks carry?
   ✦ Who drives big trucks?

✦ Tell children that drivers of big trucks have to have special licenses in order to drive the trucks.

✦ Introduce the terms cargo and freight (the products trucks transport from one place to another) to children, if you haven't already (see wagons and trains lessons), and tell them some items that might be transported by big trucks.

✦ Recall the chant learned in the lesson on trucks (see page 46) and repeat it. This time ask children to use a "big truck" voice as they chant.

Let's Go Riding by Laverne Warner
Let's go riding in a big, truck, big truck!
Let's go riding in a big, truck, big truck!
Everyone, come along!

Modifications/Accommodations

Autism: When asking the children to name things that are carried by big trucks during the review, show pictures of trucks with loads or pictures of things that trucks carry and then ask the child to name things that are carried by big trucks. During the lesson, emphasize the word *cargo*, and explain that cargo means the things big trucks carry. Sing the following song by Laverne Warner to the tune of "Farmer in the Dell" to emphasize the concept:

Big trucks carry cargo.
Big trucks carry cargo.
Hi, ho, the derry-o,
Big trucks carry cargo.

Review

Ask children to name items they believe are carried by big trucks.

Assessment Strategy

Ask each child to tell what big trucks do and to define the word *cargo*.

Speech or Language Impairments: If the child does not respond to your questions during the assessment, provide a carrier phrase such as "Big trucks ____." During the review provide pictures (pipes, machinery, hay, and others that are not typically carried by trucks) for the child to choose from that show the items that big trucks often carry,

Hearing Impairments: Seat the child across from you where he can see your mouth and face. Use pictures of things trucks carry as cargo in your discussion during the lesson. Repeat key phrases and check for understanding. Make sure that the child can clearly see the pictures as you show the book.

Visual Impairments: Describe pictures during the lesson and as you read the book. Have the children make the sounds of big trucks as they go down the highway, pretending to drive trucks. Let the child hold and feel the trucks and other objects during the lesson.

Cognitive and/or Developmental Disabilities: Use simple vocabulary and language during the lesson, repeating key concepts frequently. The song used in the autism accommodation above also will be helpful with this child. For the assessment, ask the child to tell you about cargo by showing her pictures of trucks with cargo.

Emotional Disturbance: Seat the child next to you and monitor activities closely. Have the child help you by holding materials as you finish with them. When discussing the special license needed by truck drivers, emphasize the need to be safe when driving.

Other Health Impairments/Attention Deficit Hyperactivity Disorder: Stand as you chant "Big Truck." Make sure that you have the child's attention before speaking.

Orthopedic Impairments: No accommodations are anticipated during this lesson.

Curriculum Connections

✦ **Art:** Encourage children to find pictures of big trucks from magazines and cut them out (or tear them) to glue to the street mural (see introduction activity on page 41).

✦ **Language and Literacy:** Place a copy of *Truck Talk: Rhymes on Wheels* by Bobbi Katz in the Library Center. Read various rhymes to small groups of children during the course of the transportation study.

Construction Vehicles: Diggers and Builders

Time
20 minutes

Materials
miniature building and
    construction vehicles
pictures of building and
    construction vehicles
chart and marker
Big Dig or *Diggers* by Paul
    Strickland or Richard
    Scarry's *Cars and Trucks
    and Things That Go*

Note: This lesson will be
    influenced by the types of
    transportation toys you
    have available in your
    classroom and your
    proximity to a
    construction site. Some
    children know about
    dump trucks, caterpillars,
    forklifts, cranes, power
    shovels, and other
    construction vehicles,
    while others do not.

Objectives

Children will:
1. Recognize construction machinery as a type of vehicle.
2. Identify one construction vehicle, such as a digger, by name.

Lesson

✦ Begin by asking the children if they have ever seen a building or house being built.
✦ As they respond, ask which types of machinery they have seen in action and record their names and responses on a chart. If possible, show a picture or a miniature construction vehicle as the type of machinery is mentioned.
✦ Tell the children that these types of machinery are called heavy machinery and that they do very important work when buildings are being constructed.
✦ As the discussion evolves, mention other types of machines that children may overlook. For example, tell them that garbage trucks are also a type of heavy machinery.
    Read a book about construction machinery.
✦ Tell children that construction sites are often fenced in or roped off because going inside of the sites is dangerous. "Only people who work on the machines are allowed to be around the construction work and the machines."
✦ Mention that people who work around construction sites always wear hard hats and show one, if it is available. Explain the reason why workers wear hard hats.

Modifications/Accommodations

Autism: Use pictures and objects throughout the lesson. Heavy machinery is
    often an area of high interest for children with autism, due to their interest in
    watching and hearing machines move, so enlist the child's help in telling
    the names of the equipment and what each piece of equipment does.
Speech or Language Impairments: Before the review activity, show pictures of
    heavy machinery and ask the children to name each of them as a group.
    Give each child a picture, and ask her to identify the machinery and talk
    about it, if desired. During the review activity, provide pictures for the child
    with speech or language impairments, if needed.
Hearing Impairments: Refer to pictures and objects frequently during the
    lesson. Repeat key concepts and check for understanding. Seat the child
    where she can see your mouth and face during the lesson. When reading
    the book on construction machinery, make sure that the child can see the

Review

Ask children to name as many types of heavy machinery as they can.

Assessment Strategy

Show pictures from one of the books about heavy machinery and ask individual children to name at least one of the types of equipment.

pictures as you read, and point out the machinery in the pictures.

Visual Impairments: Ask the child to tell about a type of heavy machinery that she knows about during the assessment. Having toy machinery instead of pictured machinery is helpful. While reading the book, describe the pictures as you look at them.

Cognitive and/or Developmental Disabilities: Use simple language and vocabulary during the lesson. Show toy equipment (bulldozer, crane, and so on) and demonstrate what each does using blocks. As you show pictures of heavy machinery, name each of them. Have the child repeat the names.

Emotional Disturbance: Seat the child next to you during the lesson. Emphasize the concept of safety during the lesson. Use a "What Would Happen if…" activity to help children to understand the importance of safety equipment. Examples: "What would happen if we didn't have hard hats?" and "What would happen if we didn't have safety ropes?"

Other Health Impairments/Attention Deficit Hyperactivity Disorder: Provide for movement during the activity by pantomiming how to operate heavy equipment such as a crane, bulldozer, and fork lift. State what the equipment is doing as you operate it. Make sure that you have the child's attention before speaking.

Orthopedic Impairments: No accommodations are anticipated for this lesson.

Curriculum Connections

- ✦ **Dramatic Play:** Add a few hard hats to the Dramatic Play Center so children can pretend to be construction workers.
- ✦ **Field Trip:** If possible, plan a field trip to a nearby construction site. This might be a walking tour if a construction site is in the neighborhood.
- ✦ **Sand and Water Table:** Place the construction vehicles in the classroom sand table so children can dig, dump, and build with sand.

Horseback Riding

Time
20 minutes

Materials
pictures of horses
plastic horse figurines
saddle and reins (optional)

Objectives

Children will:
1. Identify the horse as a means of transportation.
2. Understand that horseback riding as a means of transportation was more common in historical times than in current practice.

Lesson

+ Begin the lesson by asking if any of the children have ever ridden a horse.
+ As they respond, point out that most of their experiences riding horses were done for fun (or as recreation), and most of them do not ride horses every day.
+ Then tell them that before cars were invented, people rode horses to get around.
+ Explain that horseback riding was one of the only ways people were able to travel, unless they walked. Sometimes they would ride in wagons that were pulled by horses. Make sure to tell them that trains and boats were available, but horses were the most common and available form of transportation.
+ Show pictures of horses and point out the blankets, saddles, stirrups, and reins that are used to make horseback riding more comfortable.
+ Then show the saddle, if available, and talk about how the cinch is belted around the horse to keep the saddle in place. If you do not have a real saddle, show them this on a photo.
+ Talk about the rider's ability to guide the horse with the reins.
+ Ask children to stand and pretend to put a blanket on an imaginary horse, then gird the cinch around the horse, put the reins on the horse's head, and get ready to ride.
+ Demonstrate how riders say "gee" to make the horse go (or turn to the right) and "haw" to make the horse turn to the left. Riders say "whoa" to make the horse stop.
+ Then lead the children and their horses in a short "gallop" around the classroom.

Modifications/Accommodations

Autism: Use pictures and objects throughout the lesson as you explain the items used on horses. Review the words saddle, stirrups, reins, blanket, bridle, and so on prior to the assessment.

Speech or Language Impairments: During the review, use a carrier phrase for the response to why we do not use horses anymore for transportation: "We don't use horses anymore because we_____." Have the child repeat the

Review

Back in the Circle area, ask children to identify the saddle and reins and to tell what "gee," "haw," and "whoa" mean. Ask children to tell why people don't use horses as transportation as often as they did in the past.

Assessment Strategy

Ask individual children to identify any of the terms introduced in the lesson (*gee, haw, whoa, saddle, stirrups, reins*, and so on).

names of the items introduced in the lesson (saddle, stirrups, reins, blanket, bridle, and so on) and then point to each one before asking the child to name them in the assessment.

Hearing Impairments: Seat the child across from you where he can see your face and mouth. Repeat words and phrases often, checking for understanding. Refer frequently to pictures and objects in the discussion of horses. If the child uses sign language, use the sign for *horse* in the lesson.

horse

Visual Impairments: Let the child touch and feel a toy horse, blanket, reins, and saddle. If a real blanket, reins, and saddle are not available, use miniature objects found at a toy store.

Cognitive and/or Developmental Disabilities: Use simple language and vocabulary, repeating phrases frequently. During the review, show the child a car and a horse and ask him to identify the one that people use today for transportation and the one that people used a long time ago to get around.

Emotional Disturbance: Provide close supervision when the children gallop around the room. Remind the child about the ways to stop and turn the "horse" so that no one gets hurt.

Other Health Impairments/Attention Deficit Hyperactivity Disorder: Before galloping around the room, remind the children to be careful when galloping. Remind them to turn their horses when they need to so that they do not hit anyone else. Monitor this child closely.

Orthopedic Impairments: Assist the child in galloping around the room.

Curriculum Connections

✦ **Dramatic Play:** Add stick horses to the Dramatic Play Center so children can pretend to ride horses.
✦ **Fine Motor:** Encourage children to sculpt horses from playdough.
✦ **Outdoors:** Take stick horses outdoors and encourage the children to play with them.

Race Cars

Note: Before using this lesson in your classroom, consider the appropriateness and relevance for your group of children.

Time
15 minutes

Materials
model race car
pictures of NASCAR vehicles
pictures of NASCAR drivers

Preparation
Gauge how interested the children are in race cars and race car drivers prior to beginning this lesson. If you live near a racetrack, the children will probably be more familiar with race cars and races than many other children. If you feel that the children will have no knowledge of car racing, you may want to eliminate this lesson altogether.

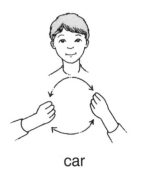

car

fast

Objectives

Children will:
1. Say that race cars are very fast.
2. Identify race cars among a set of pictures of a variety of cars.

Lesson

◆ Hold up the model race car and say, "We've talked about family cars, but this is a type of car driven by professional race car drivers."
◆ Show pictures of various race cars and tell the children that race cars travel at very high speeds on special courses called racetracks.
◆ Show pictures of race car drivers and explain that these people race cars to make money.
◆ Point out that drivers wear special uniforms and helmets when they race.
◆ If children are knowledgeable, talk about the pit crew, and how their job is to keep the race car in top condition during races.

Modifications/Accommodations

Autism: Provide pictures and toy race cars to refer to throughout the lesson. Use the following song, which is sung to the tune of "Skip to My Lou" to emphasize the fact that race cars go very fast. Because children with autism relate well to music, this is a way to help them with memory, expressive language, and concept development.

Race cars go so very fast.
Race cars go so very fast.
Race cars go so very fast,
All around the racetrack.

Speech or Language Impairments: Before having the child tell the difference between a regular car and a race car during the review, discuss this concept as a group. Divide a piece of chart paper in half. Ask the children to talk about the differences and similarities between a race car and a regular car. Write the similarities on one side and the differences on the other side.

Hearing Impairments: Seat the child across from you where he can see your face and mouth. Repeat key phrases during the lesson, checking periodically for understanding. As you show the pictures and objects throughout the lesson, make sure that the child can see each picture as you name it and talk about it. If the child uses sign language, use the sign for *car* and *fast* in the lesson.

Review

Ask the children to tell the difference between a race car and a regular car.

Assessment Strategy

From a collection of pictures of cars, ask individuals to pick out at least one race car.

Visual Impairments: As you present pictures, describe them. During the assessment, use a collection of small cars instead of pictures of cars.

Cognitive and/or Developmental Disabilities: Use simple language and vocabulary. Repeat key phrases frequently. The song from the autism accommodation above would also be helpful. Additionally, use objects during the assessment instead of pictures (see visual impairment accommodation above).

Emotional Disturbance: Seat the child next to you during the lesson. Be sure to emphasize the fact that race car drivers must have special training and wear special clothing for protection. Conduct a "What would happen if…" activity using examples such as "What would happen if race car drivers did not wear helmets?" and "What would happen if race car drivers did not wear racing suits?"

Other Health Impairments/Attention Deficit Hyperactivity Disorder: Provide opportunities for movement during the lesson. Have the children pretend (thorough pantomime) to drive race cars as you direct them: "Get in the race car. Put on the seat belt. Put on your helmet. Start the motor. Step on the gas. Go around the track."

Orthopedic Impairments: During the assessment, allow the child to respond by looking at the picture of the race car.

Curriculum Connections

✦ **Art:** Provide dowel rods and construction paper in the Art Center and encourage children to make race flags.

✦ **Dramatic Play:** Add race flags (checkered flag, caution flag, green flag) to the Dramatic Play Center so children can pretend to be race car drivers. The official set of racing flags are green, yellow, passing, black, red, white and checkered.

✦ **Outdoors:** Encourage a small group of children to use a refrigerator box to build a race car. Talk about what a soapbox derby is.

Signs and Signals

Time
20 minutes

Materials
commercial set of traffic signs (these are available in miniature size or child-sized in school supply stores and catalogs) (**Note:** If you do not have a commercial set of signs, make your own using poster board and markers) pictures of traffic signs and traffic signals

Preparation
Set up the traffic signs in the Circle Time area prior to beginning the lesson.

Objectives

Children will:
1. Identify a picture of a traffic light.
2. Identify at least one traffic sign.

Lesson

✦ Ask the children at the beginning of the lesson what they see in the Circle Time area.
✦ Ask them what traffic signs are used for.
✦ As children respond, explain that traffic signs and traffic lights are used to prevent people (drivers, passengers, and pedestrians) from getting hurt.
✦ Introduce the following signs to the children. Explain what they mean and where they are usually found:
  ✦ stop sign
  ✦ yield sign
  ✦ railroad crossing
  ✦ speed limit signs
  Note: Add any other signs you have in your collection.
✦ Talk about traffic lights. The children should be able to say that red means stop, yellow means to slow down, and green means to go.
✦ Play a game similar to Red Light, Green Light. Line up children outdoors or in a large activity room in the school. Hold up a piece of red paper, green paper, or yellow paper to indicate whether children should stop, go, or slow down.
✦ Determine where the finish line is located and use a rope to mark its place on the ground. When the game is complete, sit back down in the circle to review the lesson.

Modifications/Accommodations

Autism: Use pictures, objects, and gestures as a visual reference throughout the lesson. Develop jingles and phrases to emphasize key features of signs and signal light colors. Here are some examples written by Sharon Lynch:

Red means stop,   *Stop signs are red and have eight sides,*
green means go,   *yield signs are triangles, and*
yellow means slow.   *railroad signs form an X.*

Chant the phrases, showing each sign as you mention it. Record the chants on a tape recorder to play at a later time.

Speech or Language Impairments: During the review provide a carrier phrase and the picture of the sign if the child does not respond. For example, show a stop sign and ask what it means. If the child does not respond, say, "This sign means that we have to ____." You can also cue a response (*stop*, for example) using sign language.

stop

Review

Hold up signs (or pictures of signs) and ask the children to tell what they are, what they mean, and where they are usually located.

Assessment Strategy

Show children pictures of various traffic signs and ask them to identify at least one of the signs.

Hearing Impairments: Seat the child across from you where she can see your face. Use gestures and pictures during your explanations. Repeat key concepts frequently and check for understanding. If the child uses sign language, use the activities explained above in Speech or Language Impairments.

Visual Impairments: When playing Red Light, Green Light, say the name of the color as you hold it up. During the lesson, emphasize the shape of the signs. Allow the child to feel each sign during the lesson, review, and assessment.

Cognitive and/or Developmental Disabilities: Review the meaning of each sign several times. Then have the child find the sign that you describe. Ask the child to tell about the sign as you show it. Do the same thing with the traffic signal colors. Review the meaning, then have the child select the one that means go, slow, or stop. Finally, have the child tell the meaning of the signals.

Emotional Disturbance: Emphasize the concept of safety during the lesson, drawing attention to the fact that signals and signs are used so no one gets hurt. Review the rules of Red Light, Green Light several times and have the child tell what she would do for each color. Have several children demonstrate one at a time, including the child with emotional problems. Monitor the child closely during the activity.

Other Health Impairments/Attention Deficit Hyperactivity Disorder: Establish a consistent signal such as a raised finger to get the child's attention. Make sure that you have the child's attention before giving instructions. Before the game, demonstrate how to walk for each color. Have several children demonstrate one at a time, including the child with ADHD. Then provide close monitoring during the game.

Orthopedic Impairments: For the assessment allow the child to respond by looking at the traffic sign that you name or by naming the traffic signs. For the game, assist the child in walking or push the child in her wheelchair.

Curriculum Connections

✦ **Art:** Provide poster board patterns of stop signs, yield signs, traffic signs, and railroad crossing signs for children to trace and cut out to make their own signs.
✦ **Blocks:** Place the commercial set of signs in the Block Center for children to use as they play with their cars and blocks.
✦ **Connecting with Home:** Tell parents that you have introduced street signs and signals to their children. Ask them to talk to their children about the signs and signals they see as they drive around the community.

Rowboats

Time
15–20 minutes

Materials
picture of a rowboat
oar or paddle, if possible
Row, Row, Row Your Boat by
    Pippa Goodhart and *Cars
    and Trucks and Things
    That Go* by Richard
    Scarry
chart paper and marker

Objectives

Children will:
1. Tell how a rowboat moves through water.
2. Identify a rowboat when shown a picture of various types of boats.

Lesson

✦ Show the children a picture of a rowboat. Ask them to tell about the rowboat. Some key questions include the following: What color is it? Is it a big boat or a small boat? What is it made from? Does it have a motor? How does it move? Be prepared to help children with the answers if they need assistance.

✦ If possible, show the children an oar or paddle. Explain that a rowboat moves when a person pushes (rows) the paddle through the water.

✦ While seated, have the children sing the traditional song "Row, Row, Row Your Boat" as they move their arms to "row the boat."

✦ Read *Row, Row, Row Your Boat* by Pippa Goodhart, showing the children the rowboat in the book.

✦ Show the children pages in Richard Scarry's *Cars and Trucks and Things That Go,* pointing out the different types of boats, especially the rowboats.

Modifications/Accommodations

Autism: Since many children with autism are interested in transportation, this lesson provides an opportunity for the child to contribute. As you read the books, invite the child with autism to tell about the boats and various types of transportation if the child shows an interest.

Speech or Language Impairments: When asking the group to tell about boats and to describe the boat in the picture, ask leading questions. During the review use a question with a starter phrase if the child does not respond. It also is helpful to call on the child during the review after a few other children have responded. This helps the child with language difficulties to know why types of responses are appropriate. In the assessment, allow the child to gesture to show how a rowboat moves.

Hearing Impairments: Seat the child across from you so that he can see your face and mouth as you speak. Use gestures and refer to pictures as you present the lesson. During the story, point out the pictures as you talk about them.

Visual Impairments: As you present the pictures and books, describe the pictures.

Cognitive and/or Developmental Disabilities: Use short, simple phrases as you present the lesson. Review rowboats later in the day and on several days in the next few weeks. For the assessment, show a rowboat picture and have the child point out what makes the boat go.

Review

Make a list on chart paper of everything the children learned about rowboats. Ask the children to tell all they know about rowboats and write their responses on chart paper as they say them.

Assessment Strategy

Show the each child a page from Richard Scarry's *Cars and Trucks and Things That Go* and have him find the pictures of rowboats. Ask the child what makes the rowboat move.

Emotional Disturbance: Have the child help you turn pages as you read the stories. Affirm the child for participating in the lesson. In the lesson, emphasize safety, particularly the fact that they should get into the water only when a grownup is there. This is important for all children to understand, but the child with emotional and behavioral disorders may need to be reminded in the lesson.

Other Health Impairments/Attention Deficit Hyperactivity Disorder: If the child becomes restless during the lesson or stories, have him put materials on your desk or table for you.

Orthopedic Impairments: Assist the child with the motions in "Row, Row, Row Your Boat."

Curriculum Connections

- ✦ **Bulletin Board:** Cut out rowboats from construction paper, one for each child. Invite the children to decorate their rowboats using various art materials, such as cut straws, tissue paper, markers, and so on. Place the boats on a blue background (for water) on the bulletin board. Staple two oars on each boat and help the children write their names on cards to place beside their boats. At the top of the bulletin board, put a caption such as "Row, Row, Row Your Boat." Also, you can include the chart paper from the review activity on the bulletin board.
- ✦ **Language and Literacy:** Provide books with rowboats in them such as *Row, Row, Row Your Boat* by Pippa Goodhart and *Cars and Trucks and Things That Go* by Richard Scarry.
- ✦ **Math:** Provide laminated cutouts of rowboats and oars in the Math Center. Have the children place two oars in each rowboat. Count the boats and the oars. Then model counting the oars by twos.
- ✦ **Sand and Water Table:** Provide different types of boats in the Transportation Center for the children to play with. Also, a Water Table with different types of boats is a nice addition to the classroom.

Canoes

Time
15–20 minutes

Materials
pictures of several canoes
picture of Native Americans or Indigenous People in canoes
Boats on the River by Peter Mandel
The Boat Alphabet Book by Jerry Pallotta
oar or paddle (object or picture)

Objectives

Children will:
1. Explain how a canoe moves.
2. Identify a canoe when shown several other types of boats.

Lesson

+ Show the children a picture of a canoe and ask them to describe what they see. Show different pictures of canoes. Explain that canoes were built by the Native Americans to move through the rivers. Explain that the first canoes were built from hollowed out tree trunks and animal skins to move swiftly through the water. Show pictures of modern canoes and explain that people still use canoes today to move through the water.
+ Read *The Boat Alphabet Book* by Jerry Pallotta, pointing out the canoes.
+ Ask the children to talk about the differences and similarities between canoes the other boats in the book.
+ Show the children an oar or paddle (or a picture of an oar or paddle). Ask how the canoe moves. Discuss the fact that people have to paddle a canoe to make it go since it does not have a motor.
+ Repeat the rhyme below several times to contrast fast and slow rowing:

I Can Row a Canoe by Sharon Lynch
I can row a canoe. (motions of slow rowing)
I can row a canoe.
I can row a canoe so slow.

I can row a canoe. (motions of fast rowing)
I can row a canoe.
I can row a canoe so fast.

Modifications/Accommodations

Autism: The accommodations for children with speech or language impairments (below) will typically help this child as well. Use pictures to refer to throughout the lesson. Singing the rhyme listed above can be helpful in inviting the child with autism to participate in it.

Speech or Language Impairments: Provide a sentence starter or carrier phrase when asking questions. For example, "What makes a canoe go? It moves when you use a ____." (Point to the paddle). For the assessment, allow the child to show you how canoes move through the water if she is not able to tell you.

Hearing Impairments: Seat the child across from you so she can see your lips and face. Refer to pictures as you talk during the lesson. When reading the

Review

Ask the children to tell all they know about canoes. Write what they say on chart paper.

Assessment Strategy

Look through the book *Boats on the River* by Peter Mandel (or another book that has boat pictures in it) and ask the child to find the canoe as you look at the book. Then ask the child how canoes move through the water.

story, point out the pictures as you name and talk about them.

Visual Impairments: When showing pictures or reading the story, talk about the pictures and describe them. If you have a small toy canoe, let the child touch it and feel it.

Cognitive and/or Developmental Disabilities: Use short, simple explanations during the lesson. Review the pictures of the canoes in the books daily. Allow the child to show you how a canoe moves by gesturing on the picture if she cannot tell you.

Emotional Disturbance: Seat the child next to you during the lesson. Have her help turn the pages in the book. Affirm the child for participating. Emphasize safety and the fact that they should get into the water only when a grownup is present.

Other Health Impairments/Attention Deficit Hyperactivity Disorder: Ask the child to take materials to your desk or table if she is restless. As you finish with materials, have the child put them in the "finished box."

Orthopedic Impairments: Help the child make rowing motions during the poem.

Curriculum Connections

✦ **Art:** Cut out two identical halves of a canoe from construction paper or tagboard. Make two for each child. Use a hole punch to make a "lacing card" from the cutouts along the bottom. Show the children how to use yarn to lace up their canoes. Place the canoes on the bulletin board with blue water as the background.

✦ **Language and Literacy:** Place the books *Boats on the River* by Peter Mandel and *The Boat Alphabet Book* by Jerry Pallotta in the Library Center.

✦ **More Language and Literacy:** Provide books that show how Native Americans made canoes from tree trunks. One example is *If You Lived with the Indians of the Northwest Coast* by Anne Kamma and Pamela Johnson.

Floats

Time
15–20 minutes

Materials
picture of a float
picture of other forms of water
    transportation (boat,
      canoe, raft)
chart paper and markers
glue
colored construction paper

Objectives

Children will:
1. Identify a float from pictures of a variety of water transportation.
2. Describe a float.

Lesson

◆ Show the children a picture of a float like children use in a swimming pool. Ask if any of them have ever been on a float.

◆ Explain that a type of large float is used to go down a river. Show the children a picture of a barge and a raft and explain that they both float down the river, and that this is one way to move from one place to the next.

◆ Show the children a picture of a float and a picture of a canoe. Ask them to tell how they are different and how they are alike. Record their responses on chart paper.

◆ Sing the song below, pretending to push the pole as you sing.

My Float Is in the Pool by Sharon Lynch
Tune: "The Farmer in the Dell"
My float is in the pool,
My float is in the pool,
I can swim with my float.
My float is in the pool.

Modifications/Accommodations

Autism: Use gestures, signs, and pictures during the lesson. Repeat short explanations directed toward the child during the lesson. If the child does not respond to the open-ended questions, say, "Tell me about your float," Provide a graphic organizer to help the child tell about his float in the assessment. To do this, on a sheet of paper, write the words "color" and "where." Point to "color" and ask "What color…" and then to "where" and ask "Where do you find it?" If this organizer is used frequently it helps the child to organize a response to requests such as "Tell me about…." Use the techniques for Speech or Language Impairments below during the lesson as well.

Speech or Language Impairments: When asking the child to tell about the float, use a sentence starter or carrier phrase if the child does not respond. During the review, allow a few other children to respond first so that the child will understand the type of response that is appropriate.

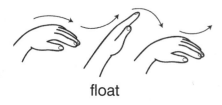

float

Review
Ask the children to tell you everything they know about floats. Write what they say on chart paper with markers.

Assessment Strategy
Show pictures of various types of water transportation and ask the children to find the float. Provide glue, blue construction paper, and colored rectangles from construction paper so the children can make their own floats. Ask each child to tell about his float. Write what the child says on an index card and tape it to his picture.

Hearing Impairments: Seat the child across from you where he can see your lips and face. Use gestures, signs, and pictures to refer to as you present the lesson. If the child uses sign language, use the signs for *float* and *water*.

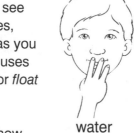

water

Visual Impairments: Explain and describe the pictures as you show them. Let the child feel the paper to construct the float in the art project. Allow the child to feel items throughout the lesson.

Cognitive and/or Developmental Disabilities: Use simple sentences and vocabulary as you describe and explain activities. In the art project, have the child tell the color of the float in his picture. Name the colors and count the rectangles before the child makes his picture for the art project. Review the concept of floats later in the day and throughout the week.

Emotional Disturbance: Seat the child near you. Have him assist you by putting materials in the "finished box" as you finish using them. Emphasize the fact that they should go in the water only when grownups are with them.

Other Health Impairments/Attention Deficit Hyperactivity Disorder: Make sure that you have the child's attention before you speak. Establish a consistent signal for getting the child's attention. During the art project, provide close supervision with the glue.

Orthopedic Impairments: The child will need help with constructing a float for the art project in the assessment activity. Using a glue brush may help the child to use the glue more effectively.

Curriculum Connections

+ **Bulletin Board:** Make a blue backing for the bulletin board. Display the children's floats on the bulletin board.
+ **Language and Literacy:** Provide books with forms of water transportation such as Richard Scarry's *Cars and Boats and Things That Go* and *Boats* by Shana Corey.
+ **Math:** Provide construction paper rectangles like the children used for their floats. Laminate the rectangles and have the children sort them by color and count them.
+ **Science:** Provide a tub of water or use a water table and give the children various objects. Ask the children to predict which ones will float or sink. Sort the objects by those that float and those that sink. Allow the children to continue this as an independent activity that you supervise.
+ **Social Studies:** Provide a map that shows rivers. Show the children where the rivers are on the map. If desired, outline the rivers on a state or local map with glue to make a raised impression when it is dry.

WATER TRANSPORTATION

Motor Boats

Time
15–20 minutes

Materials
Boats, Boats, Boats by Joanna Ruane
pictures of various types of boats
chart paper and markers

Objectives

Children will:
1. Describe a motor boat.
2. Identify a motor boat from a group of boats.

Lesson

+ Read *Boats, Boats, Boats* by Joanna Ruane or a similar book with different types of boats. The cover of this book shows a motor boat. Point out the motor and ask the children if anyone knows what this object is. If no one knows, provide clues until someone guesses the object. Explain that this boat is a motor boat and that the motor makes the boat move.
+ Ask the children to tell other ways that boats move (oars, paddles, wind).
+ Ask if anyone has been on a boat ride.
+ Talk about the sound motor boats make. Together make the whirring sound of a motor boat.
+ Ask the children if anyone knows what motors need in order to operate (gas).
+ Talk about some of the things that people use motor boats for: entertainment and leisure, traveling from one place to another, fishing, and pulling someone on water skis.
+ Gather the children into a circle and say the following poem. Go slow, and then faster as you say each line. You can do this in a circle, holding hands and going faster with each line.

Motor Boat, Motor Boat (Traditional)
Motor boat, motor boat, go so slow.
Motor boat, motor boat, go so fast.
Motor boat, motor boat, step on the gas!

Modifications/Accommodations

Autism: Transportation and motors are often areas of interest for children with autism. Direct questions to this child about boats so that she can participate. If the child does not respond use a carrier phrase. In the assessment, show the child one picture of a motor boat to describe. Use the graphic organizer described in the previous lesson to help the child to respond to the request to tell you about the motor boat.

Speech or Language Impairments: Review concepts just before asking questions about them. When asking questions, provide a sentence starter or carrier phrase if the child does not respond. For example, when you ask how boats move, first talk about other types of boats you have studied and how they move. Then ask the children how boats move.

Review

Ask the children to tell you all that they know about motor boats. Write their responses on chart paper.

Assessment Strategy

Show pictures of various types of boats or a book with various boats. Ask each child to find the motor boat. Then ask the child to tell you all about the motor boat.

Hearing Impairments: Seat the child across from you where she can see your face. Use gestures and pictures to refer to as you present the lesson. When reading the story, point out the pictures as you name them and talk about them.

Visual Impairments: When reading the story or looking at pictures, describe the pictures. As you write responses on chart paper, say the letters as you write the words. Then read each response.

Cognitive and/or Developmental Disabilities: Use short, simple sentences in your presentation of the lesson. For the review, show a picture of the motor boat before asking the child to tell about motor boats. Review the concepts of motor boats throughout the week, and have the child find motor boats in a book later in the day.

Emotional Disturbance: Have the child sit near you during the lesson. Let her assist in turning the pages of the book from time to time. Affirm the child for participating. Emphasize the fact that they should go in the water only when a grownup is there.

Other Health Impairments/Attention Deficit Hyperactivity Disorder: Make sure that you have the child's attention before you speak. Establish a consistent signal (raised finger, use of a clicker, or snapping your fingers) to get the child's attention. For the poem "Motor Boat," place the child next to you in the circle.

Orthopedic Impairments: Help the child to move with the group when you say the poem.

Curriculum Connections

✦ **Language and Literacy:** Place a variety of books that include motor boats in the Library Center. Possibilities include *Boats, Boats, Boats* by Joanna Ruane and *The Children's Book of Cars, Trains, Boats, and Planes* by Kenneth Allen.

✦ **Math:** Provide laminated cutouts of various types of boats. Have the children sort them by color and type. Ask them to count them after sorting them.

✦ **Social Studies:** Provide a map for the children to examine. Show the children the blue oceans, seas, lakes, and rivers. Invite the children to move a small boat over the water on the map while making the whirring sound of a motor boat.

Ferry Boats

Time
15–20 minutes

Materials
tan and blue construction
    paper
scissors
glue
markers
pictures of different types of
    boats, including a ferry
    boat
picture of a bridge
small toy car

Preparation
Cut out a tan "island" and
draw trees on it. Glue it to a
sheet of blue construction
paper.

Objectives

Children will:
1. Describe a ferry boat.
2. Identify a picture of a ferry boat when shown several types of boats.

Lesson

✦ Show the children the "island" picture and explain what an island is. Ask the children how a person might get to the island from another piece of land. Possibilities include flying in an airplane, going by boat, going across a bridge, swimming, or walking if the water is not too deep.

✦ Explain that there are several ways to cross the water in a car. Show a picture of a bridge. Explain that sometimes an island is too far away from other land to build a bridge, that there are not always airplanes to fly to some places, and that sometimes it is too far to walk or swim.

✦ Show the children a picture of a ferry boat. Explain that a ferry is a special type of boat that carries people and cars across the water. Ask the children to tell you about the ferry boat in the picture. Ask if anyone has ever ridden on a ferry boat.

✦ Invite the children to recite the following rhyme. Say a line, or choose a child to say a line, then have the children repeat the line together.

Going on a Ferry Ride by Sharon Lynch
Tune: "Going on a Bear Hunt"
Going on a ferry ride. (repeat)
Okay! (repeat)
Let's go. (repeat)
Want to go to an island? (repeat)
Okay! (repeat)
Let's go. (repeat)
I see a big lake. (repeat)
Can't go over it, (repeat)
Can't go under it, (repeat)
Can't go around it, (repeat)
Let's ride over it. (repeat)

Drive on the ferry boat. (repeat)
Turn off the engine. (repeat)
We're crossing the water. (repeat)
I see waves. (repeat)
I see birds. (repeat)
This is fun. (repeat)
The ferry has stopped. (repeat)
Drive off the ferry. (repeat)
We've come to the island. (repeat)
Let's go! (repeat)

Modifications/Accommodations

Autism: Show the child the pictures as you present the lesson. Invite the child to tell about the pictures. If he is not able to answer questions, then point to the item in the picture and ask the child to tell about it. During the assessment use the graphic organizer described in the previous lesson to help the child respond to the request to tell you about the ferry boat.

Review

Show the blue paper with the island. Ask the children to tell you all the ways they know to cross to an island.

Assessment Strategy

Show pictures of several types of boats. Ask each child to find the ferry boat and tell a little about it.

Speech or Language Impairments: Use a carrier phrase or sentence starter when asking questions if the child is not able to respond. For example, say, "Tell us about the ferry. The ferry carries ____." During the review, provide pictures of the types of transportation you have discussed so far, along with the ferry.

Hearing Impairments: Seat the child across from you so he can see your face. Refer to the pictures frequently as you present the lesson. Provide additional pictures of airplanes, walking, swimming, bridges, and ferries as you present the lesson. Point to the pictures as you explain about getting to the island during the lesson.

Visual Impairments: Describe the picture as you show it. For the assessment, instead of asking the child to identify the picture of a ferry, ask him to describe each picture and ask him if it is a ferry.

Cognitive and/or Developmental Disabilities: Focus on the goal of having the child identify and name a ferry. Review the picture of the ferry later in the day and throughout the following week.

Emotional Disturbance: Seat the child near you. Affirm him for participating. Let the child hold the materials for you as you finish with them. Allow different children to hold the materials each day so that all children have a turn in helping. Emphasize the fact that they should go in the water only when grownups are present.

Other Health Impairments/Attention Deficit Hyperactivity Disorder: Make sure that you have the child's attention before you speak. Establish a consistent attention signal with this child. If the child is restless, stand as you do the chant.

Orthopedic Impairments: Help the child to pat his lap during the chant. For the assessment, let the child look at the ferry to identify it. This technique, called "eye pointing" is described in Chapter 1 and allows the child who cannot use her hands for pointing to identify items by looking at them in a group of two to three objects or pictures.

Curriculum Connections

✦ **Math:** Cut out a rectangular "ferry" from construction paper. Provide die-cut or small toy cars. Invite the children to count how many cars can fit on the ferry. Encourage them to try different configurations of cars on the ferry.

✦ **Social Studies:** Provide a simple map with ferry routes, or draw a simple one. Outline the ferry routes in glue so they form a raised line when dry. Show the children the land, the ferry route, and the island or other land where the ferry goes.

Tugboats

Time

15–20 minutes

Materials

Scuffy the Tugboat by
    C. Gregory Crampton
pictures of different types of
    boats
chart paper and marker

Objectives

Children will:

1. Identify a tugboat when shown a variety of boats.
2. Explain that tugboats are small boats that help to push large boats.

Lesson

✦ Show the children the cover of *Scuffy the Tugboat.*

✦ Ask them to tell you about the tugboat. Explain that big ships and big boats cannot run their motors when they are approaching city harbors. Little tugboats must pull or push the boats to the shore so the ships can unload their goods.

✦ Some words to introduce during the story are *harbor*, *cargo*, and *dock*. As you read the story, show the pictures that are associated with these concepts.

✦ After reading the story, ask the children to tell why tugboats are important.

✦ Emphasize some concepts from the story, for example, small things are important and can do big jobs; just like Scuffy, we can be happy with who we are, even if we are not big.

✦ Sing the song below and do the motions several times and invite the children to sing along and show the motions.

I'm a Little Tugboat by Sharon Lynch
Tune: "I'm a Little Teapot"
I'm a little tugboat small and strong. (show "small" by putting hands toward floor; show "strong" by pretending to lift weights)
I'm not big and I'm not long. (show big by putting hands in the air and shaking head "no"; show long by holding arms out to sides)
When the big boats need to come to town (point hands together in front like a boat and move forward)
They are glad that I'm around. (put your fingers on your face for smile and then put hands in air)

Modifications/Accommodations

Autism: Many children with autism are very interested in boats because they move and make interesting sounds. Use this interest to build on the child's strengths. Invite the child to share about the tugboat. Use the accommodations for Speech or Language Impairments below if the child is not able to get started in talking about tugboats.

Review

After reading the story, ask the children to tell you all they know about tugboats. Write what they say on chart paper.

Assessment Strategy

Show the children pictures of different types of boats. Ask each child to show you the tugboat and tell you all about it.

Speech or Language Impairments: When asking questions about tugboats, provide a sentence starter if the child is not able to respond. Also, if the child is not able to respond to general questions or requests ("Please tell us about…"), then point to specific items in the picture and ask direct questions such as, "What is this?" or "What does this do?"

Hearing Impairments: Seat the child across from you where she can see your face. Refer to the book and to pictures as you present the lesson. As you read *Scuffy the Tugboat*, point to the pictures as you name them and talk about them.

Visual Impairments: If possible, provide a toy tugboat and let the child hold and explore it. When reading the story, tell about the pictures. For the assessment, ask the child to tell about tugboats, but omit the identification portion.

Cognitive and/or Developmental Disabilities: Use short sentences and simple vocabulary with this child. Show pictures of the tugboat later in the day and review what you have learned about tugboats. . In the assessment, limit the number of pictures to two or three. For the next week, review tugboats so the child will remember the concept.

Emotional Disturbance: Seat the child near you during the lesson. Invite her to help you by putting materials into a "finished box" after you use them. Emphasize the fact that the grownups on a tugboat wear life jackets to keep them safe around water.

Other Health Impairments/Attention Deficit Hyperactivity Disorder: Make sure that you have the child's attention before speaking. Establish a consistent signal to gain the child's attention.

Orthopedic Impairments: Assist the child with the motions to the song. For the assessment activity, have the child look at the tugboat rather than pointing to it.

Curriculum Connections

✦ **Art and Math:** Cut out different geometric shapes, such as squares, rectangles, cylinders, and trapezoids from construction paper. Have children use the shapes to construct tuboats and then glue them to blue paper.

✦ **Bulletin Board:** Place the geometric-shape tugboats on the bulletin board along with the chart paper from the review. Encourage the children to tell about their tugboats. Write what they say on index cards and staple below their boats.

✦ **Math:** Laminate the geometric shapes from the art activity (or use shapes cut from art foam). Provide a tray and invite the children to use the shapes to construct items of their choice. (**Note:** A lunch tray from a dollar store makes a good sorting tray.)

✦ **Sand and Water Table:** Provide different types of toy boats for the children to use in the water table.

Introduction: Airplanes and Jets

Time
20 minutes

Materials
model airplanes
pictures of different types of
    planes, including jets
A Day at the Airport by
    Richard Scarry

Objectives

Children will:
1. Identify that some transportation takes place in the air.
2. Name airplanes and jets as forms of air travel and transportation.

Lesson

✦ Begin the lesson by telling children that they going to learn about traveling through the air. Show model airplanes and ask, "How do people travel in the air? What do they use to fly?" Acknowledge children's answers.

✦ Show the children pictures of difference types of planes and tell children that larger planes that carry passengers are called jets.

✦ Review the word *cargo* from a previous lesson and tell children that jets often carry cargo, too, as well as passengers.

✦ Ask, "Do you know the name of the place where airplanes take off and land?" Other questions you might want to ask and answer are:
  ✦ What is the name of the person who flies the plane?
  ✦ Do you think you will ever want to fly a plane? Why?
  ✦ What are flight attendants and what do they do?

✦ Read Richard Scarry's *A Day at the Airport* (or another available selection about airplanes). Encourage the children to make comments as they look at the book, and note what they already know about airplanes and jets. Give children an opportunity to talk about any air travel they may have experienced.

✦ Introduce the following song about flying:

I Love to Fly by Laverne Warner
Tune: "Ring Around the Rosie"
I love to fly, fly around the room—-
Zoo-oom, zoo-oom, I love to fly.

✦ Ask the children to stand and move around the room, pretending to be an airplane as they sing.

Modifications/Accommodations

Autism: Many children with autism have a high interest in transportation due to the movement and sounds. Build on this interest and strength by inviting the child to tell about the types of air travel and transportation that she is familiar with.

Speech or Language Impairments: During the review, use a carrier phrase for the response to why air travel and transportation is labeled the way it is: "We use the words "air travel and transportation" to describe _____." During the review, have other children respond first so that the child will

airplane

Review

Ask the children to tell why traveling by plane is a kind of transportation.

Assessment Strategy

Using pictures of all types of transportation, ask children to select the pictures that show examples of air travel and transportation.

understand the type of response that is appropriate.

Hearing Impairments: Seat the child across from you where she can see your lips and face. Repeat key concepts and check for understanding periodically. Use pictures and objects to refer to throughout the lesson. If the child uses sign language, use the sign for *airplane*.

Visual Impairments: As you read the book *A Day at the Airport*, describe the pictures in the book verbally.

Cognitive and/or Developmental Disabilities: Use simple vocabulary and sentences throughout the lesson. Repeat key concepts. Use pictures, gestures, and signs as you present the lesson. For example, show a photograph of an airport when asking where do planes take off from and land.

Emotional Disturbance: Seat the child near you during the lesson. Let the child help by turning the pages in the book from time to time as you read the book. Affirm the child for helping and participating. Before the children pretend to fly, emphasize the fact that they need to be safe when they "fly" around the room so that they do not hurt their friends.

Other Health Impairments/Attention Deficit Hyperactivity Disorder: Establish a consistent signal to get the child's attention. Make sure that you have the child's attention before you speak. As the children move around the room pretending to fly, provide close supervision for all children, and especially for this child.

Orthopedic Impairments: Assist the child as needed to move about the room pretending to be an airplane. Encourage a child in a wheelchair to use her arms and extend them into a "flying" position while she is being moved throughout the room by a peer or teacher assistant.

Curriculum Connections

+ **Art:** Show small groups or individual children how to fold pieces of paper to make airplanes. Help them write their names on their planes.
+ **Dramatic Play:** Add props (such as hats, wing insignias, aprons, and jackets) to the Dramatic Play Center so children can pretend to be pilots and flight attendants. Airlines may give you some of these props, if asked.
+ **Language and Literacy:** Add the words *airplane*, *jet*, *runway*, *hangar*, *control tower*, *pilot*, *flight attendant*, *windsock* and others to the classroom Word Wall.
+ **More Language and Literacy:** Collect pictures of well-known air carrier logos (Delta, American, Southwest, and so on) to place in the Writing Center. Place duplicate logos for children to match. Ask older children to replicate the logos if they have had enough experience writing.
+ **Outdoors:** Let children take their paper airplanes outside during outdoor play.
+ **Science:** Place a windsock on the playground so children can observe the wind's direction.

Space Shuttles

Time
20 minutes

Materials
pictures of astronauts and space shuttles
pictures of the moon and earth (taken from space)
book about space (*Space Station* by Peter Lippman or *Roaring Rockets* by Tony Mitton)

Objectives

Children will:
1. Identify the space shuttle as a special plane that flies into space.
2. Explain that astronauts wear special clothing when they go into space.

Lesson

✦ Begin by asking children if they know what a space shuttle is (you can refer to the space shuttle as a rocket, if you would prefer).

✦ Tell the children that space shuttles are very special planes that fly into space.

✦ Ask children to tell what they think space is and then define it is as "the sky." Tell children that space is as far and wide as they can see when they look into the sky.

✦ Introduce the term *astronaut* and show pictures of astronauts wearing their space suits. Explain that the air is different in space so astronauts need special suits to be able to breathe. They also need space suits, because the temperature in space gets very cold. Space suits help the astronauts stay warm.

✦ Show the pictures of the moon and earth. Tell the children that rockets (or space shuttles) get astronauts closer to the moon, stars, and other planets.

✦ Read *Space Station* (or another available selection) to the children.

Modifications/Accommodations

Autism: Use short sentences and simple vocabulary throughout the lesson. Provide toy objects (figurines of plans, jets, rockets, and so on) to refer to throughout the lesson. Repeat key concepts and review them daily after completing the lesson. For the review, show the child pictures because children with autism often need a visual stimulus in order to respond. In the assessment, use a carrier phrase, "Astronauts need special clothing because…" rather than a why question.

Speech or Language Impairments: When asking the child to tell about space travel after the lesson, show various pictures to help elicit a response. If the child does not respond, use a carrier phrase or have the child repeat after you. Then ask the question and the child will likely respond without cues.

Hearing Impairments: Seat the child across from you where he can see your lips and face. Repeat key concepts and check for understanding periodically. Refer to pictures and objects throughout the lesson. If the child has difficulty with speech or language, use the accommodations listed above.

Review
Ask children to tell what they know about space travel after the discussion.

Assessment Strategy
Ask children on an individual basis to tell why astronauts need special clothing in space.

Visual Impairments: Describe the pictures as you read the book about space travel. Allow the child to hold and feel objects as you present them during the lesson.

Cognitive and/or Developmental Disabilities: Use simple vocabulary and sentences throughout the lesson. Repeat key concepts such as jets, astronauts, and space shuttle. Use pictures, gestures, and signs as you present the lesson. In the assessment, use a carrier phrase, "Astronauts need special clothing because…" rather than a why question.

Emotional Disturbance: Seat the child near you during the lesson. Have the child help you from time to time by turning pages in the book about space. Affirm him for helping. If the child shifts the conversation to popular (maybe violent) space creatures from the media, redirect him to the topic of the lesson.

Other Health Impairments/Attention Deficit Hyperactivity Disorder: Use a visual cue or consistent signal to get the child's attention. Make sure that you have the child's attention before you speak. Offer opportunities for movement or a stretch break throughout the lesson.

Orthopedic Impairments: Be sure the child is positioned so that he is able to fully participate in the activity presented (able to see photographs, book, and other materials).

Curriculum Connections

✦ **Art:** Add silver stars and blue or black construction paper to the Art Center so children can make representations of space.
✦ **Dramatic Play:** Add bicycle helmets to the Dramatic Play Center so children can pretend to be astronauts. Or make your own helmets out of large ice cream containers (obtained from an ice cream store). Cut out eye and nose holes and spray paint the containers with silver spray paint. **Note**: This last step is for adults only, and should be done when the children are away from the classroom.
✦ **Science:** With small groups of children, talk about the food that astronauts take into space. Tell them that the food is different because it is stored in airtight containers and the water in the food has been removed ("dehydrated"). Use Tang as an example of space food that astronauts use.

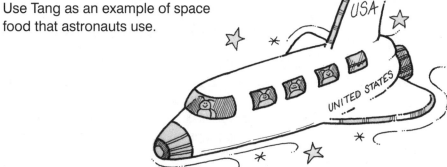

Helicopters

Time
20 minutes

Materials
pictures of helicopters (or plastic figurine, if it is available)
Budgie the Little Helicopter by Sarah Ferguson

Objectives

Children will:
1. Name the helicopter as a form of air travel and type of transportation.
2. Describe the unique features of helicopters.

Lesson

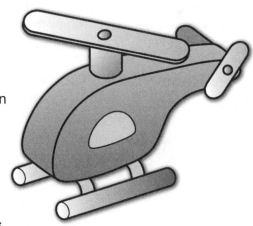

+ Show a picture of a helicopter (or a plastic figurine) and ask children if they know what special type of air travel and transportation it is. Because the propeller goes around and around on top of helicopters, they are called rotocrafts. Their wings are not fixed as in regular planes and jets.
+ Ask the children what is different about a helicopter compared to an airplane. Guide them toward making some of the following statements:
    + Its propeller is on top.
    + It's smaller than most planes.
    + It can fly up and down (unlike other planes).
    + It is noisy, because of its overhead propeller.
    + It can land on top of buildings in city areas.
    + It travels closer to the ground than jets and other planes.
+ Read *Budgie the Little Helicopter* to children and tell them that helicopters are most often used to rescue people.
+ Tell children that some police departments use helicopters to help find suspects who are running away from them.
+ Also tell children that helicopters are often used for military purposes, such as transporting injured soldiers to hospitals.
+ Ask children to stand, hold out their arms, and pretend to "hover" the way helicopters do.

Modifications/Accommodations

Autism: Use photographs to depict the various ways that helicopters are used. Photographs paired with discussion provide an additional means of teaching the concepts presented.

Speech or Language Impairments: For a child with a deficit in receptive language, simplify the vocabulary when discussing the various ways that helicopters are used: police, medical uses, and so on.

Review

As children leave Circle or Group Time, ask them to tell one thing they know about helicopters as a result of the lesson.

Assessment Strategy

Put pictures of helicopters in a collection of types of transportation. Ask individual children to find at least one helicopter among the collection.

Hearing Impairments: Be sure the child is sitting in a place where she can clearly see you as you speak. The closer the child is to the person speaking, the clearer the auditory intake will be.

Visual Impairments: Use figurines of helicopters instead of photographs. Encourage children with visual impairments to feel the figurines.

Cognitive and/or Developmental Disabilities: During the assessment, limit the number of choices available, for example, one picture of a helicopter and one picture of another form of transportation.

Emotional Disturbance: Use caution when discussing how a helicopter can be used in rescue efforts or in police efforts. A child with an emotional disturbance may have negative experiences related to this topic since there are often frightening scenes in the media that involve helicopters. Although this may not be true for all children with emotional problems, make sure that you emphasize the positive side of helicopters helping us when we are in trouble.

Other Health Impairments/Attention Deficit Hyperactivity Disorder: Allow the child to participate in the activity in a more kinesthetic manner. For example, when the children stand up and move their arms as if they were "hovering" like a helicopter, allow the child to move throughout the room. This will help her stay focused on the lesson.

Orthopedic Impairments: Be sure that the child is positioned so she may fully participate in the lesson.

Curriculum Connections

✦ **Art:** Mix olive green paint in the Art Center for children to use to paint pictures of helicopters.
✦ **Blocks:** Add plastic helicopters to the Block Center and observe how children use them in their play.
✦ **Language and Literacy:** Add *Amazing Airplanes* by Tony Mitton to the Library Center.

Parachutes

Time
15 minutes

Materials
real parachute, if available (these are made commercially for classroom use) or king-size sheet
lightweight cloth and string
plastic person figurine
Parachute Games by Todd Strong & Dale Lefevre

Preparation
Before the lesson, make a parachute-like device using lightweight cloth and string. Tie 10" strings to each corner of a square piece of cloth 12" x 12". Gather the ends of all the strings and tie all the strings to a plastic person figurine to help the parachute work more effectively. You can also make a larger parachute with a larger piece of cloth and longer strings.

Objectives

Children will:
1. Pick out a parachute from a collection of transportation pictures.
2. Identify one reason why someone would use a parachute.

Lesson

+ Hold up the parachute you made so the children can see it and then ask, "Who knows about parachutes?"
+ Allow children time to respond and then demonstrate how a parachute operates using the parachute you made.
+ Help children understand that people who use parachutes have to have lessons (instruction) before they use them. People who "sky dive" (jump from airplanes) use special planes to be able to jump from them.
+ Tell children that parachutes are designed to catch the wind and balloon upward as people fall to the ground, thus making the person fall more slowly and safely.
+ Talk about why people use parachutes. Guide the children toward mentioning some of the following reasons:
    + They're used for fun (for recreation).
    + They're used in rescue operations (for people who are lost).
    + They're used in emergencies (to escape planes about to have an accident).
    + They're used in special stunts.
+ Point out that people using parachutes fall very quietly.
+ If you have a large parachute (substitute a king-size sheet, if needed), introduce a game, for example, having the children walk or tiptoe under the parachute when a specific signal is given.
+ Tell children you will teach them other parachute games when you go outdoors.

Modifications/Accommodations

Autism: Use tangible objects during the assessment phase of this lesson. Small figurines are favorable to photographs. Limit the number of "forms of transportation" that the child is to choose from.

Speech or Language Impairments: Because the word *parachute* is long it may be difficult for the child with speech or language difficulties to pronounce. During the lesson, have the children say parachute after you one syllable at a time—*pa-ra-chute*. Accept approximations of the word during the lesson.

Review

Ask children to tell what they remember about parachute use.

Assessment Strategy

Ask individual children to identify a picture of a parachute from a collection of transportation pictures.

Hearing Impairments: Bring children with hearing impairments closer to you. Decreasing the distance between the child and the speaker will increase the probability of clearer auditory intake.

Visual Impairments: As you present pictures and books, describe them verbally. Provide physical assistance to assist the child in moving safely about during parachute play.

Cognitive and/or Developmental Disabilities: Use tangible objects during the assessment phase of this lesson. Small figurines are favorable to photographs. Limit the number of forms of transportation that the child is to choose from.

Emotional Disturbance: Monitor behaviors through proximity control. Emphasize the fact that people wear parachutes to keep them safe in airplanes and that they must be trained in how to use them.

Other Health Impairments/Attention Deficit Hyperactivity Disorder: Provide opportunities throughout the lesson for movement. For example, allow a child with attention deficits to pass out materials or gather the parachute.

Orthopedic Impairments: Provide assistance to those children with specific orthopedic impairments that may prohibit them from grasping the edge of the parachute.

Curriculum Connections

✦ **Outdoors:** Play parachute games as often as possible during outdoor play throughout the air travel and transportation unit.
✦ **Sand and Water Table:** Provide small paper umbrellas and plastic people figurines in the Sand Table. Attach strings to the umbrellas with glue so the figurines can be attached to them. Invite the children to experiment with the parachute action.

Hot Air Balloons

Time
15 minutes

Materials
Hot Air: The (Mostly) True Story of the First Hot-Air Balloon Ride by Marjorie Priceman
helium-filled balloon
picture of hot air balloons (historical versions, too, if you can find them)

Objectives

Children will:
1. Identify a hot air balloon as a form of air travel and transportation.
2. Say that hot air makes objects rise.

Lesson

✦ Hold the helium-filled balloon in front of the children and tell them that people have wanted to travel in the air for a long, long time.
✦ Explain to the children that the helium balloon is not hot. It does not have air in it. It has a special gas that is lighter than air. This makes it float.
✦ Tell them that before planes were invented, people experimented with balloon travel.
✦ Read *Hot Air: The (Mostly) True Story of the First Hot-Air Balloon Ride.*
✦ Point out that hot air makes objects rise (show the pictures in the book that demonstrate this principle).
✦ Tell children that hot air balloons don't travel very fast. They are not very reliable, either, because they bump into things.
✦ Say, "It's hard to control which way the balloon will go, and the wind will influence how it moves."

Modifications/Accommodations

Autism: During the lesson, use pictures, objects, signs, and gestures to provide visual support for the child. For the review, use a starter phrase, such as "I would like travel in a hot air balloon because…" rather than a why question.

Speech or Language Impairments: Use a lead in sentence when asking the child why he would or would not like to travel in a balloon. For example, "I would like travel in a hot air balloon because_____." "If the child still cannot respond to the request to tell whether he would like to ride in a hot air balloon, provide verbal suggestions, such as "because it's fun" or "because it's scary." Then ask the child again.

Review

Ask the children to tell whether they would like to travel in a balloon and to tell why or why not.

Assessment Strategy

Show children various pictures of modes of transportation and ask them to pick out the hot air balloon.

Hearing Impairments: Seat the child where he can see your lips and face. Repeat key concepts and check for understanding periodically. Use pictures and objects as you present the lesson. As you read *Hot Air: The (Mostly) True Story of the First Hot-Air Balloon,* point to the pictures as you name them and talk about them.

Visual Impairments: Describe the pictures as you read *Hot Air: The (Mostly) True Story of the First Hot-Air Balloon.* Allow the child to hold and feel objects as you present them during the lesson. Replace as many photographs with objects as you can.

Cognitive and/or Developmental Disabilities: During the lesson use simplified vocabulary and language, repeating phrases often. Use objects during the lesson to make it more concrete. During the assessment, limit the pictures to two or three at a time.

Emotional Disturbance: Seat the child near you during the lesson. Let the child help from time to time by turning the pages in the book as you read *Hot Air: The (Mostly) True Story of the First Hot-Air Balloon Ride.* Affirm the child for helping and participating. Emphasize the fact that people in hot air balloons must be very careful because they are way up high in the sky.

Other Health Impairments/Attention Deficit Hyperactivity Disorder: Establish a consistent signal to get the child's attention. Make sure that you have the child's attention before you speak.

Orthopedic Impairments: Position a child so that he can be involved actively in the lesson.

Curriculum Connections

✦ **Art:** Provide paper and art materials. Suggest that the children draw or paint pictures of hot air balloons.
✦ **Math:** Prepare a set of flashcards (index cards) with pictures of hot air balloons that are alike and different. Place these in the Manipulatives Center so children can match those that are alike.
✦ **Outdoors:** Attach helium-filled balloons to various pieces of playground equipment or to the fence so children can observe their movements as the wind blows.

CHAPTER

3 Pets

This topic provides a natural opportunity to develop a strong home/school connection. Children's pets are precious to them, and they will enjoy talking about their favorite animal (or animals) at school, bringing photographs of their pets to share, and learning more about pets. Asking families about their pets shows your interest in their everyday lives.

Begin with a bulletin board titled "Our Pets," matching pet photographs with their owners. (**Note**: If a child does not have a pet at home, ask family members to send a photograph of the child with a favorite stuffed animal, or you can take a picture of the child with a classroom stuffed animal.) As the unit progresses, continue to add pet pictures to the bulletin board so children can discover the unique animals they might choose as pets.

Magazine collections about animals are also noteworthy to add to the classroom library: *Paws & Claws, Pet Life, Dog Fancy, Cats & Kittens, Dog & Kennel*, and National Geographic's *Little Kids Magazine* are selections children might enjoy. You may be able to find veterinary clinics that will share their journal subscriptions with you if your school or center is unable to afford the cost of magazines. Similarly, family members might have magazines they can loan to you for the duration of the pet unit. Numerous books about pets are also available that will enhance your classroom library, providing information and stories about pets to meet the needs of the children.

When children begin to lose interest in pets, take down the bulletin board photos and collect them into an album as a keepsake of this special study. Long after you are finished with this unit, the children will be able to look through the album and find their photographs and photographs of their classmates with their favorite animals.

Of all of the topics in this book, this unit may be the most relevant and personal for your children. Remember to share information with the children in your class about the pets you have in your home or the ones you had as a child.

Introduction to Pets

Time
20 minutes

Materials
book about any pet (such as *Ginger Finds a Home* by Charlotte Voake)
pictures of all types of animals, domestic and wild
plastic animal replicas (if they are available)
black or dark blue construction paper
scissors
laminate (optional)

Objectives

Children will:
1. Name one animal that is a pet.
2. Distinguish between animals that are pets and those that are not.

Lesson

◆ Begin by telling children that they will be talking about pets for the next few days. If you have already completed lessons from Chapter 4 (Animals), you can ask children to name some animals they remember learning about.

◆ Explain that pets are animals that live in many people's homes and are different from other animals because they are tame. Say, "These animals are called domestic animals."

◆ Ask children if they have any pets and let them discuss their family pets.

◆ Point out that although most family pets are cats or dogs, other animals can be pets as well.

◆ Engage the children in a brief discussion about the responsibilities of pet owners (feeding the pet, giving it water, keeping it clean, taking it to the vet, and so on).

◆ Read *Ginger Finds a Home* or *Pizza Kittens,* both by Charlotte Voake (or substitute another book about pets).

◆ Play a game with children by holding up animal pictures or the plastic animals and asking them whether they are wild animals or pets.

◆ Introduce the children to the first verse of "I Have a Pet" (several later activities in the chapter will contain additional verses):

I Have a Pet by Laverne Warner
Tune: "The Farmer in the Dell"
I have a little pet.
It is very dear to me.
I give it food and hold it close,
So it'll remember me.

Modifications/Accommodations

Autism: Provide pictures for this child during the review. During the discussion about the responsibilities pet owners have, use pictures or objects to show what animals need.

Speech or Language Impairments: If the child does not respond to questions, use a carrier phrase, such as, "Pets are animals that live in our _____." to help him respond. If he still does not respond, have him repeat after you. Then ask the question to see if the child will respond.

Review

Ask children to name some of the pets that were talked about during the lesson.

Assessment Strategy

Prepare beforehand by cutting out animal silhouettes from black or dark blue construction paper. Laminate the silhouettes for longevity. Observe children while they match plastic animal figures (or pictures) with the animal silhouettes. Ask them informally to name the animals they know and identify those that are common pets.

Hearing Impairments: Seat the child across from you where he can see your face and mouth as you speak. Repeat what the other children say, checking periodically for understanding.

Visual Impairments: Describe the pictures when showing pictures of pets, and then have the child guess which pet you are talking about. When reading *Ginger Finds a Home*, describe the pictures. Have the child with visual impairments hold up the pictures when the children are telling whether they are wild animals or pets. This provides an opportunity for the child to participate during this part of the lesson. As each child responds, state, "Yes, a _____ is a pet, but a _____ is a wild animal." When it is the child's turn to tell whether the animal is a pet or a wild animal, present the question verbally.

Cognitive and/or Developmental Disabilities: When asking the child to match plastic animal figures (or pictures) with animal silhouettes, use only two animals and silhouettes at a time.

Emotional Disturbance: Seat the child near you. Talk about how it is important to be kind and gentle with pets. Emphasize that pets need a clean home, food, and water, and must be taken care of.

Other Health Impairments/Attention Deficit Hyperactivity Disorder: Make sure that you have the child's attention before you speak. Incorporate motions with the song "I Have a Pet." Have the child help turn pages from time to time in the book *Ginger Finds a Home* as you read it.

Orthopedic Impairments: When asking the child to match plastic animal figures (or pictures) with animal silhouettes cut from black or dark blue construction paper, allow the child to respond by looking at the animal.

Curriculum Connections

+ **Language and Literacy:** Place a number of books about pets in the Library Center. Include pet care books, too, because they usually have good pictures of children with pets.
+ **Math:** Place animal silhouette cutouts in the Manipulatives Center and ask children to identify them or match them with plastic figurines. You can also ask children to sort the animals into two categories: domestic animals and wild animals.
+ **Science:** Bring in an aquarium and fish into the classroom. Ask children to tell why fish might be classified as pets.

Time
20 minutes

Materials
aquarium with fish (brought in at the beginning of the study)
book about fish (such as *One Fish, Two Fish, Red Fish, Blue Fish* by Dr. Seuss or Marcus Pfister's *Rainbow Fish*)

Preparation
Position children in front of the aquarium as you begin this lesson or place the aquarium in the Circle Time area.

Objectives

Children will:
1. Identify a fish as a type of pet.
2. Identify one characteristic of a fish that makes it a pet.

Lesson

✦ Begin the lesson by asking children if they remember what they are learning about.

✦ Ask them to look at the aquarium and talk about what they see. Ask what the fish are doing.

✦ Show children how to make fish with their hands by positioning the palms together and moving their hands like fish.

✦ Explain that fish can be pets, though fish cannot be held like most pets. Point out that people who own fish are responsible for feeding them and cleaning their bowls or aquariums.

✦ Focus on the idea of a pet fish. Emphasize that this is not the kind of fish that people eat.

✦ Read *One Fish, Two Fish, Red Fish, Blue Fish* (or another selection) to the children and ask them to compare the fish in the book with the fish in the aquarium.

✦ Introduce the children to the next verse of "I Have a Pet":

I Have a Pet by Laverne Warner
Tune: "The Farmer in the Dell"
I have a little fish.
It is very dear to me.
I give it food and watch it swim.
He's so much fun to see.

Modifications/Accommodations

Autism: Use gestures, sign language, and pictures as you present the lesson. When you read *One Fish, Two Fish, Red Fish, Blue Fish,* have the children repeat the phrases after you.

Speech or Language Impairments: When asking the children to look at the aquarium and talk about what they see, get this child started with the phrase, "I see___," if needed. When asking what the fish are doing, use the carrier phase: "The fish are _____..." if the child does not respond. During the review, show a picture of a fish in a fishbowl for the child to relate to when answering the question.

Review

Recall the responsibilities people have to their pets. Ask children to tell what they have to do as pet owners if they have fish in their homes.

Assessment Strategy

Show various pictures of animals to individual children (including pictures of fish) and ask them to identify those that could be pets.

Hearing Impairments: Seat the child across from you where she can see your face. Use gestures and pictures as you discuss pet fish. If the child uses sign language, use the sign for *fish*.

fish

Visual Impairments: Describe the fish and aquarium. Provide a toy fish that the child can feel and hold. Describe the pictures as you read *One Fish, Two Fish, Red Fish, Blue Fish*. For the assessment, name animals and ask if they would make good pets.

Cognitive and/or Developmental Disabilities: For the assessment, show only two or three pictures at a time. During the review, use the accommodation listed above under Speech or Language Impairments, showing a picture of a fish in a fishbowl for the child to relate to when answering the question.

Emotional Disturbance: Seat the child near you during the lesson. Emphasize the fact that people have to take care of their pets.

Other Health Impairments/Attention Deficit Hyperactivity Disorder: Provide very close supervision of the child when approaching the aquarium. Talk about how to be careful around the aquarium or fishbowl since it is glass, and to be careful not to spill the water because fish must stay in the water or they will die.

Orthopedic Impairments: Help the child make the motions of a fish during the lesson.

Curriculum Connections

✦ **Art:** Add sequins or small jars of gold paint to the Art Center and encourage children to create pictures of fish for a classroom bulletin board.

✦ **Language and Literacy:** Add a log or journal to the Science Center so children can record the amount of food that is given to the fish on a daily basis.

✦ **Science:** Establish a feeding routine for the fish in the aquarium and assign individual children the responsibility for caring for the fish on a routine basis. Schedule these assignments daily or weekly, depending on the needs and interests of your children.

Snakes

Time
20 minutes

Materials
pictures of snakes
a snake replica (purchased at a novelty store or made out of playdough)
book about snakes (such as *Don't Take Your Snake for a Stroll* by Karin Ireland)

Objectives

Children will:
1. Name a snake as a pet.
2. Identify one characteristic of a snake that makes it a pet.

Lesson

✦ Begin the lesson by holding up a snake replica or a picture of a snake and asking children if they think a snake is a pet.
✦ Tell the children that some people like to have snakes as pets. Remind them that snakes cannot be petted like a cat or a dog, but that snake owners do have to feed and water their pets and keep their living quarters clean.
✦ Introduce and read the book *Don't Take Your Snake for a Stroll* (or another choice).
✦ Explain that snakes are reptiles. If you have done an animal unit, this may be a familiar term to the children. If not, tell them what a reptile is and give some examples. Tell the children that reptiles are animals that have scaly skin and crawl on their bellies or on short legs, such as lizards, turtles, alligators, and crocodiles.
✦ Emphasize that snakes that live in the wild are sometimes dangerous (or venomous) and that children should stay away from them if they ever encounter one.
✦ Introduce the children to the next verse of "I Have a Pet," then discuss what the word "slither" means.

I Have a Pet by Laverne Warner
Tune: "The Farmer in the Dell"
I have a little snake.
It is very dear to me.
I give it food and watch it slither.
He's so much fun to see.

✦ Ask children to slither around in the Circle Time area just for fun.

Modifications/Accommodations

Autism: When talking about the things that pet snakes need, provide pictures of a cage or aquarium, food, and water. As you discuss snakes, use sign language for the snake and other animals. The sign for *snake* is on the next page. Signs for other animals appear throughout this book.
Speech or Language Impairments: When asking questions, call on the child after other classmates have had a chance to model verbal responses.

Review

Ask children to tell one reason a snake might be someone's pet.

Assessment Strategy

Show various pictures of animals to individual children (including pictures of snakes) and ask them to identify those that could be pets.

Hearing Impairments: Seat the child across from you where he can see your face and mouth. Use pictures and objects to refer to as you present the lesson. Repeat the responses of classmates, checking periodically for understanding. If the child uses sign language, use the sign for *snake* in the lesson.

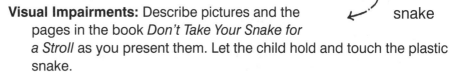
snake

Visual Impairments: Describe pictures and the pages in the book *Don't Take Your Snake for a Stroll* as you present them. Let the child hold and touch the plastic snake.

Cognitive and/or Developmental Disabilities: Use simple vocabulary and language as you discuss pet snakes. When asking the child to identify those animals that could be pets during the assessment, present the animals two at a time.

Emotional Disturbance: Seat the child next to you. Discuss the fact that although some snakes are venomous, most are not. Still, people should not pick up snakes that they see outside. Emphasize the fact that snake owners must take care of their pet snakes. Discuss the things that a pet snake needs: food to eat, water to drink, and a clean cage.

Other Health Impairments/Attention Deficit Hyperactivity Disorder: Make sure that you have this child's attention before you speak. Incorporate motions into the song "I Have a Pet," When reading the book *Don't Take Your Snake for a Stroll*, invite the child to turn the pages after you read them.

Orthopedic Impairments: Assist the child with slithering on the floor during this activity.

Curriculum Connections

✦ **Fine Motor:** Encourage children to use playdough or clay to make snake replicas during the study about pets. Just for fun, ask children to join their efforts together to make an extra long snake.

✦ **Language and Literacy:** Prior to the visit by the snake's owner (see Science activity below), brainstorm with children questions they might ask about the pet. Write the questions on a chart and the name of the child who asked the question. Use the brainstormed list as a review of the information children learned after the snake handler has left the classroom.

✦ **Science:** Invite a snake owner (perhaps a parent) to come in and show children their pet snake(s). Snake handlers often enjoy showing children larger snakes (such as boa constrictors), which might be particularly fascinating to children.

Birds

Time
20 minutes

Materials
bird in a cage, if possible
pictures of birds (or bird
   replicas)
book about birds (such as
   *The Burgess Bird Book for
   Children* by Thornton W.
   Burgess)

Preparation
Have a bird in a cage in the
Circle Time area, if possible.
Otherwise, use pictures of
birds at the appropriate times
in the lesson.

Objectives

Children will:
1. Identify that some types of birds are pets.
2. Name one characteristic of birds that make it a pet.

Lesson

✦ Ask children to name the types of pets that the class has talked about.
✦ Tell them that some people have birds as pets, and ask them to observe the bird in a cage. Point out that birds are not easy to hold and pet.
✦ Ask children what bird owners might have to do to take care of their pets.
✦ Show *The Burgess Bird Book for Children* by Thornton W. Burgess and talk about the types of birds families might own (parrots, parakeets, cockatiels, and so on).
✦ Talk about the characteristics of birds (they have wings, feathers, beaks, talons or claws, and so on).
✦ Introduce the children to the next verse of "I Have a Pet":

I Have a Pet by Laverne Warner
Tune: "The Farmer in the Dell"
I have a little bird.
It is very dear to me.
I give it food and watch it fly,
I love to hear it sing.

✦ Sing the song again, inserting the word "chirp" in place of the words in the song. Sing the whole melody using just the word "chirp."

Modifications/Accommodations

Autism: When asking the child to tell the characteristics of birds, provide a picture as a frame of reference. When asking children to name the pets that you have talked about, provide pictures if the child does not respond. Instead of the "why" question in the review, use a carrier phrase, such as, "I would like to have a pet bird because...."

Speech or Language Impairments: When asking questions provide a carrier phrase if the child does not respond. For example, in the assessment, state, "A type of bird I would want as a pet is_____."

Hearing Impairments: Seat the child across from you where she can see your face. Use pictures as a frame of reference when talking about the characteristics of birds, types of birds, and things that pet birds need.

Review

Ask children why someone might want to have a bird as a pet.

Assessment Strategy

Ask each child to name a type of bird that people might have as a pet.

Visual Impairments: Provide a stuffed animal bird for the child to feel and hold. When showing pictures during the lesson and in *The Burgess Bird Book for Children,* describe them.

Cognitive and/or Developmental Disabilities: Use simple vocabulary and short sentences. Show pictures of different types of birds. During the assessment, provide two or three pictures for the child to help her answer to the question. Review the parts of birds and types of birds daily until the child is able to name and identify each.

Emotional Disturbance: Seat the child next to you. Draw attention to the fact that bird owners must take care of their pet birds because they cannot care for themselves like wild birds. Show the child the things that pet birds need each day: a clean cage, a cover, birdseed, and water.

Other Health Impairments/Attention Deficit Hyperactivity Disorder: Incorporate movement in the song "I Have a Pet." When reading and looking at pictures in *The Burgess Bird Book for Children,* have the child help by turning pages. Make sure that you have the child's attention before speaking.

Orthopedic Impairments: No accommodations are needed for this lesson.

Curriculum Connections

✦ **Art:** Collect bird feathers to add to the Art Center so children can paint with them. Make sure they are disinfected prior to letting children use them.

✦ **Listening:** Purchase a tape or CD of birdcalls and place in the Listening Center for children's enjoyment.

✦ **Science:** Place the bird in its cage on the Science Table for children to observe at their leisure. Consider adopting a bird for the classroom.

Rabbits

Time
20 minutes

Materials
live rabbit in a cage (if
 possible)
stuffed toy rabbit
pictures of rabbits (wild and
 domesticated)
stuffed animal rabbit
The Little Rabbit by Judy
 Dunn or another book
 about bunnies

Preparation
If you secure a live rabbit for
the lesson, place it and its
cage in the Circle Time area
prior to beginning the lesson.

Objectives

Children will:
1. Identify rabbits as a possible pet.
2. Give one reason why they think rabbits are good pets to have.

Lesson

✦ Begin the lesson by asking children to tell what they think the lesson will be about today.
✦ Ask if anyone has a pet rabbit or bunny at home. Tell children that rabbits and bunnies refer to the same animal.
✦ Take the animal out of the cage and encourage the children to pet it and talk about how it feels to them (or use the stuffed animal if a live rabbit is not available).
✦ Read *The Little Rabbit* to the children.
✦ Tell the children that some rabbits live in the wild, but they can become pets if they are kept in a cage. Tell the children that rabbits hop, but they also know how to run very fast.
✦ Demonstrate to children how rabbits wiggle their noses, and ask them to wiggle their noses as a response.
✦ Ask children if they know any other stories about rabbits (for example, *The Runaway Bunny* by Margaret Wise Brown or *Listen, Buddy* by Helen Lester). Acknowledge children if they bring up the Easter Bunny.
✦ Introduce the children to the next verse of "I Have a Pet":

I Have a Pet by Laverne Warner
Tune: "The Farmer in the Dell"
I have a little bunny.
It is very dear to me.
His ears are so very long.
I love to see him run.

Modifications/Accommodations

Autism: Use pictures and objects as you present the lesson on rabbits. For the assessment, show a picture of a rabbit and ask the child to name a characteristic of rabbits.

Speech or Language Impairments: When asking questions provide a carrier phrase if the child does not respond. For example, for the assessment help the child to begin by saying, "A rabbit has_____" if the child does not respond when you ask him to tell you about rabbits. A picture of a rabbit will also help the child to respond.

Review

Sing all of the verses of "I Have a Pet" as a review of the entire unit on pets.

Assessment Strategy

Ask individual children to name a characteristic of rabbits.

Hearing Impairments: Seat the child across from you where he can see your mouth and face. When children in the classroom respond to questions or comment, repeat what they say. If the child uses sign language, use the signs for *rabbit* and *ears* in the lesson.

Visual Impairments: Allow the child to touch the live rabbit and hold a stuffed rabbit so he can understand what you are talking about. When reading *Bunny Cakes* by Rosemary Wells or another book, describe the pictures as you read.

Cognitive and/or Developmental Disabilities: For the assessment, show a picture of a rabbit and have the child describe a characteristic of rabbits. Point to the parts of the rabbit to cue the child, if needed.

Emotional Disturbance: Emphasize how it is important to be kind to rabbits and pets. Have the children show you how to pet a rabbit using a stuffed rabbit.

Other Health Impairments/Attention Deficit Hyperactivity Disorder: When singing "I Have a Pet," incorporate movement into the song. Have the child help to turn the pages from time to time as you read the book.

Orthopedic Impairments: Help the child to wiggle his nose by helping the child place a hand on the tip of his nose. Assist the child in petting the rabbit.

rabbit

ear

Curriculum Connections

✦ **Dramatic Play:** Add several sets of bunny ears (purchased or teacher-made) to the Dramatic Play Center, so children can pretend to be bunnies. Provide construction paper and small scissors so that children can create their own bunny ears. Make headbands from strips of construction paper. Help the children glue the ears onto headbands so they can wear their ears.

✦ **Science:** Place the rabbit in its cage in the Science Center for children to observe. If you have gerbils, guinea pigs, or hamsters in the classroom, ask children to touch each animal and tell which one is the softest. Record their answers on a chart.

✦ **More Science:** Locate a book that shows pictures of various animal tracks, such as *Animal Tracks and Signs* by Preben Bang. Though this book is for adults, some children will enjoy looking at the animal track pictures inside. Ask children to look for animal tracks on the playground or in their yards at home.

Hamsters

Note: If your classroom has a gerbil instead, you can adapt this lesson to fit your specific pet. If you don't have either of these animals, poll parents ahead of time to find out if any of the children have a gerbil or hamster at home that they would be willing to bring to school on the designated day for this lesson.

Time
20 minutes

Materials
live hamster (or gerbil) in a cage
pictures of a hamster or gerbil
Hamsters to the Rescue by Ellen Stoll Walsh (or another suitable book about hamsters or gerbils)

Preparation
Place a hamster (or gerbil) in a cage in the center of the Circle Time area (or position children near the hamster cage in the Science Center).

Objectives

Children will:
1. Identify a hamster (or a gerbil) as a pet.
2. Name one responsibility that hamster owners have for their pets.

Lesson

✦ Begin by asking, "Can you guess what pet we're talking about today?"
✦ Ask the children to tell what they like about their classroom hamster (or gerbil). If you do not have a classroom hamster or gerbil, ask them what they like about the borrowed animal.
✦ As children respond to the question, guide them to talk about the softness of the pet and describe how cuddly it is.
✦ Briefly discuss or review the responsibilities that pet owners have for their animals.
✦ Allow children to pet the animal (or hold it) during the discussion. Hamsters are fragile, so take care not to squeeze them at all.
✦ Present the book *Hamsters to the Rescue* or another appropriate selection.
✦ Introduce the children to the next verse of "I Have a Pet" (change the word to gerbil, if appropriate):

I Have a Pet by Laverne Warner
Tune: "The Farmer in the Dell"
I have a little hamster.
It is very dear to me.
I give it food and water, too.
He runs very fast.

Modifications/Accommodations

Autism: When asking what needs to be done to take care of hamsters, show the child the items needed to care for this animal. Emphasize that hamsters need food, water, and a clean cage. For the review activity, show the child pictures of the other animals for comparison.

Speech or Language Impairments: Provide a carrier phrase to get the child started in answering questions. For example, when asking what she likes about the hamster, say "I like_____." For the review activity, show the child pictures of the other animals for comparison. In the song "I Have a Pet," hold up a picture for each animal.

Hearing Impairments: Seat the child across from you so she can see your lips and face as you speak. When discussing the responsibilities of pet owners, show the objects needed to take care of a hamster.

Review

Make a comparison of this cuddly pet to other pets that the class has studied (birds, snakes, fish, and so on). Sing all the "I Have a Pet" verses that children have already learned.

Assessment Strategy

Add pictures of hamsters (or gerbils) and their silhouettes to the collection of animals that children have been using throughout the study. Ask individual children to match the specific animal to its silhouette and name the pet.

Visual Impairments: Allow the child to touch and pet the hamster when you present it to the class. Describe the pictures as you read the story.

Cognitive and/or Developmental Disabilities: For the assessment activity, present only two silhouettes and two pictures at a time.

Emotional Disturbance: Seat the child next to you. Show the child how to pet the hamster and emphasize being gentle with animals.

Other Health Impairments/Attention Deficit Hyperactivity Disorder: Before allowing the child to pet the hamster, make sure that the child is seated and calm. Emphasize being gentle with animals before allowing the child to pet the hamster.

Orthopedic Impairments: Assist the child to pet the hamster using hand-over-hand assistance.

Curriculum Connections

✦ **Fine Motor:** Use some of the collected pet pictures to make small puzzles. Mount the pictures on lightweight cardboard and cut them out. Laminate the pieces, so you can use the puzzles from year to year. Place them in the Manipulatives Center for children to put together.

✦ **Listening:** Make a cassette recording of the children singing "I Have a Pet" to add to the Listening Station. Consider preparing a book of pet pictures and the words of each verse to put into the Listening Station.

✦ **Science:** Place the hamster (or gerbil) in the cage in the Science Center for children to observe at their leisure. If you have purchased an animal for the classroom, assign feeding and watering duties to individual children on a rotational system.

Guinea Pigs

Time
20 minutes

Materials
pictures of guinea pigs
live guinea pig (in a cage), if
    possible
*Brian and Bob: The Tale of
    Two Guinea Pigs* by
    Georgie Ripper, *The
    Guinea Pig ABC* by Kate
    Duke, or another suitable
    book about guinea pigs

Preparation
If you have a guinea pig
available in its cage, place it
in the Center Time area prior
to the lesson or position
children in front of the guinea
pig's cage in the Science
Center.

Objectives

Children will:
1. Identify a guinea pig as a pet.
2. Name one characteristic of the guinea pig that makes it a pet.

Lesson

◆ Say to the children, "Today we're continuing our study of pets, and I think you can tell what animal we're talking about today." If a guinea pig is not available, show a large picture of the animal.
◆ When children have identified the guinea pig as the topic of discussion, describe guinea pigs as short-tailed rodents that are usually larger than gerbils and hamsters. In comparison, hamsters usually have large cheek pouches and gerbils have long hind legs that allow them to leap.
◆ Ask the children to look at the guinea pig (or picture of a guinea pig) and talk about its size and color. Tell them that the guinea pig is related to the rat because guinea pigs and rats are members of a family of animals called rodents.
◆ Read a book about guinea pigs, such as *Brian and Bob: The Tale of Two Guinea Pigs* by Georgie Ripper or *The Guinea Pig ABC* by Kate Duke.
◆ Introduce the children to the next verse of "I Have a Pet":

I Have a Pet by Laverne Warner
Tune: "The Farmer in the Dell"
I have a guinea pig.
It is very dear to me.
He's round, soft, and plump, too,
I love to feel his fur.

Modifications/Accommodations

Autism: During the review, provide a picture of a guinea pig to use as a visual reference. Use signs, gestures, pictures, and objects throughout the lesson. When discussing the distinguishing features of a guinea pig, point to the features on a picture of a guinea pig.

Speech or Language Impairments: When asking questions, provide a picture for reference. If the child does not respond, provide a carrier phrase to get the child started. Use gestures during the song to increase participation:

I have a guinea pig. (repeatedly touch nose)
It is very dear to me. (hug self by crossing arms on chest)
He's round, soft, and plump, too, (make circle with hands)
I love to feel his fur. (pet the top of one hand)

Review

Ask children to use descriptive words to describe the guinea pig.

Assessment Strategy

Add pictures of guinea pigs to the classroom collection. Ask individual children to pick out the pictures of the guinea pigs.

Hearing Impairments: Seat the child across from you where she can see your face and mouth. When talking about the distinguishing features of guinea pigs, show the children the characteristics on the guinea pig. Use pictures and objects to refer to during the lesson.

Visual Impairments: Describe the pictures as you present them during the lesson. When reading *The Tale of Two Guinea Pigs* by Georgie Ripper or *The Guinea Pig ABC,* describe the pictures in the books. For the assessment activity, have the child tell you three things about a guinea pig.

Cognitive and/or Developmental Disabilities: When using the pictures in the assessment, use only two pictures at a time. Point to the areas on a picture of a guinea pig when talking about its distinguishing features.

Emotional Disturbance: Seat the child next to you. Talk about the need to be kind to animals and pets. Show the child how to stroke the guinea pig gently to pet it. Talk about how it is important to take good care of pets, and that guinea pigs need a clean cage, water, and vegetables to eat.

Other Health Impairments/Attention Deficit Hyperactivity Disorder: Make sure that you have the child's attention before you speak. Incorporate movement into the song "I Have a Pet." When reading, *The Tale of Two Guinea Pigs* or *The Guinea Pig ABC,* invite the child to help you by turning the pages.

Orthopedic Impairments: When asking individual children to pick out the pictures of the guinea pigs, allow the child to respond by looking at the appropriate picture.

Curriculum Connections

+ **Language and Literacy:** With small groups of children, brainstorm words that describe the guinea pig. Write these on the classroom Word Wall.
+ **Music:** Sing the "I Have a Pet" song for another classroom in the building. As children sing the verses, let individual children hold up a picture of the animal they are singing about.
+ **Science:** Place the guinea pig and its cage on the Science Table for children to observe. Use caution if you let the guinea pig roam around the classroom, because guinea pigs bite if provoked.

Mice

Time
20 minutes

Materials
pictures of mice
mouse (or two) in a cage (or use stuffed animal replicas)
Mouse's First Summer by Lauren Thompson (she has a number of other mouse books that would be suitable)

Preparation
Place the mouse in its cage in the Center Time area (or have pictures or a stuffed animal mouse).

Objectives

Children will:
1. Identify mice as a suitable pet.
2. List characteristics of mice that make them appropriate as pets.

Lesson

✦ Begin the lesson by telling the children that the class is going to talk about mice as possible pets in today's lesson.
✦ Ask children what they know about mice. Some children might respond that there are mice in their attic or basement, or that they see mice outside. Explain to them that wild mice do not make good pets.
✦ Show the mouse in its cage (or the stuffed animal mouse), and tell children that domestic mice can be good pets, just like the guinea pig, hamster, and gerbil.
✦ Tell children that pet mice sometimes need to go to the vet, just like cats and dogs.
✦ Read *Mouse's First Summer* or one of Lauren Thompson's other mouse selections to the children. You could also use Arnold Shapiro's *Mice Squeak, We Speak.*
✦ Introduce the children to the next verse of "I Have a Pet."

   I Have a Pet by Laverne Warner
   Tune: "The Farmer in the Dell"
   I have a little mouse.
   It is very dear to me.
   He has the prettiest pink nose,
   I love to hold him close.

Note: The complete version of "I Have a Pet," with all the verses is on page 124 at the end of this chapter.

Modifications/Accommodations

Autism: For the assessment, give three reasons why people like mice as pets. Then ask the child why people might want mice as pets.

Speech or Language Impairments: When asking the children to tell what they know about mice in the lesson and review, give the child a hint if she does not respond. Show the child a stuffed mouse and ask her to tell you something about it.

Review
Ask children to tell what they know about having mice as pets in their homes.

Assessment Strategy
Ask individual children to tell one reason why people might want mice as pets.

Hearing Impairments: Seat the child across from you so she can see your face and lips. When talking about mice, use pictures, objects, and gestures. If the child uses sign language, include the signs for *mouse* and *pet* in the lesson.

mouse

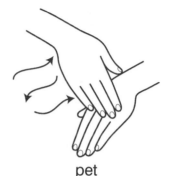
pet

Visual Impairments: Allow the child to touch the mouse when you begin talking about it. When reading *Mouse's First Summer* or another book, describe the pictures as you read it.

Cognitive and/or Developmental Disabilities: Use a stuffed mouse to talk about pet mice. Point out the body parts on the stuffed mouse.

Emotional Disturbance: Seat the child near you during the lesson. Emphasize being kind to animals and caring for pets. Have each child demonstrate how to hold and pet a mouse using a stuffed mouse.

Other Health Impairments/Attention Deficit Hyperactivity Disorder: Incorporate movement into the song "I Have a Pet." Enlist the child's help in turning pages in the book from time to time as you read it.

Orthopedic Impairments: No accommodations are anticipated for this lesson.

Curriculum Connections

✦ **Art:** Place inkpads and fine-tip markers in the Art Center so children can make thumbprint mice.

✦ **Language and Literacy:** Brainstorm with small groups of children all of the words they can think of that rhyme with mouse (*blouse, house, louse, grouse, douse*) or mice (*nice, dice, rice, lice, price, spice, thrice*).

✦ **Music:** Gather interested children together to make up a song about mice. Use a familiar tune, such as "Mary Had a Little Lamb" to assist them with their creativity.

Introduction to Cats and Dogs

Time
20 minutes

Materials
pictures of cats and dogs showing various breeds of each
small plastic cats and dogs
variety of books about cats and dogs

Objectives

Children will:
1. Identify cats and dogs as household pets.
2. Tell that there are different breeds of cats and dogs.

Lesson

✦ Tell the children that the class will be spending a few days talking about cats and dogs. Tell them that cats and dogs are popular pets.
✦ Ask children if they have a pet in their homes and, if so, what kind of animal they have as a pet.
✦ Read a book about cats and dogs, such as *Dog and Cat* by Paul Fehlner and Maxie Chambliss.
✦ Ask children to compare and contrast characteristics of cats and dogs (this strategy naturally lends itself to the use of a Venn diagram). A Venn diagram is a mathematical illustration that looks like two overlapping circles. Venn diagrams are visual tools that show how specific objects are alike and different. You can also use hula hoops to make a large Venn diagram on the floor to show the children likenesses and differences between objects.

Venn Diagram

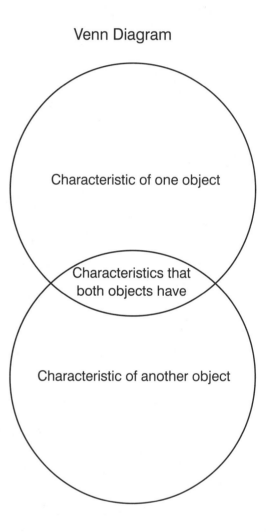

Characteristic of one object

Characteristics that both objects have

Characteristic of another object

Modifications/Accommodations

Autism: Let children with minimal verbal skills respond by choosing pictures during the lesson; provide the words for the child to say and encourage her to repeat them.

Review
Show children pictures of cats and dogs and ask them to identify each group of animals.

Assessment Strategy
Ask individual children to look at pictures of dogs and cats and point to a picture of a cat or a dog.

Speech or Language Impairments: Scaffold the child's language by directing easier responses to this child; model responses if the child does not speak.

Hearing Impairments: Seat the child where she can see your face; model correct responses if the child does not seem to understand your requests.

Visual Impairments: Use small plastic cats and dogs in addition to pictures; let the child feel and hold the cats and dogs during the lesson.

Cognitive and/or Developmental Disabilities: Simplify your language during the lesson. For example, when asking how cats and dogs are the same, say, "Cats and dogs are the same because they both have _____." If the child does not respond, point to the same feature (such as a nose) on each. If the child does not respond well to pictures, use plastic dogs and cats in the assessment and for the review, help the child sort pictures or plastic dogs and cats into piles.

Emotional Disturbance: Seat the child near you during the lesson; affirm the child for responding; direct questions to the child that you feel she would be successful in answering.

Other Health Impairments/Attention Deficit Hyperactivity Disorder: Seat the child near you as you read the book; invite specific children to help turn the pages from time to time.

Orthopedic Impairments: If the child is unable to point, ask her to look at the picture of the dog or cat.

Curriculum Connections

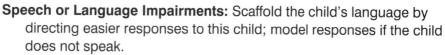

- ✦ **Art:** Trace outlines of a cat and a dog on large pieces of poster board (or butcher paper). Make one for each child. Encourage children to tear construction paper into small pieces and glue them onto the outlines in a mosaic pattern. **Note:** This activity may take several days to complete, depending on the interest and abilities of the children.
- ✦ **Math:** When children bring in pictures of their pets (see lesson), place them on a bulletin board in the correct section (Cats, Dogs, or Other Pets). After several days of collecting photographs, count the number of cats represented, the number of dogs represented, and the number of pets in the other category.
- ✦ **Special Visitor:** Many animal shelters or similar organizations have designated animals that they will bring to classrooms for children to experience firsthand. These animals are docile and enjoy being around children. Invite your local shelter to bring a dog and/or cat to spend the morning in your classroom. Allow children to interact with the animal during Center Time.

Care of Cats

Time
20 minutes

Materials
pictures of cats (optional)
stuffed toy cats

Objectives

Children will:
1. Name two things cats need that humans provide.
2. Explain why cat owners take their cats to the veterinarian.

Lesson

✦ Remind the children that any pet that lives in a home needs care in order to survive. Show the pictures of cats or the stuffed animals that are cats.

✦ Ask children to think about the needs cats have and name them (food, water, shelter, trips to the veterinarian when they are ill or need vaccinations, protection from maltreatment, opportunities to play, affection, and so on).

✦ If there are children in your class who have cats at home, ask them to tell the class about the care they or their parents provide for their cats. As they talk, write their suggestions on a chart or on a chalkboard.

✦ Introduce the song "Cat Rub" to the children.

Cat Rub by Laverne Warner
Tune: "Pop Goes the Weasel"
I love to rub my pretty cat,
She is so soft and sweet.
I rub her head and both of her ears,
Down to her feet.

✦ Remind children to be gentle with animals when they play with them.

✦ Talk to children about how cat collars and identification tags help owners find their cats when they become lost. You might want to mention that many people who let their cats outside put bells on their cats' collars to warn birds away. Cats like to catch birds, so the bell warns birds that a cat is near.

✦ Tell children that you are adding the stuffed animal cats to the Home Living Center so they can enjoy pretending to take care of them.

Modifications/Accommodations

Autism: Provide pictures when asking about the needs of cats. When talking about being gentle with cats, demonstrate with the stuffed cat and have the child show you how to pet the cat gently. For the assessment, provide pictures, if needed.

Review

Spend a few minutes reviewing about all the ways humans care for cats.

Assessment Strategy

Ask children individually to tell at least one need humans can provide for cats in their care.

Speech or Language Impairments: When asking about the needs of cats, call on the child after a few other children have responded. If needed, provide a hint by using a carrier phrase such as, "When cats are sick we take them to the_____."

Hearing Impairments: Seat the child across from you during the lesson so he can see your mouth. Provide pictures when asking about the needs of cats.

Visual Impairments: As you write the children's suggestions on a chart or on a chalkboard, say each word aloud as you write it and describe what you are writing.

Cognitive and/or Developmental Disabilities: Provide pictures when asking about the needs of cats. Repeat responses of other children several times before calling on the child with cognitive disabilities. When talking about being gentle with cats, demonstrate with the stuffed cat and have the child show you how to pet the cat gently. For the assessment, provide both verbal cues and pictures.

Emotional Disturbance: Seat the child near you and affirm participation. When talking about being gentle with cats, demonstrate with the stuffed cat and have the child show you how to pet the cat gently.

Other Health Impairments/Attention Deficit Hyperactivity Disorder: Seat the child next to you during the lesson. When writing on chart paper or chalkboard, place it close to the child so he can see you as you write.

Orthopedic Impairments: Use physical assistance to demonstrate how to be gentle in petting the stuffed cat. Allow the child to practice this several times.

Curriculum Connections

✦ **Art:** Place materials in the Art Center so children can make cat masks (lightweight paper plates, construction paper, string, markers, crayons, chenille sticks or straw for whiskers, and other art supplies). Have a "Cat Parade" when children have finished their masks.

✦ **Language and Literacy:** Place books about cats in the Library Center for children to look at. Some suggestions are Wanda Gag's *Millions of Cats* or Denise Fleming's *Mama Cat Has Three Kittens*.

✦ **More Language and Literacy:** Work with small groups to discuss words (adjectives) and phrases that describe cats and how they feel (soft, furry, speedy, love to climb, love to play, love to chase objects, scratch, claws, whiskers, and so on). Introduce the concept that cats "feel" with their whiskers when they are in small places.

Cat Behaviors

Time
20 minutes

Materials
Pretend You're a Cat by Jean Marzollo or another large book about cats
scratching post (or picture, if real scratching post is not available)

Objectives

Children will:
1. Imitate cat behaviors.
2. Demonstrate one unique movement cats make.

Lesson

◆ Begin the lesson by getting down on your hands and knees and stretching your body as taut as can be (much like a cat stretches).
◆ Ask the children if they have ever seen a cat stretch like you did. Ask what other behaviors they have seen cats perform.
◆ Read *Pretend You're a Cat* and talk about all the behaviors cats demonstrate.
◆ Spend a few minutes with the children stretching, rolling, meowing, creeping, crouching, pouncing, scratching, lapping (milk or water), scampering, climbing, purring, sleeping, and so on.
◆ Talk about what it means to take a "cat nap."
◆ Show children the scratching post (or picture of one) and tell why families place these in their homes (to prevent cats and kittens from scratching the furniture).

Modifications/Accommodations

Autism: During the lesson and assessment, provide pictures of actions that cats perform.
Speech or Language Impairments: As you demonstrate the cat behaviors, label your behaviors several times. Then ask the child what you were doing. For the assessment, have the child imitate cat behaviors before asking her favorite cat behavior.
Hearing Impairments: Seat the child where she can see your mouth and face as you present the lesson. Use gestures or pictures as you demonstrate cat behaviors. For the assessment, have the child imitate cat behaviors before asking her favorite cat behavior.

Review
Ask children to name their favorite cat behavior.

Assessment Strategy
On an individual basis, ask each child to demonstrate a specific cat behavior to you.

Visual Impairments: As you perform the cat behaviors, describe what you are doing. When reading the story, describe each page to this child.

Cognitive and/or Developmental Disabilities: Before asking the child to demonstrate a cat behavior, model it and have a classmate demonstrate it first.

Emotional Disturbance: Seat the child near you during the lesson and provide close supervision as the children model cat behaviors. Invite participation in the story reading by having the child help turn pages from time to time.

Other Health Impairments/Attention Deficit Hyperactivity Disorder: When reading the story, seat the child next to you and have her help to turn the pages. When presenting the cat actions, present them slowly and calmly, exaggerating your actions slowly.

Orthopedic Impairments: Provide physical assistance to help the child perform cat behaviors. Remind the child of behaviors they can do that do not involve a lot of body movement (closing their eyes and pretending to sleep, for example).

Curriculum Connections

✦ **Art:** Encourage children to make models of cats with homemade or commercial playdough. Display the products in a miniature Cat Circus, a child-made display of children's sculptures. If you want, add artifacts that people would see in a circus (something that resembles a big tent, three rings, or clowns, for example) to encourage children's play.

✦ **Connecting with Home:** Ask children to tear or cut out pictures of cats from magazines in their homes and bring them to school to place on a Cat Poster. Talk about all of the behaviors cats are demonstrating in the various pictures. Remind children to ask their parents' permission before tearing a picture from a magazine.

✦ **Outdoors:** Play "Kitten Chase" outdoors. Select one child to be "IT" (the chaser). The rest of the children run around the playground as if they were kittens and IT chases them. If IT tags someone, the tagged kitten helps IT chase the rest of the kittens. Every time another child is tagged, he joins the other chasers. When all of the kittens have been tagged, the game is over.

Care of Dogs

Time
20 minutes

Materials
chart paper and marker
pictures or photographs of
    dogs
Ten Dogs in the Window by
    Claire Masurel (or another
    book about dogs)
stuffed animal dogs
dog care products (water and
    feeding bowls, pet
    brushes, leashes, and so
    on)

Objectives

Children will:
1. Identify one way that humans care for their dogs.
2. Act out caring for dogs in the Dramatic Play Center.

Lesson

✦ Remind children that dogs are one of the many possible pets that families might have.
✦ Ask children to tell how they and their parents take care of their dogs (or other pets). As they make suggestions, write their responses on a chart for review later.
✦ Ask children if any one of them has a specific responsibility in caring for a dog.
✦ Read *Ten Dogs in the Window* and encourage responses from children as you read.
✦ Show children the stuffed animal dogs and the dog care products you have available. Tell them that you are going to place the items in the Dramatic Play or Home Living Center so they can pretend to be doing all the things that are needed to care for dogs (feeding them, giving them water, brushing them, washing them, giving them affection, taking them to the veterinarian's office, providing a bed for them, taking them for a walk, and so on).
✦ If necessary, demonstrate to children how to use some of the dog care products.

Modifications/Accommodations

Autism: Demonstrate how to care for dogs with the pet care items and stuffed dog. Have the child imitate your actions after you demonstrate. Describe the child's actions as she imitates them.

Speech or Language Impairments: When asking children how they take care of their pets, provide verbal cues if the child does not respond. For example, if the child does not volunteer information, ask what she does (or would do) when her dog is hungry.

Hearing Impairments: Show the child the item associated with taking car of a dog and ask the child how she helps to care for her dog. Have the child show you how to use the item with the stuffed dog.

Visual Impairments: When reading the story to the child, describe the pictures.

Cognitive and/or Developmental Disabilities: Use simple explanations and short sentences in your discussion of dog care. Show the items associated with dog care, such as a food and water bowl, leash, and brush when asking how to care for dogs.

Review
Review the chart prepared during the lesson.

Assessment Strategy
Observe children while they are in the Dramatic Play Center to determine what they learned from the discussion about dog care. For children who do not participate in dramatic play, show them a stuffed animal dog and ask them to tell what they can remember about taking care of dogs.

Emotional Disturbance: Seat the child near you during the lesson and emphasize being gentle with pets as one way to take care of them.

Other Health Impairments/Attention Deficit Hyperactivity Disorder: Ensure that you have the child's attention before giving verbal explanations. Enlist the child's help in turning the pages of the book from time to time as you read the story. Show how to use the items, such as a leash, brush, and food bowl, when caring for dogs.

Orthopedic Impairments: Have the child help you demonstrate to children how to use some of the dog care products. Use hand-over-hand assistance, if needed.

Curriculum Connections

✦ **Bulletin Board:** Encourage children to bring in pictures of their dogs (or a friend or relative's dog) to put on a classroom bulletin board. Mark their names on the back of the photographs to ensure that each child receives her contribution when they are returned. Several mathematics activities are possible with the bulletin board. Ask small groups of children to (1) count the photographs (number of dogs represented); (2) chart how many dogs are the same color; (3) identify various breeds of dogs (this will require teacher assistance); and (4) talk about the sizes of the animals.

✦ **Games:** Place duplicate flash card pictures of dogs in the Manipulatives Center for children to match. If children have the interest and ability, teach them how to play Concentration.

✦ **Special Visitor:** Invite a dog groomer to come in one day. Make arrangements to have your own dog or one of the children's dogs available for grooming. When this event is over, discuss with the children what they observed the dog groomer doing.

Dog Breeds

Note: For purposes of this lesson, concentrating on well-known breeds would be more appropriate for young children (such as Dalmatians, Collies, Beagles, and Dachshunds). An excellent resource for information about dog breeds is www.TerrificPets.com.

Time
20 minutes

Materials
pictures or photographs of various breeds of dogs (outdated dog calendars are a good source for pictures)
Any Kind of Dog by Lynn Reiser or another big book about dogs

Objectives

Children will:
1. State that there are many different breeds of dogs.
2. Identify at least one dog breed.

Lesson

✦ Show one or two pictures of dogs that are breeds children might be able to recognize and ask them to identify the breed.
✦ Tell one or two characteristics of the breed as you show their pictures. For example:

   ✦ Dalmatians are strong and muscular; they are white with black spots.
   ✦ Collies are considered to be one of the most beautiful breeds; they are great family dogs because they enjoy human companionship. They have pointed ears and when they are alert, they appear to be extremely interested and watchful. They love to be outdoors.
   ✦ Beagles love to jump and play; they make great family pets. They have short bodies with smooth coats of fur and long floppy ears.
   ✦ Dachshunds are good watch dogs. They have a long body with short legs and are often called "hot dogs" or "wiener dogs."

✦ Talk about mixed breed dogs (sometimes called "mutts") as a possible dog choice in families. Introduce the term *underdogs*, and explain why people often prefer mixed breeds (they often have good qualities of different dog breeds, they are usually inexpensive or free, and so on). (An underdog is a dog that is not a purebred. Tell them that purebred dogs usually are expensive to purchase.)
✦ Read *Any Kind of Dog* to children, encouraging discussion as you read.

Modifications/Accommodations

Autism: Present the pictured dog breeds one at a time, describing the dog's characteristics succinctly. Provide pictures of dogs during the assessment.
Speech or Language Impairments: During the review, provide verbal cues and use carrier phrases to elicit some of the things that they learned about dogs. Have the child practice naming the types of dogs with you prior to the assessment.
Hearing Impairments: Seat the child across from you where he can see your face and mouth. Use pictures and gestures when talking about specific dog breeds.

Review

Ask children to tell what they have learned about dog breeds during the lesson.

Assessment Strategy

Show individual children pictures of various dog breeds that you showed the class in the lesson and ask them to identify as many as they can.

Visual Impairments: Describe the pictures of dogs as you present them. When reading the book, describe the pictures on each page. For the assessment, ask the child to tell you about various dog breeds. If possible, use small dog figurines so the child can feel the shape of the various breeds. If those are not available, outline pictures of dogs with glue (it will dry to a clear consistency) so the child with visual impairments can feel the shape of the dogs.

Cognitive and/or Developmental Disabilities: When describing the characteristics of various dog breeds, use short, simple descriptions. For the assessment, have the child find the dog breed that you name. Present the pictures in the assessment in groups of two or three.

Emotional Disturbance: Seat the child near you as you present the lesson. Affirm participation and invite the child to help you turn pages as you read the book. Remind the child to be kind and take good care of all types of dogs, but that they should never touch a dog that is unfamiliar to them.

Other Health Impairments/Attention Deficit Hyperactivity Disorder: Show the child pictures of dog breeds one at a time. Focus the discussion on the topic as you read the book *Any Kind of Dog* to the children.

Orthopedic Impairments: When asking the child to identify types of dogs in the assessment, present two choices at a time. If needed, the child can look at the one that you name and describe.

Curriculum Connections

✦ **Language and Literacy:** Place books showing various breeds in the Library Center for children to "read." Jim Dratfield's photographs in *Pug Shots and Underdogs* are noteworthy selections. The books about Carl, a Rottweiler (*Good Dog, Carl, Carl Goes to Day Care,* and *Carl's Birthday* by Alexandra Day) are also good choices.

✦ **More Language and Literacy:** In small groups, discuss all of the words that rhyme with dog (*hog, fog, frog, log, clog, cog, bog,* and *jog*). Write the words children suggest for the classroom Word Wall.

✦ **Music:** Add a recording of "How Much Is That Doggie in the Window?" to the Music Center for children to listen to.

✦ **Writing:** Encourage children to guess the cost of a dog (use any dog breed picture) and make index card price tags to place with the picture. Help them write the name of the dog breed, if appropriate.

Dog Behaviors

Time
20 minutes

Materials
dog that can do several tricks (consider asking a parent about bringing in a pet)
Bathtime for Biscuit by Alyssa Satin Capucilli, or another book about dogs
stuffed animal dog
pictures of dogs doing tricks

Objectives

Children will:
1. Describe one behavior that dogs exhibit.
2. Demonstrate one dog behavior.

Lesson

✦ Introduce the parent (or other adult) who brought in her pet dog and ask her to demonstrate some of the tricks her dog can perform.
✦ Tell the children that teaching dogs how to do tricks takes effort, and ask the parent to explain how she trained her dog.
✦ Continue the lesson, but encourage the parent and the dog to stay for awhile so children can attempt some of the tricks (with guidance from its owner) after the lesson.
✦ Read *Bathtime for Biscuit* or another suitable book about dogs.
✦ Ask children to name some behaviors they have observed dogs do. As they suggest behaviors, ask children to imitate them (barking, stretching, playing fetch, rolling over, shaking hands, begging, sleeping, jumping, eating, drinking water, and so on).
✦ Explain that some dogs are trained for special service jobs, such as seeing eye or guide dogs for the blind.
✦ Ask children if they have ever seen a dog show. Suggest that children consider playing "dog tricks" or "dog show" when the group goes outside to the playground.

Modifications/Accommodations

Autism: Use gestures or sign language to emphasize the tricks that dogs learn to do (jump, sit, stay, roll over). When asking the children to show you some of the tricks use gestures or signs. During the assessment allow the child to respond using gestures or signs.

Speech or Language Impairments: Name and describe the behaviors that the dog performs several times during the dog demonstration. When asking the children to name some behaviors they have observed dogs do, demonstrate the action first. Then ask the child to tell you what the dog can do.

Hearing Impairments: Have the child sit across from the parent so she can see the parent's mouth. Use gestures to show the behaviors of dogs.

Visual Impairments: Demonstrate dog behaviors using a small stuffed dog.

Cognitive and/or Developmental Disabilities: Repeat the behaviors shown by the dog several times by demonstrating with a plastic or stuffed dog.

Review

Ask children to remember the dog behaviors discussed during the lesson.

Assessment Strategy

Ask individual children to name one trick that dogs might be trained to perform.

Emotional Disturbance: Have the child stand near you during the demonstration with the dog. If the children have a chance to pet the dog, remind this child to be gentle with the dog and show her how to pet the dog gently. Then guide the child as she pets the dog. Affirm the child for being gentle with pets.

Other Health Impairments/Attention Deficit Hyperactivity Disorder: Sometimes children with ADHD can become overexcited during a visit with an animal. Before the dog arrives, talk about what they need to do when the dog comes (be calm and gentle; be careful not to frighten the dog). Have several strategies to calm the child during the visit if she becomes overly excited (taking a deep breath and blowing, or crossing arms across chest and taking a deep breath). If necessary, take the child aside to calm down.

Orthopedic Impairments: This child may not be able to imitate dog behaviors. Instead, have the child tell you about the things that she saw the dog do.

Curriculum Connections

✦ **Connecting with Home:** Send a note home to parents informing them of the dog study. Request they find time to watch a dog show on television (many cable channels feature dog shows, especially channels devoted to animals). Children will probably find this activity interesting for a short period of time, so tell parents children should only watch until interest wanes.

✦ **Language and Literacy:** Spend some time with small groups brainstorming names for dogs. Write these names on a chart to display in the classroom.

✦ **Music:** Choose any well known tune to sing and invite children to "bark" the song instead of singing it ("Jingle Bells" is a great selection for this activity). If possible, record the song on a cassette for children to enjoy at another time.

✦ **Writing:** Write the names of different dog breeds on index cards. Place pictures of various dogs along with the cards in the Writing Center. Ask the children to copy the words onto sentence strips (or index cards).

Doghouses

Time
15 minutes for the lesson; children may take several days to develop the doghouse project

Materials
pictures of doghouses
large appliance box
craft knife (adult only)
paint, markers, and crayons
dog care items (see page 112)

Objectives

Children will:
1. Identify a picture of a doghouse.
2. Collaborate with others to make a doghouse as a classroom project.

Lesson

✦ Ask children where dogs live. Ask if they know what a doghouse is.
✦ Show pictures of doghouses and ask why a doghouse would be a good place for dogs to live (they are designed specifically for dogs so they protect dogs from the weather, they can be kept outdoors or in a garage, and so on). Discuss that dogs usually live inside the home, but some dogs spend most (or all depending on the type of dog it is) of their time outdoors.
✦ Teach them the following song about a doghouse (as sung from the dog's viewpoint!).

My Doghouse by Laverne Warner
Tune: "My Bonnie Lies Over the Ocean"
My house is just a little one;
It's big enough for me.
My house is just a little one;
It keeps me safe, you see.

Chorus:
When the rain comes,
My body is always D-R-Y!
When the cold comes,
I stay so cozy and warm.

✦ Show children the appliance box and invite them to work together in small groups to make a doghouse during Center Time. Use a craft knife to cut out a door in one end of the box (adult only), large enough for one or two children to enter easily.
✦ Provide guidance as the children work during the week to decorate the house, and display the finished product in the classroom. Use some of the dog care items used in the lesson on care of dogs (see Cats and Dogs—Care of Dogs on page 112) to include with the doghouse as a Special Interest Center.

Modifications/Accommodations

Autism: Use gestures or the signs for *house* and *safe* as you present the lesson on doghouses. When making the doghouse from an appliance box, model ways for the child to work on the doghouse.

house

safe

Review
Ask children to name one reason a dog might like a doghouse.

Assessment Strategy
Ask individual children to identify a doghouse among pictures of various types of houses.

Speech or Language Impairments: Call on the child after other children have modeled correct responses during the part of the lesson when you ask why a doghouse is a good place for dogs to live.

Hearing Impairments: Seat the child across from you during the presentation of the lesson where he can see your face and mouth. Use gestures or sign language as you present the lesson.

Visual Impairments: As you show the pictures of doghouses, describe them verbally. When making the doghouse, provide verbal instructions and physical prompts if needed.

Cognitive and/or Developmental Disabilities: Use simple language and repetition during your verbal explanations. When making the doghouse, provide physical assistance if needed.

Emotional Disturbance: Provide close supervision and affirm the child as he works with classmates to make the doghouse.

Other Health Impairments/Attention Deficit Hyperactivity Disorder: Remind the child about being safe when playing in the box: taking turns, only two children at a time (depending on the size of the box), and being careful with their feet so that they do not kick their friends. Adding gestures and movement to the song would be fun for all children but especially beneficial for the child with ADHD.

Orthopedic Impairments: Provide hand-over-hand assistance, if needed, to help the child make the doghouse. If motions are used with the song, help the child to do them.

Curriculum Connections

- ✦ **Art:** Add materials to the Art Center for children to build miniature doghouses (such as craft sticks, strips of cardboard, clean pint-sized milk cartons, or other small boxes).
- ✦ **Blocks:** Encourage children to build a doghouse in the Block Center.
- ✦ **Writing:** Provide markers and sentence strips for children to write dogs' names to display with the miniature doghouses or to place on the Block Center doghouse. Be prepared to facilitate children's writing when they ask how to spell dogs' names.

Visit with the Veterinarian

Note: This lesson is defined as if the veterinarian is visiting the classroom. A field trip to the veterinarian's office would be preferable but not always a possibility. Make sure that the vet is an individual who understands young children and recognizes the level of understanding they have.

Time

20 minutes (if the veterinarian comes to the classroom) one to two hours (if the children visit the veterinarian in his or her office)

Materials

tools brought by veterinarian
several stuffed animal dogs or
    cats (at least one)

Objectives

Children will:
1. Tell that a veterinarian is a doctor for pets.
2. Identify at least one job the veterinarian performs.

Lesson

✦ Before the veterinarian arrives, discuss good manners with guests: waiting, taking turns, listening. Have the children show you how to be a good listener by sitting quietly and looking at the speaker.
✦ Introduce the veterinarian and ask him or her to make a few comments about a vet's job. Provide the veterinarian with a stuffed dog or cat so he or she can share and demonstrate some basic information about examining dogs.
✦ Ask the veterinarian to reinforce the knowledge children learned in the previous lesson about dog care (regular checkups, good nutrition, sufficient exercise, keeping animals safe, and so on).
✦ Encourage children to ask questions as the veterinarian discusses his or her tasks.
✦ If time permits, ask the children to sing the "Doghouse Song" learned in the lesson about doghouses (see page 118) for their visitor.

Modifications/Accommodations

Autism: During the review, demonstrate the actions that the veterinarian performed with the stuffed animal. Using simplified language, describe what he or she did. Have several of the children demonstrate with the stuffed animal. Then have the child with autism show you what the vet did.

Speech or Language Impairments: For the assessment, use a carrier phrase to get the child started in telling what the vet did. For example, using the stethoscope, show how it is used. Then say, "Come here, little dog. We need to check your ____." Then encourage the child to tell what the vet did with the stethoscope. If the child cannot tell you, have her show you.

Hearing Impairments: Have the child sit where she can see the vet's face and observe closely what the vet is doing.

Visual Impairments: Describe what the vet is doing during the classroom visit. After the vet has finished showing what he or she does with the stuffed animal, model the actions with the stuffed animal as the child holds the animal and feels the actions with her hands.

Cognitive and/or Developmental Disabilities: Review the actions of the vet with a stuffed dog several times. Then ask the child to show you the actions. For example, say, "Show me how the vet checks the dog's ears" or "Show

Review

After the veterinarian leaves, ask children to recall what they learned during the visit.

Assessment Strategy

Ask children individually to tell one job the veterinarian performs when animals come to his or her office.

me how the vet gives the dog a shot." Use the instruments from a doctor kit to do this.

Emotional Disturbance: Have the child next to you as the vet demonstrates how he or she takes care of animals. Emphasize kindness to animals and being gentle with pets as you show the child these same actions later with a stuffed animal and instruments from a doctor kit.

Other Health Impairments/Attention Deficit Hyperactivity Disorder: Before the vet arrives, discuss using good manners with visitors. If needed, have Picture Communication Symbols (such as the line drawings from Mayer Johnson Company) or pictures to remind the children of good manners (waiting, taking turns, listening, and so on.) Remind the child to use good manners by showing the pictures as cues from time to time.

Orthopedic Impairments: Unless the child has limited speech and language, this lesson needs no adaptations for children with orthopedic impairments. For children who are nonverbal, use pictures or Picture Communication Symbols for the actions of the vet with the stuffed animal. See also the section on accommodations for Speech or Language Impairments.

Curriculum Connections

✦ **Dramatic Play:** Set up the Dramatic Play Center like a Vet's Office. Add appointment logs, stuffed animals, pretend phones, stethoscopes, bandages, animal cages, charts about cats and dogs, white veterinarian's shirts, surgery scrubs, and other props that will encourage pretend play.

✦ **Math:** Provide a variety of figurines of animals that veterinarians often tend to (cats, dogs, gerbils, hamsters, cows, horses, and so on). Encourage the children to sequence them from smallest to largest. An alternative is to use flashcards if figurines are not available.

✦ **Writing:** Prepare a large "thank you" chart to send to the veterinarian after his or her visit to the classroom. Ask the children to suggest sentences for the thank you note, which may be prepared in a large group or with a few interested children. Place the chart in the Writing Center and request all the children sign their names at the level at which they are writing. Deliver to the veterinarian at a later time.

K-9 Units

Note: This lesson will be more effective if a police officer trainer and a trained police dog are available to come to the classroom.

Time
20 minutes

Materials
pictures of German
    Shepherds
a picture of a K-9 unit

Objectives

Children will:
1. Identify that a K-9 unit is a police officer and his or her dog.
2. Understand that police dogs help police officers with their jobs.

Lesson

✦ Begin the lesson by telling children that they are going to talk about a special dog who has an important job in the community.

✦ Show pictures of German Shepherds and tell them that these dogs are often trained by police officers to be police dogs. Then introduce the term *K-9 Unit*.

✦ Tell children all of the jobs that police dogs are required to do:
    ✦ follow scent trails left by criminals,
    ✦ chase criminals when they run away from the police,
    ✦ guard criminals until the police officer can arrest them,
    ✦ find children or adults who are lost,
    ✦ search for people in a collapsed buildings, and
    ✦ rescue people from burning buildings.
Note: You may need to explain what some of the above terms mean, such as *criminal*, *scent trail*, and *guard*.

✦ Point out to children that German Shepherds are strong dogs and can run very fast. Tell them that a trainer spends several weeks making sure that a K-9 dog is trained well and follows commands easily.

✦ If a police officer trainer and dog visit and are able to do the following, go outside to the playground for a demonstration. This will enhance the children's learning about this topic.
Note: Following this procedure will add approximately 10 minutes to the lesson.

Modifications/Accommodations

Autism: Provide pictures or photographs of police dogs and some of the things that they do. Use short, simple sentences in your explanation.

Speech or Language Impairments: Use pictures and repetition when talking about the things that police dogs do. Play a game where the children pretend to be police dogs searching for a lost child. This provides a concrete example for the child with speech or language impairments, and it also would be beneficial for a child with autism or cognitive disabilities. You can use a stuffed dog to find a lost baby doll in the classroom.

Ask the group to review all the responsibilities a police dog has.

Assessment Strategy
Ask children individually to tell one job of a police dog.

Hearing Impairments: Make sure that the child is seated across from you so that he can see your face as you speak. Use pictures or photographs of police dogs and some of the things that they do.

Visual Impairments: Use a plastic miniature dog to show some of the things that police dogs do. Let the child hold on to the dog as you move it. If a real dog can make a classroom visit, speak with the trainer about letting the children touch the dog. If so, help this child touch the dog gently.

Cognitive and/or Developmental Disabilities: Use short sentences and simplified vocabulary when talking about what police dogs do. Use a stuffed or miniature dog to show some of the things that police dogs do. Refer to the accommodation for speech or language impairments above.

Emotional Disturbance: Seat the child next to you during the lesson. Speak softly in the presence of the dog and emphasize being gentle around animals.

Other Health Impairments/Attention Deficit Hyperactivity Disorder: Ensure that you have the child's attention before talking about the things that police dogs do. Use pictures when talking about what police dogs do.

Orthopedic Impairments: No modifications are anticipated for this lesson.

Curriculum Connections

✦ **Dramatic Play:** Add a police officer's hat and badge to the center as an additional prop children can use in their pretend play about dogs.

✦ **Language and Literacy:** Add *Bingo, the Best Dog in the World* by Catherine Siracusa to the Library Center.

✦ **More Language and Literacy:** Let children help collect photographs or magazine pictures of dogs who fit into special categories: seeing eye dogs, K-9 police dogs, show dogs, dogs who have received national recognition, and so on. Put them in a scrapbook and invite the children to help come up with captions for each picture.

✦ **More Language and Literacy:** Tell the children the story of Faith, a dog who was born with only two hind legs. Jude Stringfellow, her owner, taught her to walk on her two legs just like humans walk. Members of Jude's family used spoonfuls of peanut butter to encourage Faith to stand and hop toward the food. With a great deal of patience, Faith finally was able to walk. **Note:** Teachers, if you want a picture of Faith, and to learn more about her story, go to www.faiththedog.net/gallery/ to download pictures of this amazing animal to show the children as you tell Faith's story.

When all of the lessons on pets are complete, sing the "I Have a Pet" song with the children:

I Have a Pet by Laverne Warner
Tune: "The Farmer in the Dell"
I have a little pet.
It is very dear to me.
I give it food and hold it close,
So it'll remember me.

I have a little fish.
It is very dear to me.
I give it food and watch it swim,
He's so much fun to see.

I have a little snake.
It is very dear to me.
I give it food and watch it slither,
He's so much fun to see.

I have a little bird.
It is very dear to me.
I give it food and watch it fly,
I love to hear it sing.

I have a little bunny.
It is very dear to me.
His ears are so very long.
I love to see him run.

I have a little hamster.
It is very dear to me.
I give it food and water, too,
He runs very fast.

I have a guinea pig.
It is very dear to me.
He's round, soft, and plump, too,
I love to feel his fur.

I have a little mouse.
It is very dear to me.
He has the prettiest pink nose,
I love to hold him close.

Chapter 4

Animals

As you begin to study animals with the children, collect pictures of animals that were not discussed in the unit on pets. It is better to use realistic pictures of animals rather than various cartoon-like animal illustrations. Magazines such as *National Geographic Kids, Zoo Books, Wild Baby Animal*, and several others are full of great colorful pictures of the animals in their habitats. Many other nature and animal-related magazines have additional realistic pictures of animals. Create habitat scenes of jungles, rivers, oceans, forests, grassy plains, deserts, and mountainous regions on large sheets of paper and challenge the children to place the pictures of the various animals on the appropriate habitats.

Encourage the children to role-play the animals in dramatic play situations to become familiar with the characteristics of each animal. Place plastic animal figures in a Manipulatives or Math Center for the children to sort and group into different types of categories, such as "water animal or land animal," "four legs, two legs, no legs," "bigger than me, smaller than me," and so on.

You may spend many weeks with this unit. As you learn about each animal, invite the children to add their own pictures and drawings to the habitat scenes that you created. Encourage the children to add images of animals that they have not specifically studied.

There are a wide variety of books available to include in the Library Center. Examples of quality books on real animals include: *Animals* by DK Publishing, *Dangerous Animals* by John Siedensticker, *Dinosaurs* by Angela Milner, *Pony on the Porch* by Ben Baglio, *Touch and Feel Animals Box Set* by Dorling Kindersley, and *Under the Sea* by Frank Talbot.

For the children to create images of real and invented animals, set out several animal match-up cards—equal-sized animal picture cards cut in two so the children can match the upper and lower halves of different animals together.

This is a theme you can continue throughout the year. Adding information about hibernation, protective coloration, and habitats will allow children to connect with the traits of real animals as they remember the cartoon and toy animal versions of these real-life animals.

Introduction to Farm Animals

Time
20–30 minutes

Materials
plastic farm animals
box or bag
Our Animal Friends at Maple Hill Farm by Alice Provensen and Martin Provensen
paper
crayons

Preparation
Before the lesson, gather 10 different plastic farm animals and place them in a box or bag. Make sure the contents of the box or bag are hidden from view, but are accessible to children.

Objectives

Children will:
1. Identify different farm animals.
2. Make the sound of different farm animals.

Lesson

+ Gather the children together around the large box or bag. Tell them there are some special items in the bag. Select a child to reach inside and pull out one of the plastic animals.
+ Have the child name the animal and the sound the animal makes. The children repeat the name of the animal and the sound it makes.
+ Discuss each animal as it is removed from the box.
+ Once the animals are named and the sounds the make are identified, read *Our Animal Friends at Maple Hill Farm* to the children.
+ Discuss the different animals in the book and then ask the children to select their favorite animal to draw on paper.
+ While the children are drawing teach them the words to the following song:

To the Farm by Diana Nabors
Tune: "Twinkle, Twinkle, Little Star"
Horses, donkeys, cows that moo,
Chickens, goats, and piglets, too.
Fish that swim down in the pond,
Ducklings quacking all day long.
All these animals you can see
If you go to the farm with me.

Modifications/Accommodations

Autism: The child could be selected as one of the children to pull the animals from the bag throughout the lesson. Another option is for the child may be the one to hold the animals in his lap once the animal is discussed as they go on to another child to draw an animal out of the bag.

Speech or Language Impairments: Individually, have the child repeat the name of each animal after the group has determined what type of animal has been drawn from the box. Do this by asking the child to repeat the animal or asking the class as a group to name the animal. Monitor the child's verbalizations and encourage the child's speech productions.

Hearing Impairments: Seat the child so that he can see you and the children clearly as they pull out the animals and talk about them.

Review

Have the children share their pictures of the farm animals and tell why they chose to draw that animal.

Assessment Strategy

Individually, ask the children to name four farm animals and the sounds they make.

Visual Impairments: Have the child feel each animal drawn from the box.

Cognitive and/or Developmental Disabilities: Use simple words and phrases throughout the lesson and have the child repeat the names of the animals once they have been identified.

Emotional Disturbance: Invite the child to arrange the animals after they have been drawn from the box. Then review each animal from the area in which the child has placed the animals.

Other Health Impairments/Attention Deficit Hyperactivity Disorder: Establish a clear signal to get the child's attention, such as a raised finger. Make sure you have the child's attention before speaking.

Orthopedic Impairments: Ensure that the child is given proper assistance in handling the animals.

Curriculum Connections

✦ **Bulletin Board:** Begin a Farm Animals bulletin board in the classroom. Encourage children to bring photographs from home or pictures they find in magazines to add to the bulletin board during the unit study.

✦ **Language and Literacy:** In small groups, discuss farm animals the children may have seen in the community or on nearby farms.

✦ **Science:** Place the plastic animals used in the lesson on the Science Table for children to play with and explore.

Cows

Time
30–45 minutes

Materials
string
yardstick
latex gloves
water
bucket or tray
tapestry needle
Moo Cow Book by Sandra
  Boynton

Preparation
On a yardstick, loop a string
to suspend the latex gloves.
Fill each latex glove with
water and tie at the wrist end.
Suspend two or three filled
gloves from the yardstick.
Place the yardstick between
two chair backs or between
two shelves so that the gloves
are hanging and can support
a small amount of pulling
from the children. Place a
bucket or tray underneath to
catch the water.
Note: Before using latex
gloves, make sure none of
the children have latex
allergies.

Objectives

Children will:
1. Discuss traits of a cow.
2. Practice milking a "cow."

Lesson

+ Gather the children together to hear the *Moo Cow Book.* Ask the children to list things they know about cows.
+ Discuss how to milk a cow. Demonstrate using a slight tug to "milk" the latex glove. Then pierce a single hole in each finger of the glove using a tapestry needle and give a slight tug to release some of the water from the glove.
+ Give the children an opportunity to "milk the cow."
+ Sing the following song while children wait for their turn:

Milking the Cow by Diana Nabors
Tune: "Here We Go 'Round the Mulberry Bush"
This is the way we milk the cow, milk the cow, milk the cow.
This is the way we milk the cow, on the farm.

Review

Have the children discuss and review milking a cow. Place extra gloves filled with air and tied in pliable balloon fashion, in a center for the children to practice the milking technique on other occasions.

Assessment Strategy

Have a group discussion of traits of a cow and the milking activity.

Modifications/Accommodations

Autism: Encourage the child to be the one to demonstrate the process as you describe how to milk a cow.

Speech or Language Impairments: Sing the song slowly to ensure that the child can pronounce the words clearly or have the child simply say the song without singing.

Hearing Impairments: Repeat words and phrases often and be sure the child can see your face and gestures while describing how to milk the cow.

Visual Impairments: Let the child handle the materials throughout the lesson as well as have a time to examine the "glove" udder and the stream of water that is expelled from the glove.

Cognitive and/or Developmental Disabilities: Make sure to use simple language.

Emotional Disturbance: Encourage the child to participate during the lesson. Have the child turn pages for you while you read the book.

Other Health Impairments/Attention Deficit Hyperactivity Disorder: Establish a clear signal for the children to use when they wish to speak and consistently remind them of the signal.

Orthopedic Impairments: If necessary, make allowances for the child to handle materials.

Curriculum Connections

✦ **Language and Literacy:** Experiment with words that rhyme with *cow* (*now*, *bow*, *how*, *wow*, and so on.) Add the word *cow* to the classroom Word Wall.

✦ **Science:** Place pictures of different types of cows in the Science Center (such as Guernsey, Jersey, Angus, dairy, and so on). Talk to children about herds of cattle.

✦ **Social Studies:** Show pictures of milking machines and discuss how much easier the farmer's job is when he or she has a machine to milk the cows.

Ducks

Time
30–45 minutes

Materials
picture of a duck

Objectives

Children will:
1. Describe characteristics of ducks.
2. Practice walking like ducks.

Lesson

✦ Gather the children on the rug for Circle or Group Time.
✦ Hold up a picture of a duck. Ask the children to quack like a duck and stand up and waddle in place like a duck.
✦ Select one child to be "Mama Duck" and have her lead the other children around the room waddling.
✦ Let them play Follow the Leader to the playground.
✦ Once on the playground, play the group game Duck, Duck, Goose. Designate one child as "IT." IT walks around behind the circle of children, tapping each child on the head and saying, "Duck, duck, duck…" until she selects one child by saying, "Goose." The "goose" chases IT around the outside of the circle and tries to catch her before she can return to the open spot that the selected child vacated. The chasing child becomes IT and the game continues.

Modifications/Accommodations

Autism: Provide the child with various pictures of ducks and ask her what the duck is doing, or provide her with pictures of different animals and have her pick out the pictures with ducks in them.

Speech or Language Impairments: Have the child sit near you during the lesson so you can hear her clearly.

Hearing Impairments: Have the child repeat duck sounds to you to ensure she is hearing you and make sure the child can always see your face.

Visual Impairments: Provide the child with toy ducks to feel and manipulate. Also, make sure the child has an area free of obstacles to move around when acting as a duck.

Cognitive and/or Developmental Disabilities: Use developmentally appropriate language. Have the child pick out pictures of ducks from a variety of animal pictures.

Emotional Disturbance: Seat the child next to you during the lesson and participate in the game with the child next to you (you could even be a "team").

Other Health Impairments/Attention Deficit Hyperactivity Disorder: Establish a clear signal to get the child's attention, such as a raised finger. Make sure you have the child's attention before speaking.

Review
Have the children repeat the poem and perform the motions of the ducks.

Assessment Strategy
Ask the group of children to name and discuss three to five traits of ducks.

Orthopedic Impairments: Depending on the severity of the child's impairments, you may need to assist the child. If the child is in a wheelchair, make sure she has enough room to participate.

Curriculum Connections

✦ **Art:** Provide feathers (available at craft stores) for children to glue to construction paper to make pictures of ducks.

✦ **Language and Literacy:** Talk about baby ducks following their mothers in a line when they move around the barnyard. The children will listen to how the baby ducks follow the mother duck. Introduce the phrase "have your ducks in a row" to the children. This adds vocabulary development as well as concept development. The children can then practice walking around the classroom behind you or the appointed "Mother Duck."

✦ **Science:** Bring in feathers from ducks and place them on the Science Table with a shallow dish pan of water. Demonstrate to children how the feathers resist water absorption. Explain that this is one of the reasons they love to swim in water—their feathers don't get wet! Place the feathers and water pan in the Science Center.

Chickens

Time
30–45 minutes

Materials
Going to Sleep on the Farm by Wendy Cheyette Lewison or *The Chicken or the Egg?* by Allan Fowler

a hard-boiled egg and raw egg

clear glass jar, quart or larger, filled with water

10–15 plastic eggs

various materials to place in eggs (packing peanuts, pennies, small plastic toys, and so on

Preparation
Before the lesson, place different items inside the plastic eggs. Prepare the bucket or water table with at least 4" of water.

Objectives

Children will:
1. Identify characteristics of chickens.
2. Predict if selected eggs will sink or float.

Lesson

✦ Gather the children together at Circle or Group Time and read the story *Going to Sleep on the Farm* by Wendy Cheyette Lewison or *The Chicken or the Egg?* by Allan Fowler.

✦ Discuss the chickens on the farm, including that they lay eggs for the farmer.

✦ Show the children the hard-boiled and raw eggs.

✦ Pass them around and have the children discuss the similarities between the two eggs and predict the differences.

✦ Place one of the eggs in the jar of water and discuss what happens to it. Remove the egg and place the other egg in the water. (The hard-boiled egg should float midway in the water and the raw egg should sink to the bottom.)

✦ Ask the children why they think the eggs did different things in the water.

✦ Crack open the two eggs and let the children see the "inside" difference.

✦ Bring out the 10–15 plastic eggs. Explain that because they are filled with different items, some will float and some will sink.

Review

Leave the activity in the Science Center for the children to explore further. Provide paper for the children to record their findings. Encourage them to list the colors of the eggs that sink and float.

Assessment Strategy

When children are experimenting with the eggs in small groups, observe the discussion about the eggs and the actions of sinking and floating.

✦ Invite small groups of children to experiment with the eggs using a water table and tongs. Ask them to sort the eggs into two groups: those that sink and those that float.

Modifications/Accommodations

Autism: Make sure the child has ample opportunities to handle materials during the lesson.

Speech or Language Impairments: Have the child repeat phrases you use in the lesson and to name the objects that are in the plastic eggs.

Hearing Impairments: Face the child as much as possible and periodically have the child repeat things you have just stated.

Visual Impairments: Allow the child to handle materials even during the initial stages of the lesson.

Cognitive and/or Developmental Disabilities: Use language that the child can understand and have him name things that may or may not float in water.

Emotional Disturbance: Encourage the child to participate during the lesson and possibly have him assist you in placing the items into the water.

Other Health Impairments/Attention Deficit Hyperactivity Disorder: Establish a clear signal for the children to use when they wish to speak and consistently remind them of the signal.

Orthopedic Impairments: Provide the child with an area that enables him to retrieve eggs from the water.

Curriculum Connections

✦ **Math:** Place plastic eggs in the Manipulatives Center for children to count and fill with smaller objects.

✦ **Science:** Bring in chicken feathers and place them on the Science Table with the duck feathers. Invite the children to compare the two types (duck feathers are larger and more resistant to water).

✦ **Snack Time:** Let the children help prepare egg salad using any favorite recipe to eat during Snack Time. **Note:** Check for egg allergies before serving this for snack.

Pigs

Time
20–30 minutes

Materials
Piggies by Audrey and Don Wood
paper
crayons

Objectives

Children will:
1. Discuss the different characteristics of pigs.
2. Dance the Higgy Piggy.
3. Draw a pig.

Lesson

◆ Gather the children on the carpet. Read *Piggies* by Audrey and Don Wood.

◆ Have the children name the differences among the pigs in the book. You can relate the differences in the piggies to the children's differences. For example, some children have dark hair and some have light hair; some have freckles, some do not.

◆ Ask the children to form a circle and do the following "Higgy Piggy" dance.

The Higgy Piggy by Diana Nabors
Tune: "Hokey Pokey"
You put your right hoof in
You put your right hoof out,
You put your right hoof in,
And you shake it all about.
You do the Higgy Piggy,
And you turn yourself around,
That's what it's all about!
Oink!

Additional verses:
You put your left hoof in....
You put your right hamhock (hip) in...
You put your left hamhock in....
You put your snout in....
You put your curly tail in...

◆ Have the children draw their own piggy that is different from others. Encourage them to be as original as possible. Provide time for the children to share their piggy pictures.

Review

Have the children share their pig with their classmates and describe how their pig is different or "special." Then display the children's pigs around the room for others to see and discuss. Repeat the "Higgy Piggy" dance during transition times.

Assessment Strategy

Ask each child to tell you one characteristic of her pig that makes it unique.

Modifications/Accommodations

Autism: Invite the child to turn pages for you while you read the book, and make sure she receives many opportunities to be involved in the lesson.

Speech or Language Impairments: Have the child repeat phrases from the song.

Hearing Impairments: Make sure the child can see your face as the class sings the song together.

Visual Impairments: Provide a time for the child to view the book before the group reading. Discuss the pig differences to prepare the child for the group discussion. During the song/dance assist the child in finding the correct body part by highly emphasizing the body part as the teacher demonstrates what to shake.

Cognitive and/or Developmental Disabilities: Provide the child with pictures of various animals and have her sort the pictures of pigs in one pile and other animals in a different pile.

Emotional Disturbance: Seat the child close to you and monitor the activity closely. Have the child stand by you and help out as "leader" during the dance.

Other Health Impairments/Attention Deficit Hyperactivity Disorder: Establish a clear signal to get the child's attention, such as a raised finger. Make sure you have her attention before speaking.

Orthopedic Impairments: Assist the child in the dance, if necessary, and assist in the drawing of the pig.

Curriculum Connections

✦ **Art:** Prepare the following sticks in advance: Dip one half of a Popsicle stick or tongue depressor in pink paint and let dry. These are "piggies." In the Art Center, the children add faces and clothes to the piggies using thin-tipped markers and bits of construction paper.

✦ **Language and Literacy:** Add the word *pig* to the classroom Word Wall. Encourage children to think of words that rhyme with *pig* (*big*, *fig*, *gig*, *dig*, *rig*, and so on.)

✦ **Math:** Spray paint small flat stones pink. Use a permanent marker to add a snout and eyes. Place these "pigs" in the Math Center for children to group and count. (Paint them on one side or both. One-sided "pigs" will add another dimension of classification with older children.)

Sheep

Time
30–45 minutes

Materials
paper plates
scissors
sentence strips
stapler
picture of sheep
crayons
glue
cotton balls

Preparation
Cut "eye holes" in each of the paper plates. Create a "T" with the sentence strip by using about 15"–20" for the back strap and 8"–10" for the top strap. Preparing the "T" strap ahead of time will save time when fitting the mask for each child. This "T" shaped strap may be stapled or glued. The shorter strap will be attached to the top of the mask and the longer strap will go around the back of the child's head.

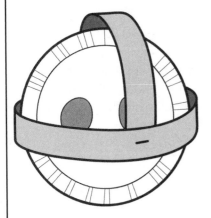

Objectives

Children will:
1. Discuss the characteristics of a sheep.
2. Create a sheep mask.

Lesson

✦ Gather the children to listen to the following poem:

Sheep by Diana Nabors
White sheep, black sheep
Out in the grass,
Enjoying the sun
Watching as the clouds float past.

✦ Show the children a picture of a sheep and ask them to name three to five things that make a sheep different from other farm animals.
✦ Tell them special facts about sheep:

Sheep usually live to be about eight years old. They hate to be alone, which is why they live in flocks (groups of sheep). Sheep are very gentle animals and are frightened easily. They flock together for protection because they can't really protect themselves. The sheep has many natural predators (animals that hunt and kill sheep for food), including coyotes, wolves, and domestic dogs. Sometimes larger animals, such as mules or llamas, are kept in the pastures with the sheep to scare off possible predators.

The people that raise and care for sheep are called shepherds. Sometimes, shepherds have dogs to help take care of the sheep. The dog learns to round up the sheep, and when one wanders from the flock, the dog brings it back! (Compiled from the Michigan Breeders Association and the American Sheep Industry)

✦ Provide paper plates (with eye holes), crayons, glue, and cotton balls for the children to create sheep masks.
✦ Assist the children in fitting their masks by stapling a back and top strap of the mask using sentence strips.

Review

Ask the children to repeat the sheep poem with you as they wear their masks.

Assessment Strategy

Individually, ask the children to tell you one fact about sheep.

Modifications/Accommodations

Autism: Provide various pictures of sheep and ask the child to describe something about each picture.

Speech or Language Impairments: Have the child repeat the poem several times and tell you an interesting detail they learned about sheep.

Hearing Impairments: Have the child in a position where he can always see your face and ask him to repeat words and phrases from the lesson.

Visual Impairments: Allow the child to handle materials, such as picture cards of sheep in the field throughout the lesson. Giving the child a piece of raw wool during the introduction of the lesson will allow this child as well as others to touch and feel the sheep's wool.

Cognitive and/or Developmental Disabilities: Provide the child with pictures of various animals and ask him to show you which pictures have sheep. Also, ask a classmate to help the child make his mask, if appropriate.

Emotional Disturbance: Make sure to keep the child close to you during the lesson. Encourage and praise the child for his efforts when making the mask.

Other Health Impairments/Attention Deficit Hyperactivity Disorder: Establish a clear signal for children to use when they wish to speak.

Orthopedic Impairments: Provide the child with an area to make his own mask and assist in placing the mask on the child if necessary.

Curriculum Connections

✦ **Science:** Place wool garments as well as an example of raw wool on the Science Table so children can feel them.

✦ **Social Studies:** Ask children to put on their sheep masks and visit another classroom to tell others what they have learned about sheep.

Donkeys

Time
30–45 minutes

Materials
*Sylvester and the Magic
    Pebble* by William Steig
picture of a donkey
white and black tempera paint
small sponges
large drawing paper
pre-cut pieces of paper
    representing various sizes
    of packages for the
    donkey to carry
tape
blindfold
pre-made picture of a donkey

Objectives

Children will:
1. Mix the paint colors of black and white to create a donkey.
2. Play Pin the Packages on the donkey.
3. Discuss the traits of donkeys.

Lesson

✦   Gather the children together to listen to the story, *Sylvester and the Magic Pebble.* Ask the children to describe the animal that Sylvester changed into.
✦   Show the children a picture of a donkey. Discuss the traits of a donkey, including some of the following facts:

   ✦   Donkeys are a class of animals called mammals.
   ✦   Donkeys are smaller than horses.
   ✦   Donkeys are surefooted, which means they tend not to trip or fall on uneven land such as mountainous or rocky trails.
   ✦   Donkeys are very strong and carry people and heavy items from place to place.
   ✦   Donkeys usually have a gray coat but can be brownish in color.

✦   Place a dish of white paint and a dish of black paint at each table.
✦   Invite the children to dip sponges into the black and white paint to create the gray color of a donkey and sponge paint donkeys.
✦   When the children are finished, play Pin the Package on the Donkey's Back (just like Pin the Tail on the Donkey). The children take turns wearing a blindfold and taping a "package" to the pre-made donkey's back.

Review

Place the Pin the Package on the Donkey and additional pre-cut packages in a center for the children to play again and again.

Assessment Strategy

Ask the children, one at a time, to tell you something about a donkey.

Modifications/Accommodations

Autism: Prior to the lesson, let the child assist you in making the donkey that will be used to play "Pin the Package on the Donkey."

Speech or Language Impairments: Ask the children to repeat information from the story and seat her close to you so you can attend to her pronunciation of words.

Hearing Impairments: Make sure the child can see you during instruction and ask her to repeat words and phrases to ensure she understands.

Visual Impairments: Have miniature donkey figures and or pictures for the child to hold and look at closely.

Cognitive and/or Developmental Disabilities: Use simple words and language and have the child repeat words and phrases to you. Also, give the child several pictures of horses and donkeys and ask her to distinguish between them.

Emotional Disturbance: Have the child assist you in handing out the materials and continually give positive reinforcement to her as she makes her donkey.

Other Health Impairments/Attention Deficit Hyperactivity Disorder: Have the child sit near you. Give her individual hand signals, and praise her when she is participating appropriately.

Orthopedic Impairments: Provide the child with an area or modification (possibly some form of an easel) that will allow her to create a donkey.

Curriculum Connections

✦ **Language and Literacy:** Invite the children to tape record the donkey's "hee haw" sound on a cassette tape to listen to in the Listening Center.

✦ **Movement:** Tell the children that donkeys can kick their hind legs very high in the air. When the children are outdoors, ask them to try standing on their hands and kicking their legs like a donkey.

✦ **Science:** With a group of interested children, talk about the differences between horses and donkeys.

Introduction to Forest Animals

Time
20 minutes

Materials
Forest Animals by Francine
    Galko
chart paper
marker

Objectives

Children will:
1. Identify animals that are found in the forest.
2. Discuss the habitat of the forest and the animals living in the forest.

Lesson

✦   Gather the children together to listen to *Forest Animals* by Francine Galko.
✦   Read the book and discuss the animals that are found in the forest.
✦   After the story, have the children list the animals that were in the book as well as other animals that they might live in the forest.
✦   Write the names of animals the children listed on chart paper.
✦   Ask the children to sit on the floor. Sing "Going Through the Forest," adding in some of the animals on the chart. You say a line, and then the children repeat the line. Add hand claps, knee slaps, and other motions as desired.

Going Through the Forest by Diana Nabors
Tune: "Going on a Bear Hunt"
Going through the forest, (children repeat)
Want to go with me? (children repeat)
Come on, let's go. (children repeat)
What will we see? (children repeat)
I see a squirrel. (children repeat)
Watch the squirrel scamper up the tree. (children repeat)

Continue the chant, adding in different animals and actions. (Suggestions: deer grazing on the grass, mole digging in the dirt, eagle soaring in the sky, possum hiding in the bush)

Out of the forest, (children repeat)
Heading for home. (children repeat)

Modifications/Accommodations

Autism: Have another adult assist the child with the hand motions during the song.
Speech or Language Impairments: Explain any new vocabulary. Encourage the child to participate in the song and state different animals found in the forest.

Review

Repeat parts of the chant throughout the days of the unit.

Assessment Strategy

Ask the children to name different forest animals. Have them draw a picture of an animal in its forest habitat. Or, if outdoor or animal magazines, such as *Ranger Rick* and *National Geographic for Kids* are available, have the children cut out animal pictures to glue next to the listed name on the chart.

Hearing Impairments: Place the child up close to the book and the reader. Be careful not to block the child's view of the book or reader's face.

Visual Impairments: Allow the child to hold the book and inspect the pictures individually before the group reading.

Cognitive and/or Developmental Disabilities: Explain any new vocabulary. Have another adult assist with the song hand motions as needed.

Emotional Disturbance: Encourage the child to think of animals in the forest to add to the chart. Praise the child for appropriate choices of animals.

Other Health Impairments/Attention Deficit Hyperactivity Disorder: Seat the child near you to help him focus on the song. Use visual cues to help the child focus.

Orthopedic Impairments: Have another adult assist the child with the song hand motions.

Curriculum Connections

✦ **Dramatic Play:** Gather puppets, including sock puppets, for the children to dramatize forest animals.

✦ **Math:** Provide a variety of pictures of forest animals for the children to sort into groups. Ask the children why they placed the animals in the groups they did.

✦ **Science:** Provide forest pictures and cut out forest animals. Help the children locate the best habitat for each forest animal (burrow, tree, root or log, clearing or thicker brush).

Squirrels

Time
30–45 minutes

Materials
Earl the Squirrel by Don Freeman
snack mix (small crackers, dry unsweetened cereal, pretzels, seeds, and dried fruit)
plastic snack bags
small pieces of brown construction paper

Preparation
Before the lesson, create small bags of snack mix, at least two or three per child. Mix together small crackers, dry unsweetened cereal, pretzels, seeds, and dried fruit. Fill each bag with 2 tablespoons of snack mix. Place the filled bags around the room so that the children can "hunt for food" during the lesson.

Objectives

Children will:
1. Discuss the characteristics of squirrels.
2. Hunt for "acorns."

Lesson

+ Gather the children together during Circle or Group Time to listen to *Earl the Squirrel* by Don Freeman.
+ Ask the children to discuss where Earl finds acorns and the things he does as he gathers acorns.
+ Ask the children why Earl must find a large amount of acorns.
+ Hold up a bag of snack mix and tell the children they will look for these "acorns" (snack mix) for the day's snack.
+ Each child looks around the room and finds two or three bags each.
+ Allow an ample amount of time (and assistance) for them to find the snacks.
+ Have the children place the snack bags on the table and then wash and prepare for snack time.
+ Discuss the difference in the way a squirrel eats acorns and the way children eat snacks. Encourage the children to practice both.

Modifications/Accommodations

Autism: Place a few snack bags near the child for easy finding. Assist the child in searching for the "nuts."

Speech or Language Impairments: Encourage the child to use complete sentences in the discussion.

Hearing Impairments: Face the child when giving directions, and ask him to repeat back the directions to ensure understanding.

Visual Impairments: Tie brightly colored tags to some of the bags so the child can find the "nuts" more easily.

Cognitive and/or Developmental Disabilities: Let the child hold one of the bags as you help him look for other bags.

Emotional Disturbance: Remind the child that each child will find two or three "nuts" and then will begin getting ready to eat the "nuts."

Review

Fill small resealable bags with small pieces of brown construction paper ("nuts") and place them in the Dramatic Play Center for the children to hide and hunt.

Assessment Strategy

Individually ask the children what they know about squirrels and their hunt for food.

Other Health Impairments/Attention Deficit Hyperactivity Disorder: Assist the child with focusing on the hunt by reminding him that once he has found two or three bags, he can return to the table to eat the snack. Use visual and auditory cues to help the child focus on the activity.

Orthopedic Impairments: Arrange an area of the room in which the child can maneuver himself to search for nuts.

Curriculum Connections

✦ **Language and Literacy:** Ask the children to dictate a class story about how they went to hunt for "nuts." Discuss preposition words such as *over*, *under*, *around*, *behind*, *near*, and *in*.

✦ **Math:** Provide time for the child to sort the items in the snack bag. Invite the children to count the items to see which type of snack they have more, less, and equal numbers of.

✦ **Outdoors:** Observe squirrels on the playground or in a park close to the center or school.

Possums

Time
20–30 minutes

Materials
Possum's Harvest Moon by
    Anne Hunter
crayons
drawing paper

Review
Encourage the children to talk about their pictures. Post the fall celebration pictures around the room.

Assessment Strategy
Ask the children questions about the forest and the animals in the forest as you read the book.

Objectives

Children will:
1. Name the different jobs the animals in *Possum's Harvest Moon* have.
2. Draw a picture of a celebration party.

Lesson

◆ Gather the children together to listen to the book *Possum's Harvest Moon*.
◆ Discuss the harvest celebration and what it takes to get ready for a celebration.
◆ Ask the children what things they could do to prepare for a celebration.
◆ Invite them to draw a picture of a fall celebration.

Modifications/Accommodations

Autism: Place art materials within the child's reach and help the child select and hold the crayons. Verbal directions to draw on the drawing paper will assist the child in focusing on the materials and activity. Assist the child in drawing as necessary.

Speech or Language Impairments: Encourage the child to speak in complete sentences as she describes her picture.

Hearing Impairments: Have the child sit near you as you read the book.

Visual Impairments: Place materials within reach of the child. Encourage the child to describe what she is drawing. Assist as needed.

Cognitive and/or Developmental Disabilities: Explain the new or difficult words to the child. Have the child give examples or use the word in a sentence during the drawing part of the lesson. Repeat directions once the child has the art materials. Ask the child to describe the picture as she is drawing.

Emotional Disturbance: Help the child focus on the task of drawing the celebration picture with the materials as needed.

Other Health Impairments/Attention Deficit Hyperactivity Disorder: Help the child individually focus on drawing the picture by cuing her with prompts such as, "What will you draw next?" "In your celebration, who else do you want to come?"

Orthopedic Impairments: Provide special grips to assist with the child's manipulation of the art materials. Allow the child to draw, using the level of drawing they may have. A drawing by a child who has orthopedic challenges may look more like a scribble than other children her age.

Curriculum Connections

◆ **Art:** Provide materials, such as paper strips and ¾ circles, for the children to make celebration hats. Provide additional construction paper and markers for children to make decorations for the party.
◆ **Dramatic Play:** Place props, such as a picnic basket filled with pretend fruit and a small tablecloth, in the Dramatic Play Center for children to act out (or retell) the story *Possum's Harvest Moon*.

Raccoons

Time
20–30 minutes

Materials
Raccoons and Ripe Corn by
    Jim Arnosky
crayons
drawing paper

Review
Discuss the traits of
raccoons, such as washing
their food before eating it,
using their paws much like
children use their hands, or
being more active in the
nighttime than the daytime.

Assessment Strategy
Have the children share their
pictures of raccoons and talk
about what the raccoons in
their pictures are doing.

Objectives

Children will:
1. Discuss the traits of raccoons.
2. Draw a picture representing the story *Raccoons and Ripe Corn.*

Lesson

✦ Gather the children together on the rug.
✦ Show the cover of the book to the children and ask them to tell what they
   know about raccoons.
✦ Read *Raccoons and Ripe Corn* and discuss the raccoon's life in the forest.
✦ Ask if any of the children have seen raccoons.
✦ Discuss what the raccoons they have seen or the raccoons on the front of
   the book are doing.
✦ Have the children draw a picture of a raccoon in the forest or in their
   neighborhood.

Modifications/Accommodations

Autism: Pre-read the story with the child. Explain any new vocabulary or
    ideas.
Speech or Language Impairments: Encourage the child to use full
    sentences when discussing the book. Explain any new words.
Hearing Impairments: Have the child sit near you as you read the book
Visual Impairments: Allow the child to view the book before the classroom
    reading.
Cognitive and/or Developmental Disabilities: Repeat the directions as
    needed.
Other Health Impairments/Attention Deficit Hyperactivity Disorder: Assist
    the child with focusing by using hand gestures and pointing out specific
    items in the book as you read.
Orthopedic Impairments: Position the child so that he has access to the art
    materials. Assist as needed.

Curriculum Connections

✦ **Art:** Make headbands with the children. Using poster board, cut out
   headbands that are 20" x 2". Measure each child's head and staple the
   headband to fit the child's head. Ask other adults to help with this task.
   Then help the children cut out gray or brown raccoon ears and black
   circles (eyes) and glue them to the headband.
✦ **Social Studies:** Invite a park ranger or someone knowledgeable about
   wildlife to come in and talk about raccoons and other small forest
   creatures.

Deer

Time
15–20 minutes

Materials
Lost in the Woods by Carl R. Sams and Jean Stoick

Review
Ask children to talk about their experiences with their classmates.

Assessment Strategy
Ask individual children to tell what they remember about the book.

Objectives

Children will:
1. Retell the story about a deer lost in the woods.
2. Discuss times they were felt that they lost and found their way, such as in a store when they may have turned around and didn't see their parent, or when they were confused as to where they were even though they were with others.
3. Discuss traits of deer, such as their antlers and their ability to leap and run fast.

Lesson

+ Gather the children together to listen to the book *Lost in the Woods* by Carl R. Sams and Jean Stoick.
+ Discuss with the children the fawn's search for his mother.
+ Encourage the children to discuss times when they were lost and what they did in the situation. Did someone help them? Did they find their own way? Children who have never been lost can talk about stories and books that feature characters that get lost (such as Snow White, Hansel and Gretel, and so on).

Modifications/Accommodations

Autism: Read the book to the child individually prior to the classroom reading.
Speech or Language Impairments: Maintain direct eye contact with the child and listen intently as she speaks. Allow the child to complete her sentence without adding words to their sentences.
Hearing Impairments: Have the child sit near you as you read. Be careful not to block the view of the book.
Visual Impairments: Provide the book to the child prior to the lesson so that she can inspect the illustrations.
Cognitive and/or Developmental Disabilities: Explain any new vocabulary or situations to the child.
Emotional Disturbance: Discuss the concept of being lost with the child before the lesson to assess if any fears are present.
Other Health Impairments/Attention Deficit Hyperactivity Disorder: Use key words to keep the child focused on the discussion
Orthopedic Impairments: No modifications are needed in this discussion lesson.

Curriculum Connections

+ **Language and Literacy:** Provide books about animals in the Library Center for children to view the animals in their habitats.
+ **Math:** Provide pictures of adult and baby animals for the child to match.
+ **Outdoors:** If possible, take a walk in the woods.

Armadillos

Time
20–30 minutes

Materials
The Armadillo from Amarillo
  by Lynne Cherry
large drawing paper
crayons or markers

Review
Invite the children to talk about their pictures. Write down what they say and post the pictures and dictations around the room.

Assessment Strategy
Individually, ask the children to describe something about the armadillo.

Objectives

Children will:
1. Discuss the traits and the habitat of the armadillo. Armadillos enjoy moist land in which to dig and burrow, such as the land near streams and ponds. They feed on grubs and insects which are found in wooded areas.
2. Draw a picture of where the child lives and an armadillo's habitat.

Lesson

✦ Gather the children together to listen to the story, *The Armadillo from Amarillo,* about an armadillo from Texas.
✦ Discuss with the children the hard outer shell of the armadillo. Explain that the protective shell protects the armadillo from the hot Texas sun.
✦ Invite the children to discuss the habitats of four different animals. Focus on the differences in the habitats mentioned in the letters from Sasparillo's cousin, Brillo.
✦ Give each child a large piece of paper with a line drawn down the middle. Have them draw their own environment and the environment of the Texas armadillo, Sasparillo.

Modifications/Accommodations

Autism: Make sure the child has plenty of time to draw her picture. Provide an alternate activity of re-reading the book individually.
Speech or Language Impairments: Specifically discuss the new vocabulary related to the environment of Texas explaining any words that are new to the child.
Hearing Impairments: Have the child sit near you when you read the book. Use hand gestures and pointing to accentuate certain parts of the story. Ask the child questions ascertain the level of understanding the child is gaining from the auditory discussion.
Visual Impairments: Provide time for the child to read the book independently.
Cognitive and/or Developmental Disabilities: Provide explanations of terms and vocabulary in the story. Allow the child extra time to draw the picture.
Emotional Disturbance: Give the child time to tell about her observations and thoughts of the armadillo and Texas.
Other Health Impairments/Attention Deficit Hyperactivity Disorder: Assist the child with focusing on the book by having her sit near you. Use visual cues to help her focus.
Orthopedic Impairments: Provide specialized straps or grips for the child to draw unassisted.

Curriculum Connections

✦ **Language and Literacy:** Ask the children if they ever send or receive letters. Encourage the child to draw pictures or "write" letters to family members. Help them write the name of the recipient on the letter.
✦ **Science:** Place pictures of armadillos in their natural habitat in the Science Center. A photo gallery is available at www.dilloscape.com/photos.html. Stuffed armadillos are also available for purchase.

Introduction to Ocean Animals

Time
30–45 minutes

Materials
2 sentence strips
set of small pictures of ocean
    animals and land animals
large pieces of drawing paper
crayons or markers

Objectives

Children will:
1. Sort pictures of animals into similar groups.
2. Discuss the differences between land and ocean animals.

Lesson

✦   Gather the children together for Circle or Group Time. Present the sentence strips, one labeled "Land" and one labeled "Ocean." Give each child a picture of an animal found on land or in the ocean.

✦   The children name the animal in the picture they are holding and decide if it is a land animal or an ocean animal. Ask children to place the picture under the correct sentence strip heading.
✦   Encourage the children to name more animals and decide if they are land animals or ocean animals.
✦   Discuss with the children the differences in the land animals and ocean animals.
✦   Give each child a piece of drawing paper. On one side, the child draws a land animal and on the other side, he draws an ocean animal. Give the children time to discuss and share their pictures with their classmates.

Modifications/Accommodations

Autism: Help the child identify his animal card by giving him two choices of names and categories from which to select. "Do you have a cat or a fish?" "Is that a land animal or an ocean animal?"

Review

Place a small set of land and ocean animal cards in the Manipulatives Center for the children to sort into appropriate groups.

Assessment Strategy

Individually, ask the children about their drawings and what traits are present in land and ocean animals.

Speech or Language Impairments: Define any unknown words and pictures. Encourage the child to use complete sentences as he describes the animals.

Hearing Impairments: Use gestures and picture cues.

Visual Impairments: Use large pictures and allow the child to sit or stand nearby to see them clearly.

Cognitive and/or Developmental Disabilities: Help the child by providing him choices (see Autism above).

Emotional Disturbance: Help the child wait for his turn to describe the animal by using hand gestures and verbal instructions.

Other Health Impairments/Attention Deficit Hyperactivity Disorder: Help the child focus on the activity by using verbal cues and hand gestures.

Orthopedic Impairments: Help the child post his picture.

Curriculum Connections

- ✦ **Art:** Encourage children to draw pictures of their favorite animals in their natural habitats.
- ✦ **Language and Literacy:** Discuss with children the differences in animals. Invite them to create "My Animal" books. After they draw pictures of different animals, help them write the words or let them dictate the words for you to write.
- ✦ **Science:** Provide picture mats of various locations, such as a forest, desert, farm, neighborhood, lake, ocean, and sky for the children to match the animals with their habitats.

Crabs

Time
30–45 minutes

Materials
small aquarium with sand
four small hermit crabs
A House for Hermit Crab by
    Eric Carle
pie tin
washable tempera paint
paper

Preparation
Before the lesson, create a living environment for the hermit crabs. A small covered, lighted aquarium with three inches of sand and a dish of water works well.

Objectives

Children will:
1. Discuss the characteristics of hermit crabs. Some hermit crabs live underwater in the ocean. Other hermit crabs live in trees near the beach.
2. Discuss the habitat of the hermit crab.
3. Create handprint crabs.

Lesson

✦ Gather the children together and show them the hermit crabs. Place the hermit crabs in the aquarium and put it where the children can see the crabs easily.

✦ Discuss the movement of the hermit crabs and their shell home.
✦ Read the story *A House for Hermit Crab.*
✦ Discuss the homes of different animals (nest, cave, and so on) and people (house, apartment, hut, and so on).
✦ Encourage the children to create their own handprint hermit crabs.
✦ Pour a small amount of washable tempera paint in a pie tin.
✦ Have the child place her hand in the paint and print a handprint on her paper.
✦ Once the handprint is dry, the child can create the shell house with crayons.

children. Provide art materials for the children to draw their observations of the hermit crabs.

Assessment Strategy
Ask the children to describe the characteristics of the hermit crab.

Modifications/Accommodations

Autism: For children who may be tactilely sensitive, let them wear a plastic glove during the painting or help them trace their handprint with a crayon.

Speech or Language Impairments: As the children observe the hermit crabs, verbalize the crabs' movements. Model using a complete sentence structure in discussions.

Hearing Impairments: Use eye contact and gestures to assist the child in full participation.

Visual Impairments: Give the child time to watch the crabs closely and discuss what he sees.

Cognitive and/or Developmental Disabilities: Use short statements and repeat directions. Allow the child to observe others making their handprints before doing it himself.

Emotional Disturbance: Explain to the child the care of the hermit crabs and the repeat the directions for making the handprint. Have the child watch others before attempting his own handprint.

Other Health Impairments/Attention Deficit Hyperactivity Disorder: Assist the child with staying on task during the painting portion by having him observe others.

Orthopedic Impairments: Guide the child in making the handprint. Make sure the materials are readily available for him.

Curriculum Connections

✦ **Language and Literacy:** On the children's crab pictures, have them write or dictate to an adult: "My crab can____." Help them complete the sentence. Then bind the pages into a class book and place it in the Library Center.

✦ **Math:** Put the children into four groups. Place the four crabs inside a small circle on a large poster board. Have each group select a crab to watch and cheer for. Set the timer for five minutes and watch the crabs. Mark on the poster board where the crabs end up at the end of the five minutes. Place the crabs back into the tank. Using inch cubes or another manipulative measuring system compare the distances of the crab movements.

✦ **Movement:** Show the children how to sit on the floor and lean back on their hands with their feet flat on the floor. Have them lift their bottoms and walk like a crab around the room without bumping into one another.

Review
Place the hermit crabs in the classroom in an area easily viewed by all

Fish

Time
20–30 minutes

Materials
small plastic snack bags
colored goldfish crackers
napkins
construction paper in a
    variety of colors
scissors

Preparation
Prior to the lesson place a
small handful of colored
goldfish crackers in a snack
bag. Make a bag for each
child. Cut out a few different
colors of fish from
construction paper.

Review
Place fish cutouts in centers
for the children to sort into
groups and count.

Assessment Strategy
Discuss with each child
individually about how she
grouped the goldfish. Have
them count one of the groups
to assess the child's ability
to use one to one
correspondence in counting.

Objectives

Children will:
1. Sort a variety of fish into similar groups.
2. Count fish using one-to-one correspondence.

Lesson

✦ Give each child a napkin and a snack bag with colored goldfish crackers.
✦ Invite the children to dump out the fish and group them by colors.
✦ Ask the children to count each small group of fish.
✦ Ask the children how many red, green, or purple fish they have.
✦ Let the children eat the goldfish for snack or save them to eat later.

Modifications/Accommodations

Autism: Help the child begin the classification/grouping of the goldfish. Use questioning skills to assist her in placing fish into the specified groups. Help from another adult may be needed to maximize the child's understanding and participation to the activity

Speech or Language Impairments: Have the child tell how many groups of fish she has, including which ones have more, less, and equal numbers.

Hearing Impairments: Face the child when giving directions.

Visual Impairments: Allow the child extra time to look carefully at the fish, group them, and count them.

Cognitive and/or Developmental Disabilities: Draw circles on a mat to help the child put fish into groups.

Emotional Disturbance: Discuss with the child that each bag may have a different amount of goldfish. Provide extra goldfish for children who have less fish than other children so that everyone has the same number of fish to eat.

Other Health Impairments/Attention Deficit Hyperactivity Disorder: Assist the child by providing a tray or mat on which the child can add, group, and manipulate the different fish. Use visual and auditory cues to help the child continue focusing until completion.

Orthopedic Impairments: Have a tray with sides and a craft stick to assist the child in sliding fish into groups.

Curriculum Connections

✦ **Language and Literacy:** Place fish books in the Library Center, including *One Fish, Two Fish, Red Fish, Blue Fish* by Dr. Seuss.
✦ **Math:** Have the children predict how many fish they have in their bag before the lesson. Then help them count and check the actual number. Once the fish are grouped, compare the groups using the terms more, less, and equal.
✦ **Science:** Add a live goldfish to the classroom if one is not already available.

Jellyfish

Time
30–45 minutes

Materials
tissue paper
scissors
picture of a jellyfish
small paper plates
art materials (ribbon, string,
    yarn, markers, and so on)
glue
stapler

Preparation
Before the lesson, cut tissue
paper into 1" x 8" strips.

Objectives

Children will:
1. Create jellyfish using
   paper plates and tissue
   paper.
2. Discuss the
   characteristics of jellyfish.

Review
Place the jellyfish art around
the room for children to
discuss during the days of
the unit.

Assessment Strategy
Ask the children to name the
    characteristics of the
    jellyfish.

Lesson

✦ Show the children the picture of a jellyfish. Ask them what they know
   about jellyfish. Ask if anyone has ever seen a real jellyfish or if they know
   anyone who has been stung. During the discussion, tell them some
   jellyfish facts (a few mentioned below). Tell them that although jellyfish
   look interesting, they should never be touched.
   Jellyfish Facts
   *Jellyfish are invertebrates (they do not have a spinal cord) and live in the
   ocean.*
   *The tentacles of a jellyfish are covered with areas that sting or kill other
   animals.*
   *The jellyfish uses its tentacles to hold its catch and as a defense from other
   ocean life.*

✦ Pass out small paper plates and art materials. Encourage the children to
   color the plate (body) and attach tissue paper strips (tentacles) with glue
   and staples. Hang the jellyfish from the ceiling.

Modifications/Accommodations

Autism: Allow the child a choice to make the jellyfish or to look at the picture.
Speech or Language Impairments: Encourage the child to use complete
    sentences and new vocabulary during the discussion.
Hearing Impairments: Face the child when talking. Have him repeat the
    directions to ensure understanding.
Visual Impairments: If needed, help the child with the gluing and stapling.
Cognitive and/or Developmental Disabilities: Give the child plenty of time to
    look at and manipulate the art materials as he creates the jellyfish.
Cognitive and/or Developmental Disabilities: Demonstrate how to make a
    jellyfish before the child designs his jellyfish. Encourage the child to be
    creative rather than duplicate your model.
Emotional Disturbance: Allow the child extra time to complete the jellyfish as
    needed.
Other Health Impairments/Attention Deficit Hyperactivity Disorder: Allow
    the child extra time to plan and create his jellyfish.
Orthopedic Impairments: Use Velcro tabs or double stick tape to assist the
    child in creating the jellyfish.

Curriculum Connections

✦ **Movement:** Give the children scarves or ribbons and invite them to move
   around the room, wiggling their "tentacles."

Seagulls

Time
25 minutes

Materials
A Day at Seagull Beach by
   Karen Wallace
copy paper
black pen or marker
copy machine
crayons
scissors
string

Preparation
Draw a basic outline of a seagull on a piece of paper. Make copies for each child in the class. If you are unable to draw a seagull, find the outline of a seagull in a coloring book or on the Internet and make copies.

Objectives

Children will:
1. Identify characteristics of seagulls.
2. Make their own seagulls using paper.

Lesson

✦ Gather the children together on the rug for story time. Show them the cover of the book *A Day at Seagull Beach.*
✦ Ask the children what they see on the cover (picture of a seagull). Discuss their experiences with seeing seagulls.
✦ Read the book and discuss the characteristics of the seagull.
✦ Discuss how the seagull swoops down to catch fish and other food.
✦ Talk about their experiences of feeding bread or crackers to seagulls at the beach.
✦ Sing the following song with the children:

Seagulls adapted by Diana Nabors
Tune: "Frere Jacques"
*I see seagulls. I see seagulls
At the beach, near the shore.
Soaring, diving, fishing.
Soaring, diving, fishing.
At the beach, near the shore.*

*I toss bread. I toss bread
To the gulls, way up high.
They swoop down and catch it.
They swoop down and catch it.
At the beach, near the shore.*

✦ Let the children color and cut out the seagull. Put a piece of masking tape or package tape on the beak of the seagull. Then use a hole punch to punch a hole in the taped beak. This taped area will provide extra support when you tie a string through the hole to make a kite seagull.
✦ Take the seagulls outside and have the children "fly the gulls" by running in an open field on the playground.
✦ If you have a limited area, have two or three children run and fly their gulls while the other children watch and sing the song. Then let others take their turn flying their gulls.

Review
Place the book in the center for future discussion.

Assessment Strategy
Ask the children where the seagulls live and how they catch their food.

Modifications/Accommodations

Autism: Assist the child in "flying" the seagull.

Speech or Language Impairments: Use varied voicing patterns, loud and soft, to accentuate the words in the poem to help the child follow along with the group to sing the song

Hearing Impairments: Face the child when giving directions. Have the child pair with a classmate while creating and flying the seagull.

Visual Impairments: You may need to tie the string through the hole for the child. Use a heavy dark line for tracing the seagull pattern to help the child see the lines to cut.

Cognitive and/or Developmental Disabilities: Provide plenty of time to create the gull. Assist the child with cutting and attaching the string. One-on-one modeling may be needed for the child to be successful. Have a classmate run with the child to assist her in staying within the boundaries.

Other Health Impairments/Attention Deficit Hyperactivity Disorder: Provide verbal and gesture clues to assist the child as she flies the seagull "kite." Provide ample space so as the child focuses on the kite, she has room to run safely.

Orthopedic Impairments: Assist the child in creating and flying the seagull as needed.

Curriculum Connections

✦ **Art:** Print pictures of seagulls from a variety of sources. Have the children cut out and glue the seagulls to paper. Invite them to draw backgrounds for the gulls.

✦ **Language and Literacy:** Ask the children to dictate a story about the travels of their seagull. Collect the stories and create a classroom book to place in the Library Center.

✦ **Science:** Use other resources, including the Internet, an encyclopedia, and other books, to find out what seagulls eat, how they catch their food, and so on.

Dolphins

Time
20–30 minutes

Materials
picture of a dolphin
chart paper
markers
Friendly Dolphins by Allan
    Fowler

Objectives

Children will:
1. Discuss the characteristics of a dolphin.
2. Retell information about dolphins they heard about in a book.

Lesson

+ Begin the lesson by asking the children what they know about dolphins. Show them a picture of a dolphin.
+ Write down what the children say on the chart paper.
+ Then ask the children what they want to know about dolphins. Use a different colored marker to write down the children's questions.
+ Read the book *Friendly Dolphins.*
+ Discuss the information in the book. Focus on answering some of the questions the children had.
+ Research with the children the rest of the unanswered questions using the Internet or books.

Modifications/Accommodations

Autism: Read the story alone with the child and discuss possible questions he may have about dolphins.

Speech or Language Impairments: Encourage the child to use complete sentences.

Hearing Impairments: Have the child sit where he can see the book easily. Face the child during discussion time. Repeat the children's questions.

Visual Impairments: Provide the child a place to sit during the story reading so that he can see the book easily.

Cognitive and/or Developmental Disabilities: Ask questions when reading the book to help children come up with questions later.

Emotional Disturbance: Encourage the child to look back through the pictures in the book to find answers to the questions.

Other Health Impairments/Attention Deficit Hyperactivity Disorder: Provide two or three note cards with question marks to cue the child on the number of questions and information pieces he should give. As he asks question, let him place the card in a selected place.

Orthopedic Impairments: No special modifications are needed in this discussion lesson.

Review
On the chart, write the answers to the questions the children asked about dolphins.

Assessment Strategy
Individually ask the children to say something they learned about dolphins.

Curriculum Connections

✦ **Art:** If any of the children have seen dolphins (or other large ocean animals) in aquariums or Sea World, invite them to bring in photographs or magazine cutouts of the animals for a classroom display in the Art Center. Children can also draw and cut out pictures of sea creatures to add to the display. Children who have seen real dolphins can tell the class their experience.

✦ **Language and Literacy:** Provide large fish-shaped paper for the children to draw and write about the dolphin. Or have parent volunteers take dictation from children about their knowledge of dolphins.

✦ **Science:** Create a "dolphin in a bottle." Place a small, deflated balloon inside a clean, empty two-liter soda bottle. Holding the balloon open, carefully add about ½ cup of water into the balloon so that it is slightly filled with water. Add one or two puffs of air into the balloon so that it is slightly inflated. Tie the end of the balloon closed (which is inside the soda bottle). Fill the soda bottle ¾ of the way with water. Add two drops of blue food coloring to the water, if desired. Tightly screw on cap. (Add hot glue to the cap before screwing it on to provide a secure seal. Note: Do this adult-only step away from the children.) Place the soda bottle on its side. Slightly squeezing the sides will allow the balloon dolphin to surface and dive.

Whales

Time
30–40 minutes

Materials
10–12 tent stakes
pictures of various whales
Whales by Seymour Simon
250"–300" of rope or
    contractors' marking tape

Preparation
Prior to the lesson find an area on the playground that is at least 25' x 100'. Stake the corners of the area.

Objectives

Children will:
1. Discuss the characteristics of a whale.
2. Create a representation of the size of the blue whale.

Lesson

◆ Gather the children together for Circle or Group Time.
◆ Ask the children what the largest animal on the earth is. If necessary, give them a hint that the animal may live in the ocean.
◆ Show them pictures of different whales.
◆ Read the book *Whales* to the children.
◆ Discuss the different characteristics of whales. Tell the children some whale facts (below) as needed for discussion.

Whale Facts
The blue whale is the largest animal in the world, even larger than the dinosaurs. They are 80'–100' long and can weigh over 100 tons. This is larger than a school bus or 18-wheeler truck.
Blue whales are thought to live to be 110 years old.
Whales live in the ocean. However, whales are mammals, not fish. Fish have scales, and whales have smooth skin. Whales have lungs to breathe air, and they give birth to their young. Fish lay eggs, and they have gills to breathe underwater.
The blue whale is blue-gray in color.
They eat small shrimp-like creatures called krill.
Some whales have teeth and some do not. Dolphins and porpoises are small-toothed whales.

◆ Take the children outside to the playground. Choose a child or two to hold one end of the contractor's tape or rope, with the excess on the ground at the beginning point. Have them start at one end of the previously selected area and walk 50 steps. (This will be about 100'.) Then add a stake and loop the tape or rope around the stake. Have them turn and walk 12 steps to add another stake, and then turn back toward the beginning point, walking another 50 steps and staking the point. Then have them walk toward the beginning stake. Add additional stakes to hold the tape or rope in place. Have the children stand, walk, skip, and move inside the area to experience the large area.
◆ Have the children step outside the area and look at the area that defines the size of a blue whale.
◆ Discuss the size of the animal.

Review

Have other adult take pictures of the children marking off the area. Post the pictures in the classroom for future discussions.

Assessment Strategy

Individually ask the children to name one trait of the whale.

Modifications/Accommodations

Autism: Pair the child with an adult or peer for the outdoor activity.

Speech or Language Impairments: Define new words and encourage the child to use the new words in the discussion.

Hearing Impairments: Provide visual clues and picture assists to allow for success both indoors and out.

Visual Impairments: Pair the child with an adult or peer for the outside activity so that the child stays within the boundaries. Provide a verbal description of the activity as it occurs.

Cognitive and/or Developmental Disabilities: Have an adult or peer assistant during the outdoor activity. Talk to the child about what is going on during the measuring experience.

Emotional Disturbance: Provide clear directions and expectations during the outside activity.

Other Health Impairments/Attention Deficit Hyperactivity Disorder: Use visual and auditory reminders to assist the child in staying safely in the area. Provide praise for correct behavior during the lesson.

Orthopedic Impairments: Have an adult or peer assist the child with walking during the activity.

Curriculum Connections

✦ **Language and Literacy:** Brainstorm as many words as possible that describe the large size of the whale (such as *huge*, *great*, *big*, *humongous*, *giant*, *monstrous*, and so on.) Add these words to the classroom Word Wall.

✦ **More Language and Literacy:** Provide large butcher paper for the children to write "whale" stories.

✦ **Math:** Provide an area in the classroom to store the string or tape used for the outdoor activity. Let the children experience the "largeness" of the tape during their play.

Starfish

Time
30–45

Materials
Starfish by Edith Thacher
   Hurd or *Starfish* by Lloyd
   G. Douglas
stars cut from poster board
   (template)
brown construction paper
sand with bits of crushed hay
   or dried grasses mixed
   with the sand.
sand

Review
Place the *Starfish* book in the
Library Center so children can
reread it. Encourage them to
describe the starfish they
made.

Assessment Strategy
Ask the children to name one
characteristic of a starfish.

Objectives

Children will:
1. Discuss the characteristics of starfish.
2. Create a starfish using a variety of art materials.

Lesson

✦ Gather the children together for center time. Read the story *Starfish* to the children.
✦ Discuss the characteristics of a starfish.
✦ Invite the children to create a starfish. Have them share star cutouts to use as tracing templates. Provide brown or tan construction paper for the children to a trace star onto. Have them cut out their star shapes, brush with thinned glue, and sprinkle with sand mixture.

Modifications/Accommodations

Autism: Provide plenty of time for the child to experiment with the art materials.
Speech or Language Impairments: Before calling on the child for responses, make sure they have the language and vocabulary they need to answer questions. Assist the child by defining and modeling desired vocabulary in your discussions and questions.
Hearing Impairments: Provide picture cues to assist the child in making the starfish.
Visual Impairments: Provide plenty of time for the child to experiment with the art materials. Place the materials close to the child.
Cognitive and/or Developmental Disabilities: Use simple vocabulary when you talk about the starfish. Let the children use their fingers to trace the shape of the starfish.
Emotional Disturbance: Provide extended time for the child to complete his starfish to his satisfaction. Some children need additional time to get it "just right." Rushing him may agitate him and disrupt his learning.
Other Health Impairments/Attention Deficit Hyperactivity Disorder: Help the child focus on the art activity by using verbal directions, and providing extra time for him to plan how he wants to design his starfish.
Orthopedic Impairments: Help the child spread the glue on the starfish with brushes or fingers.

Curriculum Connections

✦ **Art:** Place colored stars in the Art Center and invite the children to draw pictures of beaches and add "starfish."
✦ **Language and Literacy:** Provide pictures of items that begin with the /s/ sound and some items that do not have the /s/ sound in the Writing Center. Have the children group the items by sound.

Introduction to Birds

Time
15–20 minutes

Materials
Little Bird, Biddle Bird by
    David Kirk
pictures of birds

Objectives

Children will:
1. Look at pictures of different birds.
2. Name different characteristics of birds.

Lesson

✦ Gather the children together on the floor.
✦ Read the story *Little Bird, Biddle Bird* by David Kirk
✦ Discuss the trials of the little bird as he gains his independence.
✦ Discuss the physical features of the bird—the feet, beak, wings, and feathers.
✦ Explain that the bird's ability to fly is related to the size of its wings and its body size. Ostriches, for example, cannot fly because their bodies are too heavy for their wings.
✦ Look at the different pictures of birds and point out the size of the bodies and wings.
✦ Ask the children to predict if the bird can fly.

Modifications/Accommodations

Autism: individually share the book with the child. Have the child point to certain features of the bird.
Speech or Language Impairments: Encourage the child to use complete sentences during discussion about birds.
Hearing Impairments: Have the child sit near you.
Visual Impairments: Provide access to the book and pictures before, during, and after the activity to assist in understanding.
Cognitive and/or Developmental Delays: Place the pictures of birds close to the child and point to characteristics of the bird during the discussion.
Emotional Disturbance: Use hand gestures and verbal cues to help the child pass the pictures and waiting her turn in the discussion.
Other Health Impairments/Attention Deficit Hyperactivity Disorder: Give the child a picture of a bird to use during the lesson. Have her point to the characteristics on her picture as you talk about them.
Orthopedic Impairments: No specific modifications are needed in this discussion activity.

Review
Place the book in the Library Center for later reading.

Assessment Strategy
Ask the children individually to name one trait of the bird, such as having a beak, wings, feathers and two legs and feet. This can be done as the child leaves the circle area after the story and discussion.

Curriculum Connections

✦ **Art:** Invite the children to use construction paper pieces and glue to create their own bird in mosaic fashion to an outline of a bird. Have a variety bird outlines for the children to choose from.
✦ **Math:** Provide unifix squares for children to measure the body length and wingspan of pictures of birds in flight.
✦ **Movement:** Give the children scarves. Play music and encourage the children to flap their wings like a bird. Use various tempos of music and have the children move to the beat of the music.

How Birds Build Nests

Time
30–45 minutes

Materials
bird nest
one package of chocolate
    chips
saucepan
hot plate or stove (adult only)
chow mein noodles
plastic spoon for each child
muffin tins or one-cup cups
    (small Styrofoam cups cut
    to 3" high work well)
refrigerator

Preparation
Find a bird nest no longer in
use. Carefully spray it with a
disinfectant spay and place it
in a large resealable bag for
two weeks to kill any live
bugs. Melt the chocolate
chips in a small saucepan.
Allow it to cool slightly, but
keep it in the liquid state.

Objectives

Children will:
1. Examine a bird nest.
2. Create an edible bird nest.

Lesson

+ Gather the children together on
  the rug.
+ Show them the bird's nest. Tell
  them that the bird used many
  things in the environment to
  weave into a nest.
+ Point out single grass blades or
  sticks in the nest.
+ Place the bird nest in the
  Science Center for later
  inspection by the children.
+ To give the children a sense of how birds build their nests, demonstrate how
  to make edible bird nests.
    + Place a small handful of chow mien noodles in a cup or muffin tin.
    + Pour a small amount of chocolate into the cup.
    + Use a spoon to mix the chocolate and chow mien noodles and shape
      the mixture in a nest shape.
+ Invite the children to child create their own bird nests.
+ Place the nests in a cool or refrigerated place to harden.
+ Once the nest is hardened, peel away the cup or remove from the muffin tin.
+ Eat for snack.

Modifications/Accommodations

Autism: Have the child make a nest with peer assistance.
Speech or Language Impairments: Orally describe the process of making the
    bird nest as you demonstrate.
Hearing Impairments: Use hand gestures and emphasize the actions of
    making the bird nest to help the child understand the process.
Visual Impairments: Orally describe the process of making the bird nest as
    you demonstrate.
Cognitive and/or Developmental Delays: Verbally and visually demonstrate
    making the bird nest with the child. Sit beside the child and individually
    model the activity as the child makes his nest. Repeat steps as needed.

Review
Discuss the nest making procedure as the children shape their nests

Assessment Strategy
Let the children talk about how they made their nests. Have them discuss the similarities between their nest and the real bird's nest.

Emotional Disturbance: Complete the nest-making activity in small groups, offering assistance as needed.

Other Health Impairments/Attention Deficit Hyperactivity Disorder: Using individual or small group time, make the nest with the child alone to cut down on extra stimulus.

Orthopedic Impairments: Allow the child to hold spoon and assist in rotating the cup for nest making.

Curriculum Connections

✦ **Art:** Show the children how to place a small piece of corduroy or burlap under a piece of paper and rub it with an unwrapped crayon to create a nest.
✦ **Fine Motor:** Place pipe cleaners in the Manipulatives Center for children to create bird nests.
✦ **Language and Literacy:** Help the children write a class-dictated story about a nest builder (bird), the nest inhabitants (baby birds), and why they are no longer in the nest (baby birds eventually leave).

How Birds Are Hatched

Time
15–30 minutes

Materials
Chickens Aren't the Only Ones by Ruth Heller
picture cards of the hatching sequence (4 cards): egg, egg with crack, egg opening, egg open with bird coming out

Objectives

Children will:
1. Talk about bird eggs and the hatching process.
2. Sequence pictures of eggs hatching.

Lesson

✦ Gather the children together and read the story *Chickens Aren't the Only Ones.*
✦ Discuss the various creatures that hatch from eggs.
✦ Talk about the hatching process of the bird, pecking from the inside to crack the shell.
✦ Place the four hatching sequence cards in front of the children in the wrong order.
✦ Call on children to place the cards in the correct sequence.

Modifications/Accommodations

Autism: Let the child hold a blown egg to feel the fragility of it. Ask him to tap the egg with a pencil gently to begin the crack, and then harder to open the eggshell.

Speech or Language Impairments: Use a variety of words for the cracking of the eggshell to increase the child's vocabulary.

Hearing Impairments: Visually cue the child to attend to the story and activity by pointing and gesturing to the book, speaker, and sequence cards.

Visual Impairments: Cue the child to the story and activity using your voice and sound. Use volume and pitch of your voice to accentuate specific words in the story and to assist the child in sequencing the life cycle of the hatching of eggs.

Cognitive and/or Developmental Delays: Give the child a blown egg and allow him to tap the egg and crack it open.

Emotional Disturbance: Give the child a blown egg to feel it and tap it lightly until cracks appear.

Other Health Impairments/Attention Deficit Hyperactivity Disorder:
Provide verbal and hand signs to help the child wait his turn in the sequencing activity. Have the child sit near you so that you will know if the child is attending to the story.

Orthopedic Impairments: Help the child handle the cards to place them in the correct order, or have the child verbally tell a friend how to sequence the cards.

Review
Place the sequence cards and the book in centers for children to access later.

Assessment Strategy
Ask the children to tell how birds are born.

Curriculum Connections

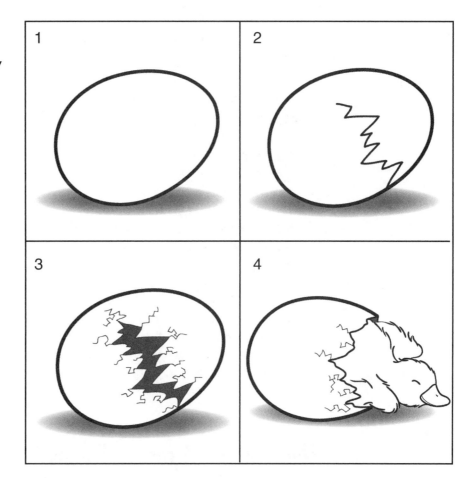

+ **Language and Literacy:** Have the child fold a sheet of manila paper into four sections. Draw a stage of eggs hatching in each of the squares. Have the child write a word or a phrase about what is happening in each section of the paper.
+ **More Language and Literacy:** Read *Horton Hatches the Egg* by Dr. Seuss.
+ **Science:** Call your county extension office and ask them to deliver eggs and an incubator to your classroom so the children can see the hatching of real eggs.

Migration

Time
30–45 minutes

Materials
chart paper for group story
drawing paper
crayons and markers

Objectives

Children will:
1. Discuss the migration of birds and how weather plays a part.
2. Illustrate migrating birds.

Lesson

✦ Gather the children together on the rug.
✦ Ask the children where animals go in the winter. Ask them where they go when it is cold outside.
✦ Ask the children if they know where birds go when it is cold.
✦ Explain that many birds move to warmer climates in the fall. The children in the South may see different types of birds in the fall and winter due to migration and the children in the North may see fewer birds.
✦ Invite the children to dictate a class story of a bird flying South for the winter and then returning to its home.
✦ Have the children illustrate the chart story and post it on the wall.

Modifications/Accommodations

Autism: This is a difficult concept. Discuss the movement of birds using a paper mat moving up and down to show the child the movement a birds wings make. Allow the child to hold a mat in each arm moving up and down to feel the movement of the air.

Speech or Language Impairments: Encourage the child to use the words migration and hibernation in their discussion. Use these words in the questions to the children to model how to use the words and to reinforce the usage of the new words,

Hearing Impairments: Have the child sit in an area where she can have an unobstructed view of the speaker. Use gestures to help the child focus on the information and understand the information.

Visual Impairments: Use auditory cues to help the child participate in the discussion. Provide markers for the drawing activity; markers provide greater contrast visually and are seen more easily.

Cognitive and/or Developmental Delays: Explain that the birds know instinctually where to go and when to return to their homes. Help them understand that the birds are not lost.

Review
Place the story and the illustrations in the classroom for child to read later.

Assessment Strategy
Have each child tell about the bird they drew to illustrate the class story.

Emotional Disturbance: Encourage the child to stay on topic in the story dictation by providing sentence beginnings for the child to complete as they add to the story.

Other Health Impairments/Attention Deficit Hyperactivity Disorder: Provide verbal and nonverbal cues, such as hand and thumbs-up gestures, to assist the child in participating and turn taking.

Orthopedic Impairments: Provide materials within reach of the child.

Curriculum Connections

✦ **Math:** Create word problems for the children to solve using a bird's migration. For example, "There were five birds in the tree. Three of them began their migration on Monday. How many were left in the tree?"

✦ **Science:** Discuss other animals that hibernate or migrate in the cold months. Have children select animal pictures and place them in "stay" or "migrate" piles.

✦ **Social Studies:** Discuss travels of people during the holidays and in the winter months. "Do some families travel to a new place to be with friends and family for the holidays?" "Where do many people vacation in the winter?" Relate families' travels to the need to be in a warmer climate for the birds.

Hummingbirds

Time
30–45 minutes

Materials
clear plastic soda bottles
scissors
pictures of hummingbirds
tapestry needle (adult only)
waxed string or fishing line
1-cup measuring cup
red food coloring
light corn syrup, such as Karo
    syrup
water

Preparation
Before the lesson, cut the soda bottles in half. Both halves of the bottle can be used for this activity if the lid is secured to the top of the bottle. Cut scallops into the cut edge of one of the bottle halves.

Objectives

Children will:
1. Look at hummingbird pictures and discuss facts about hummingbirds.
2. Make a hummingbird feeder.

Lesson

✦ Gather the children together to look at the pictures of hummingbirds.
✦ Tell them that hummingbirds are the smallest type of bird. Some are about 3 ½" long. (Show them an object that is 3" long as a point of reference.) Others are as tiny as bumblebees. Even though they are small, they can fly up to 50 miles per hour. They can fly backwards or hover in mid-air. Their wings beat so quickly, one can't see them move. Because hummingbirds hover rather than land when they feed, their feeders are unlike other bird feeders.
✦ Show the children the bottle half with scalloped edges. (This allows the birds to get closer to the nectar.) Use a small piece of a coffee stir stick attached to a clay ball to represent the hummingbird head and beak. Show the child how this thin straw like beak can reach in the side of the feeder to get to the nectar.
✦ Give each child a bottle half. Some children will use the top half and some will use the bottom half. Demonstrate how to use scissors to cut scalloped edges on the bottle. Help the children cut scalloped ridges in the open end of the soda bottle.
✦ Use a tapestry needle to poke three holes in the side of each bottle half. (This is step for adults to do.) Help the children thread the waxed string or fishing line through the holes.
✦ Help each child tie the ends of the fishing line together to create a hanger for the bird feeder.
✦ Mix 4 cups of water, 2 cups of light Karo syrup, and 10 drops of red food coloring together. The red color attracts the humming birds.
✦ Hang the bird feeders outside in the trees. Fill each feeder with the nectar mixture. Fill each feeder just below the scalloped edges.
✦ Watch the hummingbirds.

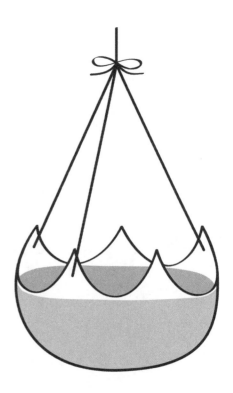

Review

Watch the birds attracted to the feeders over a few weeks. If no hummingbirds are attracted to the feeders, the children can watch the other insects and birds that may be attracted to the feeder. The children can draw pictures of hummingbirds feeding and place these pictures near the window and the bird feeder.

Assessment Strategy

Have each child tell about the birds they see and how the hummingbird is different from other birds.

Modifications/Accommodations

Autism: Give the child extra time in threading the string and selecting the site for her bird feeder.

Speech or Language Impairments: Have the child identify the wings, beak, and body of the hummingbird from pictures. Encourage the child to use complete sentences when sequencing the activity of making the hummingbird feeder after the child has finished.

Hearing Impairments: Use visual prompts when demonstrating the making of the bird feeder. Have another adult help the child with the steps of making the bird feeder.

Visual Impairments: Verbalize the process of making the bird feeder. As the child makes the feeder, verbalize the current step as well as the following step.

Cognitive and/or Developmental Delays: Pair the child with another child when creating the bird feeders.

Emotional Disturbance: Have extra materials available for mishaps. Have the child select his feeding sight and verbalize where she wants to place the feeder before going out to hang it.

Other Health Impairments/Attention Deficit Hyperactivity Disorder: Ask the child to state the directions and the procedure before she begins. Refocus the child (if necessary) by asking her what she should do next.

Orthopedic Impairments: Provide materials at the level appropriate for the child. Offer assistance in the creation of the feeder.

Curriculum Connections

✦ **Art:** Let the children draw pictures of hummingbirds.
✦ **Language and Literacy:** Help the children dictate a story about what the hummingbird sees in its travels.
✦ **Math:** Figure out how far the hummingbird can fly during the school day.

Introduction to Insects

Time
15–20 minutes

Materials
100 Things You Should Know About Insects and Spiders by Steve Parker

Objectives

Children will:
1. Listen to and discuss information on insects.
2. Name the three main parts of the insect.

Lesson

+ Gather the children together for Circle or Group Time.
+ Ask them if they can name an insect.
+ Record all of the children's answers on the board.
+ Then ask them if they know what makes an insect an insect.
+ Read the book *Insects and Spiders* by Steve Parker.
+ Emphasize that insects have a hard exoskeleton that protects a softer interior, and that the adult insect is divided into three main parts: the head, thorax or chest area, and abdomen the lower tummy area (top, middle, and bottom).

Modifications/Accommodations

Autism: Help the child make the hand motions. Model the hand motions for the child, or hold the child's hands to help him make the movements. Ask the child forced-choice questions to allow him to participate in the discussion. These questions will be either-or questions allowing the child the modeled vocabulary to complete his answer.

Speech or Language Impairments: As you read the book, define any unknown words and relate them to the children's experiences by giving an example. Encourage the child to participate in discussion, and use the new words, by providing introductory phrases for the child to complete.

Hearing Impairments: Provide an area in which there are few distracters to the speaker and where the child can see your mouth, which will allow the child to use facial cues for any lip reading cues to assist in the child's understanding of auditory information. Stand near the child during the song to assist as needed.

Visual Impairments: Seat the child close to you during the story reading or allow him to preview the story before group time. If possible, provide a duplicate copy of the book for the child to follow along in.

Cognitive and/or Developmental Delays: Provide time for the child to repeat the song with assistance of motor movements. The assistance will be at an individually appropriate level. Some children will need to be near the teacher to watch her movements, some may need the teacher or another adult verbalizing the needed movements and some children may need hand-over-hand assistance to make each of the movements.

Review
Have the children sing the song "Head, Thorax, Abdomen" while making the suggested movements.

Head, Thorax, Abdomen
adapted by Diana Nabors
Tune: "Head, Shoulders, Knees, and Toes"

Head, thorax, abdomen, abdomen. (touch head with both hands, then the chest and the abdomen)

Head, thorax, abdomen, abdomen. (touch head, chest, and abdomen)

Insects have three parts, yes ma'am. (hold up three fingers)

Head, thorax abdomen, abdomen. (touch head, chest, and abdomen)

Assessment Strategy
Note children's participation and ability to name the three main parts of the insect.

Emotional Disturbance: Show the child the book and sing the song (with movements) for him before the group lesson. Point out the parts of the insect.

Other Health Impairments/Attention Deficit Hyperactivity Disorder: Provide a carpet square for the children to use as a movement area during the song and possibly during story time.

Orthopedic Impairments: Provide visual and physical assists in the song movements.

Curriculum Connections

✦ **Art:** Provide fingerpaint and paper. Have the children make three fingerprints, one on top of the other, like an insect body. After the paint dries, invite the children to use markers to add legs, antennae, and wings to their insects.

✦ **Language and Literacy:** Give the children a variety of magazines or books to find pictures of insects. Have them point out the head, thorax, and abdomen of each. This will help them to realize that the three parts are not uniform in size.

✦ **Math:** Cut out or photocopy 10 insect pictures. Make two matching cards for each insect. Put all the cards facedown and invite children to play Concentration by matching pairs of insects.

Ants

Time
15–20 minutes

Materials
Two Bad Ants by Chris Van
  Allsburg
fingerpaint
painting paper

Objectives

Children will:
1. Listen to and discuss to the story of *Two Bad Ants* by Chris Van Allsburg.
2. Discuss how ants might see the human world.

Lesson

✦ Gather the children together to listen to the story *Two Bad Ants.*
✦ Have the children discuss what life might be like as an ant. Discuss what the world would look like to an ant.
✦ Ask questions such as:

   ✦ What would seem to be a river to an ant?
   ✦ What might seem to be a mountain to an ant?
   ✦ What might be a snowstorm to an ant?
   ✦ What would be a home for an ant?

✦ Invite the children to use fingerpaint to make fingerprint ants (three fingerprints) and then illustrate the ant in the human world having an adventure.)

Modifications/Accommodations

Autism: Discuss ants with the child prior to the lesson. Assist the child in making the three fingerprints. If the child is tactilely defensive, provide the three fingerprints for him to add insect parts.

Speech or Language Impairments: Encourage the child to discuss ants he may have seen and the traits of ants.

Hearing Impairments: Provide a place for the child to see the speakers during the discussion. If the speaker's voice is low, repeat the major points for the child.

Visual Impairments: Provide an extra copy of the book for the child to use during the story time. Allow time for the child to read and re-read the book, focusing on the illustrations.

Cognitive and/or Developmental Delays: Discuss the ant and the difference of its world and the child's world. Help the child in relating size of items. Have the child order three doll-sized bowls next to a doll and then order three adult-sized bowls in front of the child.

Emotional Disturbance: Provide verbal support to the child as he discusses an ant's point of view.

Discuss the child's illustration and let her share the illustration with others.

Assessment Strategy
Individually prompt children to participate in the discussion of the ant's perspective of the world.

Other Health Impairments/Attention Deficit Hyperactivity Disorder: Assist the child with taking turns and accepting other ideas during the discussion.

Orthopedic Impairments: Provide assistance in making the three fingerprints. Encourage the child to perform as much of the art work as desired.

Curriculum Connections

✦ **Math:** Using small plastic ants found in may toy stores, have the children count ants into piles of five.
✦ **Music and Movement:** Invite the children to march around the room singing the song below:

The Ants Go Marching (Traditional)
The ants go marching one by one, hurrah, hurrah
The ants go marching one by one, hurrah, hurrah
The ants go marching one by one,
The little one stops to suck his thumb
And they all go marching down to the ground
To get out of the rain, BOOM! BOOM! BOOM!

…two…tie her shoe…
…three…climb a tree…
…four…shut the door…
…five…take a dive…
…six…pick up sticks…
…seven…pray to heaven…
…eight…shut the gate…
…nine…check the time…
…ten…say "The end!"…

✦ **Snack:** Make Ants on a Log. Spread peanut butter or cheese spread on a celery stick and top with raisins.

Review

Mosquitoes

Time
10–15 minutes

Materials
2–4 pictures of mosquitoes
2–4 pictures of water
    collection areas—pots,
    bowls, and toys
child-safe mosquito repellant
citronella spray or candles
eucalyptus oils

Objectives

Children will:
1. Identify pictures of mosquitoes.
2. Discuss mosquito bites and how to treat the bites.

Lesson

◆ Gather the children together on the floor.
◆ Show them a picture of a mosquito and ask them what kind of insect they see.
◆ Help them identify the head, thorax, abdomen, and other noticeable features of the mosquito.
◆ Ask them what they know about mosquitoes. Most will tell about the bites they have gotten or the mosquitoes they have squashed. Explain that the mosquito has a proboscis, a long pointed tube that allows the mosquito to bite people and animals. It sucks blood without being felt until the small red bump it makes begins to itch. Only the female mosquito bites and sucks blood, which is needed to assist in the egg development.
◆ Explain that mosquitoes are hatched from eggs left in standing water. Show pictures of common standing water locations, such as flower pots, bowls, and outdoor tools and toys.
◆ Ask the children what their families do to prevent mosquito bites or care for bites. If the children do not focus on how their families have them cover their exposed skin or applications of repellents you may want to add information about covering their body with hat, long sleeves, and pants, mosquito repellants for people and pets, the use of citronella or eucalyptus sprays or candles to protect areas as well as the use of a fan to create a gentle breeze. Mosquitoes do not like moving air.

Modifications/Accommodations

Autism: Provide one-on-one discussion about mosquitoes before the lesson. Ask the child forced choice questions to include her in the discussion.
Speech or Language Impairments: Provide time for the child to add to the discussion. Ask the child questions about her experiences with mosquitoes to allow her a chance to add to the discussion.
Hearing Impairments: Restate children's discussions. Have the child sit near you and allow her to move around to see the speaker during the discussion.
Visual Impairments: Provide a time for the child to touch and explore the materials prior to the group time. Provide one on one discussion time with the child.

Review

Have the children discuss what they can do to avoid mosquito bites if they are going into an area where there may be many mosquitoes, such as a field, near a lake or river, or wooded area early in the morning or at dusk when the air is still and more humid, and care for the bites they may get. Let them draw a picture of how they can help. (Empty water from collection sites in the area, cover their bodies, and so on.)

Assessment Strategy

Have each child tell about her drawing.

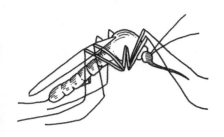

Cognitive and/or Developmental Delays: Ask the child about her experiences with mosquitoes prior to the lesson. Then allow the child to restate her experiences during the group time.

Emotional Disturbance: Have the child discuss the pictures and the materials before the lesson or allow her to discuss the items one-on-one with you after the lesson.

Other Health Impairments/Attention Deficit Hyperactivity Disorder: Provide one-on-one time for the child to discuss mosquitoes with you.

Orthopedic Impairments: Provide art materials at the level of the child for independent work.

Curriculum Connections

✦ **Literacy and Language:** Using a mosquito net, create an area for the children to read, draw, or write about insects.

✦ **More Literacy and Language:** Read the story *Mosquito Bite* by Alexandrea Siy. Have the children draw a picture of a child with a mosquito bite and tell a story to a friend about how the child in the picture can take care of the mosquito bite.

✦ **Science and Health:** Have the children use soap and water to wash their hands and arms before applying a lotion of eucalyptus oil. This will encourage the children to care for their own skin with and without insect bites.

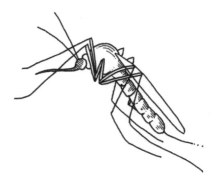

Flies

Time
15–20 minutes

Materials
Hi, Fly Guy by Tedd Arnold
A variety of Art Center
material such as pipe
cleaners, straws, pieces
of poster board,
construction paper, small
boxes and jars, scissors,
rubber bands, wax paper
squares, glue, crayons,
markers

Objectives

Children will:
1. Listen to and discuss a story about a fly—*Hi, Fly Guy* by Tedd Arnold.
2. Discuss pets and why insects are not good pets.

Lesson

✦ Gather the children to listen to the book *Hi, Fly Guy,* a fictional story about a boy who wants to make a fly his pet.
✦ Discuss the ways that the fly in the story made a good pet and the ways that a real fly would not be a good pet.
✦ Have the children use classroom materials to make a cage for the insect of their choosing. Provide pipe cleaners, paper, poster board strips, small boxes and jars.
✦ Have the children draw and cut out their paper insect to keep in their cage.
✦ Have the children share with the others about their pet and how they can care for the pet.

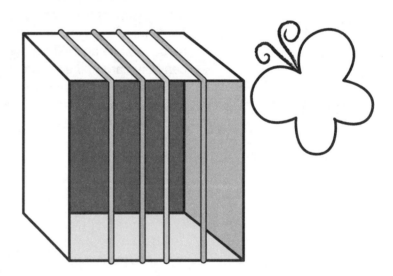

Modifications/Accommodations

Autism: Talk with the individual child about flies.
Speech or Language Impairments: Encourage the child to use complete sentences during the discussion.
Hearing Impairments: Speak clearly, and read with variance in your voice to assist the child in understanding the story.

Review
Have the children list the reasons they could not have a real live fly as a pet.

Assessment Strategy
Ask the children individually to list the qualities of a good pet.

Visual Impairments: Provide a time for the child to view the book and ask questions before the lesson. Place the book in the Library Center for individual exploration after the lesson

Emotional Disturbances: Encourage the child to talk about insects as pets and provide the child with possible options of a pet and pet cage he might build. Continuously check with the child to keep him on task and help in any needed problem-solving strategies as the child makes the cage and pet.

Cognitive and/or Developmental Delays: Provide lead phrases to help the child participate in the discussion.

Other Health Impairments/Attention Deficit Hyperactivity Disorder: Provide support in turn taking during the discussion. This can be done using hand signals and gestures, such as a thumbs-up sign to reinforce correct waiting for turns.

Orthopedic Impairments: Help the child by providing a buddy for making the cage and insect. Provide specialized grips for the child to be successful in holding the crayons, markers, and scissors.

Curriculum Connections

✦ **Literacy and Language:** Have the child dictate or write a list of care instructions or rules for handling their chosen insect. Have the child tell others what his insect needs and how others should handle the insect. Provide time for children to view and care for each others paper pets.

✦ **Movement:** Give each child two small scarves. Invite them to "fly" around the room or outdoors.

✦ **Music:** Invite the children to sing the song "Shoo Fly, Don't Bother Me."

Grasshoppers

Time
20–30 minutes

Materials
Are You a Grasshopper? by Judy Allen
pictures of grasshoppers

Objectives

Children will:
1. Identify characteristics of grasshoppers.
2. Listen to *Are You a Grasshopper?* by Judy Allen.

Lesson

✦ Gather the children together to listen to the book *Are You a Grasshopper?* by Judy Allen.

✦ Talk about the characteristics of grasshoppers that the book mentions, such as they change their exoskeletons at least four times in their lives. The grasshopper's body covering does not grow with it. When the grasshopper grows too large for the outer coating, it must shed the exoskeleton or outer coating to continue to grow. Grasshoppers have pegs on their legs that when rubbed against the wings or other legs make chirping sounds, and they have small suction-like cups on their legs to allow them to hold onto stems and branches.

✦ Show examples of other insects or reptiles that shed their exoskeletons ("skin"). Use a suction cup to show how grasshoppers hold on to things.

✦ Show the pictures of grasshoppers and point out the length of a grasshopper's legs. Discuss the long jumps that they make.

✦ Invite the children to practice hopping in place like a grasshopper.

✦ Provide lively music for the children to hop around the room as a grasshopper as you chant:

Hop, hop, hop little grasshopper,
Hopping through the grass.
Stop, stop, stop little grasshopper,
Rub your legs to sing.

Modifications/Accommodations

Autism: One-on-one, read and discuss the story with the child prior to or after the group time.

Speech or Language Impairments: Define unfamiliar words and use pictures to describe new concepts.

Hearing Impairments: Provide verbal restatements of the children's discussion for the child to hear.

Visual Impairments: Let the child look at and experience the materials and book after the group time.

Review

Ask each child to state one trait about the grasshopper she has learned today.

Assessment Strategy

Ask each child to tell one thing about a grasshopper as she leaves the group setting for the next activity.

Cognitive and/or Developmental Delays: Discuss and use picture cues of grasshoppers in their natural environment to assist in new concepts. Provide pictures of grasshoppers at flight, at rest, and singing.

Emotional Disturbance: Provide time for the child to discuss grasshoppers with a peer or with you.

Other Health Impairments/Attention Deficit Hyperactivity Disorder: Provide verbal instructions to assist the child in jumping in place.

Orthopedic Impairments: Assist the child in jumping or bending her legs like a grasshopper. If the child is unable to use her legs, help her experience the movement by verbalizing the motions of classmates. Then have the child move a part of her body in response to the chant. This can be her arms, fingers, or head.

Curriculum Connections

✦ **Fine Motor:** Give each child a 1" square of card stock paper to fold in half. Let the children experiment with different folds to hop their paper across the table. (To make papers that hop, help the children fold the paper in half diagonally then fold the tip back accordion style. Using the tip as the pressure point the child can hop the cricket along.)

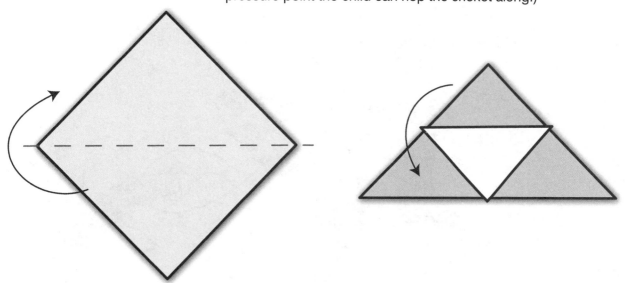

✦ **Language and Literacy:** Provide a tape of nature sounds, including crickets or grasshoppers chirping and other insect noises.

✦ **Math:** Ask the children to hop one time and then have the other children measure how far the child hopped or the child can measure the distance of hops of the card stock cricket by using small blocks.

Caterpillars and Butterflies

Time

story and discussion: 20–30 minutes
observation: 21 days.

Materials

From Caterpillar to Butterfly by Deborah Heiligman
painted lady butterfly caterpillars (can be purchased from educational/science websites or catalogues)
butterfly habitat, available from school supply catalogs and companies
paper
crayons

Objectives

Children will:
1. Observe the growth of a caterpillar and its metamorphosis to a butterfly.
2. Listen to and discuss the story *From Caterpillar to Butterfly*.

Lesson

✦ Read the story *From Caterpillar to Butterfly* by Deborah Heiligman to the children.
✦ Discuss the changes the caterpillar goes through in the story.
✦ Show the children a cup of five to seven caterpillars.
✦ Put the caterpillars in their habitat and discuss the care of the caterpillars.
✦ Provide paper and crayons for the children to record the daily changes of the caterpillars as the view the habitat over the next 21 days.
✦ Discuss the chrysalis of the caterpillar and how still it is. Talk about what changes the caterpillar might be experiencing in the chrysalis.
✦ Once the caterpillars have changed into butterflies, observe them for a few days before releasing them into the wild.

Modifications/Accommodations

Autism: Introduce the live caterpillars to the child and discuss the care and procedures for observing them without touching.
Speech or Language Impairments: Encourage the child to use complete sentences during the discussion time.

Review

Re-read the story or have the children talk about the sequence of the change of the caterpillar into a butterfly.

Assessment Strategy

Have the children sequence the stages of metamorphoses of the caterpillar using pre-made cards showing the stages of metamorphosis

Hearing Impairments: Have the child sit where he can see you reading the book and is able to move his body to see the children talking during discussion.

Visual Impairments: Give the child an extra copy of the book to look at as you read to the group. Provide the child with a magnifying glass to view the caterpillars without disturbing the environment.

Cognitive and/or Developmental Delays: Discuss the care of the caterpillars and the procedure for observing without touching the caterpillar's environment.

Emotional Disturbance: Discuss observing the caterpillars without touching them.

Other Health Impairments/Attention Deficit Hyperactivity Disorder: Discuss one-on-one with the child the need for the caterpillars to live undisturbed in their environment. Place the caterpillars in an easy-to-observe place with a "no-hands" border made of masking tape around the habitat.

Orthopedic Impairments: Place the caterpillars where the child can view them easily.

Curriculum Connections

✦ **Art:** Encourage the children to create butterflies using watercolors and coffee filters. After the filters dry, show the children how to twist a pipe cleaner around the middle of the filter to form "wings" and "antennae" of the butterfly.

✦ **Math:** Have the children place five different-sized caterpillars in order from longest to shortest. Make these caterpillars out of felt or braided pipe cleaners.

✦ **Science:** Find simple pictures of the stages of a caterpillar's metamorphosis and make copies for all the children. Have the children glue the pictures in order on a strip of paper.

Introduction to Reptiles

Time
20–30 minutes in each of two
separate settings

Materials
three sheets of chart paper
marker
*How to Hide a Crocodile and
Other Reptiles* by Ruth
Heller

Objectives

Children will:
1. Identify characteristics of reptiles.
2. List different reptiles.

Lesson

✦ Gather the children on the rug for story time. Show the children the cover of the book and discuss what they think the other reptiles might be.
✦ Record all of their thoughts on a piece of chart paper.
✦ Read the story *How to Hide a Crocodile and Other Reptiles* by Ruth Heller.
✦ Discuss the traits of a reptile. Add to the children's discussion using the facts below:

Reptile Facts
Reptiles have scaly, dry skin and breathe air using their lungs.
Many reptiles have teeth and claws on their feet.
Reptiles shed their skin as they grow.
Most reptiles lay eggs.
Baby reptiles usually look like small adult reptiles.
Reptiles are cold-blooded and often hibernate during periods of cold weather.
The reptile family includes turtles, lizards, snakes, and crocodiles.

✦ Record the traits of reptiles on a second sheet of chart paper.
✦ Invite the children to draw a small picture of a reptile. Glue their drawings to the third piece of chart paper.

Modifications/Accommodations

Autism: During the assessment, provide various photographs of reptiles and ask the child to select one and name it.
Speech or Language Impairments: During the assessment, name a reptile and ask the child to point to the corresponding photograph.
Hearing Impairments: Seat the child across from you where she can see your face and mouth. Repeat words and phrases often, checking for understanding. Refer frequently to pictures and objects in the discussion of reptiles.
Visual Impairments: Provide small, inexpensive, plastic toy reptiles (found at toy stores or dollar stores) for the child to examine closely. Show the child fabric pieces and other textured materials when describing the texture of a reptile's skin.

Review
Ask the children as a group to create and dictate a story about reptiles. This chart story is then added it to the class library.

Assessment Strategy
Individually, ask the children to name a reptile.

Cognitive and/or Developmental Disabilities: Use simple language and vocabulary, repeating phrases frequently. During the review, show the child photographs and invite him to dictate a phrase to add to the story.

Emotional Disturbance: Involve the child in the lesson by having her turn the pages of the book during story time.

Other Health Impairments/Attention Deficit Hyperactivity Disorder: Establish a clear signal to get the child's attention, such as a raised finger. Make sure you have the child's attention before speaking.

Orthopedic Impairments: Make sure the child can see the book when you read it.

Curriculum Connections

✦ **Art:** Cut out a large crocodile shape from poster board and place it in the Art Center. Provide various shades of green construction paper for children to tear into small pieces and glue to the crocodile shape.

✦ **Science:** Provide picture cards of a variety of animals. Encourage the children to sort the reptiles from the rest of the animals.

✦ **More Science:** Bring in a baby turtle or other reptile as a new class pet. Let the children suggest names for the turtle and then vote to determine what the turtle's name will be. Observe the turtle in its new habitat.

Turtles

Time
20–30 minutes

Materials
stuffed toy turtle
12" x 18" paper
scissors
Little Turtle and the Song of the Sea by Sheridan Cain
crayons

Preparation
Before the lesson, cut pieces of 12" x 18" paper in half to create 6" x 18" strips. Fold each 6" x 18" strip into four squares in a row.

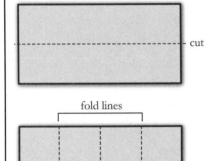

fold lines

Review
In small groups, encourage the children to discuss their drawings. Place the book in the Library Center.

Assessment Strategy
In small groups, ask the children to list three of the obstacles the turtle faced and how the turtle overcame these obstacles.

Objectives

Children will:
1. Discuss the challenges turtles face as they grow.
2. Draw pictures of turtles.

Lesson

✦ Gather the children on the rug. Show them a stuffed toy turtle and ask them what they think they will be talking about today. Ask them to tell what they know about turtles.
✦ Read the book *Little Turtle and the Song of the Sea* by Sheridan Cain.
✦ Discuss the story. Ask the children to tell the challenges the turtle faces when heading towards the sea, his motivation, and the obstacles he faces when he reaches the sea.
✦ Give the children a folded sheet of paper (6″ x 18″) and crayons. Ask them to draw the sequence of the baby turtle's difficult day that is described in the book.

Modifications/Accommodations

Autism: Throughout the lesson, provide various pictures of turtles and ask the child to point out the differences among the pictures.
Speech or Language Impairments: Have the child tell you only one obstacle the turtle faced during the assessment phase. If the child is hesitant, name one obstacle and ask the child if this is or is not an obstacle the turtle faced.
Hearing Impairments: Make sure the child can clearly see you and ask him periodically to repeat what you have said.
Visual Impairments: Find small replicas of turtles at a toy store or dollar store and other items to display the texture of the turtle's shell.
Cognitive and/or Developmental Disabilities: Use simple vocabulary when discussing the turtle. Show the child pictures of various animals and ask him to identify the turtle pictures.
Emotional Disturbance: Seat the child next to you and monitor activities closely. Let the child help you by holding the materials as you finish with them.
Other Health Impairments/Attention Deficit Hyperactivity Disorder: Establish a clear signal for the children to use when they wish to speak and consistently remind them of the signal.
Orthopedic Impairments: No accommodations are anticipated during this lesson.

Curriculum Connections

✦ **Language and Literacy:** Teach the children the poem "I Had a Little Turtle."
✦ **More Language and Literacy:** Encourage the children to describe the turtle using words that begin with the letter "t" (*tiny, terrible, teeny, tough,* and so on).

Snakes

Time
20–30 minutes

Materials
15–20 plastic snakes
number cards (0–5)
pictures of snakes
Snakes by Seymour Simon

Review
Place plastic snakes and number cards in a center for the children to play with.

Assessment Strategy
Assess the children based on group discussion and their participation in the number/snake concept match.

Objectives

Children will:
1. Name the different characteristics of snakes.
2. Count from 1–10 using snakes.

Lesson

✦ Gather the children in a circle to discuss snakes. Show them a plastic snake.
✦ Have the children list as many things that they can about snakes.
✦ Show the children the pictures of different snakes or read the book *Snakes* by Seymour Simon.
✦ Pass out the plastic snakes for the children to hold, one snake per child. Show them the six number cards (0–5) and explain that they are going to place the correct number of snakes on each card.
✦ Place the cards in the front of the room. Two at a time, let the children place their snakes on cards.
✦ Once the children have placed their snakes on the cards, have them count the snakes on each card and adjust the number of snakes, if needed.

Modifications/Accommodations

Autism: Ensure that throughout the lesson the child has many opportunities to handle the materials.

Speech or Language Impairments: During the assessment, say the numbers for the child and have her match the snakes on the correct number. This oral modeling of the numbers matching the quantity will assist the child in numeral language.

Hearing Impairments: Seat the child near you so she can see your face and mouth. Repeat important information several times.

Visual Impairments: Allow the child to handle the snakes throughout the lesson.

Cognitive and/or Developmental Disabilities: During the assessment, provide different toy animals and have the child pick out only the snakes or all of the animals that are not snakes. When handing out materials, let the child assist you.

Other Health Impairments/Attention Deficit Hyperactivity Disorder: Provide verbal cues and hand gestures to assist the child in attending to the activity.

Orthopedic Impairments: If necessary, help the child pick up and place the snakes on the card.

Curriculum Connections

✦ **Fine Motor:** Place playdough in the Art Center and encourage the children to make snakes.
✦ **Science:** Prepare picture cards of a variety of snakes to place in the Manipulatives Center and ask children to match them based on snakes' coloring and markings.

Lizards

Time

Group activity: 30–45 minutes
Repeated observations:
    5 minutes each

Materials

small aquarium with screen top
sticks and foliage
water source (small jar lid or
    frequent misting of foliage)
reptile pellets or live worms
large resealable bag
leaf
3–5 lizards (purchased from
    pet store)
small magnifying glasses
quarter sheets of drawing
    paper
crayons
lizard outlines (black line
    drawing of a lizard)
All About Lizards by Jim
    Arnosky

Preparation

Before the lesson, set up the lizard environment by adding foliage, and sticks to a small aquarium. Make sure to add water and small reptile pellets. Place a leaf in a large resealable bag and mist the sides with water. Save the bag to put the lizard in right before the lesson. Draw two outlines of a lizard and color them to match an area of the room. Hide them in plain view. For example, color one red and place it on a red shelf or poster in your room, and make another striped and place it on a zebra on an alphabet chart. Do this before the children arrive.

Objectives

Children will:
1. Observe lizards in their habitat.
2. Discuss protective coloration.

Lesson

✦ Gather the children on the rug to see the new addition to the classroom.
✦ Ask the children where they have seen lizards before and what they know about lizards.
✦ Place one lizard in a large resealable bag filled with air and misted with water. (**Note** The lizards should be kept in the bags for only a few minutes.)
✦ Allow the children to carefully pass the bag around to see the lizard. Ask them to discuss the physical features of the lizard. Focus on the feet, tail, skin texture, facial features, tongue, and coloration.
✦ Carefully add the lizard to the aquarium with the other lizards.
✦ Read the book *All About Lizards* by Jim Arnosky.
✦ Discuss protective coloration. Invite the children to look around room for the two hidden lizards. Give them hints, if needed.
✦ Give each child a small black-line outline of a lizard. Have the children color their lizard to match an area of the room and then hide it in the area.

Modifications/Accommodations

Autism: Provide photographs and computer-generated images for the child to use during the lesson.
Speech or Language Impairments: During the lesson name the parts of a lizard and have the child point to the part on a picture of a lizard.
Hearing Impairments: Refer frequently to pictures and the real lizards, while constantly checking for understanding. Strategically place the child so that he can see you when you speak.

Review

The children try to locate other children's lizards around the room for the next few days.

Assessment Strategy

Ask each child why he colored his lizard the way he did.

Visual Impairments: Provide small toy lizards for the child to handle.

Cognitive and/or Developmental Disabilities: Use simple vocabulary. Ask the child to pick out pictures of lizards from pictures of a variety of animals.

Emotional Disturbance: Provide close supervision when the child is handling the lizard and remind him of the importance of being careful with the animal.

Other Health Impairments/Attention Deficit Hyperactivity Disorder: Provide extra time for the child to view the lizards in the aquarium. Allow the child some individual time to talk with you about the lizards so you can learn what he knows about lizards.

Orthopedic Impairments: If necessary, assist the child in holding or touching the lizard.

Curriculum Connections

✦ **Outdoors:** Watch for lizards on the playground or in a nearby park.
✦ **More Outdoors:** Talk to the children about how fast lizards can run. At periodic intervals during outdoor play, call out "run, lizards, run." The children run as fast as they can around the playground perimeter when they hear your signal.
✦ **Science:** Place sandpaper and other rough textured material in the Science Center for children to feel. Talk about the rough skin that most reptiles have.

Crocodiles and Alligators

Time
20–30 minutes

Materials
poster board or card stock
marker
scissors
There's an Alligator Under My Bed by Mercer Mayer
green construction paper
crayons

Preparation
Before the lesson, create tracing templates out of poster board or card stock paper. The template should be half the size of a piece of construction paper (4 ½" x 12"). Make the top of the template a straight line (this will be placed on the fold of the construction paper for tracing). Draw a wide-curved "U" shape, about 3" long, on the lower part of the template. Attach 2" rectangles to the base of the "U." Cut out the template.

Objectives

Children will:
1. Identify traits of alligators and crocodiles.
2. Create their own alligators or crocodiles.

Lesson

◆ Gather the children for story time.
◆ Show them the book There's an Alligator Under My Bed by Mercer Mayer. Encourage them to talk about things under their beds, both real and make-believe.
◆ Read the story and discuss alligators. Include information from the facts below:

Crocodile and Alligator Facts
Crocodiles and alligators are the largest reptiles in the world.
They live in warm, wet places such as Louisiana and Florida.
They use their sharp teeth and powerful jaws to capture their food.
They eat insects, frogs, fish, turtles, and birds.
Crocodiles and alligators are different:
◆ *Alligators have a wide, flat heard and a rounded nose. Their head looks like the letter U. Their teeth are sharp and when they close their mouth the lower teeth cannot be seen.*
◆ *Crocodiles have more of a pointed snout. Their head looks more like a baseball bat. The lower teeth of a crocodile can be seen even when they shut their mouth tightly.*

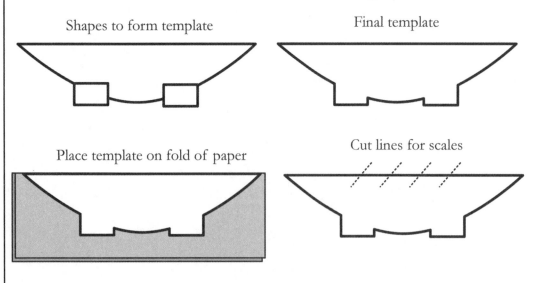

Shapes to form template

Final template

Place template on fold of paper

Cut lines for scales

◆ Invite the children to make their own alligator or crocodile.
◆ Give each child a sheet of green construction paper folded lengthwise (4 ½" x 12").
◆ Help the children place the tracing template at the top fold of the paper and trace around the template.
◆ Let the child cut out tracing, keeping their paper folded.

Review

Have the children name their alligator and tell a story about the "alligator under their bed."

Assessment Strategy

In small groups, have the children discuss one or two traits of alligators and crocodiles.

✦ Help each child snip five angled cuts in the folded straight line of the paper (this will become the alligator's back).
✦ The children open the folded paper and bend back the angled snips (to make a rough scaly back of the alligator).
✦ Encourage the children to draw a mouth, teeth, and eyes on their alligator.

Modifications/Accommodations

Autism: Use pictures and toys of alligators and crocodiles throughout the lesson and have the child periodically tell you if a certain picture or toy is an alligator or another animal.

Speech or Language Impairments: Whenever you say alligator or crocodile throughout the lesson, have the child point to a corresponding picture.

Hearing Impairments: Place the child close to you during instruction so she can see your face and mouth. Check for understanding during the lesson.

Visual Impairments: Let the child touch and feel a letter U and a bat to understand the differences in the heads of the animals. Also, find small toy alligators and crocodiles that the child can hold and manipulate.

Cognitive and/or Developmental Disabilities: Use simple words and phrases during the lesson, and provide pictures of crocodiles and alligators.

Emotional Disturbance: Encourage the child to work with others and monitor the group closely with constant reminders of how a group should work together.

Other Health Impairments/Attention Deficit Hyperactivity Disorder: Have the child sit near you during the discussion part of the lesson. Provide individual assistance as the child makes the reptile.

Orthopedic Impairments: Encourage the children within the groups to assist the child in making the alligator's head, but make sure they give only the necessary assistance.

Curriculum Connections

✦ **Art:** Draw a large shape of a crocodile or alligator on a piece of poster board and place it in the Art Center. Invite the children to use markers and crayons to draw pictures of animals that crocodiles and alligators in their habitat.
✦ **Language and Literacy:** With small groups of children, retell the story of *There's an Alligator Under My Bed*. Invite them to substitute other animal names for the alligator.
✦ **Math:** Ask children to look at pictures of various reptiles and identify which ones are large and which ones are small.

Dinosaurs

Time
30–45 minutes

Materials
How Big Were the Dinosaurs?
    by Bernard Most
3–5 pictures of dinosaurs
    from the book
measuring tape (50"–100")
chalk or tent stakes
colored string or police
    (caution) tape
tent stakes

Objectives

Children will:
1. Discuss the size of different dinosaurs.
2. Create a representation of a dinosaur's size.

Lesson

✦ Gather the children together and read them the story *How Big Were the Dinosaurs?*
✦ Discuss the sizes of the dinosaurs in the story.
✦ Using three to five drawings from the book, have the children sequence the dinosaurs according to size.

✦ Take the book outside and measure different dinosaurs' sizes using a measuring tape and chalk (on blacktop) or tent stakes (on grassy or soft area).
✦ Let the children help with the measuring and marking with chalk or stakes.
✦ Encourage the children to run from one end of the dinosaur shape to the other.
✦ Ask the children to name items that are the same size as dinosaurs.

Review
Discuss the different dinosaur sizes and items of similar sizes that the children are familiar with.

Assessment Strategy
In small groups, ask the children to sequence the dinosaur cards by size.

Modifications/Accommodations

Autism: Ensure that the child can see the drawings from the text and give him copies of the drawings to have during the discussion.

Speech or Language Impairments: When you move outside, be sure that the child is near you and that you give instructions where the child can see you. **Note**: Do not stand with the sun behind because the sun will be in the child's eyes.

Hearing Impairments: Constantly refer to the names of the dinosaurs in the drawings and have the child point to the one you are discussing to ensure that she understands you.

Visual Impairments: Provide the child with images of other animals that he is familiar with. Explain the massive size of some dinosaurs in relation to the size of the familiar animals. This can be demonstrated by using different plastic animals and dinosaurs.

Cognitive and/or Developmental Disabilities: Use several pictures of dinosaurs during the review and have the child tell which one is the largest and the smallest and repeat several times with different pictures.

Emotional Disturbance: Provide close supervision when the child is running and continually remind the child of the objective.

Other Health Impairments/Attention Deficit Hyperactivity Disorder: Have the child help hold the dinosaurs to give the child a specific task during the lesson.

Orthopedic Impairments: Assist the child in moving during the lesson as needed.

Curriculum Connections

✦ **Language and Literacy:** Place children's books or a child's encyclopedia showing pictures of dinosaurs in the Library Center or classroom library.

✦ **More Language and Literacy:** Add the word dinosaur to the classroom Word Wall. Encourage children to say descriptive words that describe the dinosaur (*huge*, *slow*, *big*, *large*, *lumbering*, *scary*, and so on.)

✦ **Science:** Talk to interested children about the megalosaurus, a dinosaur called the "giant lizard." Provide additional dinosaur names and the meaning of each name for continued dinosaur discussion.

Introduction to Amphibians

Time
10–15 minutes

Materials
pictures of frogs, toads, salamanders, and newts
Why Frogs Are Wet by Judy Hawes

Objectives

Children will:
1. Talk about the characteristics of amphibians.
2. Name different amphibians.

Lesson

◆ Gather the children to discuss amphibians. Show them pictures of frogs and toads.

◆ Ask the children how frogs and toads are similar. Have them focus on the size of the hind legs and the smoothness or roughness of the skin. Then tell the children that toads are actually a type of frog.

◆ Show the children pictures of newts and salamanders.

◆ Talk about the similarities between salamanders and newts, focusing on the smooth bodies, short legs, and web-like feet. They are very similar to each other, and depending on the area of the world they are found, the same amphibian is called either a salamander or newt.

◆ The salamander and newt are shaped like chameleons or lizards, which are reptiles that the children may see in their yards or other outdoor areas. The salamander and newt must live near or in water. Their skin is smooth without scales and they have no claws (lizards have claws to climb).

◆ Frogs, toads, salamanders, and newts are all similar in that they live part of their life in the water and part on land. This type of animal is called an amphibian. Stress that the amphibians must have water in order to live rather than just enjoying a swim as some other animals do.

◆ Read the book *Why Frogs Are Wet* by Judy Hawes. Discuss the information in the book. Continually relate the information to frogs, toads, salamanders, and newts.

◆ Provide a variety of plastic or rubber frogs, newts, salamanders, and toads for the children to hold and look at as they listen and discuss the traits of the amphibians.

Modifications/Accommodations

Autism: Use objects and pictures as you present the lesson.

Speech or Language Impairments: Call on the child to answer questions after one or two children have modeled the type of responses. If the child has difficulty responding to questions about how the amphibian examples are similar, provide a carrier phrase or sentence starter.

Hearing Impairments: Make sure to seat the child across from you so she can see your mouth as you speak. As you present the various amphibians in the lesson, show the child pictures or objects associated with the concepts.

Review

Place the pictures and book in the Science Center to increase discussion during the unit on amphibians.

Assessment Strategy

Encourage the discussion of the traits of amphibians and the term amphibian.

Visual Impairments: When showing pictures to the group, describe them in detail. Provide small vinyl frogs or salamanders for the child to feel and hold.

Cognitive and/or Developmental Delays: Use simple language and vocabulary as you present the lesson. Review the concept of amphibians later in the day. Throughout the unit, review amphibians to ensure that the child learns and retains the concept. If she has difficulty remembering word *amphibians*, have her point out amphibians when you show pictures of animals.

Emotional Disturbance: Seat the child next to you during the lesson. Enlist her help by letting her hold the pictures, put them away, or give objects to classmates.

Other Health Impairments/Attention Deficit Hyperactivity Disorder: Make sure that you have the child's attention before you speak. Establish a clear signal to get the child's attention before speaking.

Orthopedic Impairments: No accommodations are anticipated for this lesson.

Curriculum Connections

✦ **Art:** Invite the child to draw pictures of water and the amphibians living in the water.

✦ **Math:** Provide plastic or laminated pictures of amphibians for the children to count and sort.

✦ **Social Studies:** Provide a blue sheet of paper (water) and a brown sheet of paper (land). Also, give the child a set of laminated paper frogs and eggs. Have the children sort the frogs onto the brown paper and the eggs onto the blue paper. Talk about the fact that the frog eggs need water in order to live, but some frogs live mostly on land.

Wide-Mouthed Frogs

Time
45 minutes–1 hour

Materials
The Wide-Mouthed Frog by Keith Faulkner
paper lunch bags
6" green construction paper circles cut in half (1 per child)
8" green construction paper circles cut in half (1 per child)
1" x 4" strips of green construction paper (2 per child)
½" x 8" strips of red construction paper (1 per child)
2" white construction paper circles (2 per child)
crayons

Objectives

Children will:
1. Respond to the story *The Wide-Mouthed Frog.*
2. Create wide-mouth frog puppets using paper bags.

Lesson

✦ Gather the children to listen to the story *The Wide-Mouthed Frog* by Keith Faulkner.
✦ Read the story with the help of your paper bag frog. Discuss the story with the children.
✦ Invite the children to sequence the story by naming what the frog came across first, next, and last.
✦ Discuss what frogs eat.
✦ If time permits, say the following rhyme using the paper bag frogs.

The Little Green Frog (Traditional)
Bak-gloom went the little green frog one day (tongue licks to right)
Bak-gloom went the little green frog (tongue licks to left)
Bak-gloom went the little green frog one day (tongue licks to right)
And his eyes went bak-bak-gloom. (tongue out, nodding head up and down)

Modifications/Accommodations

Autism: Use objects, pictures, or line drawings (frogs, flies, mosquitoes, and so on) to assist the child in attending as you present the lesson. Use the accommodations described below if the child has difficulty responding to questions.

Speech or Language Impairments: Call on the child to answer questions after one or two children have modeled the appropriate type of responses. If the child has difficulty responding to questions, provide a carrier phrase or sentence starter. For example, when you ask, "What do frogs eat?" provide the sentence starter for the response, "Frogs eat ___," holding up the picture, if needed.

Hearing Impairments: Make sure that the child is seated across from you so he can see your mouth as you speak during the lesson. As you present the lesson, show the child pictures or objects associated with the discussion. Use gestures or sign language as you explain the life cycle of the frog.

Visual Impairments: Provide a vinyl frog for the child to feel and hold. When showing the children pictures and reading the book, describe the pictures to the child.

Review
Place the book in the Library Center for the children to read with their frog puppets.

Assessment Strategy
Encourage children to describe sequence the story. Use the book as a tool to remember the sequence of animals.

Cognitive and/or Developmental Delays: Use simple language and vocabulary as you present the lesson. Review the concept of frogs later in the day and throughout the week to make sure he retains the concept. Help the child learn to sequence the life cycle of the frog.

Emotional Disturbance: Seat the child next to you during the lesson. Enlist his help by letting him hold materials, put them away, or give objects to classmates. Have the child assist in turning pages as you read the book.

Other Health Impairments/Attention Deficit Hyperactivity Disorder: Establish a clear signal to get the child's attention, and make sure you have his attention before you speak. Supervise closely and assist the child in making the frog puppet.

Orthopedic Impairments: Physically assist the child with the motions to the song.

Curriculum Connections

✦ **Dramatic Play:** Provide an area for the children to create puppets and present a puppet show.

✦ **Language and Literacy:** Invite the children to draw what their frog does during the day. Have them use invented spelling to write a story under the pictures. If the children are unable to use invented spelling, have them dictate the story to you or another adult.

✦ **Science:** Discuss and sort the different things that a frog eats. Provide small plastic bugs for the child to sort.

Five Wide-Mouthed Frogs

Time
30–45 minutes

Materials
frog counters (available from school supply catalogs and stores) or other manipulatives (5 per child)
construction paper
crayons
chart of "Five Wide-Mouthed Frogs" chant

Objectives

Children will:
1. Use manipulatives to make groups of 1–5.
2. Participate in a chant.

Lesson

✦ Have the children sit in an area where they have space to work, such as a table or an open floor space.
✦ Prepare math mats with the children. Give each child a piece of construction paper. Have them draw a line down the middle of the paper. On one side of the paper, they draw waves of water; on the other side, they draw a log. Help the children, if needed.
✦ Give each child five frog manipulatives.
✦ Sing the "Five Green Wide-Mouthed Frogs" chant with the children as the children move frogs on their math mats to represent the math problem. Discuss other situations of frogs jumping into the pond.

Five Wide-Mouthed Frogs by Diana Nabors
I have five wide-mouthed frogs
They are sitting on the logs,
Into the water, jumped two frogs
How many are left on the logs?

(Repeat the chant, substituting the "five" and "two" with other numbers as the children use their math mats to represent the math problem.)

✦ Give the children different math problems using the mat and frog manipulatives. For example, tell them to put four frogs on a log. Children count out four frogs and put them on the log. Then say a number (under four) and children move that number of frogs into the "water." How many frogs are now on the log?
✦ Repeat different situations and have the children recreate the stories on their mats about five to seven times.

Modifications/Accommodations

Autism: Show the child the movement of the frogs as you say the chant. Then have the child move her own frogs as you chant. Model the responses before asking the child to move the frogs on her own.
Speech or Language Impairments: Have the child repeat the chant one line at a time after you say each line. Show her how to move the frogs, and then

Review

Have the children make up a story/math problem to create on their mats. Place math mats and frog manipulatives in the Math Center.

Assessment Strategy

Watch the children closely as they create different math problems individually.

have her perform the action independently.

Hearing Impairments: Seat the child across from you so she can see your mouth as you speak. As you present the lesson, make sure the child associates the manipulatives with the chant. Use facial and voice exaggeration as you chant about the frogs that are left.

Visual Impairments: As you chant, encourage the child to touch the frog manipulatives.

Cognitive and/or Developmental Delays: Use simple language and vocabulary as you present the lesson. Focus on the concepts of more and less, and counting the five frogs.

Emotional Disturbance: Before you begin the lesson, talk about being kind to animals and treating frogs gently. Remind her to be gentle with the frog manipulatives. Seat the child next to you during the lesson.

Other Health Impairments/Attention Deficit Hyperactivity Disorder: Keep your voice calm during the activity. Seat the child next to you, and demonstrate how to move the frogs. Begin with an adaptation of the chant:

One wide-mouthed frog
Sitting on a log,
Out of the water jumped one frog.
How many frogs are sitting on the log?

Let the child get used to handling the frogs gently before giving her more frogs.

Orthopedic Impairments: Physically assist the child in moving the frogs during the lesson, if needed. Then have the child tell you which frogs to move if she is unable to move them on her own.

Curriculum Connections

✦ **Language and Literacy:** Have the children make up addition and subtraction math stories. Record the stories in written story form using words written on strips of paper and in math problem form writing the number sentence.

✦ **Math:** Encourage the children to add the numerals and number sentences to the manipulative stories they have created, such as $4 + 1 = 5$.

✦ **Science:** Provide a magnifying glass and invite the children to examine a "log" (stick) and leaves of plants that live in the water. Talk about the fact that frogs live in the water and need logs and plants in order to live. Ask the children what other things frogs need in order to live.

Frogs

Time
30–45 minutes

Materials
Hop Jump by Ellen Stoll Walsh
CD or tape of children's music
hula hoops, bath towels, or large carpet squares

Objectives

Children will:
1. Hop, twist, jump, and dance around the classroom.
2. Listen to the story *Hop Jump* by Ellen Stoll Walsh.

Lesson

✦ Gather the children to listen to the story *Hop Jump* by Ellen Stoll Walsh. After the story, discuss how the frogs moved.
✦ Move to an area where each child will have room to move. Place large carpet squares, bath towels, or hula hoops on the floor so each child can see his own space.
✦ Turn on the music and call out movements for the child to practice (such as hop, jump, or dance).
✦ Continue the discussion by having them move "like the frogs did." This can be done by having the children sit in jumping position. Ask them a question about the frog. Once a child has answered the question then the class can chant "Jump, Frog, Jump" and all children take one more jump. Repeat this discussion activity 6–8 times. Then end it with "Jump, Frog, jump, jump, jump, jump, sit."

Modifications/Accommodations

Autism: Show pictures or line drawings of the various actions (hopping, jumping, twisting, and dancing).

Speech or Language Impairments: Show the child how to jump, hop, twist, and dance, using pictures of the actions as you perform them. Then have the child jump, hop, twist, and dance when you show the picture of the action.

Hearing Impairments: Make that sure the child sits across from you so that he can see your mouth as you speak during the lesson. As you present the lesson, show the child pictures associated twisting, jumping, hopping, and dancing. Use gestures as you explain the actions.

Visual Impairments: When showing the group pictures and reading the story *Hop Jump*, describe the pictures. Using a toy frog, show the child how to twist, jump, hop, and dance, letting the child feel the frog as you move it.

Cognitive and/or Developmental Delays: Use simple language and vocabulary as you present the lesson. Show the child how to jump, hop, twist, and dance. Review the concepts of twisting, jumping, hopping, and dancing later in the day and throughout the following week.

Review

Place the book in the Library Center for continued enjoyment.

Assessment Strategy

Watch the children as they move: twisting, hopping, jumping, and dancing.

Emotional Disturbance: Seat the child next to you during the lesson. Remind the child of the classroom rules before the children begin to jump, hop, twist, and dance. Ask them to move carefully so they do not hurt their friends when doing the actions.

Other Health Impairments/Attention Deficit Hyperactivity Disorder: Make sure that you have the child's attention before you speak. Establish a clear signal to get the child's attention before speaking. If the child becomes restless during the lesson, have him put materials on your desk.

Orthopedic Impairments: Physically assist the child with the actions of twisting, jumping, and hopping.

Curriculum Connections

✦ **Movement:** Discuss with the children the need for rest and exercise. Talk about the ways the children exercise in their usual daily routines. Encourage the children to think of new ways to exercise and demonstrate.

✦ **Language and Literacy:** Have the children draw pictures of frogs moving in different ways. On the picture, the child writes or dictates to an adult, "My frog can _____."

✦ **Music:** Provide tapes or CDs with music that emphasizes the movements of jumping, twisting, hopping, and dancing.

The Life Cycle of Frogs

Time
30–45 minutes

Materials
Frog by DK Publishing or
   From Tadpole to Frog by
   Wendy Pfeffer
drawing paper
crayons

Objectives

Children will:
1. Listen to and discuss to the story *Frog* by DK Publishing or *From Tadpole to Frog* by Wendy Pfeffer.
2. Draw the four stages of frog development.

Lesson

✦ Show the children the front of the book and ask them what they know about frogs and how they change as they grow.
✦ Ask questions about how frogs are born and where they live.
✦ Begin the story, stressing the change from egg to tadpole to frog.
✦ After the story, discuss the changes mentioned in the book.
✦ Give a piece of drawing paper to each child.
✦ Demonstrate how to fold the paper in half and then half again. It does not matter if the folds are exact.
✦ Have the children open the sheet and turn it so that the larger area is at the bottom, if sections are different in size.
✦ Invite the children to draw frog eggs in the top left section of the paper, then draw a line to the top right section and draw a tadpole. Then have the child draw a line down to the bottom right of the paper and draw a changing tadpole (a tadpole with legs). Then draw a line to the left bottom section of the paper and draw a frog. They can finish by drawing a line upward to show that adult frogs lay eggs.

Modifications/Accommodations

Autism: Use pictures of the life cycle of the frog to assist the child as you present the lesson. Review the pictures and have the child put them in order before asking her to draw the life cycle of the frog. Use the accommodations described below for Speech or Language Impairments if the child has difficulty responding to questions.

Speech or Language Impairments: Call on the child to answer questions after one or two children have modeled the type of responses. If the child has difficulty responding to questions, provide a carrier phrase or sentence starter.

Hearing Impairments: Make sure that the child is seated across from you so she can see your mouth as you speak during the lesson. As you present the lesson, show the child pictures associated with concepts and use gestures as you speak.

Visual Impairments: When showing the group pictures and reading the story, describe the pictures.

Assessment Strategy
Observe the children as they listen and discuss the story. View the final product for representation of the frog life cycle.

Cognitive and/or Developmental Delays: Focus on the concepts of frog, egg, and tadpole. Use pictures to sequence before having the child draw pictures of the frog, tadpole, and egg.

Emotional Disturbance: Seat the child next to you during the lesson. Enlist her help by letting her hold materials, put them away, or give objects to classmates. Provide close supervision as she draws pictures of the egg, tadpole, and frog.

Other Health Impairments/Attention Deficit Hyperactivity Disorder: Make sure that you have the child's attention before you speak. Establish a clear signal to get the child's attention before speaking. If the child becomes restless during the lesson, have her put materials on your desk. During the activity of drawing the life cycle of the frog, provide supervision and assistance. Ask the child to tell you about each picture as she draws it.

Orthopedic Impairments: Physically assist the child with the picture of life cycle of the frog, using pictures for the child to glue on the page rather than drawing.

Curriculum Connections

✦ **Language and Literacy:** Include various books about the frog life cycle in the Library Center for the children to view and compare.

✦ **Math:** Provide plastic frogs and laminated circles (frog eggs) for counters. Ask the child how many eggs the frog will lay. Then count out the number of eggs.

✦ **Science:** Set up a small fish tank with tadpoles and have the children observe the development of the frog.

Review
Post the children's drawings for future discussions.

Salamanders

Time
30–40 minutes

Materials
Salamander Room by Anne Mazer
Aquarium with lid and warming light
Sand, leaves, dirt, small twigs, grass
Bucket
Live salamander from the pet store
Saucer for water/lake
Bowl for food.

Objectives

Children will:
1. Listen to and discuss the story *Salamander Room* by Anne Mazer.
2. Discuss and create the habitat of a salamander.

Lesson

✦ Gather the children together to listen to and discuss the book *Salamander Room* by Anne Mazer.
✦ After reading the book, discuss with the children the environment a salamander needs as a pet. Focus on needed plants and water.
✦ Ask if the salamander would be a good pet for the classroom or home, or if it would be better kept in the wild.
✦ Take the children outside. Have the children use small shovels or spoons to scoop up a small quantity of sand, leaves, and dried grass to place in a bucket.
✦ After returning to the classroom, pour the sand mixture on to the bottom of the aquarium. Place a twig and saucer of water and food in to the aquarium.
✦ Have the children draw pictures of salamanders to cut out and place on the outside of the aquarium
✦ Then have the children look at the environment for the salamander to see if they want to make any modifications before adding a real salamander.
✦ Let children make final adjustments. Then add the salamander.
✦ Have the children watch and care for the salamander for a few weeks.
✦ Place the salamander in the Science Center for continued observation.

Modifications/Accommodations

Autism: Use pictures or drawings when discussing salamanders. Use accommodations below for Speech or Language Impairments if the child has difficulty responding to questions during the lesson.

Speech or Language Impairments: Call on the child to answer questions after one or two children have modeled the type of responses. If the child has difficulty responding to questions, provide a carrier phrase or sentence starter.

Hearing Impairments: Make sure that the child is seated across from you so that he can see your mouth as you speak during the lesson. Use gestures as you talk about where salamanders live and what you need in order to keep a salamander as a pet.

Visual Impairments: When showing the group pictures and reading the story, describe the pictures.

Review

Place the book with the other pictures and books from the unit in the Library Center for discussion and viewing. Provide paper for drawing and recoding the salamander's activities in the Science Center.

Assessment Strategy

Listen to reasons the children give for what needs to be in the salamander's environment for a high quality of life. Have the children individually write a note to welcome the new class pet.

Cognitive and/or Developmental Delays: Use simple language and vocabulary as you present the lesson. Review the concept of salamanders later in the day. Throughout the following week, review salamanders to ensure that the child learns and retains the concept.

Emotional Disturbance: Seat the child next to you during the lesson. Discuss what pets need and how to handle pets. Ask the child to show you how to touch a salamander using a plastic salamander.

Other Health Impairments/Attention Deficit Hyperactivity Disorder: Make sure that you have the child's attention before you speak. Establish a clear signal to get the child's attention before speaking. Have the child show how to touch a salamander (gently) using a picture or plastic salamander.

Orthopedic Impairments: No accommodations are anticipated for this lesson.

Curriculum Connections

✦ **Language and Literacy:** Provide books that include salamanders and other types of amphibians. Some examples include *Salamander Room* by Anne Mazer, *Frog (Watch Me Grow Series)* by DK Publishing, and *From Tadpole to Frog* by Wendy Pfeffer.

✦ **Math:** Provide sets of plastic or laminated salamanders for the children to sort by color or type.

✦ **Science:** In the classroom, set up an aquarium with everything that is needed for a salamander. Put a salamander inside and keep it as a class pet. Each day, have a selected child care for the salamander including the job to feed the salamander and give it water.

Introduction to Arachnids

Time
20–30 minutes

Materials
About Arachnids: A Guide for Children by Cathryn P. Sill
crayons
drawing paper

Review
Have the child individually describe why they chose to place their drawing under the specific label. Have the child point out specific features of their drawing that assists in classifying the arachnid in that grouping.

Assessment Strategy
Have the children discuss the arachnid they drew. Provide additional pictures of arachnids for the children to add to the groupings.

Objectives

Children will:
1. Discuss information about arachnids.
2. Draw a spider and count the legs.

Lesson

✦ Gather the children and read the book *About Arachnids* by Cathryn P. Sill.
✦ Talk about arachnids: they have eight legs, one or two body parts, an exoskeleton, and no antennae.
✦ Show the children the pictures in the book of the most common arachnids—spiders, scorpions, ticks, and mites.
✦ Have the children select one of the common arachnids and draw it on drawing paper. Ask him to describe which arachnid he drew and count the eight legs.
✦ Place label signs in areas of the room, (spiders, scorpions, ticks, mites) and have the children choose where their drawing should be grouped. Have the child affix their drawing under the appropriate label.

Modifications/Accommodations

Autism: Individually present the information about arachnids. Try to ease any fears or concerns. Assist with drawings.

Speech or Language Impairments: Explain any new vocabulary. Encourage the child to use the new vocabulary during discussion. Encourage complete sentences.

Hearing Impairments: Have the child sit near you as you read. Face the child during discussion. Visually cue the child in the art activity by pointing to features that the child may need to draw.

Visual Impairments: Provide time for the child to examine the book. Make sure art materials are within the child's reach.

Cognitive and/or Developmental Delays: Provide explanations of new terms. Provide information to ease fears or concerns.

Emotional Disturbance: Answer questions to ease any fears.

Other Health Impairments/Attention Deficit Hyperactivity Disorder: Provide plenty of discussion time for the child to discuss his drawing and his experiences with arachnids.

Orthopedic Impairments: Make sure all materials are within the child's reach.

Curriculum Connections

✦ **Art:** Place black or brown chenille sticks in the Art Center for the children to use to create a spider.
✦ **Science:** Place several non-fiction books about arachnids in the Science Center for child exploration.

Spiders

Time
30–45 minutes

Materials
The Very Busy Spider by Eric
    Carle
construction paper
pencil
crayons
clear or light-colored glitter
glue

Preparation
Make a spider web to use as
a model. Draw the web on a
piece of paper and trace the
lines using glue. Add glitter
and let dry.

Objectives

Children will:
1. Listen to, discuss, and
    chorally assist in reading
    to the story *The Very Busy
    Spider* by Eric Carle.
2. Create a spider web
    using glue and glitter.

Review
Place the book The Very
Busy Spider in the Library
Center for re-readings.

Assessment Strategy
Ask the children about the
work the spider does as it
spins a web.

Lesson

✦ Gather the children to listen to the story *The Very Busy Spider.*
✦ Discuss the characteristics of the spider and the spider's work of weaving a web.
✦ Show the children the spider web you made as a model.
✦ Give each child a piece of construction paper. Demonstrate how to draw a spider web. Encourage the children to draw their webs attached to trees or fence posts.
✦ Help the children trace their spider webs with glue. Have them work in small groups of three to five children. (Holding the glue bottle so that it touches the page will deliver a thin trail of glue.)
✦ Invite the children to sprinkle their spider web with clear glitter.

Modifications/Accommodations

Autism: Use hand-over-hand assistance to create the spider web. Vocalize cues such as, "Shake, shake, shake the glitter."

Speech or Language Impairments: Encourage complete sentences during discussion of the spider.

Hearing Impairments: Use hand and picture cues to help the child follow directions.

Visual Impairments: Provide an opportunity for the child to touch the glitter web created by you.

Cognitive and/or Developmental Delays: Discuss the process of adding glue to the spider web. Talk about how the glitter sticks to it.

Emotional Disturbances: Provide time for the child to individually discuss with you her spider creation and any encounters the child may have had with spiders previously.

Other Health Impairments/Attention Deficit Hyperactivity Disorder: Provide time for the child to talk with you about her spider creation and any encounters she may have had with spiders previously.

Orthopedic Impairments: Use adaptive equipment to help the child create a spider web.

Curriculum Connections

✦ **Music:** Sing "The Itsy Bitsy Spider" with the children and do the actions.
✦ **Science:** Add a real spider to the classroom. Use a large glass jar with a secure lid (poke holes in the lid) or other secure observation tank. Place a spider in the tank with natural materials such as sticks, grass, and pieces of bark. Observe the spider for a few days before releasing it outdoors.

Introduction to Zoo Animals

Time
20–30 minutes

Materials
Zoo by Gail Gibbons
drawing paper
crayons

Objectives

Children will:
1. Listen to a story about the zoo and what it takes to keep the animals safe and comfortable.
2. Discuss what they know about zoos.

Review
Have the children brainstorm what they must do as zoo workers of their newly created zoo.

Assessment Strategy
Have the children name one job at the zoo that helps the animals and one job that helps visitors to the zoo.

Lesson

✦ Gather the children together to listen to the story *Zoo* by Gail Gibbons.
✦ Invite the children to discuss times they have visited the zoo or knowledge they have about a zoo from other sources, TV, movies, friends, and other books.
✦ Have the children decide on 4–5 main areas of the zoo that they would like to visit on a trip to the zoo, such as the monkey area, the reptile house, or the aquarium area.
✦ Split the children into 4–5 groups.
✦ Give each group a large piece of butcher paper. Have the children draw and design the habitat for this area. And draw the animals that will live in the area. This is a group mural picture.
✦ Place all murals together around the room for the children to "visit" the zoo.

Modifications/Accommodations

Autism: Use picture cues to assist the child in understanding zoo jobs and the zoo animals. Point to parts of the story to help the child stay on target.

Speech or Language Impairments: Provide time for the child to tell the class about their zoo knowledge.

Hearing Impairments: Have the child sit near you as you read. Use the picture cues to assist the child in understanding.

Visual Impairments: Pre-read the book with the child or provide an additional copy for the child to view during the group reading.

Cognitive and/or Developmental Delays: Point out and discuss the pictures in the book as you read about the zoo. Ask the child questions about the zoo to assess his understanding of the zoo.

Emotional Disturbance: Use voicing, such as alternating pitch and volume, to keep the child alert and focusing on the lesson. Many times lowering the pitch of your voice, slowing the rate of your speech as well as lowering the volume has children listen more intently.

Other Health Impairments/Attention Deficit Hyperactivity Disorder: Provide time for the child to discuss his trip to the zoo or what he would like to see at the zoo as the other children begin the group art activity.

Orthopedic Impairments: Provide all art materials, book, drawing paper and picture clues at the level of easy access for the child.

Curriculum Connections

✦ **Language and Literacy:** Add children's dictations to their zoo pictures and combine all the pictures into a class book, titled "Our Trip to the Zoo." Add it to the classroom library.
✦ **Math:** Ask the children to name as many zoo animals as they can. List the animals on the board. Count the number of animals on the list.
✦ **Science:** Describe the types of homes the zoo animals have. Using picture cards, group the animals into "like" habitats.

Giraffes

Time
20–30 minutes

Materials
Giraffes Can't Dance by Giles
    Andreae
picture cards of various
    animals, including giraffes

Objectives

Children will:
1. Move like different
    animals, including the
    giraffe.
2. Identify and name
    characteristics of different
    animals, including the
    giraffe.

Lesson

✦ Have the children sit on the floor. Invite them to name different animals
    and record the list on the board or chart paper. If they do not mention the
    giraffe, cue them to think of tall animals, or animals with long necks.
✦ Encourage them to stand and move in their space like an animal you
    name (choose three to five animals). Cue the children by telling them
    different characteristics that will help them move. Include the giraffe last.
✦ Have the children sit back down. Read them the story *Giraffes Can't
    Dance* by Giles Andreae.
✦ Talk about the way the animals in the story moved compared to how they
    moved. Discuss additional characteristics of the giraffe.

Modifications/Accommodations

Autism: Stand near the child to assist in movements. Use pictures of animals
    and model animal movements for the child to use as she moves.
Speech or Language Impairments: Define any new words.
Hearing Impairments: Use gestures and picture cues to help the child
    participate in the lesson.
Visual Impairments: Provide a copy of the book for the child to use during
    story time.
Cognitive and/or Developmental Delays: Use verbal cues to help the child
    participate.
Emotional Disturbance: Allow the child to watch if she is not comfortable
    participating in the movement. Let her hold the animal card for the class if
    she is not participating in the movement.
Other Health Impairments/Attention Deficit Hyperactivity Disorder: Have
    the children sit on the carpet squares while you read the story.
Orthopedic Impairments: Help the child with any movements. Let her place
    her hands on your and move like the animal.

Review
Place the book and animal
cards in the Movement
Center for children to recreate
the movements.

Assessment Strategy
Watch the children as they
dance and move as various
animals.

Curriculum Connections

✦ **Art:** Have the children draw a giraffe and then cut and glue different
    shaped brown tissue paper pieces to the giraffe to show the distinct and
    different patterns on each giraffe.
✦ **Movement:** Place the picture cards in the center for the children to
    recreate the movements. Add taped music to enhance this activity.

Elephants

Time
30–45 minutes

Materials
drawing paper
crayons or markers

Objectives

Children will:
1. Draw a picture of an elephant.
2. Listen to a story about and elephant

Lesson

◆ Gather the children together on the floor and ask them what they know about elephants without showing a picture cue.
◆ Spend about five minutes allowing the children to give traits of the elephant.
◆ Tell the children the following story, which was adapted from John Godfrey Saxe's poem, "The Blind Men and the Elephant."
◆ Tell the children the story using hand gestures, differentiated voicing, and dramatization as you "become" each of the blind men. Use pictures of a brick wall, a spear, a snake, tree trunk, fan, and a rope as you tell the story (optional).

"The Blind Men and the Elephant" adapted by Diana Nabors
Once upon a time, six men who could not see were walking and came across an elephant. Each man touched the new creature to find out more about this new animal called "elephant."

The first man walked to the side of the elephant and exclaimed, "The elephant is like a wall—sturdy, wide, and tall."

The second man was near the front of the elephant and his hands felt the long smooth tusk of the elephant. He cried out, "Oh, no, that is not correct. The elephant is like a spear, smooth and sharp. That my friends, is very clear."

The third man, standing near his friend, felt the trunk against his skin. He reached out and remarked, "No, no, I fear you have made a mistake. What I feel here is much like a very large snake."

The fourth man, shorter than his friends, reached downward and felt the animal's knee. "Goodness, gracious, me, I know that we cannot see, but you must use your senses like me. This elephant is sturdy, rough skinned, and round, very much like a tree."

The fifth man reached out. His hands landed on the elephant's ear moving back and forth. "My friends, I am not sure you have a good grasp of this new animal called "elephant." It is clear to any man, what I feel with my hand is large and moves the air much like my own hand fan."

Curriculum Connections

+ **Art:** Find a puzzle of an elephant. If you don't have a commercially made puzzle, make your own by cutting a poster or large picture into puzzle pieces. Give each child a piece of the elephant puzzle to draw. Put the various drawings together in a collage-type picture.
+ **Dramatic Play:** Make several sets of large elephant ears from poster board and glue on a headband for children to use in the Dramatic Play Center.
+ **Language and Literacy:** Find other versions of "The Blind Men and the Elephant" to add to the Library Center.
+ **Math:** Have the children match pictures of a wall, spear, fan, tree, snake, and rope to the correct elephant body parts.

Review
Have the children continue discussing the traits of the elephant as they draw. They can also discuss why they think each of the blind men had a different opinion of what the elephant was.

Assessment Strategy
Have the children individually name one physical trait of an elephant.

The sixth man, holding the elephant's tail, cried out. "My brothers, our thoughts are so different. What I hold in my hand is not of the same scope. I have here a long and knotted rope. To your views of this large beast, I must say, nope, you are not right; the elephant is much like a rope."

In the end, each of the six blind men was partially correct in his idea of an elephant. And each of them was also wrong.

+ Talk about the story with the children. Talk about specific features of the elephant as well as the parable itself.
+ Show them a picture of an elephant.
+ Invite the children to draw a picture of their view of the elephant. The may take on the role of one or more of the blind men and add a feature of the elephant as seen by the blind men.
+ Post the pictures in the classroom for further discussion.

Modifications/Accommodations

Autism: Provide time after the story for the child to look at the pictures and retell the story individually before he draws the elephant picture.

Speech or Language Impairments: Encourage the children to use complete sentences as they talk about the elephant and the story.

Hearing Impairments: Provide picture clues at each part of the story to depict the thoughts of the blind men.

Visual Impairments: Have the pictures large enough for the child to see clearly or have a time when the child can look over the pictures after the oral story has been told.

Cognitive and/or Developmental Delays: Have the child help retell the story using pictures or flannel pieces and flannel board.

Emotional Disturbance: Help the child listen to the story by providing picture clues and gestures, such as hand signals, to show the child she is aware of him and his needs as well as reinforcing his appropriate behavior of listening, attending and discussing.

Other Health Impairments/Attention Deficit Hyperactivity Disorder: Provide a picture of the elephant with features distorted as the blind men saw the elephant. Pre-tell the story individually.

Orthopedic Impairments: Use specialized grips around crayons.

Hippopotamuses

Time
20–30 minutes

Materials
Mama by Jeanette Winter
pictures of hippopotamuses
in their natural habitat

Objectives

Children will:
1. Discuss the problems of the baby hippopotamus in the story *Mama*.
2. Point out the similarities and differences between the hippopotamus, elephant, and rhinoceros.

Lesson

✦ Read the book *Mama* by Jeanette Winter.
✦ Discuss the concerns of the baby hippopotamus and the situation he finds himself in. Discuss his wants and needs. What was the hippopotamus' misunderstanding as he searched for his mama?
✦ Discuss the importance of friends to help the hippopotamus feel comfortable. Ask children, "Who helps and comforts you?"
✦ Show a picture of a hippopotamus.
✦ Using the facts below, give information about the hippopotamus.

Hippopotamus Facts
The word hippopotamus *means "river horse."*
The hippopotamus lives in lakes, rivers, and swamps in Africa.
The hippopotamus has a barrel-shaped blue-gray body, a pink belly, large head, and short stumpy legs.
It is the second largest land animal (the elephant is the largest), and eats about 100 pounds of plants and grass each day.
Even though it is very large and usually moves very slowly, it can run on land faster than a human can.
It spends its day in the water and climbs out of the water at night to rest on land.
The hippopotamus' ears, nostrils, and eyes are on top of its head, which allows it see and breathe while in the water.

✦ Have children compare similarities and differences in the hippopotamus, elephant, and rhinoceros.
✦ Have the child use clay or playdough to shape a hippo. This can be done is a child-directed fashion or you can help the children by telling them or showing them how to make it. Making a hippopotamus out of clay or playdough: Take a fist-sized piece of clay and shape the barrel of the hippopotamus body. Take four small balls to add for the short legs. Add a medium-sized ball for a head. Pinch two ears and poke two eyes. The nostrils and mouth can be made using a straw or other object. Each child can add specific details to her hippopotamus.

Review
Have each child talk about her hippopotamus and describe what it can do.

Assessment Strategy
Have the children name one thing about the hippopotamus.

Modifications/Accommodations

Autism: Read the story to the child individually, pointing out the needs of the hippopotamus and his new friend.

Speech or Language Impairments: Encourage the child to use complete sentences during the discussion.

Hearing Impairments: Use gestures and visual cues.

Visual Impairments: Provide an extra copy of the book or plan time for the child to view the book prior to the lesson.

Cognitive and/or Developmental Delays: Stress the concept of friendship and how the new friends comforted the hippopotamus rather than the concept of loss.

Emotional Disturbance: Prior to the lesson read the story to the child. Focus on the new friendships that the hippopotamus made along the way.

Other Health Impairments/Attention Deficit Hyperactivity Disorder: Use eye contact and hand gestures to keep the child focused on the lesson.

Orthopedic Impairments: Pre-knead and shape the playdough or clay for the child to be easily successful. The child may need one-on-one assistance by an adult.

Curriculum Connections

✦ **Language and Literacy:** Encourage the child to draw pictures of those who help her. Let the children discuss their drawings with their classmates.

✦ **Math:** Challenge the children to draw a set number of pictures of hippos. Choose a number based on the numerals children in your class already know.

✦ **Science:** Have the child list similarities and differences between the hippopotamus and other animals. Provide picture cues to assist.

Camels

Time
20–30 minutes

Materials
cardboard egg cartons
scissors
brown construction paper
How the Camel Got Its Hump
    by Justine Fontes and
    Ron Fontes
art supplies (brown paint,
    markers, glue, paper)

Preparation
Before the lesson, cut paper egg cartons into one and two "hump" pieces. Cut ½" x 2" strips and 2" squares of brown paper. (The strips will be used for the camel's legs and the squares can be used for a tail and head for the camel.)

Review
Ask the children about the camel characteristics on their camel pictures.

Assessment Strategy
Have each child name one or two characteristics of the camel.

Objectives

Children will:
1. Describe one characteristic about a camel.
2. Make a camel using paper and art supplies.

Lesson

◆ Gather the children together at Circle or Group Time. Ask them if they know what a camel looks like.
◆ Read the story *How the Camel Got Its Hump* by Justine Fontes and Ron Fontes.
◆ Provide art supplies, cardboard "humps," and brown paper strips and squares for the children to design their own camels. They will use the egg carton as the body and hump attaching a head, legs, and a tail to the egg carton.

Modifications/Accommodations

Autism: Use voicing strategies and picture clues to keep the child engaged in the activity.

Speech or Language Impairments: Explain any new vocabulary. Provide the needed vocabulary words in your questions and provide a choice of one or two answers to have the child choose the correct answer. This will allow the child to participate more fully.

Hearing Impairments: Face the child during reading and discussion. Repeat the questions and discussion of the other children, if needed.

Visual Impairments: Let the child read the book prior to the class reading.

Cognitive and/or Developmental Delays: Explain any new concepts. Use pictures in the book to demonstrate new concepts.

Emotional Disturbance: Have the child sit near you or another adult for any needed assistance.

Other Health Impairments/Attention Deficit Hyperactivity Disorder: Ask questions during the story. This helps keep the child listening and attending to the story. Ask the child to tell you how she will make the camel before doing it to assist her in sequencing.

Orthopedic Impairments: Provide all materials within the reach of the child.

Curriculum Connections

◆ **Movement:** Show children how to put their hands on the floor and their buttocks in the air to walk like camels.
◆ **Science:** Provide other books about camels and other desert animals in the Science Center for the children to view. Also provide a dish pan of sand for the children to make handprints and footprints in the sand.

Monkeys

Time
30–45 minutes

Materials
Five Little Monkeys Jumping on the Bed by Eileen Christelow

6 monkey masks, hand-held or sentence strip headbands (see below of ways to make monkey masks to be used in this lesson)

Preparation
Make monkeys masks by drawing or copying monkey faces. Make six monkey puppets—one for each of the five little monkeys and a sixth one for the mama monkey. Make a doctor monkey by drawing or copying a monkey face and adding a stethoscope around the monkey's neck. Make these stick puppets by attaching them to tongue depressors, or make headband puppets by attaching each monkey face to a separate sentence strip. Staple or paper clip the sentence strips to fit the child's head.

Review
Place the masks and book in the Dramatic Play Center.

Assessment Strategy
Ask the children what the monkeys were doing on the bed and what they should have been doing.

Objectives

Children will:
1. Listen and discuss to the book *Five Little Monkeys Jumping on the Bed.*
2. Act out the story *Five Little Monkeys Jumping on the Bed.*

Lesson

✦ Read the book *Five Little Monkeys Jumping on the Bed.* As you read the book, invite the children to chime in with the predictable words.
✦ Pass out five little monkey masks and a mama monkey mask. Read the story again and have seven selected children act out the story using the masks. Discuss the mischief the monkeys were engaged in.
✦ Repeat the activity with new children acting the parts.

Modifications/Accommodations

Autism: Stand with the child to assist him with dramatization of the story. Model the correct dramatization.

Speech or Language Impairments: Encourage the child to chorally read the story aloud with you and other children in the re-readings.

Hearing Impairments: Use the masks as cues to the story. Use hand gestures and physical movements to assist the child in participation.

Visual Impairments: Stand near the child and use hand cues, smiles, and nods as well as accentuated body movements to assist the child in participation.

Cognitive and/or Developmental Delays: The frequent re-readings will assist the child in participation.

Emotional Disturbance: Allow the child to chose which monkey he would like to re-enact first in the group of seven. This will avoid a confrontation or disappointment not "getting" the desired prop/character.

Other Health Impairments/Attention Deficit Hyperactivity Disorder: Assist the child in the dramatization of the story through whole group interaction or small group interaction with his peers.

Orthopedic Impairments: Assist the child with large motor movements as needed.

Curriculum Connections

✦ **Language and Literacy:** Provide this book as well as the book *Five Little Monkeys Sitting in the Tree* in the Library Center for children to read. The children will read and discuss the monkey's actions and similarities to the monkey books.
✦ **Math:** Provide small monkey pictures found on the internet or cut from magazines in the Math Center for the children to count, add, subtract, and group.

Big Cats

Time
20 minutes

Materials
pictures of various big cats (lion, tiger, panther, leopard, and so on)
John Archambault and Bill Martin, Jr.'s *A Beautiful Feast for a Big King Cat* or another big book on big cats

Objectives

Children will:
1. Say that big cats are wild animals that live in forests, grasslands, deserts, and jungles.
2. Name at least one big cat.

Lesson

✦ Begin by asking children if they know what a "big cat" is. (**Note**: This lesson focuses on lions, tigers, panthers, and leopards as big cats, but listen carefully to your children's suggestions and follow their lead in developing the lesson.)

✦ Tell children that big cats are not house pets. They are animals in the cat family that live in forests, jungles, grasslands, and deserts.

✦ Show children pictures of various big cats.

✦ Ask children to identify the characteristics of the animals that place them in the cat family.

✦ Tell children that the size, speed, and other physical features of big cats allow them to chase, catch, and eat other animals.

✦ Read *A Beautiful Feast for a Big King Cat.* Encourage discussion as you read the book to the children.

Modifications/Accommodations

Autism: During the lesson, ask questions that the child can respond to by pointing to pictures. If the child can speak, simplify your questions and wait for her to respond. If needed, model appropriate responses.

Speech or Language Impairments: If the child does not respond to questions about big cats, provide a carrier phrase such as, "Cat's feet are called ____," or "Look at the cat's paws. On their paws cats have ____." Wait for the child to respond. If the child does not respond, provide a verbal model. Use pictures as you present information throughout the lesson and review.

Hearing Impairments: Seat the child where she can see your mouth during the lesson. Provide pictures to refer to as you speak. For the review, provide pictures as a way to get the child started in responding to the request to tell what she learned about big cats.

Visual Impairments: Provide plastic big cats instead of pictures. Let the child feel and hold the animals.

Cognitive and/or Developmental Disabilities: Limit the choices of pictures to two during the assessment activity. Shorten the period that the child listens to the story if needed.

Review

Ask the children to tell what they learned about big cats during the lesson.

Assessment Strategy

Using pictures as clues, ask individual children to identify one or more of the big cats.

Emotional Disturbance: Have the child seated near you. Affirm the child for participating and responding. Ensure success by directing items to her at her level. Emphasize that big cats are wild animals and that they are animals that we should not touch.

Other Health Impairments/Attention Deficit Hyperactivity Disorder: During the story, seat the child near the book where she can see it easily. Enlist her help periodically in turning pages. If the child becomes fidgety during the story, ask her to put materials on your desk, or you can have the children take a stretch break

Orthopedic Impairments: During the assessment, if the child is unable to identify big cats by pointing or speaking, have her look at the big cat that you name.

Curriculum Connections

✦ **Field Trip:** If possible, arrange a field trip to a nearby zoo so children can observe big cats. Encourage parents to take their child to the zoo if organizing a field trip is not an option in the classroom.

✦ **Language and Literacy:** Show children the book *The Lion King* by Disney. In small groups, develop a discussion with children about their memory of the story using the pictures in the book. Ask them to draw pictures or dictate stories about the book. Collect their efforts into a class book to place in the Library Center.

✦ **Math:** Place animal figurines in the Manipulatives Center. Ask children to sort the big cats from other pets.

5 Celebrating People

This unit provides an opportunity for children to explore the traditions of people in the United States and other countries. The unit begins with a study of two things common to children everywhere, the food we eat and the clothes we wear. The lessons then move to exploring life in the United States, different foods, clothing, and languages, and then the diversity of family traditions everywhere.

Begin the unit with a mural made of bulletin board paper. Divide the mural horizontally into thirds. In the middle of the first section, place a picture of children. As you explore foods and clothing, add images of these items in the first section of the mural to the right of the children. After discussing languages, traditions, and music with the children, add additional pictures relating to these topics to the left of the picture of children, still in the first section of the mural. Be sure to discuss the pictures as you put them up, and refer to earlier pictures as you introduce new ones. Involve the children in the process of selecting photographs to put on the mural, and enlist their help in putting pictures up as well. Relevant pictures can be found in magazines as well as on the Internet.

Before introducing Living in America, put a picture of the map of the United States on the second portion of the mural. As you discuss various aspects of living in America, add related pictures, such as images of the flag, the president, the military, the White House, ballots, and fireworks, to the second section of the mural.

Finally, use the third section of the mural to place pictures relating to the various celebrations that the children discuss and learn about throughout the units. Include pictures and photographs of classroom celebrations, family celebrations, and birthdays in this section of the mural.

Each lesson in this unit includes suggestions for related books. Providing relevant books before, during, and after the specific lessons helps to build prior knowledge and stimulates the children's memory of the classroom study. After you introduce music in a lesson, include samples of this music, and samples of other music, in the classroom Listening Center. When you study different languages, invite friends or family members who are bilingual to visit the classroom and teach the children some basic vocabulary in the language that they speak. Classroom visitors can also share their holidays, traditions, and celebrations.

After completing the unit, move the mural to another location in your school or center, such as an indoor hallway or recreation area. As you pass the mural, point out the various pictures, reminding the children of your previous discussions and activities from the unit.

Introduction to People We Meet

Time
20 minutes

Materials
Best Friends by Charlotte
    Labaronne
paper lunch bags
construction paper
scissors
yarn
glue
markers
chart paper and marker or dry
    erase board and dry-
    erase marker

Objectives

Children will:
1. Learn how to meet new people.
2. Explain one way to make a new friend.

Lesson

✦   Introduce the lesson by reading the story *Best Friends* by Charlotte
    Labaronne.
✦   Talk about Alex the Alligator wanting a friend. Louise the Lion is new at
    school and Alex wants her to be his friend.
✦   Ask the children some key questions about the story, for example:
    ✦   Why was Alex lonely?
    ✦   What did Alex do to get Louise to notice him?
    ✦   How do you think Louise felt as a new student at school?
    ✦   What are some things that we can do when we meet new people?
    ✦   Can Alex and Louise become friends, even though one is a lion and the
        other an alligator?
    ✦   What can we do to make new friends?
✦   Everyone needs friends. Children have a chance to meet new people at
    school and at home.
✦   Discuss how everybody has differences: different hair or eye color, height,
    gender, and so on. Ask the children how we are all the same.
✦   Emphasize that everyone is special. We all have things that we are good at,
    things we like, and things to share with other people.
✦   Make people puppets using lunch bags. Decorate the bags with
    construction paper cutouts, yarn, glue, and markers. Later, after the
    puppets are dry, have the children use the puppets to show how they can
    meet new friends.

Modifications/Accommodations

Autism: As you read the story, point to the pictures in the story relating to key
    concepts. Emphasize the concepts of loneliness, friendship, meeting new
    people, and being noticed.
Speech or Language Impairments: Have other children model responses
    before calling on this child. If he is unable to respond spontaneously during
    the two-person puppet play, whisper some key responses for the puppet to
    use.
Hearing Impairments: Seat the child across from you so he can see your face.
    Use signs, gestures, and pictures during the lesson.

Review

Introduce the following song:

What Can I Do When I Meet You? by Sharon Lynch
Tune: "My Bonnie Lies over the Ocean"
What can I do when I meet you?
What can I do to be friends?
What can I do when I meet you?
I can be friends with you when I ___. (share, for example)

The first time you sing this song, fill in the blank with share. Invite the children to fill in with their own words. If they need help at first, suggest some possible words to use: *help*, *play*, *work*, *draw*, or other action words. Ask each child to tell one way to make a new friend.

Assessment Strategy

Have two children at a time put on a puppet show to demonstrate how to make a new friend.

Visual Impairments: Describe the pictures as you read the story. Help the child make the eyes, nose, hair, and mouth for the puppet.

Cognitive and/or Developmental Disabilities: Keep your sentences short and use simple vocabulary. Repeat key concepts. Model responses if the child does not answer.

Emotional Disturbance: Seat the child next to you during the lesson and affirm participation. Model the way to meet new people and make new friends during the puppet plays.

Other Health Impairments/Attention Deficit Hyperactivity Disorder: Make sure you have the child's attention before speaking. Have the group stand to sing the song.

Orthopedic Impairments: Assist the child in making the puppet. Use a glue brush to help the child make the puppet. If the child has an adaptive grip for crayons or markers, assist the child in using it as independently as possible.

Curriculum Connections

✦ **Art:** Invite the children to make friendship bracelets using yarn and small plastic charms. They can make one for themselves and one to give a friend.

✦ **Language and Literacy:** Place books in the Library Center about friendship, meeting new people, and the fact that all of us are special. Some suggestions include *A Bad Case of Stripes* by David Shannon, *Clifford's First School Day* by Norman Bridwell, *Perfect Porridge: A Story About Kindness* by Rochel Sandman, *Make New Friends* by Rosemary Wells, *Clifford's Best Friend* by Norman Bridwell, *I Like Me* by Nancy Carlson, *Will I Have a Friend* by Miriam Cohen.

✦ **Math:** Prepare a name chart with all of the children's names on it. Each morning count the total number of children in the class, the number of children who are present, and the number of children who are absent.

✦ **Social Studies:** Place books about children from a variety of cultures and countries in the Library Center. Some suggestions include *Hairs/Pelitos* by Sandra Cisñeros, *Meet Danitra Brown* by Nikki Grimes, *One Afternoon* by Yumi Heo, *In My Momma's Kitchen* by Jerdine Nolen, *Angel Baby* by Pat Cummings, *My Pal Al* by Marcia Leonard, *Uptown* by Bryan Collier, *Hooray! A Pinata!* by Elisa Kleven, *Abuela* by Arthur Dorros, and *Pablo's Tree* by Pat Mora.

Foods People Eat

Time
15–20 minutes

Materials
variety of finger foods (cheese cubes, chunks of fruit, crackers, and so on)
paper plate
chart paper and markers
pictures of different foods
drawing paper
crayons and markers

Objectives

Children will:
1. Remember and describe what they ate for dinner.
2. Talk about their favorite food.

Lesson

✦ Put a variety of finger foods on a paper plate, and invite each child to choose one item to eat. Be sure to have enough items that each child will have a choice of finger foods. Some choices include cubes of cheese, apple chunks, small crackers, and grapes.

✦ Explain that people eat different foods, and that not everyone picked the same snack to eat.

✦ Every family enjoys different types of food (based on taste preferences, health consciousness, cultural backgrounds, and so on). Ask the children what they ate for dinner last night.

✦ On chart paper, write each child's name. Ask each child to make a quick drawing of what they ate last night.

✦ With the children, count the number of things that everyone ate.

✦ Ask if anyone ate the same thing for dinner.

✦ Show pictures of different types of food. Magazines are good sources for pictures. Be sure to include common foods, as well as those that are different from what the children typically eat at school.

✦ Ask the children which food they like best. After each response, say, "___'s favorite food is ____."

Modifications/Accommodations

Autism: The child may not know what she ate for dinner last night. Discuss this with the parent, or try to elicit a response by stating, "For dinner last night we ate ___." When asking about lunch, use the statement, "For lunch we will eat ___." If you know what the child will eat at school, talk about this earlier in the day.

Speech or Language Impairments: Use a carrier phrase as a sentence starter when asking what the child ate last night or will eat for lunch. For example, "For dinner last night we ate ___."

Hearing Impairments: Seat the child where she can see your face and mouth. Repeat what other children say to ensure that she can hear their thoughts.

Visual Impairments: Tell the child what snack items are on the plate and let her choose the snack. When showing the child food pictures, describe them verbally. Ask if she wants help with her drawing and provide assistance, if needed.

Review

Review the children's responses from the chart paper. Ask them if they know what they are going to eat for lunch.

Assessment Strategy

Give each child markers or crayons and drawing paper and ask her to draw her favorite food. Write the sentence "_____'s favorite food is _____."

Cognitive and/or Developmental Disabilities: Use short, simple sentences in your explanation. Show different types of food pictures and ask if she ate them last night. Provide common choices of lunch foods when asking what she will eat for lunch.

Emotional Disturbance: Seat the child next to you. Before offering the snack item, remind the child to take one snack. Affirm him/her for following directions.

Other Health Impairments/Attention Deficit Hyperactivity Disorder: Make sure that you have the child's attention before giving instructions. If the child becomes restless, ask her to put an item on your desk or throw something in the trash.

Orthopedic Impairments: Help the child to select the snack food. Provide hand-over-hand assistance for the drawing activity in the assessment.

Curriculum Connections

✦ **Dramatic Play:** Provide plastic food and empty food boxes in the Home Living Center. Be sure to include foods that the children may not have seen before, including ethnic foods, as well as familiar foods.

✦ **Language and Literacy:** Provide books about food in the Library Center. Some examples include *Food for Thought* by Joost Elffers and Saxton Freymann, *Gregory the Terrible Eater* by Mitchell Sharmat and Jose Aruego, *Now I Eat My ABC's* by Pam Abrams, and *Too Many Tamales* by Gary Soto.

✦ **Math:** When working with quantitative concepts, provide die-cuts or cutouts of food items for counting.

✦ **Social Studies:** Provide foods that people in other countries eat. Include some of these at snack time if they are available in your area.

Clothes People Wear

Time
15–20 minutes

Materials
suitcase or bag
summer and winter clothes
chart paper and marker
large paper
paint
paintbrushes
easel

Objectives

Children will:
1. State one reason for wearing clothes.
2. Name two to three articles of clothing.

Lesson

◆ Put summer and winter clothing in a small suitcase or bag.
◆ Gather the children in a circle. Explain that we wear clothes to protect our body, keeping it safe and warm.
◆ Remove each item of clothing from the suitcase, one at a time, asking if we wear it in cold weather or hot weather.
◆ Talk about how different types of clothing protect our body from the sun, the rain, the cold, and so on.
◆ Ask what would happen if we didn't have coats, shoes, gloves, boots, sandals, shorts, raincoats, or bathing suits.
◆ Give each child a turn to paint their favorite clothes at the easel.

Modifications/Accommodations

Autism: Make two cards, one with the symbol of a sun and the word "hot" and the other with a picture of an ice cube and the word "cold." After discussing the clothing, sort them into two piles (one for hot weather and the other for cold weather), asking the child where to place the clothing.

Speech or Language Impairments: Call on the child after others have modeled the expected response. Use carrier phrases.

Hearing Impairments: Seat the child across from you where he can see your mouth and face. Use signs (for hot and cold), symbols, pictures, as well as the "hot" and "cold" symbol cards when classifying clothing for hot and cold weather.

hot

cold

Review

Ask the children to name some of the reasons why we wear clothes. Write their responses on chart paper.

Assessment Strategy

After the children paint their pictures, have them tell you about their pictures and why we wear clothes. Write their responses on cards and staple or tape them to their pictures when they are dry.

Visual Impairments: Let the child touch the clothes as you remove them from the bag.

Cognitive and/or Developmental Disabilities: Keep your language simple and direct. Repeat key phrases such as "We wear clothes to protect out bodies." Instead of asking "why" questions, ask the child "who," "when," and "what" questions.

Emotional Disturbance: Seat the child beside you during the lesson. Let him help put away the materials in a "finished box" as you complete each activity. Supervise closely when the child is painting.

Other Health Impairments/Attention Deficit Hyperactivity Disorder: Make sure that the child is looking at you before speaking. Establish a consistent cue (either a clicker, snapping your fingers twice, or clapping your hands) to get the child's attention.

Orthopedic Impairments: Help the child paint at the easel. Provide a brush holder if the child is able to use it; otherwise use hand-over-hand assistance.

Curriculum Connections

✦ **Art:** Suggest that children draw and decorate pictures of clothing items associated with various celebrations: sombreros at Cinco de Mayo, green clothing on St. Patrick's Day, or cowboy hats at rodeo time.

✦ **Math:** Provide pictures of people wearing a variety of clothing. Have the children sort them in different way. For example, winter or summer clothes, by type of clothing (dresses, shoes, socks, pants), clothes used for special events (sports attire, dance attire). Help them count the number in each group.

✦ **Social Studies:** Place books about children in other lands in the Library Center. When looking at them, discuss the clothing the children wear.

Languages People Use

Time
15–20 minutes

Materials
globe or world map
CD with songs from other
   lands (in other languages)
   and CD player
chart paper and marker

Objectives

Children will:
1. Identify what language or languages they speak.
2. Name two languages.

Lesson

✦ Show the children a globe (or world map) and talk about "our big round world." Invite the children to tell what they know about the world or earth.

✦ Explain that the blue parts of the globe are water (oceans, rivers, lakes, and so on) and the other areas are land (different countries where people live).

✦ Talk about the different languages spoken in other countries. Mention that many people can speak more than one language.

✦ Play a CD or tape with a song in another language. Some examples are "Frere Jacque," "Un Elephante," "El Sapito," or "De Colores." Explain what the words mean, and sing it in English as well. Most CDs sold in the US have the words in English on the inside cover.

✦ Talk about the languages that people speak in your area, such as Spanish, French, Urdu, Hebrew, Farsi, and others. Ask the children what language they speak at school and at home.

✦ Make a list of the languages that the children in your classroom speak.

✦ Show the children the country where each language is spoken on the globe. If the children in your class only speak English, show them the globe and name languages that are spoken in other countries as you point them out on the globe.

Modifications/Accommodations

Autism: In the assessment activity, call on this child after others have had a chance to respond. Review the languages that you have talked about. Then ask the child what language she speaks. Then ask her to name another language that others speak while showing the globe. If the child does not understand this question, then start the sentence with, "What language does Josefina speak? Josefina speaks ___," so that the child can complete the sentence.

Speech or Language Impairments: Call on the child in the assessment after others have had an opportunity to respond and model responses. Provide a carrier phrase ("At home I speak ___.") in response to the assessment question about the child's home language.

Review

Talk about the language that they speak at school and at home. Count to six in English and in Spanish (uno, dos, tres, cuatro, cinco, seis). If Spanish is not the more common language in your area, count in the most common second language in your area. Have the children repeat after you and then count with you.

Assessment Strategy

Write each child's name on a chart table. Ask the children what language(s) they speak and write their responses on the chart next to their name. Ask the child what other languages people speak.

Hearing Impairments: Seat the child across from you where she can see your face. When playing the CD or tape with a song in another language, let the child listen on a headset (use a signal splitter so everyone can hear the song).

Visual Impairments: Let the child feel the globe as you discuss it. If using a map, it is helpful to have the countries outlined with school glue to provide a tactile representation of the boundaries of the countries. When writing on chart paper, describe what you are doing.

Cognitive and/or Developmental Disabilities: Use simple language and repetition. Have the child repeat several times during the counting activity. When counting at later times, review counting in Spanish or the other common second language in your area.

Emotional Disturbance: Seat the child close to you and affirm her for participating. Enlist the child's help in turning on the tape recorder or CD player.

Other Health Impairments/Attention Deficit Hyperactivity Disorder: Make sure that you have the child's attention before speaking. If the child becomes restless, ask her to put materials on a shelf of put something in the trash for you.

Orthopedic Impairments: No accommodations are anticipated for this child in this lesson.

Curriculum Connections

✦ **Language and Literacy:** In the Library Center, place books about other countries and books in another language. Two examples are *Cuento Hasta Diez* by Lisa Miles and *La Casa y El Hogar* by Alastair Smith.

✦ **More Language and Literacy:** Set up a CD player or tape player with music in other languages.

✦ **Math:** Provide counters and count with the children in Spanish or another common language in your area.

✦ **Social Studies:** Provide a world map or globe in a center. Place different colored cards on the globe or map to tell where different languages are spoken.

Traditions Families Have

Time
15–20 minutes

Materials
items or pictures of items associated with specific holidays or celebrations
calendar
pictures related to a holiday, for example, a turkey, cornucopia, and a pumpkin pie for Thanksgiving; or a jack-o-lantern, costume, and black cat for Halloween
picture of a birthday cake and candles
paper
markers and crayons

Preparation
Send home a note to parents prior to a holiday such as Thanksgiving or winter holidays. Explain in the note that you will be talking about family traditions at school. Ask parents to list a few things that their family does during the holiday.

Objectives

Children will:
1. Identify something that their family does on holidays.
2. Describe one tradition that their classroom family has.

Lesson

✦ Before an upcoming holiday, show items or pictures of items associated with the holiday. For example, show a turkey, cornucopia, and a pumpkin pie for Thanksgiving; or a jack-o-lantern, costume, and black cat for Halloween.
✦ Explain that during holidays, families celebrate in a variety of ways. When families do special things at special times, these are "family traditions."
✦ Invite the children to share special things that their family does during a specific holiday.
✦ Read some of the notes from families describing what they do during holidays.
✦ Show a picture of a birthday cake, and talk about celebrating each child's birthday.

Modifications/Accommodations

Autism: Use a consistent phrase to describe traditions. For example, when talking about Thanksgiving, say, "At Thanksgiving, one tradition we have is eating pumpkin pie" and "In January, one tradition we have is talking about snowmen." Use pictures during the discussion.

Speech or Language Impairments: Call on the child after others have had a chance to model responses. If needed, let the child respond by pointing to pictures. For example, show a snowman, a heart, and a flower, and ask, "Which one of these is a Valentine's day tradition?"

Hearing Impairments: Make sure the child is seated across from you where he can see your face. Use gestures and pictures during the discussion.

Visual Impairments: Describe each picture as you talk about traditions. For the assessment activity, put the drawing paper, crayons, and markers on a tray to provide a boundary for locating the materials.

Review

Discuss what a family tradition is: it is something special that families do at special times. When celebrating holidays, people have traditions at home and traditions at school. Ask the children to tell about a family tradition for the upcoming holiday, as well as a school tradition.

Assessment Strategy

Provide the children with drawing paper, markers, and crayons. Ask them to draw a picture about a family tradition. Ask them to tell about their picture and write what they say on the back of the picture.

Cognitive and/or Developmental Disabilities: Use short, simple phrases when presenting the lesson. Repeat key information. If the child does not respond to question, let him respond by pointing to pictures.

Emotional Disturbance: Seat the child next to you during the lesson. Encourage participation and have the child assist you with materials by handing you items and putting them back in the box.

Other Health Impairments/Attention Deficit Hyperactivity Disorder: Make sure that you have the child's attention before speaking. If the child becomes restless, use the statement, "We are almost finished" (if it is toward the end of the lesson). If the child is restless early in the lesson, take a break and invite all the children to stand up, stretch and bend, and then sit down.

Orthopedic Impairments: Assist the child in drawing the picture using hand-over-hand assistance, or provide an adaptive holder to help the child hold the marker or crayon.

Curriculum Connections

✦ **Art:** Provide die-cuts of items associated with various holiday traditions for the children to decorate in the Art Center. Include a variety of art materials, such as sequins, rickrack, braid, yarn, markers, crayons, glue, and paint.

✦ **Language and Literacy:** Provide books on holidays and traditions in the Library Center. Some suggestions include *Going to New Orleans to Visit Weezie Anna* by Mary Beth Pisano' *Milly and the Macy's Parade* by Shana Corey; *Miriam's Cup: A Passover Story* by Fran Manushkin; *When Mindy Saved Hanukkah* by Eric Kimmel; *My First Kwanzaa* by Deborah Chocolate; *The First Night* by B.G. Hennessy; and *Gracias the Thanksgiving Turkey* by Joy Crowley.

✦ **Math:** In the Math Center, include counters that are associated with traditions. Some possible counters include snowmen, turkeys, candles, and flags.

✦ **Social Studies:** Provide books that show traditions in other countries and cultures in the Library Center. Some possible books include *The First Americans* by Anthony Aveni, *Feliz Navidad* by Jose Feliciano, *A Doll for Navidades* by Esmeralda Santiago, *Ruby's Wish* by Shirin Yim Bridges, and *Gracias el Pavo de Thanksgiving* by Joy Crowley.

Music People Enjoy

Time
15–20 minutes

Materials
CD or tape player
CDs or cassette tapes of
    various genres of music
    including children's music
chart paper or dry-erase
    board and marker

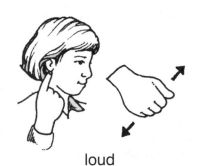

loud

soft

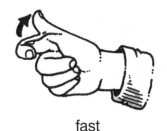

fast

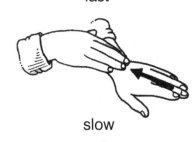

slow

Objectives

Children will:
1. Describe the music they like.
2. Identify different genres and tempos of music.

Lesson

✦   Gather the children in a circle and ask them to put on their "listening ears" because they will be listening to different kinds of music. Explain that some music is fast and some is slow.
✦   Play a children's song and ask the children if it is fast or slow. Repeat this with several songs, making sure that the songs are either very fast or very slow to emphasize the concept.
✦   Invite the children to move and dance to the music so that the concepts will be contrasted.
✦   Play loud and soft music, and ask the children if the music is loud or soft.
✦   Play short selections of different types of music (classical, rock, country, soul, Tejano), and invite the children to describe each type.

Modifications/Accommodations

Autism: Have the child move with the music, describing it as fast or slow during the lesson. Use your voice to demonstrate soft and loud music during the lesson. Sign language or gestures are a great help in describing music as fast, slow, soft, or loud. Signs also are helpful when asking the child to describe the music.

Speech or Language Impairments: When asking the child to describer the music, use a carrier phrase to help him begin: "This music sounds ___." Call on the child after several other children have responded.

Hearing Impairments: A signal splitter (available at music stores or electronics stores) is helpful so that the child can listen on a headset and the other children can hear the music as well. Make sure the child can see your face and mouth for the discussion during the lesson.

Visual Impairments: As you write responses on chart paper, describe what you are doing.

Cognitive and/or Developmental Disabilities: Repeat key words several times: *loud*, *soft*, *fast*, *slow*. Emphasize the terms and use movement during the music, describing the music as fast or slow.

Emotional Disturbance: Seat the child near you during the lesson and affirm him for participating.

Review

Play selections of children's music and ask the children to describe the music.

Assessment Strategy

Ask the each child to tell what kind of music she likes best and her favorite song. Write their favorites on chart paper or a dry-erase board.

Other Health Impairments/Attention Deficit Hyperactivity Disorder: Use shakers or other instruments during the lesson to emphasize fast and slow, and to maintain engagement.

Orthopedic Impairments: Physically assist the child in moving to the music and dancing.

Curriculum Connections

✦ **Art:** Provide materials for children to make musical instruments. For example, make drums using empty coffee cans or oatmeal containers. Cover with construction paper and decorate.

✦ **Math:** Give each child an instrument and invite them to count beats with you.

✦ **Music:** Provide CDs or tapes of children's songs in other languages. Provide music from other countries and cultures.

✦ **Social Studies:** During music time, provide instruments from a variety of countries, such as maracas, castanets, drums, marimba, rain stick, pan flute, and others.

Introduction to Living in America

Time
20–30 minutes

Materials
America: A Patriotic Primer by
    Lynne Cheney
paper
crayons

Objectives

Children will:
1. Name different qualities that make America great.
2. Make an ABC book of things they like in America.

Lesson

+ Gather the children together during Circle or Group Time. Ask them if they know the name of the country in which they live and if they give the name of their neighborhood, city, or state. Encourage them to think of the larger area in which they live. Understanding the difference between a neighborhood, city, state, and country is above the conceptual knowledge of many young children. They should be able to state that they live in America.

+ Encourage them to think of symbols or things that they know about America. If the children have difficulty, ask them what colors represent America or the flag. If necessary, read them a story about different symbols and special things about America.

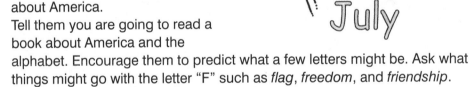

+ Tell them you are going to read a book about America and the alphabet. Encourage them to predict what a few letters might be. Ask what things might go with the letter "F" such as *flag*, *freedom*, and *friendship*.

+ Read *America: a Patriotic Primer* with the children.

+ Discuss American symbols and traits highlighted in the book.

+ Have the children think of American symbols or traits that begin with the same sounds as their names. Invite them to draw the items on sheets of art paper. Record each child's dictation on the bottom or the drawing. It would be helpful to have another adult assist with this.

+ Place the pages in alphabetical order and staple or bind together. It is fine to have duplicate alphabet letters. If you have missing letters, insert a blank page with the letter written at the top of the page for children to complete later, if they choose.

Modifications/Accommodations

Autism: Individually discuss American symbols and qualities. Help the child select the item she wishes to draw. Use yes-or-no questions to encourage child's participation if language is limited.

Review
Place the book in the Library Center for children to reread and look at during center times.

Assessment Strategy
Ask each child to identify two American traits or symbols.

Speech or Language Impairments: Encourage the children to use complete sentences. To help children understand American characteristics and symbols, relate the characteristics to children's daily lives. For example, an application of freedom of choice is the children's ability to choose the center activity they wish to work on or to choose who to play with.

Hearing Impairments: Have the child sit near you as you read the book. Use hand gestures and point to pictures.

Visual Impairments: Provide an additional copy of the book for the child to look at as you read. Assist with art materials as needed.

Cognitive and/or Developmental Delays: Explain any new concepts and characteristics using classroom situations or pictures to assist understanding.

Emotional Disturbance: Provide time prior to the lesson for the child to look at the book and ask questions before the class discussion.

Other Health Impairments/Attention Deficit Hyperactivity Disorder: Have the child sit near you as you read the book to encourage her attention. Use gestures and eye contact to keep the child focused on the topic.

Orthopedic Impairments: Provide materials at the child's level.

Curriculum Connections

✦ **Art:** Ask the children to draw pictures of themselves and their family in a place they have visited in the United States. Glue these pictures to a map of the United States.

✦ **Just for Fun:** Ask children to wear red, white, and blue clothing on a predetermined date to celebrate being Americans. During this day, plan additional patriotic or "red, white, and blue" activities, such as play geography games; eat red, white, and blue snacks; make red, white, and blue art projects, and so on.

✦ **Social Studies:** Display a map of the United States. Talk about the different areas of the country and see if the children know anything about these places, including friends or family that may live there.

The Flag

Time
30–45 minutes

Materials
Red, White and Blue: The Story of the American Flag by John Herman
white butcher paper (3' x 5')
blue butcher paper (18" square)
glue
pencil
red and white paint
paper plates
paper towels
small sponge cut into star shape

Preparation
Before the lesson design a template for the American Flag. Glue an 18" square of blue butcher paper in the top left corner of a piece of 3' x 5' white butcher paper. With a pencil, draw the 13 stripes (the children will paint these during the lesson). Pour red paint on two paper plates and white paint on two paper plates.

Objectives

Children will:
1. Listen to and discuss the book to *Red, White and Blue: The Story of the American Flag* by John Herman.
2. Use paint activities to create a classroom flag.
3. Discuss the history of the American flag.

Lesson

✦ Read the story *Red, White, and Blue: The Story of the American Flag.* During the story, highlight the changes in the American flag over time.
✦ Ask the children to tell different things they know about the American flag. If they do not state the number of stripes and stars, ask questions and use the book to count the number of stars and stripes on the current American flag.
✦ Show the children the American flag template.
✦ Tell them they will be adding stripes and stars to the flag.
✦ One at a time, have the children tell you something they learned about the flag. Then have them take turns dipping their hands, palms down, in the red paint. Show them how to make two handprints on the (fingers together) to fill in the red stripes of the flag.

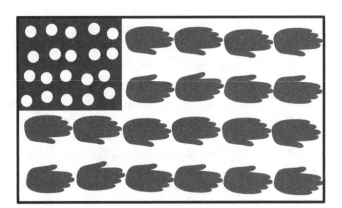

✦ After each child makes handprints, give the child a paper towel to wipe off the excess paint. Children then wash their hands with soap and water in the sink.
✦ Once the red stripes are dry, have the children use the star sponge stamps dipped in white paint to stamp two to three stars each on the flag for the 50 stars.
✦ Fly the flag in your classroom.

Assessment Strategy
Individually ask each child to
say one thing they learned
about the American flag.

Modifications/Accommodations

Autism: If the child is tactically defensive or is uncomfortable with placing his hand in paint, provide a hand-shaped sponge for him to make handprints. Talk with the child about the concepts and the process as he participates. For example, say to the child, "Dip the sponge in the red paint. Press, Press. Now put it on the stripe. Press, press. You added color to the flag's strip. Let's do it again."

Speech or Language Impairments: Model complete sentences using the new vocabulary. As the child works on the flag describe what he is doing. This will assist his comprehension of new vocabulary and sequence of information.

Hearing Impairments: Model the hand printing for the child or have the child watch another child make his handprints. Provide gestures and picture clues.

Visual Impairments: Provide materials within the child's vision field. Discuss the materials and the location of paint and paper.

Cognitive and/or Developmental Delays: Have the child watch another child make handprints and stars.

Emotional Disturbance: Give the child a choice of stamping his hands or using a sponge to print hands. Or have him trace and cut out handprints to glue to the flag.

Other Health Impairments/Attention Deficit Hyperactivity Disorder: Have the child repeat the directions to reinforce the sequence of steps.

Orthopedic Impairments: Make sure materials are accessible to the child. For example, bring the paper to the child rather than moving the child to the paper.

Curriculum Connections

✦ **Art:** Place red, white, and blue paints in the Art Center for the children to make their own flags.

✦ **Language and Literacy:** Have the children draw pictures of the flag and dictate a sentence about it. Compile the pictures into a class book.

✦ **Math:** Count the stars of the flag. Place the star stamp in the Math Center so the children can stamp and count the stars.

LIVING IN AMERICA

The President

Time
20–30 minutes

Materials
Duck for President by Doreen Cronin
pictures of the current president and vice president

Objectives

Children will:
1. Listen and discuss the story *Duck for President* by Doreen Cronin.
2. Discuss the responsibilities of the president of the country.

Lesson

✦ Gather the children to listen to the story *Duck for President* by Doreen Cronin.
✦ Discuss with the children that the president is the leader of the country.
✦ Ask the children to name the new responsibilities that Duck has when he becomes President.
✦ Show a picture of the current president and vice president.
✦ Discuss what they think the president and vice president do in their positions.
✦ If it is an election year, add pictures of the top candidates for president and vice president.
✦ Ask the children what they would do if they were president of the United States.

Modifications/Accommodations

Autism: Individually discuss the office of president with the child. Read and discuss the book with the child.

Speech or Language Impairments: Encourage the child to use complete sentences during discussion time.

Hearing Impairments: Have the child sit where she can see the book and your face as you read.

Visual Impairments: Provide an extra copy of the book for the child to look at during the class reading

Cognitive and/or Developmental Delays: Explain any unknown words. You may want to use questioning skills to help the child make some choices in what she would want to do as president. This will help the child make a choice and participate in the discussion.

Emotional Disturbance: Individually discuss the idea of the president and encourage the child to participate.

Other Health Impairments/Attention Deficit Hyperactive Disorder: Use visual cues to help the child attend to the book and stay on task. Cues may include pointing to the book and using hand gestures to show the child she is doing what she should and gestures to help the child remain focused on the topic.

Orthopedic Impairments: None needed for this lesson.

Review

Place the book and pictures in an area of the classroom for the children to discuss and examine.

Assessment Strategy

Ask the children what they would do if they were president. Ask the children what they think the most important thing about the Presidency is.

Curriculum Connections

✦ **Language and Literacy:** Have the children draw and write about what they would do if they were president for a day.
✦ **Math:** Challenge interested children to look at coins and identify presidents using the pictures of past presidents. Allow the children a time to vote for a class leader for a day. Have the children count the ballots and discuss concepts of majority and more and less.

Ballot

☐ **Jeremy**   ☐ **Angela**

☐ **Keith**   ☐ **Tyler**

☐ **Rebecca**   ☐ **Tasha**

☐ **Michael**   ☐ **Jada**

☐ **Lewis**   ☐ **Antwoinette**

☐ **Melissa**   ☐ **Tara**

✦ **More Math:** Challenge interested children to look at coins and identify presidents on the coins using the pictures of past presidents.
✦ **Social Studies:** Have the children look at pictures of past presidents. Have them discuss traits to help them remember physical features.

The White House

Time
15–20 Minutes

Materials
pictures of the White House
    and other houses
computer with Internet access
    (optional)
art paper
crayons

Objectives

Children will:
1. Identify the White House from photographs.
2. Discuss what life might be like in the White House.

Lesson

✦   Show the children pictures of different houses. This can include photographs of different-sized homes, homes and apartments, doghouses, birdhouses, anthills, and caves. If possible, use pictures of the children's homes. Ask the children who or what might live in each type of home.
✦   Then show the children a picture of the White House and explain that it is a very important house. Ask them if they know who lives in the White House.

✦   Explain to them that part of the White House is for living, part of the White House is for "having company," and part of the White House is for working.
✦   Discuss the things they think go on in the White House.
✦   Let them draw a picture of themselves visiting or working at the White House. As they dictate a sentence about their picture, write their words on the drawing.

Modifications/Accommodations

Autism: Individually discuss the houses and the White House with the child. Have the child identify the White House from the other pictures.
Speech or Language Impairments: Provide the child with sentence starters for him to use to tell about his picture. Encourage him to use complete sentences.

Review

Place the pictures in the classroom for the children to look at and discuss later.

Assessment Strategy

Individually show each child the picture of the White House and have him tell something about it.

Hearing Impairments: Have the child sit near the speakers so that he can participate fully.

Visual Impairments: Have the child look at the pictures before the lesson. Discuss the different pictures in detail so that the child can focus on the details of the pictures. Use verbal dialogue to describe the pictures and the White House.

Cognitive and/or Developmental Delays: Individually discuss the function of the White House. Have the child describe what he would like to do in the White House.

Emotional Disturbance: Sit the child near you and affirm the child's appropriate behavior and participation.

Other Health Impairments/Attention Deficit Hyperactivity Disorder: Provide time for the child to focus on the pictures and plan what he would do in the White House.

Orthopedic Impairments: Use specialized grips to help the child draw a picture. Place all materials at the appropriate level and distance for ease of use.

Curriculum Connections

- ✦ **Art:** Provide boxes in a variety of sizes and white tempera paint so children can make their own "white houses."
- ✦ **Language and Literacy:** Have the children make a class book with individual pages: "If I lived in the White House, I would _____."
- ✦ **Social Studies:** Have individual children locate Washington, DC on a map. Gather other pictures of buildings in Washington, DC for the children to explore and learn about. If possible, get a walking map of Washington, DC that highlights different buildings and exhibits.

Voting

Time
15–20 Minutes

Materials
paper
markers

Objectives

Children will:
1. Discuss voting and choosing.
2. Vote for a class activity.

Lesson

✦ Gather the children together on the floor. Tell them that they will choose a special thing to do today. Remember to include all children in this activity because it is focused on the concept of voting and the majority rule.

✦ Explain that in America one of the ways American citizens choose is to vote. Each child will get to vote for their choice of what to do today.

✦ Brainstorm a list of reasonable things to do, for example:
  ✦ "shoes off" time in the classroom
  ✦ extra time outdoors
  ✦ special music or drama time
  ✦ decorating cups for snack time

✦ Narrow down the options to three or four choices and write them on piece of paper.

✦ Designate an area of the room for each choice. For example, "This corner where you stand if you choose the "shoes off" choice; this corner is the extra outdoors time choice; and so on.

✦ Have the children move to the part of the classroom that represents their choice.

✦ Once the children have all selected their choices, go to each area and help the children in the group count themselves. Write the results on the paper next to the choice.

✦ Explain to the children that the class had a majority vote for one choice. Ensure them that if they were not in the majority group, they will get to participate in the choice, and they will have another time during the year to vote again.

Modifications/Accommodations

Autism: Use forced-choice, yes-or-no questions to help the child select her choice.

Speech or Language Impairments: Use complete sentences as you model correct expanded speech to explain the process of voting to the children.

Hearing Impairments: Use picture cues to help the child with voting.

Visual Impairments: Help the child move to her voting choice location.

Review

During the day find additional reasons for voting, such as deciding which book to read—book "A" or book "B." Have the children move to an area of the room to show their choice of book (to vote for a specific book).

Assessment Strategy

Ask the children why they are getting the reward and how they voted for the reward.

Cognitive and/or Developmental Delays: Discuss the voting process with the child. If the child's choice was not the majority choice, discuss the benefits of the selected choice and the possibility that her choice might be selected at a different time.

Emotional Disturbance: Before the lesson, discuss the voting process. During the voting discuss the benefits of each of the selections. Tell the child there will be other voting times during the year.

Other Health Impairments/Attention Deficit Hyperactivity Disorder: Help the child make her choice and understand the majority selection.

Orthopedic Impairments: Help the child move to her voting choice location.

Curriculum Connections

✦ **Art:** Use the location voting strategy to vote for the type of art materials the class will use in the Art Center the following week.

✦ **Language and Literacy:** Use the voting strategy to vote for next story time book.

✦ **Social Studies:** Discuss with small groups of children why it is important to use the "majority rule" process when voting.

Book A	Book B

Fourth of July

Time
20–30 minutes

Materials
pictures of Fourth of July celebrations
poster board
small wooden dowel rods or sturdy plastic straws
construction paper
crepe paper streamers and ribbons
tissue paper
red, white, and blue cutouts, sequins, flags, and other small paper and plastic patriotic items that can be easily glued
pipe cleaners
glittered foil
wire tinsel with stars
markers, crayons, and paint
scissors
glue

Objectives

Children will:
1. Decorate items for a Fourth of July parade.
2. Discuss Fourth of July celebrations.

Lesson

✦ At Circle or Group Time, ask the children how their families celebrate the Fourth of July.
✦ Talk about getting together with their family and friends, having picnics, watching parades and fireworks displays, and other celebrations.
✦ Show the children pictures of Fourth of July celebrations (parades, fireworks).
✦ Discuss what children would like to do on the next Fourth of July.
✦ Explain to them that the Fourth of July is a birthday celebration. Ask the children if they know whose birthday it is. Explain that the United States has a birthday every year on the Fourth of July. They all get to celebrate. Explain that one custom of celebration is a parade. Many towns have Fourth of July parades. Ask the children if they have ever watched a parade or participated in a parade.
✦ Tell the children that they will get to participate in a parade but first they need to make the decorations and hats for the parade.
✦ Provide materials for the children to make and decorate hats, banners, and flags to use in a Fourth of July parade.
✦ Encourage children to use their creativity to create hats, headbands, flags, and banners.
✦ You may provide a few examples of a red, white, and blue headband or a hand-held flag, but allow the children time with free expression and creation using the art materials.
✦ Have a parade around the school!

Modifications/Accommodations

Autism: Give the child an opportunity to create decorations for the parade. Provide plenty of time and a variety of materials for the child to select from.
Speech or Language Impairments: Encourage the child to use complete sentences during discussions.
Hearing Impairments: Provide hand cues and visual cues to assist the child in participating in the discussion. Have the child near you in the parade to help him will communication and directions.
Visual Impairments: Provide a variety of materials. Let the child parade with a classmate.

Review

Ask each child what they have made and encourage them to wear or display each as they show their spirit in a Fourth of July parade around the school.

Assessment Strategy

Ask each child individually about the reason to have a Fourth of July Celebration and what he would like to do to celebrate.

Cognitive and/or Developmental Delays: Provide plenty of time for the child to design his own parade hats and decorations. Encourage and praise the child's attempts.

Emotional Disturbance: Provide time and encouragement as the child designs the parade decorations.

Other Health Impairments/Attention Deficit Hyperactivity Disorder: Encourage the child to be creative in designing their parade decorations. Orthopedic Impairments: Assist the child in moving with the parade. Provide the materials for making the decorations within reach.

Curriculum Connections

✦ **Art:** Create fireworks art. Use an eyedropper to drop one drop of paint onto a sheet of paper. The child blows on the drop to create "fireworks bursts." Use multiple colors and multiple drops to create a beautiful display.

✦ **Movement:** Provide red, white, and blue streamers and invite the children to dance and move to a rousing march recording.

✦ **Language and Literacy:** Encourage the children to tell stories of their favorite birthday celebrations.

Introduction to Celebrations

Note: This theme can be introduced at any time of the year, not just before a holiday. One teacher tells the story about a four-year-old who insisted that the class have a Halloween party in mid-July. When he continued (over a period of days) to ask his teacher to organize a celebration, the teacher let the class spend an entire morning decorating the classroom with orange and black paper, and then had a mid-summer Halloween party!

Time
25 minutes

Materials
Franklin's Thanksgiving by Paulette Bourgeois, or another book about a celebration
holiday props (tableware, paper goods, streamers, decorations, candles, hats, and so on)

Objectives

Children will:
1. Explain that a celebration is a special occasion spent with families and friends.
2. Describe a celebration they have experienced.

Lesson

✦ Explain that the class will be talking about various celebrations for a few days. Ask them if they know what a celebration is.
✦ Following the children's discussion, tell them that any special event that is not usual or routine is considered a celebration. Name some common celebrations the children may have overlooked.
✦ Introduce the book *Franklin's Thanksgiving* (if it is available). Explain that the story is about a celebration. Then read the book to the children and encourage them to make responses about the book's illustrations.
✦ Show some of the holiday props and ask children if they can match them with specific celebrations.
✦ Place the props in the Dramatic Play Center for them to play with during Center Time.

Modifications/Accommodations

Autism: Use concrete objects and real-life examples to reinforce the activities in this lesson.

Speech or Language Impairments: When reviewing the sequence of events in the book, use picture cards. Limit the number of events to sequence to an appropriate number at the child's knowledge level.

Hearing Impairments: When presenting information about celebrations, use nonverbal communication to reinforce verbal messages. Integrate simple sign language into all parts of the lesson, such as the signs for *book* and *celebrate*.

book   celebrate

Review

Review the sequence of the book, asking specific questions about what happened in the story.

Assessment Strategy

While children are playing with the celebration props in the Dramatic Play Center, conduct formal assessments by asking individuals to identify props and match them to various holidays and celebrations.

Visual Impairments: Allow children to touch and manipulate the various props presented during the lesson. When reading the story, verbally describe the actions and features in the photographs.

Cognitive and/or Developmental Disabilities: Limit the number of props for children to match to celebrations to a number that is appropriate to the child's cognitive level.

Emotional Disturbance: The child may need special supervision when transitioning from one activity to another.

Other Health Impairments/Attention Deficit Hyperactivity Disorder: Allow the child additional opportunities to move throughout the lesson. For example, have the child with attention difficulties place the props in the Dramatic Play area.

Orthopedic Impairments: Position the child at an appropriate level so that she can see the photographs in the story and actively participate in the lesson.

Curriculum Connections

✦ **Bulletin Board:** Display pictures of celebrations on a classroom bulletin board. Talk to children individually or in small groups about celebrations they might recognize by looking at the pictures. Encourage them to draw pictures of celebrations to add to the bulletin board.

✦ **Language and Literacy:** With small groups of children, introduce the term *anniversary*. Tell them that couples celebrate their marriages by recognizing their anniversaries every year. Ask the children to find out when their parents were married and if they have anniversary celebrations. Children of divorced parents need sensitivity when discussing this topic with them. Say, "Some parents decide not to stay married, so they stop having anniversaries." Point out to children that birthdays are anniversaries of their birthdates.

✦ **Music:** Add CDs or cassette recordings of music commonly played during a parade or at the circus in the Music Center.

Family Celebrations

Time
25 minutes

Materials
pictures of family celebrations
chart paper and marker
Pizza by Saturnino Romay

Objectives

Children will:
1. Name one family celebration.
2. Describe how their families celebrates a specific holiday (such as Thanksgiving or the Fourth of July).

Lesson

✦ Begin the lesson by telling children that families have special celebrations that may or may not be similar to other families' celebrations.

✦ Identify one specific tradition that you have in your own family that will possibly be unique to you (such as always celebrating Thanksgiving at your grandmother's house or having a Fourth of July picnic every year).

✦ Ask children what types of celebrations they have in their homes. You might want to send out an informal survey to parents prior to this lesson to find out the most common family traditions your children's families celebrate. This will help you prepare the following chart accordingly.

✦ Prepare a chart that shows the most common family celebrations. Draw pictures with the headings to help the children understand the categories. Be prepared to show children where to place tally marks when the discussion evolves. Here is an example:

Sunday Dinner	Going to the Park	Birthdays
Always eat at home	Go every Saturday with members of the family	Always have a cake
Always eat out	Invite cousins or neighbors to go to the park	Always have a party
Always order pizza	Plan a special picnic for a family reunion	Never have a party

✦ As children talk about their family celebrations, call on individual children to make tally marks in the appropriate places on the chart as a summary of the discussion.

✦ Be prepared to read the book *Pizza* if this celebration is a tradition for some families.

- **Language and Literacy:**
Ask individual children to
dictate sentences to you
describing a family
celebration they enjoy.
This activity will take
several days to complete,
and you may want to
invite parents to help out
with the story collection.
Put the completed stories
into a scrapbook or make
a classroom book titled
"Our Family
Celebrations." Share the
book with parents when
they visit the classroom
and show it to your
principal or director. Call
on children to share the
stories themselves if they
wish.

Review

Spend a little time at the end
of the lesson talking about
the events that are the most
popular among children's
families (based on tally mark
results).

Assessment Strategy

Informally, ask individual
children to describe one of
their family celebrations.

Modifications/Accommodations

Autism: Use visual cues to assist the child in transitioning from one part of the
activity to another. For example, use a hand signal to indicate that it is time
to move from the chart paper activity to story time.

Speech or Language Impairments: Use verbal and visual cues to help the
child prepare for his turn in the lesson.

Hearing Impairments: Face the child when
speaking and clearly articulate your
speech. Supplement this activity by adding
simple sign language, such as for the
words *celebrate* and *party*.

Visual Impairments: Supplement photos and
tally marks on the chart with tactile items.
For example, tape a candle to the chart for
birthday celebrations. Verbally describe the
photographs presented in the book.

Cognitive and/or Developmental Disabilities:
During the assessment phase of the
lesson, ask the child to bring a photo from
home of a celebration.

celebrate

party

Emotional Disturbance: Seat the child closer to you so you can monitor
his behavior.

Other Health Impairments/Attention Deficit Hyperactivity Disorder: Allow
the child ample opportunities for movement throughout the lesson. This
can be accomplished by asking the child to help with gathering props or
turning pages of the book.

Orthopedic Impairments: Help the child make tally marks on the chart, if
needed. Position the child to encourage full participation in the activities.

Curriculum Connections

- **Art:** Place plain paper hats in the Art Center with books of stickers,
markers, and chalk for children to decorate. You may want to work with
small groups of children and show them how to roll paper into cone
shapes to make hats, using 24" square pieces of paper. If desired, provide
glitter and glue (place newspaper under the art tables for easy cleanup).
- **Connecting with Home:** Invite parents to send in photographs showing
family celebrations. Display the photos in a classroom scrapbook or on a
bulletin board. Ask parents to write down children's remembrances of
family get-togethers to accompany the photos. At school, with individual
children or in small groups, ask children to tell about their stories and
pictures. Remember to mark these photographs carefully so you can
return them at the end of the study.

Birthdays

Time
20 minutes

Materials
A Birthday Basket for Tia by
    Pat Mora, *Every Year on
    Your Birthday* by Rose A.
    Lewis, or another book
    about birthdays
brown, green, and red
    construction paper
scissors
birthday party props (plates,
    napkins, cups, party hats,
    and so on) to place in the
    Dramatic Play Center

Preparation
Make a classroom "Birthday
Tree." Cut out a tree from
brown construction paper
and a few leaves from green
construction paper. Attach the
tree and leaves to a bulletin
board. Cut out apples from
red construction paper.

Objectives

Children will:
1. Name their birth dates.
2. Describe how they celebrate their birthdays.

Lesson

◆ Begin by asking children why they enjoy celebrating their birthdays.
◆ Talk about the how families celebrate birthdays (having a special dinner, blowing out candles on a birthday cake, singing "Happy Birthday," receiving presents, and so on).
◆ One of the most popular songs in America is "Happy Birthday." Sing the song with the children (substitute "Happy birthday, everybody" for the third phrase of the song).
◆ Read *A Birthday Basket for Tia* (or another available selection) and discuss the story as you read it.
◆ Show them the classroom Birthday Tree. Explain that you will add birthday apples to the tree whenever a child in the class celebrates a birthday.
◆ When a child has a birthday, write her name and birthday on an apple cutout and place it on the tree. Be sensitive to children whose families choose not to celebrate birthdays.

Modifications/Accommodations

Autism: Provide visual cues to help children transition from one activity to another.
Speech or Language Impairments: Offer children choices for how they might celebrate their birthday ("Do you eat cake or cupcakes?") or offer leading sentences such as "On my birthday my family celebrates by...."
Hearing Impairments: Teach simple sign language for the "Happy Birthday" song, including the signs for happy birthday and you. Place the child closer to you when you are reading or giving directions.

Happy Birthday

you

Review

Ask children to tell why birthday parties are considered celebrations.

Assessment Strategy

Individually ask children what their birth date is.

Visual Impairments: Verbally describe the photographs in the book A Birthday Basket for Tia. Focus attention on the details of the photographs including colors and sizes of objects portrayed.

Cognitive and/or Developmental Disabilities: During the assessment, tell the child her birth date and then have the child repeat her birth date to you.

Emotional Disturbance: Offer praise and encouragement for participation in the activity.

Other Health Impairments/Attention Deficit Hyperactivity Disorder: Allow children to move their bodies (clapping, dancing) when singing the birthday song. A child with attention difficulties may benefit from holding the book as you read the story.

Orthopedic Impairments: Position the child so that she may actively participate in the activity.

Curriculum Connections

✦ **Art:** Encourage children to make birthday cards for their parents to give to them during the surprise birthday party (or to take home if parents are unable to attend). Provide construction paper, markers, stickers, chalk, paint, and other art media.

✦ **Dramatic Play:** Add birthday party props to the Dramatic Play Center so children can pretend to have a birthday party.

✦ **Social Studies:** Have a surprise birthday party for the children's parents. Designate a day and time during the celebration unit for the party. Invite the parents to come to school for a class presentation and surprise them with cupcakes and punch. Ask parents to RSVP so you can plan accordingly. Purchase (or bake) cupcakes and give children an opportunity to decorate at least one cupcake to give to their parent (or two if both parents are coming).

Holiday Celebrations

Time
20 minutes

Materials
holiday props (many of the props used in the Introduction to Celebrations on page 242 are appropriate to use for this lesson)
Kids Around the World Celebrate! by Lynda Jones

Objectives

Children will:
1. Name one holiday they celebrate.
2. Tell that holidays are special days they usually spend with family and friends.

Lesson

✦ Remind children that the topic of discussion for the past few days has been celebrations and ask them to recall what they have talked about so far.
✦ Talk about an upcoming holiday that most people in America enjoy (Thanksgiving is a good choice). Note from one of the authors: Several years ago, I did informal interviews with children in preschool and in kindergarten classrooms, and what I discovered was that they believed that holidays meant "being away from school."
✦ Ask children to recall memories of Thanksgivings past and tell them that holidays are a great time for families to get together.
✦ Introduce *Kids Around the World Celebrate!* to the children and let them talk about the various holidays that are presented in the book.
✦ Tell children that most holidays are special times when they stay at home and spend time with their families.
✦ Show the collection of props and review with children the holidays they represent.
✦ During Center Time, make and decorate holiday cookies with children who choose to participate.

Modifications/Accommodations

Autism: When reviewing the topics of discussion previously presented, offer lead-in sentences. For example, "Yesterday we talked about a holiday that we celebrate when we turn a year older. This is called our _____."
Speech or Language Impairments: Frequently check for understanding and ask children to repeat various key points.
Hearing Impairments: Eliminate as much background noise as possible. Place the child close to you.
Visual Impairments: Allow the child to touch and manipulate the various props presented in the activity.
Cognitive and/or Developmental Disabilities: Ask clear and specific questions that you are sure the child can respond to. This will help in building the child's confidence and increase his desire to participate.
Emotional Disturbance: Provide frequent feedback and offer praise for active participation in the activity.

Review
Ask the children to brainstorm holidays they have experienced during the school year.

Assessment Strategy
Informally poll individual children to learn what holidays they recall. Ask them to tell why the holidays they name are special.

Other Health Impairments/Attention Deficit Hyperactivity Disorder: Have a child with attention difficulties hold the book while you read or help with measuring during the curriculum extension activities.
Orthopedic Impairments: Position child so that he can see the book.

Curriculum Connections

✦ **Art:** Bring a "holiday" tree to the classroom and encourage children to make ornaments to represent an upcoming holiday (red hearts for Valentine's Day or green balls for St. Patrick's Day). Let children decorate the tree any way they deem suitable. Provide string, yarn, construction paper, glue, crayons, markers, ornament hangers, confetti, glitter, sequins, beads, chenille, and pipe cleaners.

✦ **Connecting with Home:** Invite parents who want to share a cultural celebration with the children to come to school and talk about their favorite holiday. Cinco de Mayo, Hanukkah, and Kwanzaa are celebrations that families might want to discuss. Collaborate with the parents prior to their coming to school about food items that they might share (or that the children could prepare as a snack).

✦ **Science:** Invite small groups of children to gather around a clean table and use commercial cookie dough to make holiday cookies. Have a variety of cookie cutter shapes (hearts, ovals, flags, pumpkins, turkeys, trees, and so on) so children can choose the holiday shape they want. Place their efforts on cookie sheets and bake in an oven until done. Make sure the cookies are marked with their owners' names to ensure each child having his or her cookie at snack time. Bake a few additional cookies for children who choose not to participate in the cooking experience.

CELEBRATIONS

Rodeos

Time
25 minutes

Materials
cowboy hats and ropes
White Dynamite and Curly Kidd by Bill Martin, Jr. and John Archambault (or another children's book about rodeos)
rodeo barrels (trash cans will substitute if barrels aren't available)

Objectives

Children will:
1. State what a rodeo is.
2. Identify one event commonly observed in rodeos.

Lesson

✦ Draw attention to the lesson by wearing a cowboy hat and carrying a rope.
✦ Ask children if they know who might wear a hat like this and use ropes.
✦ Tell them that the lesson is about a special type of celebration, a rodeo. A rodeo is a celebration that usually happens at the end of a trail ride or in connection with a county fair.
✦ Ask if any of the children have ever attended a rodeo and allow them to tell what they know about them.
✦ Read *White Dynamite and Curly Kidd* to the children, allowing them to talk about the pictures as you read.
✦ Tell children that other events at rodeos are calf-roping, bareback racing, team roping, barrel racing, saddle bronco riding, chuck wagon races, and having special entertainers. (Note: Another book that shows pictures of rodeo events, though written for older children, has great illustrations to show to children: *Bill Pickett: Rodeo-Ridin' Cowboy* by Andrea Davis Pinkney.)
✦ Tell the children that they will be having pretend barrel races on the playground. Set up the rodeo barrels on the playground prior to children going outside to encourage participation.
✦ Tell children that most rodeos begin with a parade. Ask them to stand and move around the classroom as if they were in a rodeo parade (you can be the grand marshal leading the parade).

Modifications/Accommodations

Autism: Supplement the activity with various props that center around the rodeo theme. Concrete items will reinforce learning. When assessing learning, allow the child to select a photo that depicts a rodeo event.
Speech or Language Impairments: Use a lead-in sentence when asking children to tell about rodeo experiences. For example, "At the rodeo we see people wearing _____."
Hearing Impairments: Face the child when speaking. Strategically place the child where she can be least distracted by outside activities.
Visual Impairments: Allow the child to touch and manipulate the various rodeo items. Verbally describe the photos in *White Dynamite and Curly Kidd.*

Review
Return to the circle for a few minutes to review the lesson on rodeos.

Assessment Strategy
Ask children to name at least one rodeo event they recall from the lesson.

Cognitive and/or Developmental Disabilities: When assessing learning allow the child to describe what they see in a photograph of a rodeo event. Ask the child to tell you what she sees in the photograph.

Emotional Disturbance: Review class rules. Provide positive reinforcement for following class rules and actively participating in the lesson.

Other Health Impairments/Attention Deficit Hyperactivity Disorder: Have a child with attention difficulties lead the rodeo parade. Provide multiple opportunities for movement throughout the lesson.

Orthopedic Impairments: Assist child as needed in order to increase participation in outside rodeo events. Make sure the child feels comfortable asking for assistance. You may ask, "Is there anything I can do to make you more comfortable when you are doing the barrel race?"

Curriculum Connections

+ **Dramatic Play:** Place cowboy hats and ropes in the Dramatic Play Center for children to use to pretend to be cowboys. Add other cowboy paraphernalia (such as cowboy vests, cowboy boots, bandannas, shirts, and so on), if available.
+ **Outdoors:** Use the preset barrels to pretend to have barrel races. The main focus of this activity is allowing children time to run while pretending to be horses (or riders). The emphasis should be on running without indicating who are "winners" or "losers."
+ **More Outdoors:** Invite a parent (or an older child) who has roping expertise to visit the classroom to demonstrate roping skills. Any instruction would need to be given with a small group of interested children. Not all children should be expected to participate in this event.

At Home and at School

Developing children's interest in food, clothes, and toys should not take much effort. Children begin at very early ages to form opinions about the food, clothes, and toys they like. Over time, these preferences become more evident, both at home and at school.

One delightful aspect of food-related themes is that they give children the opportunity to taste and discuss new as well as familiar foods. Not only do such activities enhance language and vocabulary skills, but the children learn about many scientific and mathematical concepts when they prepare food to eat and share with others. Following a rebus recipe chart also helps children connect print with pictures, an early form of reading. Organizing the sale of a booklet of recipes that are family favorites to the children's families is a good fundraising project, both for schools and individual classrooms (and, of course, this kind of activity encourages family participation in an ongoing school project).

Although clothing is unimportant to some children, a few children are particular about the clothing they wear. Some opinions children have about clothes, especially about what is "in fashion," are heavily influenced by older siblings, as well as by what children see on television and in clothing stores. The materials and activities in these units expose children to various types of clothes and fabrics people use to make clothes. The vocabulary children acquire about clothes and the differences among clothing pieces should be the main objectives for unit.

Studying children's toys should help children learn about all the varieties of toys that are available to them for play. Some children might even try toys that they often do not choose, thus expanding concepts about their world they may have previously overlooked. Taking time to graph children's favorite toys and recording the reasons they enjoy certain toys will introduce the children to the scientific process of data collection. You might also want to help children classify toys into categories, such as toys for dramatic play, toys for imagination, or toys for physical activity. Studying the construction of toys (how they are put together) and their special features continues to add to the children's understanding of scientific data collection.

Sharing information about these units should be easy, and will likely foster learning that positively affects children's attitudes and choices.

Introduction to Food

Note: This unit on food is an excellent way to introduce health concepts to young children, and it also gives you an opportunity to teach the children about the cultures of the children in your classroom. Check for food allergies prior to serving any food to the children.

Time
20 minutes

Materials
popcorn popper and kernels
chart paper and marker
    (optional)
One Hungry Monster: A Counting Book in Rhyme by Susan Heyboer O'Keefe, or another book about food
pictures of food (available as part of the *Preschool Photo Activity Library* by Pam Schiller, or another source of pictures of food)

Preparation
Begin popping popcorn as children gather for Circle or Group Time (or cook other food with a delicious aroma) so they can smell the aroma of the food.

Objectives

Children will:
1. Tell that the reason people eat is because their bodies need food.
2. Name three foods that are good for their bodies.

Lesson

✦ Ask the children, "What do you smell? How do you know it is popcorn?"
✦ Tell children that popcorn is a type of food.
✦ Ask them to name other foods that smell good to them and show them pictures of food as children mention them. If you wish, write the children's responses on a chart.
✦ As the children brainstorm, tell them that our bodies need food to work effectively. Say, "Just like cars need gasoline to run, our bodies need food to keep us going. Food gives us energy. It helps us grow, and it keeps us healthy."
✦ Ask the children if their mouths are watering (or salivating) as they smell the popcorn. Talk about yummy food.
✦ Tell them that our bodies enjoy food and when we smell something we like to eat, we often salivate. Explain what salivation means.
✦ Share *One Hungry Monster: A Counting Book in Rhyme* or another book about food.
✦ Repeat some of the rhymes children remember from the book.
✦ Transition to the snack table to enjoy the popcorn.

Modifications/Accommodations

Autism: Use the sign for *popcorn* (individual fingers popping up alternately) as the popcorn begins to pop. As you talk about the smell of popcorn, point to your nose. Because "why" questions and definitions are difficult language tasks for children with autism, use an alternate assessment, such as, "Draw something that your body needs to grow" or "Show me where you salivate."

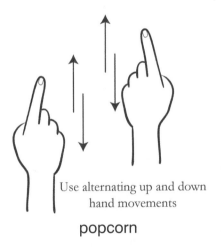

Use alternating up and down hand movements

popcorn

Speech or Language Impairments: For the assessment, show the child an array of pictures and ask him to select something that his body needs to grow. Instead of defining the word *salivate*, ask him to show where he salivates by pointing (hold up your finger to prompt the child to point).

Review

As children are eating their popcorn, ask them to recall the foods that they talked about during Circle or Group Time.

Assessment Strategy

Ask individual children to tell why food is important to our bodies. Ask them to define the word salivate.

Hearing Impairments: Seat the child near the popcorn as it begins to pop so that he can hear it. While reading the story, make sure that the child can see both your lips and the pictures as you read. Check periodically while reading the story to be sure he understands.

Visual Impairments: Describe the pictures of food as you show them. While reading the book (*One Hungry Monster: A Counting Book in Rhyme* or another book), comment on and describe the pictures.

Cognitive and/or Developmental Disabilities: Preteach the vocabulary smell, food, salivate. After the lesson, review the vocabulary frequently (at least every few days). Have the child repeat the rhymes after you when reviewing the rhymes from the book. Use one of the alternate assessments described in Speech or Language Impairments or Autism with the child.

Emotional Disturbance: When popping the popcorn, provide close supervision for this child. Even though all children need close supervision around a cooking area, the child with emotional problems may require additional vigilance. Make sure that the child is seated and waiting before you give him popcorn to eat.

Other Health Impairments/Attention Deficit Hyperactivity Disorder: If the child becomes restless after the story, stand up as you review the rhymes after reading the book. When transitioning to the snack table, call on a few children at a time to move. While this is a useful transition technique for many children, it is especially important to have planned transitions with this child.

Orthopedic Impairments: Help the child move to the snack table. When reading the book, make sure that he is positioned so that he can see the pictures.

Curriculum Connections

+ **Art:** Begin a classroom display that will continue throughout the food study. Use a bulletin board or a series of posters that the children develop. Label the first section "Foods We Enjoy." Invite children to draw or cut out pictures of foods they like to eat and glue the pictures onto the display (bulletin board or poster board).

+ **Connecting with Home:** Send a survey home with children to learn from the children's families about any foods that are unique to their culture that they would be willing to share with your class. This expands the children's opportunities to share information about their unique cultures.

+ **Social Studies:** With small groups of children, talk about when people get together and enjoy food (family reunions, picnics, religious activities, birthday parties, and so on.) Add party hats to the Dramatic Play Center or Home Living Center for children to use to pretend to have a party.

Meat

Note: When presenting this lesson, be sensitive to families who are vegetarians because of their religion or for any other reason.

Time

20 minutes

Materials

samples of various foods (fruits, dairy, vegetables, and so on)

photographs of meat products

The Meat Eaters Arrive by Suzan Reid, or another suitable book about meat

large poster showing the food pyramid (a copy is available at http://www.mypyramid.gov/downloads/MiniPoster.pdf)

Objectives

Children will:

1. Identify that meat is a category on the food pyramid.
2. Name one meat product.

Lesson

✦ Ask the children to participate in a taste test for a food survey.
   Note: Let children decide whether or not they want to participate in the taste test. It is okay if some of the children do not want to taste the food you have displayed.

✦ Invite them to take small bites of the foods and select the one they prefer. Mark their responses on a chart labeled "Our Favorite Foods." (Children who do not participate in the tasting can say which foods they prefer eating at home.) Consider blindfolding the children for the taste test. However, this decision should be based on the developmental maturity of the children in your class (some children are frightened by blindfolds).

✦ Tally the results. Say, "In this class, our favorite food is _____."

✦ Show the children food pyramid poster and point out the various categories, telling the children that today the discussion will focus on the meat section.

✦ Tell children that meat provides protein, which is an important part of our diets because it helps build muscle and body strength. (Technically, protein is an element composed of several amino acids, but you may not want to be this detailed with young children.)

✦ Name other foods that provide protein, such as eggs, dairy products, and some vegetables, such as legumes.

✦ Tell children that nuts are high protein foods.

✦ Introduce and read *The Meat Eaters Arrive* to the children.

✦ Summarize the lesson by reminding children that meat contains protein, an important nutrient that helps bodies grow strong and healthy.

Modifications/Accommodations

Autism: Show the child pictures of different types of foods and play a game of "Find the Meat." Show the pictures of food and say, "Find the meat" as you show each picture. When the food picture shows meat, slap the deck and say, "Here's the meat." This activity is also useful for other children who may need extra instruction as well as for those who have expressive language difficulties.

Speech or Language Impairments: For the assessment, depending on the ability of the child, have her select the meat pictures from groups of three to four pictures.

Review
Ask the group to tell why meat is important for their bodies.

Assessment Strategy
Ask individual children to name one of the foods shown on the food pyramid.

Hearing Impairments: During the story *The Meat Eaters Arrive*, point to the pictures as you read. Make sure that the child can see your lips and mouth as you speak and read the story.

Visual Impairments: Describe the pictures on the food pyramid as you show it. When you read *The Meat Eaters Arrive*, describe the pictures in the book.

Cognitive and/or Developmental Disabilities: Show the child pictures of different types of foods. Sort them into two stacks—those that are meats and those that are not. Model the process, saying, "Is this meat?" and answering yes or no as you put them into stacks. Have the child do this with you and then review the pictures, with the child putting them into the correct pile.

Emotional Disturbance: Seat the child near you during the lesson and while you read *The Meat Eaters Arrive*. Stress the fact that meat helps us to be healthy and that it is good for our bodies to grow strong. Although this is an important fact for all children, it is particularly important for children with emotional disturbance because they tend to select and eat "junk food" more often than other children.

Other Health Impairments/Attention Deficit Hyperactivity Disorder: When reading the story *The Meat Eaters Arrive,* make sure that the child is attending and seated where she is near the book. If the child becomes restless, have everyone take a stretch break and then finish the story.

Orthopedic Impairments: Make sure that the child is positioned so that she can see the pictures when you read the story *The Meat Eaters Arrive.*

Curriculum Connections

✦ **Art:** Label a chart "Our Favorite Meat." Ask the children to cut out (or draw) pictures of meat products to glue on the chart. Add the chart to the classroom display begun during the introductory lesson.

✦ **Fine Motor:** Developing fine motor skills provides children with the hand skills that they need when they begin to write. Crack pecans or walnuts for the children and place them on the Discovery Center so children can remove the meat in the nuts to eat. This activity will enhance their fine motor development. Save the shells for children to glue onto paper (or poster board) to make an art collage in the Art Center.
Safety note: Check for allergies to nuts before setting up this activity.

✦ **Science:** At the Discovery Center, show small groups of children pictures of cat and dog food. Talk to the children about pet food containing meat. Discuss the importance of meat (and proteins) for keeping animals strong and healthy, just like meat is helpful to humans' bodies.

Milk and Milk Products

Note: If you learn through the survey you sent home (see Introduction to Food on page 254) that a child is lactose intolerant, be sensitive to his needs as you present this lesson. As in the previous lesson, be aware of and sensitive to children whose families are vegetarians.

Time
20 minutes

Materials
poster of the food pyramid
picture of a cow or dairy farm
The Milk Makers by Gail
    Gibbons, *Milk: From Cow
    to Carton* by Aliki, or any
    other book about milk
empty, clean containers of
    dairy products (milk, ice
    cream, cottage cheese,
    cheese, yogurt, and so
    on)

Objectives

Children will:
1. Identify that milk is part of the dairy group on the food pyramid.
2. Name at least one milk product.

Lesson

✦ As children gather for Circle or Group Time, show them the food pyramid poster. Point out the various parts of the poster. Say, "Yesterday, we talked about the meat food group. Today we're going to talk about the milk and cheese food group and why we need to drink and eat these products."

✦ Ask children if they remember the nutrient in meat that is important to humans. Tell them that milk also has protein in it (as well as calcium, which helps the bones and teeth, and vitamins and minerals).

✦ Explain that reason babies need a lot of milk or formula because they are growing very fast and they need the nutrients in milk to help them become strong.

✦ Ask children if they know where milk comes from. Show the picture of the cow (or dairy farm) and tell children that cows provide the milk we drink daily.

✦ Read *The Milk Makers* by Gail Gibbons, *Milk: From Cow to Carton* by Aliki, or any other book about milk to the group.

✦ Afterwards, ask children if they know what food items are made from milk. As each dairy product is mentioned, show the empty container from the collection you have available.

Modifications/Accommodations

Autism: Use pictures or clip art to assist the child as you present the lesson. Use the accommodations described below for Speech or Language Impairments if the child has difficulty responding to questions. For the assessment, have the child select a milk product from a group of pictures.

Speech or Language Impairments: Call on the child to answer questions after one or two children have modeled the type of responses. If the child has difficulty responding to questions, provide a carrier phrase or sentence starter. For example when you ask, "Where does milk come from?" provide the sentence starter for the response: "Milk comes from _____." If the child has difficulty naming a milk product in the assessment, provide names some foods and then ask him to name a milk product.

Hearing Impairments: Make sure that the child is seated across from you so that he can see your mouth as you speak during the lesson. As you present the lesson, show the child pictures associated with milk products. Use gestures or sign language, such as the signs for *milk* and *cow*, during the lesson.

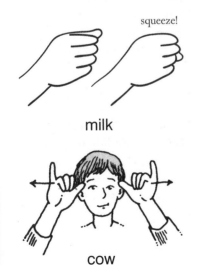

squeeze!

milk

COW

Review

Ask the group to mention things they remember about the book.

Assessment Strategy

Ask individual children to name at least one milk product.

Visual Impairments: When showing the group pictures and reading the book, describe the pictures.

Cognitive and/or Developmental Disabilities: Use simple language and vocabulary as you present the lesson on milk and milk products. For the assessment, show the child several pictures and ask him to find the milk product. Review the concept of milk products during lunch. Throughout the following week, review milk products during meals to ensure that the child learns and retains the concept.

Emotional Disturbance: Seat the child near you during the lesson. Enlist his help by letting him hold materials, put them away, or give objects to classmates. Emphasize the fact that milk helps our bodies to be strong and healthy, and that it is good for us. During lunch or snack time, affirm the child for choosing milk products.

Other Health Impairments/Attention Deficit Hyperactivity Disorder: Make sure that you have the child's attention before you speak. Establish a clear signal to get the child's attention before speaking. Have the child stand up and point to items on the food pyramid chart during the lesson.

Orthopedic Impairments: Make sure that the child is positioned so that he can see the pictures during the lesson.

Curriculum Connections

✦ **Art:** Continue the ongoing classroom display (see Introduction to Food on page 254) by adding a section (or chart) labeled "Milk Is Good for Us." Ask children to cut out (or draw) pictures of dairy products to glue to the display.

✦ **Language and Literacy:** Introduce the poem "The Purple Cow" by Gelett Burgess to the children. Talk about the absurd possibility that purple cows would provide purple milk.

✦ **Snack:** Serve cheese cubes, slices of cheese, or string cheese. Ask the children what nutrients in cheese are important for their bodies. Remind children that milk and milk products are a category of food that humans need every day. Serve leafy green vegetables (especially spinach) that have calcium for children who do not like to or are unable to drink milk.

Fruit and Vegetables

Time
20 minutes

Materials
a picture of a cornucopia filled with fruits and vegetables (or a real one, if possible)
an assortment of fruits and vegetables
Eating the Alphabet: Fruits & Vegetables from A to Z by Lois Ehlert
food pyramid poster

Objectives

Children will:
1. Name at least one fruit or vegetable.
2. State that fruits and vegetables are a food group.

Lesson

✦ Begin the lesson by showing the picture of the cornucopia. Explain that the word *cornucopia* means "horn of plenty." Say, "The word plenty means 'a lot.' When we have plenty of something, such as food, we have a lot of food." The cornucopia is a symbol of food and abundance.

✦ Ask children if they know when Americans celebrate having plenty of food. If they don't mention Thanksgiving, tell them the holiday.

✦ Show the fruits and vegetables and ask children to identify them. Tell them the names of items they may not recognize.

✦ Show the food pyramid and explain that fruits and vegetables make up a large part of it. Fruits and vegetables contain numerous vitamins and minerals that are important for the body's health.

✦ Explain that some fruits and vegetables also provide fiber for the body, which is essential to good health. The fiber in fruits and vegetables fills you up, moves food through the body, and helps you feel full quickly.

✦ Share the alphabet book about fruits and vegetables with the children. Because of the photographic nature of this book, a leisurely look at its contents is a good strategy to use.

✦ Encourage children to talk about the foods as you show them the pictures in the book. Invite them to discuss the fruits and vegetables they like and the ones they are familiar with. Ask, "Are there foods in the book that you have never eaten?"

✦ As children respond to this question, make a note to yourself to bring in specific fruits and vegetables that are unfamiliar to the children in your class.

Modifications/Accommodations

Autism: Use pictures of food and the foods themselves to refer to as you present the lesson. During the review, show pictures of various food groups. Then ask the child to tell you the categories of food after you have sorted them into groups. Use the accommodations described below for Speech or Language Impairments if the child has difficulty responding to questions.

Speech or Language Impairments: Call on the child to answer questions after one or two children have modeled the type of responses. If the child has difficulty responding to questions, provide a carrier phrase or sentence starter. For example when you ask, "Are there foods in the book that you have never eaten?" provide the sentence starter for the response "I have

- **Snack:** Place containers of fruits (bananas, apples, berries, pineapple slices, peaches, and so on) on the snack tables along with spoons and small bowls. Invite the children to make individual fruit salads for their morning snacks. Include a carton of yogurt, too, so children can have a dressing for their salad. Remind the children that yogurt is a milk product.
- **Social Studies:** Ask your grocery store manager for discarded produce posters to put up in your classroom. These posters would be a wonderful addition to your classroom Cooking Center, or you could use them to develop a special interest Grocery Store Center. Ask children to determine where the posters belong in the classroom and provide tools so they can hang the posters up. Assist them as necessary.

Review

Ask children to name the food groups that they have talked about for the last few days (meats, milk and milk products, fruits and vegetables).

Assessment Strategy

Ask individual children to tell what their favorite fruits and vegetables are.

never eaten ___," while showing the child pictures of foods. Show the child the picture of the food pyramid when asking which food groups the class has already learned about in the review section of the lesson. During the assessment, provide pictures of fruits and vegetables before asking the child to tell her favorite fruit and vegetable.

Hearing Impairments: Make sure that the child is seated across from you so that she can see your mouth as you speak during the lesson. As you present the lesson on fruits and vegetables, show the child pictures associated with concepts. During the lesson, use

fruit   vegetable

gestures or sign language for *fruit* and *vegetables*, if the child is learning sign language.

Visual Impairments: Let the child feel actual fruits and vegetables in the cornucopia. As you read the alphabet book, describe the pictures.

Cognitive and/or Developmental Disabilities: Use simple language and vocabulary as you present the lesson on fruits and vegetables. Review the concept of fruits and vegetables later in the day. Throughout the following week, review fruits and vegetables to ensure that the child learns and retains the concept. Provide pictures of fruits and vegetables and help the child sort them into groups of fruits and vegetables. Make sure that there is a good variety of plastic food in the Home Living Center, and point out the fruits and vegetables when the child is playing in this center.

Emotional Disturbance: Seat the child near you during the lesson. Emphasize the need to eat healthy foods like fruits and vegetables. At lunch, encourage the child to at least try fruits and vegetables when they are served. Affirm her for trying the fruits and vegetables.

Other Health Impairments/Attention Deficit Hyperactivity Disorder: Make sure that you have the child's attention before you speak. Establish a clear signal to get the child's attention before speaking. If the child becomes restless during the lesson, have her put materials on your desk.

Orthopedic Impairments: No accommodations are anticipated for this lesson.

Curriculum Connections

- **Art:** Continue the classroom display by adding a section titled "Fruits and Vegetables Are Good for Us." Ask children to draw (or cut out) pictures of fruit and vegetables to glue to the display.

Bread

Time
20 minutes

Materials
loaf of bread
box of cereal
pictures of breads and grain
 products (such as
 crackers)
Bread and Jam for Frances by
 Russell Hoban, or another
 similar title

Objectives

Children will:
1. Identify bread as a category on the food pyramid.
2. Name foods that are made from grains.

Lesson

✦ Tell the children that today they are going
   to learn about another category on the
   food pyramid known as breads and
   grains.
✦ Point to the bread section of the food
   pyramid and tell children that this group
   is the largest section in our diet. Bread
   and cereals are filling, and they help
   people feel full.
✦ Show the book *Bread and Jam for
   Frances* to children and read it to them,
   allowing them to make comments as they
   listen to the story.
✦ Talk about the different types of bread that children
   might eat during the day, reminding them that they
   often eat toast or cereal every morning for breakfast.
✦ Point out that pasta, hamburger and hot dog buns,
   pizza dough, and crackers are part of the bread
   category.

Modifications/Accommodations

Autism: Use pictures to assist the child as you present the lesson. Before
   assessing the child, review the types of bread by showing pictures of them.
   As you go through the pictures, name them. Use the accommodations
   described below for Speech or Language Impairments if the child has
   difficulty responding to questions during the review.
Speech or Language Impairments: Review the different types of bread while
   showing pictures of them. Show the child various food pictures and sort
   them into piles of those that are in the bread and grains category and those
   that are not.
Hearing Impairments: Make sure that the child is seated across from you so
   that he can see your mouth as you speak during the lesson. When reading
   Bread and Jam for Frances, point to the pictures as you read and name
   them. As you present the lesson on breads, make sure that the child can
   see the pictures on the food pyramid as you talk about them.

Review

Ask children to name a bread product that they eat on a regular basis.

Assessment Strategy

Ask individual children to point to the bread and grains category on the food pyramid.

Visual Impairments: Describe the different types of breads as you talk about them. As you read the book *Bread and Jam for Frances*, describe the pictures.

Cognitive and/or Developmental Disabilities: Use simple vocabulary and language as you talk about bread. Show the children pictures of the different types of bread. Use the technique mentioned above in the Speech or Language Accommodations where you sort food pictures into piles of those that are breads and those that are not. Review the different food groups on the food pyramid prior to the assessment. During snacks and meals, point out the foods that are in the bread and grain group.

Emotional Disturbance: Seat the child near you during the lesson. Enlist his help by letting him turn the pages from time to time in the book *Bread and Jam for Frances*. Emphasize the fact that bread and grains are good for us and help our bodies to stay healthy.

Other Health Impairments/Attention Deficit Hyperactivity Disorder: Make sure that you have the child's attention before you speak. Establish a clear signal to get the child's attention before speaking. During the assessment, remind the child to wait his turn by using the sign for *wait*.

wait

Orthopedic Impairments: For the assessment, have the child look at the place on the food pyramid where the bread and grain group is. This will work best if you have a large chart for the food pyramid. If your food pyramid is smaller, you can confirm the food group that the child is looking toward by asking him, "Is it this one?" as you point to the food group that he is looking toward.

Curriculum Connections

✦ **Art:** Continue the classroom display by asking children to draw or cut out pictures of breads to glue onto the section labeled "Breads Are Good for Us."

✦ **Connecting with Home:** Encourage the children's families to purchase various types of breads for children if at all possible.

✦ **Science:** Use crescent-shaped dinner rolls as a base for a berry tart. Help children assemble fresh berries and sugar onto the rolls and then place another triangle on top of the mixture. Bake in an oven at 350° for approximately 15 minutes. Have tarts as a mid-morning snack (or for lunch).

Safety Note: Bake the tarts in a safe area that is away from the children. Be sure tarts are safe for children to handle before serving them for snack or lunch.

Desserts/Sweets

Time
10–15 minutes

Materials
a carrot (or another
    vegetable)
a piece of candy
pictures of desserts (pies,
    cookies, cakes, and ice
    cream)
pictures of fruits, vegetables,
    meats, breads, and dairy
    products

Objectives

Children will:
1. Name two desserts.
2. Explain why desserts need to be eaten in moderation.

Lesson

◆ When children come to Circle or Group Time, have a piece of candy and a carrot on the floor for them to see.
◆ Begin the lesson by asking children to name the two items of food they see in front of them.
◆ Ask them which of the two items is healthier. Explain that the carrot is healthier to eat because it is a vegetable that is high in vitamins and develops good eyesight.
◆ Explain that candy often has a great deal of sugar in it. Say, "Too much candy and other sweets are not good for our bodies. A little bit of sweet food is okay to eat, but too much can harm your body. Sweets are bad for your teeth, and they do not contain many nutrients. Too many sweets can give you a stomach ache, too."
◆ Remind the children that protein-rich foods (meats, milk, and milk products) and foods high in fiber (fruits and vegetables) are better for us to eat than sweets because our bodies need healthy foods.
◆ Tell them that sodas and many juice drinks are usually very high in sugar.
◆ show the children pictures of all types of foods and ask the children to identify which ones are healthy to eat.

Modifications/Accommodations

Autism: When asking the child to name desserts, show pictures of items that are desserts and some that are not. Have the child find the desserts and then name them.

Speech or Language Impairments: When asking the children which food they like to eat when you introduce the lesson, hold up both items. Provide a sentence starter, such as "I like to eat ___," if the child is hesitant to respond. For the review, show pictures of desserts before asking her to name the desserts that she likes to eat.

Hearing Impairments: Make sure that the child is seated across from you so that she can see your mouth as you speak during the lesson. As you present the lesson, show the child pictures or objects associated with desserts. As you present the lesson, use gestures or sign language for *dessert* if the child is learning sign language.

dessert

Review

Ask children to name desserts they enjoy eating.

Assessment Strategy

Show individual children pictures of various types of foods. Ask each child to select the ones that are healthy to eat.

Visual Impairments: When showing the foods, let the child touch them or let her hold plastic food items during the lesson.

Cognitive and/or Developmental Disabilities: Use simple language and vocabulary as you present the lesson. Review the names of selections of healthy desserts after meals. For the assessment, limit the choices to two or three pictures.

Emotional Disturbance: Seat the child next to you during the lesson. Emphasize the fact that we need to eat foods that are good for us and help us to grow healthy and strong. Remind the child that we may want to eat two desserts because they taste good, but we need to only eat one dessert. Show the child a piece of fruit and candy and ask her to find the healthy dessert.

Other Health Impairment/Attention Deficit Hyperactivity Disorder: Emphasize the fact that food helps our bodies to stay healthy. When we eat too many sweets, it is not good for our bodies, and we may have trouble paying attention and finishing the things that we need to do. Emphasize the fact that we can eat healthy desserts.

Orthopedic Impairments: When asking the children to identify foods that are healthy to eat, have the child identify them by naming or looking at them (eye pointing by looking toward the healthy one).

Curriculum Connections

✦ **Art:** Finalize the classroom display by placing a section on the bulletin board labeled "Foods That Are Good for Our Bodies." Have children draw pictures of healthy foods and add them to the display.

✦ **Connecting with Home:** Provide nutritional information for the children's families in a weekly newsletter. Or obtain health brochures from a nutritionist (or a county extension agent) to send home to the children's families. Encourage parents to talk to their children about eating healthy foods.

✦ **Science:** Place the pictures used in the lesson in the Discovery Center. Have the children sort them into two categories: "Foods That Are Good for Our Bodies" and "Foods That Are Not Good for Our Bodies."

Introduction to Clothes

Time
15–20 minutes

Materials
box or bag
clothes
clothing items
non-clothing items such as
    crayons, toy cars, blocks,
    or other items in the
    classroom (used in the
    review)
drawing paper and markers

Objectives

Children will:
1. Identify three articles of clothing.
2. Describe the clothes they are wearing.

Lesson

✦ Before children arrive, place the clothes in the box or bag.

✦ At Circle or Group Time, show the children the box and ask them to guess what is inside of it. Give them clues such as, "The things inside the box are made of cloth," and "Some of the items have buttons." Give the final clue, "The items are things you wear." If children guess specific articles of clothing, respond, "There is a (the item the child named) inside the box but there are other things too." Remove each article of clothing from the box and ask the children to name it and talk about it.

✦ Teach the children the following chant, which is similar to "Going on a Bear Hunt."

Let's Get Dressed by Sharon Lynch
Gonna put on my clothes, (children repeat)
Okay, okay.
Let's go. Let's go.
First put on my underwear, (children repeat and pantomime)
Okay, okay.
Let's go. Let's go.
(Repeat with shirt, pants, socks, shoes)

Now it's time to play,
Okay, okay.
Let's go. Let's go.
Run, run, run. (children repeat and pantomime)
Play all day. (children repeat and pantomime)
Okay, okay.
Let's go. Let's go.

Additional verses:
Time for a bath. (children repeat and pantomime)
Take off my shoes. (children repeat and pantomime)
Take off my socks. (children repeat and pantomime)
Take off my pants. (children repeat and pantomime)
Take off my shirt. (children repeat and pantomime)
Got to take a bath. (children repeat and pantomime)
Put on pajamas. (children repeat and pantomime)
Now it's time for bed. (children repeat and pantomime)
Goodnight.

- **Math:** Cut out different article of clothing, such as shoes, hats, and socks, from different colors of construction paper. Provide these clothing cutouts and challenge the children to sort them by color. Arrange the items by color on poster board to create a bar graph.

Review

Place an article of clothing or a non-clothing item in the bag or box without children seeing you. Choose a volunteer to feel the item without looking. Ask him if it is clothing and if he knows what it is. Repeat with the other children, using other items.

Assessment Strategy

Provide drawing paper and markers and ask each child to make a picture of his favorite clothes. Help the child write the name of the clothing on the back of the picture. Then ask each child to tell about the clothes he is currently wearing.

Modifications/Accommodations

Autism: When introducing the lesson, give clear, direct clues about what is in the box when addressing this child. When asking the child to name and describe clothing, call on several other children first so they can provide a model of the appropriate responses.

Speech or Language Impairments: When removing the clothing from the box, model several responses and then ask the child to name the clothing and describe it. Provide more clues if the child needs them. If needed, tell the child the name of the clothing and have him repeat it.

Hearing Impairments: Seat the child across from you where he can see your face and mouth. Use gestures or some basic signs for clothing items, such as *shirt* and *pants*, if the child is learning sign language.

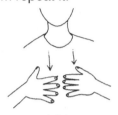

shirt

Visual Impairments: Let the child touch and feel the items during the lesson. The child may need some assistance in the pantomime during the chant.

Cognitive and/or Developmental Disabilities: Speak in short, simple sentences during the lesson. The child will likely need suggestions of types of clothes to draw during the assessment activity.

pants

Emotional Disturbance: Seat the child next to you. Affirm him for participating. Maintain close supervision during the assessment activity. Ask the child questions with that are likely to be familiar to him, questions that he will be successful answering.

Other Health Impairments/Attention Deficit Hyperactivity Disorder: Make sure that you have the child's attention before speaking or giving instructions. Have the children stand up during the chant.

Orthopedic Impairments: This child may need assistance with pantomime during the chant. Also, the child will need hand-over-hand assistance in making the picture during the assessment.

Curriculum Connections

- **Dramatic Play:** Provide clothing for various types of occupations in the Dramatic Play Center.
- **More Dramatic Play:** Provide doll clothes and dolls of both genders in the Home Living Center.
- **Language and Literacy:** Provide books and stories that include pictures about clothing, such as "The Three Little Kittens," "The Emperor's New Clothes," "Little Red Riding Hood," and *Mrs. McNosh Hangs Up Her Wash* by Sarah Weeks.

Shirts

Time
15 minutes

Materials
shopping bag
different types of shirts
box of children's clothing

Objectives

Children will:
1. Identify shirts from an array of different types of shirts (T-shirt, tank top, button-up shirt).
2. Identify the parts of a shirt: sleeves, neck, collar, buttons, front, and back.

Lesson

✦ Show the children a shopping bag filled with shirts and have them guess what is in the bag. Give the children clues until someone guesses that there are shirts in the bag.

✦ Take three different types of shirts out of the bag, one at a time: a child's T-shirt; a woman's flowered, button-up blouse; and a men's polo shirt.

✦ Ask the child who might wear each of these shirts.

✦ Talk about how the shirts are the same and how they are different.

✦ Ask the children to show you the various parts of the shirt, such as the sleeves, neck, collar, buttons, front, and back.

✦ Ask the children to find someone in the class who has a shirt with sleeves, a shirt with a collar, and a shirt with buttons.

✦ Ask the children to locate the front, back, and neck of their clothing. Talk about the fact that they all are probably wearing clothing with a front and a back.

✦ Sing the following song with the children:

Put Your Finger on Your Shirt by Sharon Lynch
Tune: "If You're Happy and You Know It"
Put your finger on your shirt, on your shirt.
Put your finger on your shirt, on your shirt.
Put your finger on your shirt, put your finger on your shirt,
Put your finger on your shirt, on your shirt.

✦ Repeat the verse, substituting neck, sleeve, front, back, and so on into the song.

Modifications/Accommodations

Autism: During the shopping bag part of the lesson, provide simple clues to help this child guess. For the assessment, model finding the shirts and then have the child do it independently. Repeat this with naming the parts of a shirt.

Review

Play Simon Says, and say, "Simon says, 'Touch your shirt.'" Repeat with other parts of the shirt.

Assessment Strategy

Show each child a box of children's clothing and ask her to find all of the shirts. Then ask her to show you a sleeve, neck, front, back, button, and collar.

Speech or Language Impairments: When asking how the shirts are the same, begin with the carrier phrase, "They both ___. " When asking how they are different, use the carrier phrase, "This one is red, but the other one is ___." For the song, accept the child's gestures if she is not able to sing the song.

Hearing Impairments: Seat the child across from you where she can see your face. Use gestures or pictures when talking about shirts.

Visual Impairments: Assist the child in touching and finding the various parts of the shirt. If needed, help with the motions of the song.

Cognitive and/or Developmental Disabilities: Use short, simple sentences and explanations in the discussion of shirts. Repeat key words such as *front*, *back*, *neck*, *collar*, *buttons*, and *sleeve*. For the assessment, show the clothing one at a time and ask if it is a shirt. Then ask the child to show you the various parts of the shirt.

Emotional Disturbance: Seat the child next to you and affirm her participation and appropriate behavior. When you finish with an item, have the child put it in the "finished box." When playing Simon Says, do not omit the word Simon for any direction.

Other Health Impairments/Attention Deficit Hyperactivity Disorder: Ensure that the child is looking at you before you speak or give instructions. Stand up to sing the song.

Orthopedic Impairments: Assist the child in locating the parts of her clothing and with the motions of the song.

Curriculum Connections

✦ **Art:** Give the children cutouts of a body and ask them to draw a shirt and clothing using markers and decorations such as yarn, rickrack, and buttons.

✦ **Language and Literacy:** Place a drawing of a shirt on the bulletin board. Label the shirt and its parts: front, neck, collar, buttons, and sleeve. Have the children name the parts of the shirt when you refer to the picture. Describe parts of the shirt in the picture and have the child guess which part you are talking about.

✦ **Math:** Provide construction paper cutouts of shirts in a variety of colors and sizes. Have the children sort the shirts by color. Then have them sort the shirts by size.

✦ **Social Studies:** Provide pictures of clothing from other countries. Invite the children to describe the clothes, including the shirts.

Pants

Time
15–20 minutes

Materials
small suitcase
various types and sizes of
    pants
other clothing items
chart paper or dry-erase
    board and markers
picture cards of a variety of
    clothing

Objectives

Children will:
1. Identify pants from other articles of clothing.
2. Describe pants (by telling that you wear them on your body, that they cover your legs).

Lesson

◆ Show the children a small suitcase and ask them to guess what you might pack in it. Provide hints to help the children guess pants.

◆ Ask the children who is wearing pants today. Then ask them to tell about the pants they see children wearing.

◆ Show the children several pairs of pants and ask who might wear them. Examples include pants for infants, jeans, women's pants, men's trousers, athletic pants, and children's pants. Ask the children to tell about each pair of pants.

◆ On a chart, make three columns to list the characteristics of pants. In the first column, write things that pants always have (such as two pants legs), and in the second column, write things that pants sometimes have (such as a zipper). In the last column, write things that pants never have (such as sleeves).

◆ Have the children help you complete the chart. Name the item, such as a zipper, and ask if pants always, sometimes, or never have a zipper.

Things Pants Always Have	Things Pants Sometimes Have	Things Pants Never Have

counting by ones and twos.

Review
Have the children choose cards with pictures of clothing. Ask them if they have a picture of pants or another type of clothing.

Assessment Strategy
Have individual children help you pack a suitcase for a pretend trip. Place shirts and socks in the suitcase, and then ask the child to help you find three specific pairs of pants; for example, a pair that is a specific color, a pair with a zipper, and a pair with pockets. Then ask the child to help you make a list of the pants that he packed. As the child describes the pants, write down what he says.

Modifications/Accommodations

Autism: When introducing the lesson, provide simple, direct clues to help the child guess what is inside the suitcase. Call on the child after others have responded to questions.

Speech or Language Impairments: Show the child items he may not know the names of, such as zipper or elastic. Before the review activity, preview the pictures of the articles of clothing.

Hearing Impairments: Seat the child across from you so he can see your face and mouth. Refer to clothing and pictures of clothing during the lesson.

Visual Impairments: Describe pictures and allow the child to touch and feel items and articles of clothing.

Cognitive and/or Developmental Disabilities: Use short, simple sentences in your explanations. Repeat correct responses. Show the child the items that he may not know the names of. During the assessment, limit the number of pairs of pants for the child to choose from in packing the suitcase.

Emotional Disturbance: Seat the child near you. Enlist his help by having him put materials in the suitcase as you finish with them. Affirm him for helping and for appropriate behavior.

Other Health Impairments/Attention Deficit Hyperactivity Disorder: Make sure that you have the child's attention before speaking or giving instructions. When doing the individual assessment, have this child participate first and then let him go to centers.

Orthopedic Impairments: This child may need help in drawing cards during the review activity and in packing clothes during the assessment.

Curriculum Connections

+ **Dramatic Play:** Provide pants worn by people with different kinds of occupations, such as surgical scrubs, clown pants, football pants, and so on.
+ **Games:** The classic *Ants in the Pants* or *Ants in the Pants Cootie Game* both provide practice in fine motor skills for children ages four and older.
+ **Language and Literacy:** Provide books in the Library Center about clothing and pants. Some suggestions include *The Emperor's New Clothes* by Hans Christian Andersen and Virginia Lee Burton, *Clothing Around the World* by Kelly Doudna, *Mrs. McNosh Hangs Up Her Wash* by Sarah Weeks, *Ella Sarah Gets Dressed* by Margaret Chodos-Irvine, and *Animals Should Definitely Not Wear Clothing* by Judi Barrett. Ask the child to choose a book to be read to the class, or let the children select a book that she can check out and take home.
+ **Math:** Provide cutouts of pants in a variety of colors and sizes. Have the children sort them by color and size. Then count the total number of legs,

Dresses

Time
20 minutes

Materials
Ella Sarah Gets Dressed by Margaret Chodos-Irvine
pictures of different types of dresses
paper
markers
bear cutout (see illustration) from construction paper for each child
small paper dresses for each bear

Objectives

Children will:
1. Explain what a dress is.
2. Describe different characteristics of dresses.

Lesson

✦ Read the book *Ella Sarah Gets Dressed* by Margaret Chodos-Irvine.
✦ Discuss what Ella Sarah wants to wear and the different outfits her family wants her to wear.
✦ Review the pictures in the book as you talk about the clothing. Explain that people wear a dress by itself instead of two pieces of clothing like shirts and pants. Some people may wear a jumper, which is a dress with a shirt under it.
✦ Ask the children, "Who is wearing a dress today?" If someone is wearing a dress, discuss what her dress looks like and if it is long or short.
✦ Talk about all of the different styles, colors, and lengths of dresses. Show pictures of different types of dresses, including dresses worn by people in other parts of the world.
✦ Provide paper and markers and ask the children to design a dress.
✦ If any boys or girls are reluctant to do this, provide an alternative by asking them what type of clothing they would like to draw. Affirm them for drawing their clothing picture.

Modifications/Accommodations

Autism: Use gestures or simple signs, such as the sign for *dress*, as you read the story and discuss dresses. Point to parts of dresses in the pictures as you talk about them. Show the child pictures of clothing, including several different dresses. Ask the child to find the dresses.

Speech or Language Impairments: During the assessment activity, provide a carrier phrase to help the child describe the dress, such as "This dress is ____." If the child has difficulty describing the dress during the assessment, provide suggestions by asking, for example, "Is it long or short?" or "Is it red or green?"

Hearing Impairments: Seat the child where she can see your face as you discuss dresses and read the story. Refer to the pictures frequently as you read the story.

Visual Impairments: Describe the pictures as you read the book. For the assessment, let the child feel a small cloth dress and describe it.

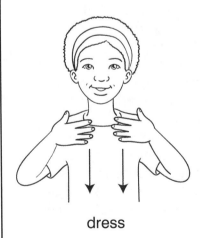

dress

Review

Dress the bear cutouts by giving the children their own bear cutout and little construction paper dresses to fit the cutout. Let each child choose a dress, decorate it, and glue it onto her bear.

Assessment Strategy

Show each child pictures of different types of dresses and ask her to pick a dress and describe it.

Cognitive and/or Developmental Disabilities: Use short sentences and simple language as you discuss dresses. For the assessment activity, ask the child to find the dress that is ____ (name a characteristic of the dress such as long, short, red, and so on).

Emotional Disturbance: Seat the child close to you. Provide close supervision during the review activity of dressing the bear.

Other Health Impairments/Attention Deficit Hyperactivity Disorder: Make sure that you have the child's attention before speaking and giving instructions during the activities. Enlist the child's help in turning the pages from time to time during the story.

Orthopedic Impairments: Assist the child in using markers to make her own dress and in dressing the bear. If necessary, provide hand-over-hand assistance.

Curriculum Connections

✦ **Art:** Cut sponges into dress shapes. Invite the children to dip the sponges into paint and create dress prints on paper.

✦ **Language and Literacy:** Take an imaginary walk through a clothing store. "Let's go to a clothing store. We can find all of the dresses we talked about in class. We are passing through the shirts, and now the pants, and the shoes. Here are our dresses. These are the colorful dresses, and these are the plain dresses. Here are the short dresses. Does anyone see the long dresses? What do think you will see in the clothing store?"

✦ **Math:** Provide construction paper dresses in different colors and lengths. The children sort the dresses that are alike and count the number of dresses in each group. Make a graph on a sheet of poster board by lining up all of the dresses by color. Then make a graph by lining up all of the long, medium, and short dresses.

✦ **Science:** Provide pieces of cloth from dresses of different materials and colors and a magnifying glass for the children to inspect the pieces of cloth.

Shoes and Socks

Time

15–20 minutes

Materials

Shoes by Elizabeth Winthrop or *Shoes, Shoes, Shoes* by Ann Morris

different types of shoes and socks

bag

small shoe such as a doll shoe

five washcloths

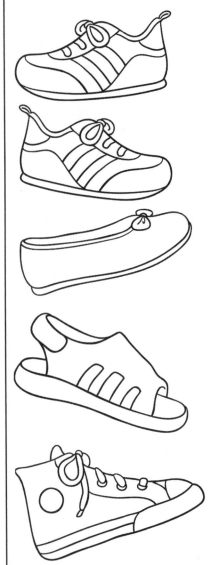

Objectives

Children will:

1. Distinguish between shoes and socks.
2. Describe a pair of shoes or socks.

Lesson

◆ Read *Shoes* by Elizabeth Winthrop or *Shoes, Shoes, Shoes* by Ann Morris. Ask the children to show their socks and shoes.

◆ Remove different types of shoes from a bag, one at a time. Ask the children to describe them. Use a variety of shoes, such as slippers, sneakers, men's dress shoes, high heels, baby shoes, sandals, flip flops, ballet slippers, and so on.

◆ Ask who might wear each type of shoe and what the person might do when wearing them.

◆ Show different types of socks (athletic socks, slipper socks, dress socks, and so on), and ask the children to tell about them.

◆ Ask how shoes and socks are similar and different.

◆ Talk about what would happen if we didn't have shoes and socks.

Modifications/Accommodations

Autism: Provide pictures or clip art to refer to during the lesson. For example, when asking who might wear a type of shoe, show the child pictures of people who might wear it.

Speech or Language Impairments: When asking how shoes are similar, begin with the carrier phrase, "They both _____," and then have the child tell how they are similar. When asking how they are different, say, "This one is big but that one is _____." In the child is unable to respond during the review, provide suggested descriptions such as, "Is it big or little?" or "Is it black or white?"

Hearing Impairments: Seat the child across from you so that he can see your face and mouth. Provide objects and pictures to refer to as you present the lesson.

Visual Impairments: Let the child feel and touch the shoes and socks as you show them to the class. During the assessment activity let the child feel what is under each washcloth.

Cognitive and/or Developmental Disabilities: During the game for the assessment, use three washcloths instead of five. The accommodations under Speech or Language Impairments also are appropriate for this child.

Emotional Disturbance: Before the activity where the children find the person with the mate to their shoe or sock, remind them to walk and not run.

Review

Give each child a shoe and have him find the child holding the other shoe in the pair. Have each pair of children tell about their shoes. Repeat this game with socks. Explain that shoes and socks come in pairs because we have two feet.

Assessment Strategy

Play Find the Shoe by placing a small shoe under one of five washcloths while the child hides his eyes. Place other objects such as a small toy car, a block, or other objects commonly found in the classroom under the other washcloths. The class counts to 10 and then child finds the shoe. This activity promotes both memory and self-control because it requires the child to remember what he was searching for and to stay focused on what he is looking for. Give every child a turn to play. Repeat this game later in the day or the next day with Find the Sock.

Other Health Impairments/Attention Deficit Hyperactivity Disorder: Make sure that you have the child's attention and when you read the story. Have the child help to turn the pages of the book from time to time.

Orthopedic Impairments: Provide physical assistance for the game Find the Shoe. When finding a partner with the same shoe or sock during the lesson, the child may need physical assistance as well.

Curriculum Connections

✦ **Art:** Have the children decorate construction paper shoes with yarn, markers, sequins, string, and braid.
✦ **Dramatic Play:** Provide shoes worn by people from different occupations and cultures for the Dramatic Play Center. Suggestions include cowboy boots, work boots, moccasins, white nurse's shoes, high heels, dance shoes, and so on.
✦ **Language and Literacy:** Put books in the Library Center about shoes. Some suggestions include *The Soles of Your Feet* by Genichiro Yagyu; and *Shoes, Shoes, Shoes* by Ann Morris. Ask the child to choose a book to be read to the class, or let the children select a book to check out and take home.
✦ **Math:** Provide pairs of socks for matching and counting. Model counting by ones and twos.

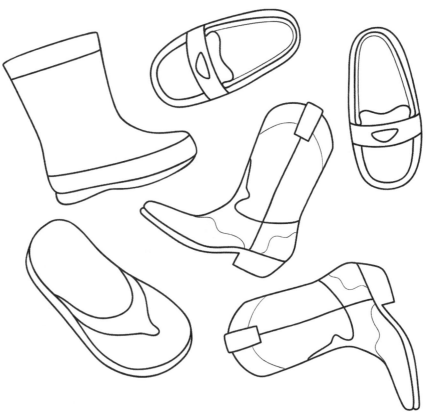

Hats

Time
15–20 minutes

Materials
hat
hatbox or cardboard box
different types of hats

Objectives

Children will:
1. Explain why and when people wear hats.
2. Select a hat when shown different types of clothing

Lesson

✦ Place a hat inside a hatbox or cardboard box. Show the children the box and ask them to guess what is inside. Provide clues to help them to guess.

✦ Ask the children to tell you what they know about hats.

✦ Show different types of hats and ask the children to talk about who might wear each type of hat.

✦ Explain that we wear hats to protect our heads from the sun, cold, rain, and so on.

✦ Show hats with brims and talk about how they keep the sun out of our eyes.

✦ Show a knit cap and explain how it keeps our head warm in the winter when it is cold outside.

✦ Recite the following fingerplay with the children:

My Hat, It Has Three Corners (author unknown)
My hat, it has three corners, (put hand on head, then show three fingers)
Three corners has my hat (put hand on elbow, then on head)
And had it not three corners (show three fingers, then put hand on elbow)
Then it would not be my hat. (shake head side to side and put hand on head)

✦ Repeat several times to encourage the children to participate.

Modifications/Accommodations

Autism: Use the sign for *hats* or pictures of hats to help the child as you talk about hats. For the assessment, use the carrier phrase, "People wear hats because _____" instead of the "why" question if the child has difficulty with "why" questions.

Speech or Language Impairments: For the assessment, provide a sentence starter rather than a "wh" question, For example, say, "We wear these hats when it is _____," or "These are hats we wear in the winter. Those are hats we wear in the _____." Then ask when we wear the particular type of hat.

Hearing Impairments: Seat the child across from you where she can see your face. Make sure that you refer to concrete objects or pictures during the discussion of hats.

Visual Impairments: Allow the child to touch and feel the hats. During the song, help the child make the motions at first.

hat

Review

Give each child a hat and let each child have a turn to describe her hat.

Assessment Strategy

Provide several winter hats and summer hats. Ask the children, one at a time, to help sort them into piles (cold weather and hot weather). Then ask the child when and why people wear these hats.

Cognitive and/or Developmental Disabilities: Use short, simple sentences in your discussion of hats. For the assessment, help the child sort the hats into piles for hot weather and cold weather. Then ask the child to do this with less assistance.

Emotional Disturbance: Seat the child next to you during the discussion. Affirm participation and have her hold the items in a "finished box" as you finish using them.

Other Health Impairments/Attention Deficit Hyperactivity Disorder: Make sure that you have the child's attention before you begin speaking or showing him the items used in the lesson. Have the children stand up to sing the song.

Orthopedic Impairments: For the song, help the child make the motions. For the assessment activity, help her place the items into the piles.

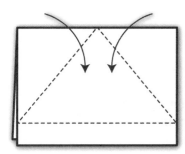

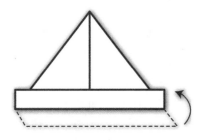

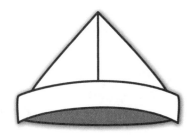

Curriculum Connections

+ **Art:** Make three-cornered hats with the children. Demonstrate each step and help the children as needed. Take a double sheet of newspaper and fold it in the middle. With the fold at the top, fold the corners down to meet in the center. This makes a triangle on top of two rectangle flaps. Then fold the flap up in the front and bend the corners over. Turn the hat over. Repeat with the other flap to make a triangle. Then open the hat in the middle. Push the two end points together with the center poking out to form a square. The bottom points on the square become flaps. Then fold the front one up so the point meets the top point of the triangle. Finally, turn the hat over and fold up the other point.

+ **Dramatic Play:** Provide hats from many countries and cultures in the Dramatic Play Center (for example, a sombrero, top hat, hijab, cowboy hat, a pirate hat, and a German Alpine hat). Talk about where the hats are worn.

+ **More Dramatic Play:** Provide hats from different occupations in the Dramatic Play Center and discuss who wears each type of hat.

+ **Language and Literacy:** Provide books including hats in the Library Center. Some suggestions include *The Cat in the Hat* by Dr. Seuss; *Aunt Flossie's Hats (and Crab Cakes Later)* by Elizabeth Fitzgerald Howard; *Caps, Hats, Socks, and Mittens: A Book About the Four Seasons* by Louise Borden; *The Hat* by Jan Brett; and *Miss Hunnicutt's Hat* by Jeff Brumbeau. Ask the child to choose a book to be read to the class, or let the children select a book to check out and take home.

+ **Math:** Provide hat cutouts of different colors. Invite the children to sort them by color or line them up on poster board with lines drawn to create a bar graph.

Sweaters and Coats

Time

15–20 minutes

Materials

small suitcase with a coat and a sweater in it

pictures of jeans, shirts, socks, sweaters, and coats

pictures of different weather conditions (snow, rain, sunshine)

Objectives

Children will:

1. Identify a coat or sweater when presented with different types of clothing.
2. Describe a coat or sweater and why it is worn.

Lesson

✦ Show the children a small suitcase and tell them you are going on a trip where it is cold. Ask them to guess what you will pack in your suitcase.

✦ Provide hints until someone guesses a coat.

✦ Open the suitcase and take out a coat. Ask the children about the coat, pointing to items on the coat to elicit comments.

✦ Next, ask them what you would bring if the weather was cool, but not cold. Provide hints until they guess that it is a sweater.

✦ Open the suitcase and take out the sweater. Ask the children to describe the sweater.

✦ Ask how a coat and sweater are similar and different.

✦ Say the following chant with the children:

We're Going Up North by Sharon Lynch
Tune: "Going on a Bear Hunt"
We're going up north (children repeat)
Okay, okay.
Let's go. Let's go.
I feel a wind. (children repeat)
Now I'm getting cool. (children repeat)
Gotta get a sweater. (children repeat)
Put on the sleeves. (children repeat)
Button up the buttons. (children repeat)
Okay, okay.
Let's go. Let's go.
I feel something cold. (children repeat)
I see something white. (children repeat)
It's starting to snow. (children repeat)

Now I'm freezing cold. (children repeat)
Gotta get my coat. (children repeat)
Put on the sleeves. (children repeat)
Pull up the hood. (children repeat)
Zip up the zipper. (children repeat)
Now I'm nice and warm. (children repeat)
I see a house. (children repeat)
Let's go inside. (children repeat)
It's warm inside. (children repeat)
Take off the coat. (children repeat)
Take off the sweater. (children repeat)
I'm getting tired. (children repeat)
I'm ready for bed. (children repeat)
Let's go to sleep. (curl up and pretend to sleep)

Review

Provide pictures of sweaters, coats, and different weather conditions. Ask the children to match the weather pictures with the pictures of sweaters and coats.

Assessment Strategy

Show individual children pictures of coats, jeans, shirts, socks, and other clothing items. Ask the child to find the coat and tell when he would wear a coat. Also, ask him to describe the coat. Repeat at a later time with sweaters.

Modifications/Accommodations

Autism: When asking the child to guess what is in the suitcase, provide simple hints such as, "You wear it when it's cold." To elicit comments, call on the child after others have modeled the response. Point to something on the coat or sweater and ask him to tell about it.

Speech or Language Impairments: When asking how a coat and sweater are similar, provide a carrier phrase such as, "They both _____," and then ask the child how they are the same. If the child cannot repeat the words during the chant, encourage the child to at least do the motions.

Hearing Impairments: Seat the child across from you so that he can see your mouth and face. Refer to objects as pictures as you present the lesson.

Visual Impairments: Let the child feel the suitcase, coat, and sweater. Describe the pictures verbally.

Cognitive and/or Developmental Disabilities: Speak in short, simple sentences. For the assessment, use objects or realistic pictures. Instead of describing the items, ask him to find the one that is blue, or to find the one that has a zipper, and so on.

Emotional Disturbance: Seat the child near you. Make sure that you make eye contact with him during the chant and encourage him to participate. Emphasize the importance of wearing coats and sweaters in cold weather to stay warm.

Other Health Impairments/Attention Deficit Hyperactivity Disorder: Make sure that you have the child's attention before beginning instruction. Use a visual cue or tap to get his attention before giving him instructions. If the child seems restless, have all the children stand for the chant "We're Going Up North."

Orthopedic Impairments: Provide physical assistance for the child to pat his lap and make motions during the chant "We're Going Up North." During the review matching activity, the child may need physical assistance as well.

Curriculum Connections

✦ **Language and Literacy:** Provide books that include coats and sweaters in the Library Center. Give the children turns to select books to be read to the class during another part of the day. Some titles include *A New Coat for Anna* by Harriet Ziefert, *Charlie Needs a Cloak* by Tomie dePaola, and *Joseph's Amazing Coat* by Teddy Slater.

✦ **Science:** Provide a magnifying glass so the children can look at samples of fabric and yarns used for making coats and sweaters.

✦ **Social Studies:** Provide small plastic knitting needles and yarn to show how sweaters are made. Try to get a sample of sheep's wool or goat mohair for the children to see what wool coats and sweaters are made from.

Mittens and Gloves

Time
15–20 minutes

Materials
Hats, Socks, and Mittens: A Book about the Four Seasons by Louise Borden
gloves and mittens
various types of gloves (gardening glove, rubber glove, leather glove)
construction paper
markers
decorations, such as rickrack, braid, and sequins (optional)
glue

Objectives

Children will:
1. Identify why and when we wear gloves and mittens.
2. Tell how mittens and gloves are the same and different.

Lesson

◆ Read *Caps, Hats, Socks, and Mittens: A Book about the Four Seasons* by Louise Borden. Talk about why we need to wear mittens and gloves.
◆ Show the children a glove and a mitten. Ask them how they are the same and how they are different. Emphasize that they both protect us from the cold.
◆ Show different types of gloves (gardening glove, rubber glove, leather glove). Talk about who uses them and when.
◆ Ask what would happen if we did not have gloves.

Modifications/Accommodations

Autism: Use pictures or clip art to support concepts in the lesson as you discuss them. Demonstrate how gloves and mittens protect your hands by having the child hold a piece of ice with and without a glove.

Speech or Language Impairments: Instead of "wh" questions, use carrier phrases, such as "We wear glove to _____," or "We wear mittens in the _____." Then you can ask the "when" or "why" questions. Use this technique in the lesson and in the assessment. If the child is not able to respond to the questions, then provide several responses to choose from, such as, "Do we wear mittens in the winter or summer?" or "Do we wear gloves when we are cold or when we are hot?"

Hearing Impairments: Seat the child so that she can see your mouth and face. Hold up the glove or mitten close to the child so that she sees what you are referring to as you present the lesson.

Visual Impairments: Let the child feel the gloves and mittens. Describe the pictures as you read the book.

Cognitive and/or Developmental Disabilities: Use simple, short sentences, repeating concepts that you present to the large group. Provide verbal cues during the assessment. If the child does not understand the "when" and "why" questions, then have her repeat, "We wear mittens and gloves when it is cold to keep our hands safe and warm)." Use the carrier phrase technique in the Speech or Language Impairments.

Emotional Disturbance: Seat the child close to you and affirm appropriate behavior. Emphasize that we wear gloves and mittens to keep our bodies safe and warm.

Review

Show the children pictures of mittens and gloves. Ask the children to identify each picture. Count the "fingers" in the glove and the mitten. Ask how many fingers go into the thumb and the pad of each mitten. Ask how the mittens and gloves are the same, and then ask how they are different.

Assessment Strategy

Help individual children trace around their hand on a piece of construction paper (fingers apart to make a glove and fingers together to make a mitten). Ask why people wear gloves or mittens. Write their responses on the back of their pictures. Ask them to decorate their gloves or mittens with rickrack, braid, or sequins.

Other Health Impairments/Attention Deficit Hyperactivity Disorder: Be sure that you have the child's attention before speaking or demonstrating concepts. Enlist the child's help in turning the pages in the book from time to time as you read it.

Orthopedic Impairments: Help the child decorate her glove or mitten, if needed.

Curriculum Connections

✦ **Dramatic Play:** In the Dramatic Play Center, provide dress-up clothing for cool weather. Include several sets of gloves and mittens of different sizes for this center.

✦ **Language and Literacy:** Provide books in the Library Center that include mittens and gloves. Some selections include *What's the Weather Today?* by Allan Fowler, *Math for All Seasons* by Greg Tang, and the children's classic story "The Three Little Kittens" (many versions available). Allow different children to select a book to be read to the class.

✦ **Math:** Provide several pairs of gloves and mittens for independent matching. Using mittens, count the number of fingers in the pads of each pair of mittens and the number of thumbs in each pair. Use gloves to demonstrate counting by fives. (Note: The goal of this activity is not to teach children to count by fours with mittens or fives with gloves, but to demonstrate different ways of counting.)

✦ **Social Studies:** Provide different types of gloves and discuss who wears them and why. Show gloves such as knit gloves, leather gloves, rubber dishwashing gloves, surgical gloves, gardening gloves, and heavy winter gloves.

Introduction to Toys

Note: In preparation for the toys theme, send a note home to families announcing that the class will have a Toy Fair at the end of the unit. Explain that children can bring one toy, with the child's name on it, to school on an assigned day.

Time
20 minutes

Materials
variety of age-appropriate toys
sheet or small blanket

Objectives

Children will:
1. Describe a favorite toy.
2. Name at least three toys.

Review
As children move to Center Time, ask each child to name a favorite toy.

Assessment Strategy
Using the toy display, ask individual children to name specific toys.

Lesson

+ Begin the lesson by asking children to name a favorite toy. Ask individual children to tell why it is their favorite. Tell the children about your favorite toy as you were growing up.
+ Show the toys that you collected for the lesson and display them in the circle. Ask the children to cover their eyes for a moment as you cover one of the toys. Call on a volunteer to identify the toy that has been covered.
+ Continue this game until all of the children have had an opportunity to play.

Modifications/Accommodations

Autism: During the assessment ask the child to point to a specific toy instead of naming it. For example, "Can you show me the teddy bear?"

Speech or Language Impairments: Use a lead-in sentence when asking about why a toy is a child's favorite. For example, "My teddy bear is my favorite toy because _____."

Hearing Impairments: Show a picture or a sample toy when you talk about your favorite toy when you were a child. As you talk about each toy, show it or point it out to the child.

Visual Impairments: Allow the child to feel the toys on display. When covering up a toy, allow the child to feel the selected toy and to make a guess based on the tactile experience.

Cognitive and/or Developmental Disabilities: Use only three toys when playing the guessing game. Limiting the number of toys displayed increases the chance of the child guessing correctly.

Emotional Disturbance: Explain the rules about handling toys. During the assessment, explain that we must take good care of the toys. Check for understanding on how to handle the toys by asking the child to restate the rules.

Other Health Impairments/Attention Deficit Hyperactivity Disorder: Provide frequent feedback for appropriate participation in the activity and for keeping focused on the lesson.

Orthopedic Impairments: Position the child so that he has access to all the toys that children are bringing in. Be sure he is in an optimal position to participate in the activity.

Curriculum Connections

+ **Art:** Ask interested children to prepare signs for the upcoming Toy Fair.
+ **Blocks:** Add wheel toys to the Block Center to enhance children's play.
+ **Language and Literacy:** Place encyclopedias showing historical toys in the Library Center for children to study.

Dolls

Time
20 minutes

Materials
dolls, including older dolls
teacher-made corncob doll
(or another historical doll
that might be available)
favorite doll of yours, if
available
William's Doll by Charlotte
Zolotow

Objectives
Children will:
1. Describe their favorite dolls.
2. Identify a historical doll.

Review
Ask the children questions about William's Doll, such as
✦ What toys did William have?
✦ Who bought him his toys?
✦ Why did he want a doll?
✦ Who came to visit?
✦ What did Grandmother do for William?
✦ How did William feel about having his new doll?

Assessment Strategy
Ask individual children to describe a doll they own. (If children do not have a doll, ask them to describe a favorite toy or a stuffed animal.)

Lesson

✦ Tell the children that dolls have been popular children's toys for many years.
✦ Discuss how children of both genders enjoy playing with dolls.
✦ Read *William's Doll* by Charlotte Zolotow.
✦ Show children a historical version of a doll and tell them again that dolls have been favorite toys for many years. Show them the corncob doll, if available, and explain how children played with these types of dolls a long time ago because store-bought dolls were expensive and not always easy to find. Encourage children to ask their parents if they had favorite dolls when they were growing up and show the children your favorite doll, if available.

Modifications/Accommodations

Autism: During the assessment, you may need to have the child show her doll rather than describe it.

Speech or Language Impairments: During the assessment, ask direct questions about the doll. For example, you might ask the child what color the doll's hair is or how big the doll is.

Hearing Impairments: Have the child sit close to you when you read the book.

Visual Impairments: Allow the child to hold the dolls. The child can use the various textures of the dolls to discriminate between each of them.

Cognitive and/or Developmental Disabilities: When reviewing the story, allow the child to look at the photos in the book when responding to the questions.

Emotional Disturbance: Review rules on how to properly handle the dolls. Role play the way to carry and hand dolls to each other.

Other Health Impairments/Attention Deficit Hyperactivity Disorder: Review rules on how to properly handle the dolls. Role play the way to carry and hand dolls to each other.

Orthopedic Impairments: Position the child so that she has access to the dolls. If a child is unable to clearly see or touch the dolls, move the dolls closer to her.

Curriculum Connections

✦ **Art:** Provide materials in the Art Center and encourage children to make dolls or doll clothes.
✦ **Dramatic Play:** Add additional dolls to the Home Living Center. Remember to include dolls from many cultures and dolls with special needs. Consider setting up a nursery in the center. Include a crib or cradle, empty containers of baby powder and baby lotions, and diapers.

Cars and Trucks

Time
20 minutes

Materials
several toy cars and trucks
pictures of cars and trucks
(these may be found at
car dealerships)

Objectives

Children will:
1. Identify a toy car and truck.
2. Compare differences between cars and trucks.

Lesson

◆ Invite the children to the circle by moving around the room, pretending to drive a car and asking the children to join you.
◆ Move to the circle area and ask children to find their places.
◆ Have the toy cars and trucks and pictures on display in the circle. Ask them what they think the lesson is about.
◆ Ask, "Do you like to play with cars and trucks?" "Why?"
◆ Describe one or the toys or one of the pictures and ask a child to pick out the item you are describing. For example, say, "I'm looking at a picture of a big red truck that is driving through mud. Can you find it?"
◆ Continue this activity until most or all of the children have had a turn.
◆ Stand in the circle and ask children to pretend to drive a vehicle while reciting the following chant.

I Like Cars, I Like Trucks by Laverne Warner
I like cars. I like trucks.
I like playing with both of these toys.
I like cars. I like trucks.
They make such wonderful noise!

Modifications/Accommodations

Autism: Use visual cues or picture cards to help the child transition between the activities in the lesson.
Speech or Language Impairments: A child with a language impairment may have a difficult time coming up with descriptive words during the assessment phase of the lesson. Allow other children to respond first and limit the number of toys presented to the individual or group.

Review

As children leave the circle, ask them whether they prefer cars or trucks and to say why.

Assessment Strategy

With individual children or small groups of children, play the description game used in the lesson to determine how well each child uses clues to locate specific items.

Hearing Impairments: When you say the chant and when pretend to drive around the room, stay close to the child with hearing impairments so that he can hear the chant and learn it.

Visual Impairments: When asking the child to find one of the toys in the room, be sure to use very specific words to assist this child. For example, use position words, such as "to the left," "by the door," and so on. Do not use cues that require vision, such as "the red truck" or "the blue truck." Use actual toys rather than pictures for the child. Allow him time to use his tactile abilities to find the object.

Cognitive and/or Developmental Disabilities: Offer choices for why a child likes to play with cars and trucks. For example, say, "Why do we like to play with trucks? Is it because they roll, or they are big, or they make neat noises?"

Emotional Disturbance: Before pretending to drive around the room, remind the children to drive safely, not too fast. We do not want to have an accident. As the child with emotional problems pretends to drive, supervise him closely.

Other Health Impairments/Attention Deficit Hyperactive Disorder: Remain close to the child while he pretends to be a car or truck. Your presence will serve as a reminder to remain focused on the lesson.

Orthopedic Impairments: If a child is in a wheelchair, be sure that the arrangement of the furniture in the room gives him the space to move about while pretending to be a car or truck.

Curriculum Connections

✦ **Math:** Place cars and trucks in the Manipulatives Center for children to sort using various attributes (color, model, or type) or put them in order by size.

✦ **Outdoors:** Take cars and trucks to the playground for the children to play with.

✦ **Sand and Water Table:** Add cars and trucks to the sand table. Provide dump trucks and other vehicles that lend themselves to sand play.

TOYS

Teddy Bears

Time
20 minutes

Materials
collection of soft fabrics (enough for every child to have a piece of cloth)
variety of stuffed animals, including at least one teddy bear

Objectives

Children will:
1. Identify a teddy bear among several toys.
2. Explain why they like (or don't like) teddy bears.

Lesson

- ✦ Begin the lesson by talking about things that are soft. Ask children to name some objects that are soft.
- ✦ Give each child a piece of soft fabric. Ask them to feel it and rub it against their face or skin.
- ✦ Ask children to tell why they like soft fabric.
- ✦ Show them a teddy bear and tell them that it is soft.
- ✦ Ask how many children have teddy bears at home. Call on individual children to describe their teddy bears.
- ✦ Ask why they like their teddy bears.
- ✦ Teach them the following song about teddy bears (or use the traditional "Teddy Bear, Teddy Bear" song):

Teddy Bears by Laverne Warner
Tune: "London Bridge"
Teddy bears are fun to hug, fun to hug, fun to hug.
Teddy bears are fun to hug; they're soft and fuzzy.

Teddy bears are oh so soft, oh so soft, oh so soft.
Teddy bears are oh so soft; I love to hold them.

Modifications/Accommodations

Autism: Some children with autism tend to exhibit stereotypic behavior when given specific textures. For example, they may rub objects repeatedly for 20 minutes or more, while ignoring other events in the classroom. If a child is presented with the soft fabric and seems to be rubbing it against her skin for a prolonged period of time, collect the material. Although the fabric will not harm the child, it may cause her to lose the focus of the lesson.

Speech or Language Impairments: Provide children with articulation disorders the opportunity to practice the song beforehand. If possible, send the lyrics of the song home with the child earlier in the week.

Review

Ask children to say one thing they like about teddy bears.

Assessment Strategy

Ask each child to point to the teddy bear in a display of several stuffed animals.

Hearing Impairments: Use simple sign language, such as the signs for *teddy bear*, *hug*, and *soft*, to support the song.

Visual Impairments: During the assessment, allow the child to touch each object before selecting the teddy bear.

Cognitive and/or Developmental Disabilities: Provide the child with specific choices as to why she likes soft toys.

Emotional Disturbance: Encourage active participation in the activity.

Other Health Impairments/Attention Deficit Hyperactive Disorder: Provide opportunities for the child to move throughout the lesson.

Orthopedic Impairments: Be sure the child is positioned in a manner so she can participate fully in the activity.

teddy bear

hug

soft

Curriculum Connections

✦ **Art:** Place the soft fabric pieces used in the lesson in the Art Center and encourage children to make teddy bears with them.

✦ **Language and Literacy:** Add books about bears to the Library Center. Remember to include *Ask Mr. Bear* by Marjorie Flack and *Corduroy* by Don Freeman.

✦ **More Language and Literacy:** Invite children who are experimenting with print to write a story about their teddy bears.

Balls

Time
20 minutes

Materials
variety of balls

Objectives

Children will:
1. Identify a ball from a collection of toys.
2. Use gross motor skills to throw and catch a ball.

Lesson

◆ Hold up a ball and ask children to identify it.
◆ Ask children how balls move (they roll).
◆ Encourage children to tell how they use balls (in games, to bounce, rolling them, throwing them to one another, and so on).
◆ Ask children to stand. Toss the ball to a child and ask him to toss it back to you. Continue to toss the ball to various children, giving every child an opportunity to catch and toss the ball.
◆ Create pairs of children; the two children stand about 6' apart. One child rolls (or tosses) the ball, and the other child catches the ball. Emphasize the skill of rolling (or tossing) and catching, telling children that accuracy is more important than speed. If pairs of children have difficulty with this skill, intervene and demonstrate how to roll (or toss) the ball and then catch it. **Note:** Consider rolling the ball if you are inside, and tossing or throwing the ball if you are outside.
◆ Play this activity for a few minutes.

Modifications/Accommodations

Autism: When asking children to identify characteristics of balls, use a multiple choice format. For example, "Is a ball round or square?"
Speech or Language Impairments: When asking children to tell how they use balls, allow a few children to respond first. This simple modification will serve a model as to how the child should respond.
Hearing Impairments: Place the child closer to the speaker and use simple sign language to support key words in the lesson, such as the signs for *ball*, *catch*, and *toss*.

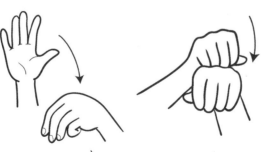

ball   catch   toss

Review

Call on individual children to tell you one characteristic of balls. Ask each child to point to a ball in a collection of toys.

Assessment Strategy

Ask individual children to catch a ball and then throw it back to you.

Visual Impairments: A child with a visual impairment may have a difficult time catching a ball that is thrown to him. In this case, sitting children in pairs of two with legs spread apart (V-shaped) and rolling the ball to each other is more appropriate. The diamond-shaped area created by the two children facing each other will serve as a boundary that keeps the ball within the child's reach.

Cognitive and/or Developmental Disabilities: After giving the directions, check to be sure the child understands what to do. Restate the directions, if necessary.

Emotional Disturbance: Have children participate in a role model activity that demonstrates appropriate use of the ball when rolling, tossing, or throwing it to each other.

Other Health Impairments/Attention Deficit Hyperactive Disorder: Use proximity control when children are in pairs tossing or throwing the ball. Stand close to the child and remind him to toss or throw carefully so that his friend can catch the ball.

Orthopedic Impairments: Apply stabilizing, gripping materials to the balls so a child with grasping and gripping difficulties can participate. For example, place Velcro on the ball and on a glove that the child wears.

Curriculum Connections

✦ **Art:** Add small balls and two or three pans of tempera paint to the Art Center. Demonstrate how balls can be dipped in paint and then rolled onto paper to make intriguing art designs.

✦ **Just for Fun:** Ask children to collect round objects from home to put in a special display titled "Round Things." Show the children how to roll paper or playdough into round shapes to add to the center. Bring in sweet gum balls or acorns from the playground to put on the table. Continue this display until the study of toys is completed.

✦ **Outdoors:** Spend time with small groups of children demonstrating other ball skills, such as rolling them on the ground, bouncing them to other children, throwing them long distances, volleying the balls, or throwing them in the air and catching them.

Blocks

Time
15–20 minutes

Materials
variety of classroom blocks

Objectives

Children will:
1. Learn about stamp pads.
2. Identify at least one use for blocks.

Lesson

✦ Show the children the collection of blocks and identify blocks as toys.
✦ Ask children what they like to do with blocks.
✦ Show various ways that blocks can be used:
   ✦ as foundations for inclined planes;
   ✦ as foundations for shelves or tables;
   ✦ as platforms for roads for cars and trucks;
   ✦ in buildings, towers, and bridges;
   ✦ substitutes for other objects (for example, planes or machines);
   ✦ as steps or stairs; and
   ✦ as fences or enclosures.

Modifications/Accommodations

Autism: Provide positive reinforcement for participation in the activity.

Speech or Language Impairments: During the assessment phase of the lesson, provide a group of objects, some of which are toys. For example, provide a spoon, a pencil, and a block and ask her to find the toy. If the child does not locate the block as a toy, explain that toys are things that we play with. Then ask her to find the toy.

Hearing Impairments: Be sure the child is sitting in a place where she can clearly see you as you speak. The closer the child is to the person speaking, the clearer her auditory intake will be.

Visual Impairments: Allow a child with a visual impairment to manipulate and feel the positions of the blocks as you discuss how blocks can be used.

Cognitive and/or Developmental Disabilities: Simplify the vocabulary used in describing the ways blocks can be used. Words such as *foundations*, *inclines*, *enclosures*, or *platforms* may need to be explained or substituted. When using this vocabulary in the lesson, always pair the easier word with the more difficult one. For example, when using the word *foundation*, state that blocks can be used as a foundation or *bottom* for buildings. Although this is helpful for all children, it is especially important that this child have the added information. Also, use gestures in your discussion. For example, when talking about a *tall tower*, make a gesture upward with both hands as you speak.

Review

Ask each child to tell how she uses blocks when she plays with them.

Assessment Strategy

Ask each child whether blocks are toys. Ask for an explanation if any child responds with "no."

Emotional Disturbance: Review safety issues regarding blocks. For example, remind children that throwing wooden blocks (or any blocks or toys) can be dangerous.

Other Health Impairments/Attention Deficit Hyperactive Disorder: Allow the child to participate in the activity in a more kinesthetic manner. For example, she can help set up the blocks in an incline position. Allow the child to move throughout the activity to help keep her focused on the lesson.

Orthopedic Impairments: Apply gripping materials to the blocks for children with a significant fine motor disability, in particular, a child with difficulty gripping or grasping objects.

Curriculum Connections

+ **Art:** Add stamps and stamp pads to the Art Center for children to use in their creative endeavors. Consider also adding a block from the Block Center so children can experiment with making block prints.
+ **Connecting with Home:** Ask the children's families to point out cement blocks or other construction blocks as they drive or walk with their children around their community.
+ **Outdoors:** Take blocks outdoors on occasion to enhance children's play experience on the playground.
+ **Transitions:** As children move to another part of the building, ask them to look for evidence that blocks are used in construction (a brick is a block shape, for example, and some buildings are constructed with blocks of cement).

Playdough

Time
10 minutes

Materials
playdough (purchased or teacher-made)

Objectives

Children will:
1. Use playdough to craft a sculpture of their choice.
2. Explain why they enjoy or don't enjoy using playdough.

> **Note:** Some children do not like the smell of commercial playdough. The following is a salt dough recipe to use that children could help you make in the classroom:
>
> 4 cups flour
> 1 cup salt
> 1 ½ cups hot water (from tap)
> 2 teaspoons vegetable oil
>
> Mix the salt and flour, then gradually add the water and vegetable oil until the dough becomes elastic. Knead the dough until it's a good consistency, adding either flour or water to get exactly when you want.
>
> This recipe will allow children to form art creations that will harden when dry (or can be baked at 200° for about an hour).

Lesson

✦ Show children the playdough and ask them to identify what it is.
✦ Ask if they have ever played with playdough before.
✦ If they have, ask them if they enjoyed playing with the dough. If they did enjoy it, ask them what they enjoyed about it.
✦ Place the dough in the Art Center, and invite the children to create a figure during Center Time.

Modifications/Accommodations

Autism: Be sensitive to a child's tactile needs. Some children with autism are tactilely defensive towards things that are sticky. Increasing the amount of flour in the dough often works. However, some children might prefer to wear disposable gloves when playing with the playdough.

Speech or Language Impairments: Avoid open-ended questions when asking about the playdough. Instead provide two choices for the child to select from.

Review

As children leave the circle area, ask each child to tell what art creation they plan to make. Allow children a choice about participating with playdough. If children cannot respond to this question, give them an opportunity to experiment with the playdough and then ask the question again.

Assessment Strategy

Ask children to place their playdough sculptures on display in the classroom.

Hearing Impairments: Make sure that the child can see your mouth when you are speaking in case a child is lip reading.

Visual Impairments: Instead of showing the child the playdough, give him some playdough to smell and touch. After allowing the child time to manipulate the dough, ask him what it is and if he has ever played with playdough.

Cognitive and/or Developmental Disabilities: When reviewing the activity and asking children what they plan to make, you may need to guide the child into making a decision.

Emotional Disturbance: If concerns of unacceptable behavior exist, keep the child nearby. Reinforce positive behaviors.

Other Health Impairments/Attention Deficit Hyperactive Disorder: Use visual cues to direct a child's attention back to the task.

Orthopedic Impairments: Make sure to place the playdough is within the child's reach.

Curriculum Connections

✦ **Art:** Add cookie cutters and jar lids to the Art Center and invite children to experiment with the playdough in a variety of ways. Add textured objects, such as slotted spoons, forks, mesh wire, and plastic toys. These objects make interesting designs on playdough.

✦ **Connecting with Home:** Tell families that playing with playdough helps develop children's fine motor skills. Encourage them to purchase playdough for use at home or share your recipe with them.

✦ **Dramatic Play:** Place playdough in the Home Living Center so children can use it to make pretend food items.
   Note: Playdough is difficult to get out of carpets, so you may want to place a painter's drop cloth on the floor if the area is carpeted.

Toy Fair

Time

approximately 1 minute for each child in the class

Materials

paper and markers
display table (or classroom area devoted for display)
signs and decorations
favorite toys brought from home
refreshments (donated by families, or prepared by you and the children the day before)

Preparation

Send home information about the fair in a note or a class newsletter. Ask parents to let their children bring their favorite toy to class on the day of the Toy Fair. Tell families the day and time to come to class. Remember to be sensitive to children who may not have the same number or quality of toys as others in the class. Provide paper and markers and help the children make invitations for their families. The day before the Toy Fair, let the children help prepare a display area for the toys. Encourage them to prepare signs and decorations for the area.

Objectives

Children will:
1. Share information about their favorite toys.
2. Name at least three different types of toys.

Lesson

+ As the children arrive with their toys on the designated day, have them place their toys in the display area.
+ Greet families as they arrive at the designated time. Provide a sitting area by the circle area.
+ Let each child present her toy to the group. Ask her to describe her toy and tell what makes it special. Some children may not want to speak in front of a large group. It is okay for some children not to participate.
+ Serve refreshments after the presentation.

Modifications/Accommodations

Autism: Use visual cues to help the child transition from one speaker to another. Also, give the child ample time to prepare to transition into her sharing time.

Speech or Language Impairments: A child with a significant speech or language impairment may not feel comfortable speaking in front of the group. Allow the child's family member to help her or use close-ended questions to lead the child in the discussion.

Hearing Impairments: Add simple sign language, such as the signs for *teddy bear*, *hug*, and *soft*, to the song "Teddy Bears" to increase the child's participation. All children in the class can learn to use the signs.

teddy bear

hug

soft

Review

Invite several children to share some of the information they have learned during their study of toys. As a group, have the children recite the chant from Cars and Trucks on page 284, or sing the "Teddy Bears" song on page 286.

Assessment Strategy

Ask individual children as they are leave for the day what their favorite toy is and why.

Visual Impairments: Allow the child to sit closer to the toy area so that she can have a closer view of the toys.
Before or after each child shares her toy, provide a few minutes for this child to feel the object. This can be done by passing each toy around to all children (if the children agree to it—some children may not want to share, which is okay).

Cognitive and/or Developmental Disabilities: Provide choices to the child to guide her when sharing. For example, "Allie, is this your favorite toy because it is soft or because you can take it outside?"

Emotional Disturbance: Provide positive reinforcement for the child's participation in the activity.

Other Health Impairments/Attention Deficit Hyperactive Disorder: Place the child close to you (proximity control) to help her maintain appropriate behaviors.

Orthopedic Impairments: Position the child so she can participate fully in the activity.

Curriculum Connections

✦ **Language and Literacy:** Ask children to bring their favorite classroom toys to Circle or Group Time one day and each give one reason they chose the toys they selected. You may want to try this with a small group initially, if children are not familiar with this format.

✦ **More Language and Literacy:** With small groups of children, ask for comparisons between someone's favorite toy and a similar toy found in the classroom. Write down children's descriptions of the likenesses and differences.

✦ **Math:** Ask small groups of children to develop a graph showing the class's favorite toys.

CHAPTER
7

Literature, Rhythms, and Rhymes

Books, nursery rhymes, and music are naturally very popular with children. You may have noticed children poring over books in the Library Center and heard them singing while they play by themselves or with others. For days and weeks after reading "The Gingerbread Man," you may hear the children shouting, "Run, run, as fast as you can; you can't catch me, I'm the Gingerbread Man." Families also report that children sing their favorite songs and rhymes on the very days they learn them.

One reason children do this is because words are fun! Children love phrases that are repetitive and tickle their tongues. Studying favorite books, stories, nursery rhymes, and music provides children with memories they carry with them throughout their lives. Many adults can remember a favorite book that was read to them when they were young. And most can still sing a song or two they learned as a child. When people mention that they liked "The Three Billy Goats Gruff" or "B-I-N-G-O" as children, others can relate immediately to those experiences because of their own familiarity with those books or songs.

The activities in this chapter introduce children to vocabulary that they might not have heard before, and they encourage the children to enjoy hearing and repeating words and phrases. Terms such as *the characters in a story* or the *tempo of a song* are helpful for children to know and learn because such terms stimulate a working knowledge of things they will need to understand when they grow older. These activities do not intend to make the children memorize specific phrases, but rather to expose children to words and phrases for future reference.

Expanding on the information children learn in the classroom will be easier if you explain to family members the nature of the lessons you are presenting to their children. Consider doing this by sending families weekly newsletters or by telling family members about the lesson when they arrive to pick up their children at the end of the day. For example, you could say, "Today we had a discussion about the plot in the book *Curious George*." Most family members will appreciate your efforts to teach their children new words and concepts that will improve the children's lives when they enter more formal educational settings.

Remember to focus on the playful and enjoyable aspects of the topics in this chapter. Children are sure to enjoy them, and many will remember the books, stories, rhymes, and songs you teach them for their entire lives.

Introduction to Books

Time
20–25 minutes

Materials
popular children's book
big book
variety of books that
    demonstrate various
    genres (a picture book,
    poetry book, shape book,
    predictable book,
    humorous book, and so
    on)
chart paper or dry-erase
    board and marker

Objectives

Children will:
1. Explain what books are.
2. Name a favorite book.

Lesson

+ Hold up a popular book the children enjoy and ask, "What is this thing called?"
+ Tell the children that books come in a variety of shapes and sizes.
+ Describe some genres of children's books, for example:
    + This is a shape book, because it is in a round shape.
    + We can make predictions about the print on the page with this book. That's the reason we call it a predictable book.
    + This book only has pictures in it, so we call it a wordless book.
    + Poetry books only have poems in them.
+ Read one of the books to children, preferably one that they already know and enjoy. Ask what kind of book it is.
+ Remind children that two types of literature exist—fiction and nonfiction.
+ Emphasize to children why it is important to take good care of books. Show the children a book that is torn or worn out and explain that the book will need repair.
+ Point out the various parts of the book: the binding, the book's spine, the front and back covers of the book, and the pages in the book.
+ Ask children to name some of their favorite books. Record their answers on chart paper or a dry-erase board.

Modifications/Accommodations

Autism: Use picture icons to support each part of the lesson. For example, when discussing each part of the book, have an icon of that part available. Make the lesson as concrete as possible by allowing the child to manipulate the books demonstrated (for example, picture books, shape books, and so on). A story about how to take care of a book would be a great addition to this lesson.

Speech or Language Impairments: During the assessment, ask the child to point to the parts of the book rather than to name them.

Hearing Impairments: Place the child close to the speaker. Decreasing the distance between the speaker and the child will increase the auditory input that the child receives.

Visual Impairments: Allow the child to feel the books as the discussion is taking place. For instance, if showing a shape book, the child can feel the edges of the book to determine what shape it is. When telling the children

Review

As children leave the circle area, ask them to tell one thing they learned about books.

Assessment Strategy

The review could serve as an assessment strategy, or at another time, ask them to identify the various parts of a book.

about the parts of the book, be sure to place the child's hand directly on the corresponding part. For example, when discussing the spine of the book, rub the child's hand across the spine of the book.

Cognitive and/or Developmental Disabilities: Break down this lesson into smaller parts and teach it over a period of several days. Make sure that the child understands each part before moving on to the next concept. When discussing predictions, play a simple game about predicting. For instance, blow up a balloon and then put a pin next to it. Ask the children what will happen if you prick the balloon with the pin. The prediction is that the balloon will pop. During the assessment, ask the child to point to the parts of the book rather than to name them.

Emotional Disturbance: If you anticipate that the child may exhibit a behavior problem, keep him close to you so you can monitor his behavior.

Other Health Impairments/Attention Deficit Disorder: Provide chances for the child to move throughout the lesson, such as asking him to bring a book or a pencil, and so on. Provide visual cues to remind the child to stay focused and attentive to the lesson.

Orthopedic Impairments: Make sure the child is positioned so he can see and access the materials used in the lesson.

Curriculum Connections

✦ **Language and Literacy:** Read *The ABC Bunny* by Wanda Gag. If children are experimenting with learning the alphabet, ask them to sort books in the Library Center according to the beginning alphabet letter of each title.

✦ **More Language and Literacy:** Use a cassette recorder to record children telling a story based on one of their favorite books. Invite everyone to listen to the recorded stories.

✦ **More Language and Literacy:** With small groups of children, compare book covers from an assortment of books. Ask the children to say which books they would prefer to read based on their covers. Introduce the words artist and illustrator.

✦ **Science:** Have teacher-made books in the Science Center for children to record information they are observing (growth of a plant or how many times a classroom pet is fed).

Favorite Books

Time
15 minutes

Materials
books children enjoy
list of children's favorite
    books from previous
    activity (see page 298)

Objectives

Children will:
1. Name at least one favorite book.
2. Describe why the book is a favorite.

Lesson

✦ Begin reading a favorite book the children have enjoyed throughout the year. Stop after reading a few pages and ask, "Why is this one of your favorite books?"

✦ Remind the children that the class has named some of its favorite books in a previous lesson and show the chart that was used to record their favorite books.

✦ Begin a graph to allow children to select three favorite books. After children have made a tally mark next to their favorites, count which book is the most popular for the class.

✦ Hang the chart in the classroom as a reminder to the children about their selections.

Modifications/Accommodations

Autism: Allow the child to thumb through a book and point to her favorite part of the book instead of having to think and share this information without the pictures within the book to guide or remind him of the storyline.

Speech or Language Impairments: Offer a child with a language impairment a choice as to why a book is her favorite. For example, "Is the story about the three little pigs your favorite book because the wolf blows the houses down or because the pigs are so smart in what they do?"

Hearing Impairments: Use simple sign language to support the discussion. Words such as *book* and *favorite* are easy to sign. Speak clearly and place the child in close to the speaker during the lesson.

book

favorite

Review

As children leave the circle area, ask them to name a favorite character from a book.

Assessment Strategy

At various times throughout the day, invite small groups of children to view the favorite book chart. Ask them to explain what the chart means.

Visual Impairments: Use raised objects, such as puffy stickers, instead of creating tally marks on a graph. The raised stickers allow a child with a visual impairment to tactilely determine the number of votes in each graph column.

Cognitive and/or Developmental Disabilities: When presenting previously created graph of the children's favorite books, have several of the books represented in the graph available to show during the discussion.

Emotional Disturbance: Remind children of the rules about getting up during a lesson and waiting on her turn. Praise the children for waiting for their turns to mark on the chart.

Other Health Impairments/Attention Deficit Hyperactivity Disorder: Move a child with inattention or impulsivity closer to you during all parts of the lesson. Allow the child to get chart paper, pens, and so on. This will give her an opportunity to move around without being disruptive to the class.

Orthopedic Impairments: Be sure to place the chart within reach of the child. If the child is unable to make her tally marks on the chart, have a peer assist her.

Curriculum Connections

+ **Connecting with Home:** Have children ask their families what their favorite books were when they were children. If possible, invite parent volunteers to come in and read their favorites to the children.
+ **Dramatic Play:** Provide props for the children's favorite book. Suggest that the children reenact the book.
+ **Language and Literacy:** Use a cassette recorder to record the children's favorite book. Provide multiple copies of the book in the Listening Center so several children can listen to the recording as they look through the book. Use a bell or other signaling system to indicate when a page needs to be turned.

Words in Books

Time
20 minutes

Materials
The Napping House by Audrey Wood or any other book that is familiar to the children
flashcards with the words granny, child, and sleeping written on them, or words related to the book you are reading

Objectives

Children will:
1. Point out specific words in books.
2. Explain what words do.

Lesson

◆ Begin reading a book that children have heard before during the year, such as *The Napping House* by Audrey Wood.
◆ As you read the book, call attention to the words in the book. Explain that the words tell the story you are reading.
◆ Whenever you read the words granny, child, or sleeping, hold up the flash cards for children to see. Explain that these are words written by the author. **Note:** Make your own word flashcards by printing the words on blank index cards.

Modifications/Accommodations

Autism: When presenting flashcards with the words granny, child, or sleeping, pair the word with a picture or icon. Be sure that when you indicate that a work in on the card that you point to the word and not the icon. The icon is only used to bring meaning to the printed word.

Speech or Language Impairments: When asking a child to read a word before leaving Circle or Group Time, offer the child two choices. Is this word cat or man? When selecting the words for the child to choose from, select a word which is depicted with a photograph on the same page that the word appears.

Hearing Impairments: Speak clearly during reading and when saying the words on the flashcards. If a child is using sign language, sign the words on the flashcards (such as *granny*, *child*, and *sleeping*). Words such as *granny* may need to be signed as *grandmother*.

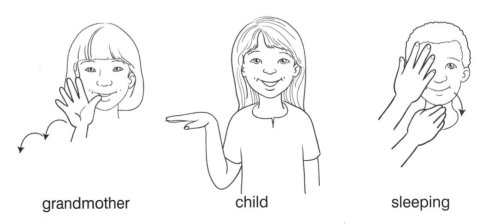

grandmother   child   sleeping

Review

As children leave the circle area, ask them to "read" one of the words introduced in the book. If a child cannot name a word, tell him that he can practice this skill at another time.

Assessment Strategy

Use the flashcards with individual children to assess whether he can match the words on the cards to the words in the book.

Visual Impairments: Use Braille on flashcards and allow the child to feel the words as you are showing them to the class. If Braille is not a preferred method, use large, black print or textured print on the cards presented. The size of the flashcards should depend on the child's level of visual impairment.

Cognitive and/or Developmental Disabilities: Highlight words in the book that are focus words. Use concrete objects to support the written flashcard word. Provide choices as to which word is presented. For example, during the assessment ask, the child to point to the word that starts with "D" instead of reading a word.

Emotional Disturbance: Reinforce positive behaviors during activity. Although all children need positive reinforcement, this is especially true for children who have emotional disturbances.

Other Health Impairments/Attention Deficit Hyperactivity Disorder: Use proximity control to help remind the child to stay focused on the lesson. During the review, ask the child to hold the book. This will help the child remain focused on the activity.

Orthopedic Impairments: Place flashcards of words directly within view of the child. Be sure he is positioned to see the story and words being presented.

Curriculum Connections

✦ **Connecting with Home:** Send a note home to parents explaining how to create print books with their children. Choose print examples that children would be able to recognize, such as cereal boxes, food containers, store and restaurant logos, toy labels, and so on. Ask parents to help their child cut out pictures or brand names from boxes, labels, and advertisements that the children can "read." Set aside a specific day for children to bring in their books to "read" to their classmates.

✦ **Language and Literacy:** Provide flannel pieces to represent all of the characters in the book *The Napping House.* Let the children retell the story using a flannel board.

✦ **More Language and Literacy:** Use a cassette recorder to record *The Napping House* for the Listening Center. Provide multiple copies of the book so several children can listen to the recording as they follow along in the book. Use a bell or other signaling system to indicate when to turn a page.

✦ **Writing:** Place blank flashcards in the Writing Center with markers. Encourage the children to copy any words they learned from *The Napping House.*

Numbers in Books

Note: Most children's books do not have numbered pages. In order to do this lesson, you will need books that have page numbers.

Time
15 minutes

Materials
Over in the Meadow by Olive A. Wadsworth
books with page numbers (first grade primers, textbooks, or story collections)

Objectives

Children will:
1. Point to a page number in a book.
2. Give a reason why numbers are used in books.

Lesson

✦ Begin reading a book that mentions numbers, such as *Over in the Meadow* by Olive A. Wadsworth. Focus children's attention on the number of animals that are mentioned on each page.
Note: Try to use a book that the children know so the children learn something new about a book they already know.
✦ Continue reading the book. Point out as you turn each page that "This is page one," "…page two," "…page three," and so on.
✦ When the book is finished, ask the children what page numbers might be used for. Explain that we can find specific pages in books if we know the page numbers.
✦ Show the children a first grade primer and point out the page numbers in the book. If appropriate for the children in your class, explain how page numbers let a reader turn to a specific page. Say, "If everyone is looking at a copy of the same book, we can all turn to the same page if we need to."

Modifications/Accommodations

Autism: Allow other children to respond to their favorite part of the story as a means to model expected behavior and responses. Offer two choices as to which part of the story was a favorite. For example, if the story selected is about a duck who finds a hidden treasure, then ask, "Was your favorite part of the story when the duck fell in the hole looking for the treasure, or when the duck danced on one foot after it found the treasure?"

Speech or Language Impairments: Use a lead-in sentence when asking child to respond to her favorite part of the story. For example, "My favorite part of the story was_____."

Hearing Impairments: Speak clearly and face the child when reading the selected book. Annunciate clearly when discussing the numerals on the page. Repeat the numerals when pointing to them.

Visual Impairments: Add Braille numbers to the bottom of each page number so that a child with a significant visual impairment may participate in activity; those children with visual impairments not utilizing Braille would benefit from selecting a Big book with larger page numbers.

Review

Before leaving the circle area, ask children to tell what their favorite part of the book was. Ask the children to "quack" as they transition to their next activity.

Assessment Strategy

Individually, ask children to find a specific page number in a book that has numbered pages.

Cognitive and/or Developmental Delays: During the assessment phase of the lesson, provide a choice to the child. For example, ask, "Is this page number 1 or 3?" Review counting with the child. If the child has a severe cognitive delay, ask her to select a page number and help her find the page in the book.

Emotional Disturbance: Offer praise throughout lesson for appropriate listening, sitting, and correctly identifying selected page numbers. If a child exhibits unacceptable behavior, place the child closer to you.

Other Health Impairments/Attention Deficit Hyperactivity Disorder: Place a child who is having a difficult time maintaining attention to the task closer to the teacher during the story time. Utilization of carpet squares for children to sit on provides a visual reminder to children as to where they are supposed to sit.

Orthopedic Impairments: if children are to turn pages and point to page numbers add a tactile element to the bottom of the pages. For example a piece of felt or Velcro enables a child with grasping difficulties to turn a page more easily. Board books are often easier to manipulate pages in too.

Curriculum Connections

- ✦ **Art:** Add sandpaper numbers to the Art Center for children to use to make rubbings.
- ✦ **Language and Literacy:** Place the book *Over in the Meadow* in the Library Center for children to look at later. Encourage children to retell the story to one another.
- ✦ **Fine Motor:** Provide sandpaper numerals in the Manipulatives Center for children to trace with their fingers. Let children practice writing numerals using stencils.
- ✦ **Writing:** Add words from the book to the Word Wall to encourage children to refer to them as they "write." Add number words as well as *beaver*, *lizard*, *bask*, *turtle*, *dig*, *owl*, and so on.

Authors

Note: If you have been routinely reading to children throughout the year, it should be easy to introduce the term *author*.

Time
20 minutes

Materials
several children's books by the same author
flip chart and marker

Objectives

Children will:
1. Name one author they enjoy.
2. Name one book title by their favorite authors.

Lesson

✦ Show children a book that they have heard before by a familiar author; for example, Eric Carle. Tell the children that the author of the book is Eric Carle. **Note:** Reading a familiar book allows you to focus on another concept about the book that children might not know—in this instance, the author's role.

✦ Hold up other books by Eric Carle and ask, "Who remembers who the author of these books is?" Then ask, "Who knows what an author is?" "Do you know anyone who is an author?"

✦ Share one of the class books children have developed throughout the year and ask, "Who are the authors of this book?" Comment that anyone can be an author.

✦ Ask if they would like to write a letter to Eric Carle. Let the children dictate a group letter to Eric Carle. Write their words on a chart or have individual children dictate letters to parent volunteers. Consult the Internet for Eric Carle's address.

Modifications/Accommodations

Autism: Allow other children to start the dictation process when writing a letter. This will serve as a model as to what is expected of the child. Frequently remind the child about the book that the class created and how each person in the class is an author. This will make the lesson more meaningful to the child.

Speech or Language Impairments: When asking direct questions about authors, such as who knows what an author is, use a lead-in sentence. For example, "An author is a person who_____." In addition, provide fill-in-the-blank sentences such as, "An author is a person who_____ books."

Hearing Impairments: When holding up the books by the same author, be sure that the book is not blocking your mouth. If you block the child's view of your lips, it makes it difficult for the child to read your lips and participate in the activity.

Visual Impairments: Allow the child to hold the books that are shown to the class. Allowing the child to hold the book will provide him with the opportunity to bring the books closer to his eyes. Using big books when possible will assist the child in utilizing any limited vision he has.

Review

Ask children to name their favorite books. Tell the children the authors' names as each book is mentioned.

Assessment Strategy

Ask individual children to explain what an author does.

Cognitive and/or Developmental Disabilities: During assessment phase, provide the child with a choice as to the correct answer. For example, "Does an author write the words or draw the pictures in the book?"

Emotional Disturbance: Offer praise for participation in the activity when the child responds correctly when identifying the role of the author.

Other Health Impairments/Attention Deficit Hyperactivity Disorder: Monitor impulsivity or inattention through proximity control. Ask the child to hold up the various books that are being shown to the class.

Orthopedic Impairments: Position child so that materials and the story are accessible him. After a book is held up, place it within the child's grasp.

Curriculum Connections

✦ **Language and Literacy:** Focus on a popular author by placing several titles by the same author in the Library Corner. Authors might include Bill Martin, Jr.; Mem Fox; Tana Hoban; Leo Lionni; Eric Hill; Mercer Meyer; and so on.

✦ **More Language and Literacy:** Invite the children to become authors by providing them with paper and writing implements.

✦ **Math:** Create a graph with small groups of children showing who their favorite authors are.

What Makes a Story?

Time
25 minutes

Materials
"The Three Billy Goats Gruff"
(many versions available)
or any well-known book
the children have heard
multiple times

Objectives

Children will:
1. State at least one component of a story (plot, setting, beginning, middle, or end).
2. Identify a specific part of a story.

Lesson

✦ Show the children a book of the story "The Three Billy Goats Gruff."

✦ Say to the children, "I know that you know what happens in this book. Who can tell me what happened at the beginning of the book?

✦ After the children respond, ask them what happens in the middle of the book and at the end of the book.

✦ Explain that there are three main parts of a book: the beginning, the middle, and the end.

✦ Then tell the children that when the three parts of a story are put together, it is called the plot. Explain that the plot includes all the things that happen in the story.

✦ Explain children that the setting is the place where the story happens. In "The Three Billy Goats Gruff," the setting is a bridge between two pastures.

Modifications/Accommodations

Autism: Prepare sequence cards with pictorial depictions of the beginning, middle and end of the story. Place cards in the proper sequence when telling the story.

Speech or Language Impairments: When assessing the children's learning, use lead-in sentence such as, "In the beginning of the story, the Little Red Hen...."

Hearing Impairments: Place child near you as you read. Be sure that your mouth is in clear view to the child. This will benefit those children using lip reading to support the child's auditory intake.

Review

Ask children to describe the beginning, middle, and end of another favorite story (or what happened first, second, and last). Ask what the plot is and where the setting is placed. Good stories to suggest are "The Little Red Hen" or "The Three Little Pigs."

Assessment Strategy

With individuals or small groups, ask children to identify the beginning, middle, or end of another well-known story.

Visual Impairments: Select a big book version of "Three Billy Goats Gruff." Also, place the child close to the front of the book so that the photographs are clearer. Use supporting props, such as toy goats, while reading the story. Allow the child to manipulate the props as the story is being told.

Cognitive and/or Developmental Disabilities: When telling the story, use as many concrete objects as possible, including a toy troll, toy goats, a plastic bridge, and so on. Stress the beginning, middle, and end by placing the concrete objects in the correct order. Use objects for retelling purposes. For higher functioning children, use sequence cards instead of objects.

Emotional Disturbance: Offer a suggestion to the child as to which story to retell. For example, if you suggest that the child retell "The Three Little Pigs," this controls the content of the story that is being presented.

Other Health Impairments/Attention Deficit Hyperactivity Disorder: Provide the child with several opportunities to move throughout the lesson. For example, a child with ADHD could assist in getting materials or moving any utilized props into the story telling area.

Orthopedic Impairments: Be sure the child is positioned so that she can participate in discussions and clearly see the story. If concrete items, such as a toy bridge or toy trolls are being used, place them on a child's wheelchair tray after holding them up for the class to see.

Curriculum Connections

✦ **Art:** Ask small groups of children to use large pieces of paper to draw the beginning, middle, or end of a familiar book. Then review the parts of the book at Circle or Group Time and use the children's art to put the plot into sequential order.

✦ **Connecting with Home:** Send home a note to parents explaining that children are learning about the terms setting and plot and identifying the beginning, middle, and end of stories. Ask them to point these out to the children as they read them books. Tell parents to encourage their child to do this on their own.

✦ **Language and Literacy:** Invite children to "research" their books to find settings that are similar (in forests, in homes, at school, in make-believe places, and so on). Organize books with similar settings into groups and prepare sentence strip labels for children to use as markers for the books.

Who Are the Characters in a Story?

Time
20 minutes

Materials
"The Three Billy Goats Gruff" (many versions available) or any book children have read numerous times

Objectives

Children will:
1. Name characters in a specific book.
2. Identify a favorite storybook character.

Lesson

✦ Show the children a book of the story "The Billy Goats Gruff" and review the terms setting and plot from the previous lesson.

✦ Tell them that there are also characters in the book. Explain that characters are the people or the animals in a book. The characters are what a book is about. Say, "For example, in the story "Goldilocks and the Three Bears," the characters are Papa Bear, Mama Bear, Baby Bear, and Goldilocks. The story tells what the characters do."

✦ Ask children to identify the four characters in the story. Help them as needed (the little billy goat, the middle billy goat, the big billy goat, and the troll).

✦ Tell children that all stories have characters. Ask them to identify characters in other well-known stories.

Modifications/Accommodations

Autism: Have felt pieces of the characters in the book available. As the story is read and a new character is introduced, place the felt piece on a felt board. When asking children who the characters in the book are, allow the child to respond by pointing to the felt piece. Make the lesson as concrete as possible by using dolls or puppets of the characters.

Speech or Language Impairments: Allow other children to identify characters in well known stories first as a means of providing a model for the child. Provide choices to a child as to well known characters in a book. Say, "In 'The Three Little Pigs,' is one of the characters a pig or a rabbit?"

Hearing Impairments: Speak clearly and face the child when explaining the content of the lesson. Be sure to keep your hands away from face in an effort to keep mouth clear for lip reading. When identifying the characters in the various stories or books, use sign language for familiar books, such as *pig* in "The Three Little Pigs" or *goat* in "The Three Billy Goats Gruff." If you use sign language with the child, add the signs for *little* and *big*.

Visual Impairments: Move the child closer to you as you read the book. If a big book is available, it is a more advisable choice than a book in a standard size. Larger pictures will help the child understand the content.

little

big

Review

Ask the group to name the four main characters in "The Three Billy Goats Gruff."

Assessment Strategy

Individually ask children to name a favorite storybook character from another book they enjoy.

Cognitive and/or Developmental Disabilities: Read the book at the start of the lesson, marking the pages with visual depictions of the characters with a sticky note. Throughout the book specifically state that each animal or person is a character in the book. As the characters appear in the book, ask the child to point to each character.

Emotional Disturbance: Reinforce positive behaviors such as appropriately responding to who are the characters in the book. Specifically offer praise for exhibiting proper sitting and using acceptable voice levels during the lesson.

Other Health Impairments/Attention Deficit Hyperactivity Disorder: If a child has a difficult time with impulsivity, place a lap pad on his lap to remind him to stay seated. The lap pad is created by filling a small pillow case with beans and sewing up the side. The weight acts as a physical reminder to remain seated. When presenting felt pieces or concrete items to represent the characters in the book, have the child help to hold the pieces of felt or objects.

Orthopedic Impairments: Be sure the child is positioned to see the book clearly and to engage in discussions at the same physical level as the other children.

Curriculum Connections

+ **Connecting with Home**: Consider having a special dress-up day for children to dress up like their favorite storybook characters. Send home a note to families and ask them to help their child with this and to visit that day, if they wish.
+ **Dramatic Play**: Listen carefully as children identify favorite storybook characters during the lesson. Then add related props to the Dramatic Play Center so children can act out their favorite roles. Make comments to children as they use the props such as, "I see you enjoy the Goldilocks character, because you dressed like her."
+ **Language and Literacy**: Individually or in small groups, ask children to identify characters in a familiar story. Write their responses on a chart or poster to share with their peers at the end of the day.

Making Our Own Books

Time
15 minutes

Materials
construction paper
white paper
markers
stickers or stamps
old magazines
scissors
glue
hole punch and string or
    staplers

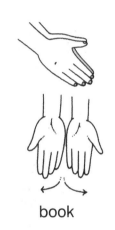

book

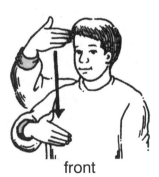

front

back

Objectives

Children will:
1. Identify components of books (front and back covers, pages, and illustrations.
2. Construct a simple book independently.

Lesson

♦ Ask the children, "What have we been learning about for the past few days?" If they don't respond with books, gently remind them of the topic.
♦ Review some of the story terminology that children have learned about (plot, setting, characters, and so on.)
♦ Tell them they will each have an opportunity to construct a book if they choose.
♦ Talk about the parts of a book (front and back covers, pages and illustrations). Explain what the terms illustrations and illustrator mean.
♦ Demonstrate how to put a book together. Put a few white pages between two pieces of construction paper and staple them together or punch holes in the sides and tie string through.
♦ Brainstorm story ideas and tell children they can write or dictate a story to put on the pages of their books. They can use markers to illustrate their stories and book covers, or they can cut out pictures from magazines to glue to the pages. Remind them to think of book titles to add to the cover.
♦ Put the materials in the Art Center and tell the children they can make their own books during Center Time if they wish.

Modifications/Accommodations

Autism: When reviewing the parts of a story, select a specific story, such as "The Three Little Pigs." Use concrete items, such as three toy pigs, Lincoln Logs, and a wolf. Identify the elements of the story and pair the items with the parts of the story. For example, when discussing the characters, show the toy pigs and the toy wolf. Offer choices for the child during the assessment strategy. Ask, "Is this the front cover or the back cover?"

Speech or Language Impairments: No specific modifications necessary. However, as with all children, encourage participation in the activity. A child with a speech or language impairment may be hesitant to participate in discussion. Offering her for participating in the activity will increase the likelihood that she will continue to be involved in the activity.

Review
Ask individual children to name a specific part of a book that you have read during the unit as you point to it.

Assessment Strategy
Observe children as they construct their books and ask them to name parts of the book as they work.

Hearing Impairments: Use the signs for *book*, *front*, and *back* during the lesson.

Visual Impairments: When the child makes a book in the assessment, be sure that the child can see the materials. If possible, provide large paper or textured paper for the child to use.

Cognitive and/or Developmental Disabilities: Instead of asking a child to name a specific part of the book, say the part of the book and ask the child to point to it. "Can you point to the front cover of the book?"

Emotional Disturbance: Provide positive reinforcement for appropriate classroom behavior. If you are concerned the child may not use scissors appropriately, monitor her cutting activities or do not provide scissors. Reviewing the rules of scissor usage will benefit all children.

Other Health Impairments/Attention Deficit Hyperactivity Disorder: Provide opportunities for movement throughout the activity. For example, have the child move to the front to turn pages of the book.

Orthopedic Impairments: Provide opportunities for movement throughout the activity. For example, have the child move to the front to turn pages of the book. Remind children that when using scissors they should be seated and not move about the room with scissors in their hands.

Curriculum Connections

✦ **Language and Literacy:** Display children's books in the Library Center or on a special table. Ask children from other classrooms to come to see the books the children have made.

✦ **More Language and Literacy:** Compare the children's books with real books. Ask them how they are the same and how they are different.

✦ **Math:** Use the information about how the books are similar and different (see More Language and Literacy above) to form a graph showing the results (for example, books with red covers, books with stickers on the front, books that only have a few pages, and so on).

✦ **Writing:** Place blank books in the Writing Center for children to use to practice their writing skills.

Introduction to Nursery Rhymes

Note: At the beginning of this unit of study, locate a reliable Mother Goose nursery rhyme book to use throughout the unit. A good choice is Iona Opie's *My Very First Mother Goose,* but other excellent volumes are available.

Time
15 minutes

Materials
a book of nursery rhymes

Objectives

Children will:
1. Say what nursery rhymes are.
2. Name one nursery rhyme character.

Lesson

✦ Begin singing "Hickory Dickory Dock" as children come to Circle or Group Time.
✦ Tell the children that this song is a nursery rhyme. Explain that they will be learning about nursery rhymes for a few days.
✦ Say, "We are going to learn about some special people, such as Little Miss Muffet, Old Mother Hubbard, and Jack and Jill." Name as many nursery rhyme characters as you want. Flip through the nursery rhyme book and show the pictures as you talk about the characters.
✦ Ask if any child knows a nursery rhyme and allow him to share with the group. Share your favorite nursery rhyme, too.
✦ Explain that nursery rhymes are short poems that have been around for many years. Say, "I bet your mom or dad or caretaker know some nursery rhymes. Ask them tonight which ones they can remember."
✦ Explain that these special verses are usually referred to as Mother Goose nursery rhymes. (**Note:** Though historians are unsure of the origin of the name Mother Goose, some believe that she was an actual woman named Bertha, who was married to English royalty. "Queen Bertha" loved to tell stories.)

Modifications/Accommodations

Autism: Use motions, clapping, and gestures as you say the nursery rhymes.
Speech or Language Impairments: Say the nursery rhyme and then ask the children to say it with you. Repeat this process and have the children say the last word of each line.
Hearing Impairments: Seat the child across from you so he can see your lips and face as you say the rhyme. Refer to the pictures as you present them and talk about the nursery rhyme characters.
Visual Impairments: Describe each picture of the nursery rhyme characters as you present them.
Cognitive and/or Developmental Disabilities: Repeat the nursery rhyme and song "Hickory Dickory Dock" several times. Ask the child to say it along with you, going very slowly, one line at a time. Review the song and rhyme each day until he can say it with you.

Review

Ask children to name nursery rhymes they might know.

Assessment Strategy

Show pictures of nursery rhymes to individual children and ask them to tell what a nursery rhyme is.

Emotional Disturbance: Seat the child next to you and affirm him for participating. Have the child hold up the pictures to get him involved in the lesson.

Other Health Impairments/Attention Deficit Hyperactivity Disorder: Have the children stand and imitate motions as you sing "Hickory Dickory Dock."

Orthopedic Impairments: This child should not need any accommodations for this lesson.

Curriculum Connections

✦ **Connecting with Home:** Send home a note to parents and ask them to share the name of at least one nursery rhyme they enjoyed when they were children. Begin a graph or chart (sample below) to show the children's favorite rhymes. As the study progresses, invite children to place tally marks next to their favorite rhymes. Add picture clues to the chart so children can easily "read" the chart for themselves.

Nursery Rhymes	Parent Favorites	Children's Favorites
"Little Miss Muffet"	♥ ♥ ♥	♥ ♥
"Old Mother Hubbard"		♥ ♥ ♥ ♥
"Jack and Jill"	♥ ♥ ♥ ♥	♥ ♥ ♥ ♥
"Little Boy Blue"	♥ ♥	♥ ♥ ♥
"Humpty Dumpty"	♥ ♥ ♥ ♥	♥ ♥ ♥ ♥

✦ **Language and Literacy:** Fill the Library Center with as many versions of Mother Goose nursery rhymes as you can find. Nursery rhymes support literacy development in wonderful ways (rhymes, rhythms, alliteration, sense of story, and memory development). If possible, spend as much quality time in the center sharing rhymes with children who are interested in hearing them.

✦ **Music:** Add a CD collection of nursery rhyme songs to the Listening Center for children to enjoy. Most tunes to nursery rhymes are difficult for preschoolers' voices, so listening becomes a better experience for them. **Note:** "Twinkle, Twinkle, Little Star" and "Mary Had a Little Lamb" are appropriate melodies for young children. Consider creating new words to sing to these familiar tunes (sometimes called invented songs). For example, sing "Old King Cole" to the tune of "Mary Had a Little Lamb." Invite children to make up make up their own tunes, and record them on a cassette recorder.

"Little Miss Muffet"

Time
20 minutes

Materials
"Little Miss Muffet" nursery rhyme
picture of Miss Muffet (use a picture in a Mother Goose book)

Objectives

Children will:
1. Describe the problem that occurs in the "Little Miss Muffet" rhyme.
2. Recite at least one line from the "Little Miss Muffet" rhyme.

Lesson

- ✦ Show the children the picture of Miss Muffet and tell the children who she is.
- ✦ Ask, "What is she sitting on?"
- ✦ Explain that a *tuffet* is a cluster of grasses or a bunch of close-set plants.
- ✦ Explain that *curds and whey* are like a soft cheese or sour yogurt.
- ✦ Ask the children to listen to the rhyme to see if they can identify Miss Muffet's problem (or dilemma).
- ✦ Read the nursery rhyme, and ask for children's responses about the problem Miss Muffet encountered. Brainstorm other reactions Miss Muffet could have had to her problem.

Little Miss Muffet
Little Miss Muffet sat on a tuffet,
Eating her curds and whey.
Along came a spider and sat down beside her,
And frightened Miss Muffet away.

- ✦ Ask the children if, in real life, a spider would come and sit beside them.
- ✦ Pair children and give each child in the pair a role as either Miss Muffet or the spider. Repeat the nursery rhyme and ask the pairs to act out the story. The children can act out the rhyme as many times as they desire.

Modifications/Accommodations

Autism: Write the poem on chart paper, with small drawings (like icons) above the following words: *Little Miss Muffet, tuffet, eating, curds and whey, spider,* and *frightened*. Recite the poem several times and point to the words as you recite it. Have the child recite it aloud with you as you say it slowly.

Review

Ask the children to tell the story of "Little Miss Muffet" in their own words.

Assessment Strategy

Assess individual children by asking each child to repeat as much of the "Little Miss Muffet" nursery rhyme as she can.

Speech or Language Impairments: Say the poem one line at a time and have the child repeat the line after you. Then say the poem while leaving off the last word of the statement, having the child complete it. Then have the child say the poem with you.

Hearing Impairments: Make sure that the child can see your face and mouth as you say the rhyme. Use pictures and gestures as you present the poem and the concepts.

Visual Impairments: Describe the picture of Miss Muffet and the tuffet as you show them to the class.

Cognitive and/or Developmental Disabilities: Use simple language, vocabulary, and short sentences in your explanations. The key concepts that you should focus on are *sitting*, *eating*, *spider*, and *frightened*. Have the child point to pictures that demonstrate these key concepts. Have the child pantomime eating, sitting, and frightened after you demonstrate them. Review the poem several times a day for the first week; later review it weekly.

Emotional Disturbance: Seat the child next to you. Have her give you materials and pictures during the lesson. Affirm her for participating. Talk about how Miss Muffett felt when she saw the spider. Discuss what the child can do when she is frightened.

Other Health Impairments/Attention Deficit Hyperactivity Disorder: Make sure that you have the child's attention before speaking. Talk about what the child can do when she is frightened.

Orthopedic Impairments: Assist the child physically to reenact Little Miss Muffet.

Curriculum Connections

✦ **Art:** Place Styrofoam balls (spray-painted black while the children are not around) and chenille sticks in the Art Center for children to experiment with making spiders. Or, they can roll black construction paper into balls and add chenille stick legs.

✦ **Language and Literacy:** Work with small groups of interested children and show them the word muffet. Demonstrate how muffet becomes tuffet by placing a "t" over the "m". Experiment with other letters to form other make-believe words, such as *cuffet, duffet, guffet, huffet, juffet ,luffet*, ruffet, *wuffet*, and so on. Explain to children that these are "just for fun" words and that they are not real words.

✦ **Snack:** Serve yogurt to the children. Ask them to describe how it tastes. Do this activity in small groups or individually.

"Old Mother Hubbard"

Time
25 minutes

Materials
picture of Old Mother
    Hubbard
stuffed animal dog
toy dog bones
"Old Mother Hubbard" rhyme

Preparation
Before the children arrive,
hide several toy dog bones
throughout the classroom.

Objectives

Children will:
1. Say that a cupboard is a kitchen cabinet.
2. Identify the Old Mother Hubbard's dilemma or problem.
3. Recite at least one line from the "Old Mother Hubbard" rhyme.

Lesson

✦ Begin by asking children to tell what a *cupboard* is and define the word, if necessary. Show children the picture of Old Mother Hubbard and point out the cupboard.

✦ Tell them that Old Mother Hubbard has a problem. Ask them to listen closely to the nursery rhyme to determine her problem. Use a stuffed dog and toy dog bone as props as you recite the rhyme (hide the bone behind your back at an appropriate time during the rhyme).

Old Mother Hubbard
Old Mother Hubbard went to the cupboard,
To find her poor dog a bone.
When she was there, the cupboard was bare,
And so the poor dog had none.

✦ Ask the children about Old Mother Hubbard's dilemma. Brainstorm ways that she could solve the problem.

✦ Play a follow-the-directions game with the children by calling on individuals to find the hidden bones in the classroom. Give specific directions for each child, asking the other children to watch to see if the child is following directions. Examples include:
  ✦ A bone is hidden in the Art Center under the easel.
  ✦ A bone is hidden behind the Library Center table.
  ✦ A bone is hidden beside a large block in the Block Center.
  ✦ A bone is hidden in the classroom dollhouse.

✦ Tell the children that the bones will be available for small groups to hide during Center Time.

Modifications/Accommodations

Autism: During the review and assessment, write the poem on a chart table with drawings above key concepts. Some of the drawings to be used include the following: Mother Hubbard, cupboard, dog, bone, and none (0).

Speech or Language Impairments: Recite the poem several times before assessing the child's learning. Then recite the poem, omitting the last word of each line and asking the child complete the line.

Hearing Impairments: Seat the child across from you where he can see your face and mouth. Use pictures and gestures to reinforce concepts as you present them.

Visual Impairments: Let the child feel the stuffed dog and bones. Verbally describe Mother Hubbard, the cupboard, and other items in the picture. During the hiding game, provide verbal cues such as, "You're getting warmer/colder," "It is somewhere to your right/left," and "It is higher/lower."

Review

Ask children to tell the story of "Old Mother Hubbard" in their own words.

Assessment Strategy

Informally invite individual children to tell anything they remember about the rhyme. Encourage them to recite as much of the rhyme as they can.

Cognitive and/or Developmental Disabilities: Use short sentences and simple vocabulary. Emphasize the following key concepts: *Mother Hubbard*, *cupboard*, *dog*, *bone*, and *bare*. Show pictures and have the child identify each of them. Review the poem daily until the child can say it with you. Then review it each week.

Emotional Disturbance: Seat the child next to you during the lesson. Enlist his help in holding materials. Provide close supervision during the game where you hide the bone to ensure that the child does not become rambunctious.

Other Health Impairments/Attention Deficit Hyperactivity Disorder: Make sure that you have the child's attention before speaking, showing pictures, or asking the child to do something. Have the children stand up and use motions as you say the poem. Some possible motions include the following:

Old Mother Hubbard (cup both hands around your face to make a bonnet)
cupboard (opening motion)
dog (pet a dog)
bone (both hands eating a bone beside your mouth)
when she got there (hands making running motion)
bare (hands palms up in front of you)
none (head down making a sad face)

This technique of using motions will also help other children with disabilities, such as speech or language disorders, autism, and cognitive disabilities.

Orthopedic Impairments: Help the child move about the classroom to locate the bone during the hiding game.

Curriculum Connections

✦ **Art:** Place dog bones (use various sizes) and one large piece of poster board in the Art Center. Encourage interested children to trace the dog bones onto various colors of construction paper and cut them out. Invite them to glue the bone cutouts onto the poster board however they wish. After the project is complete, show the poster to the class and tell them that Old Mother Hubbard's dog now has enough bones to eat.

✦ **Connecting with Home:** Tell the children's parents they heard the "Old Mother Hubbard" rhyme and ask them to show children their kitchen "cupboard."

"Jack and Jill"

Time
20 minutes

Materials
picture of Jack and Jill
empty pail
"Jack and Jill" nursery rhyme

Objectives

Children will:
1. Describe the dilemma or problem that occurs in the "Jack and Jill" rhyme.
2. Recite at least one line from the "Jack and Jill" rhyme.

Lesson

◆ Begin the lesson by asking the children if they know what a crown is. Explain that the word *crown* in the Jack and Jill rhyme means the top of the head. You may also need to explain what the words *fetch* and *pail* mean.

◆ Say the rhyme, and ask the children what the problem is in the nursery rhyme. Ask them why they think Jack and Jill may have fallen down.

Jack and Jill
Jack and Jill went up the hill
To fetch a pail of water.
Jack fell down and broke his crown,
And Jill came tumbling after.

◆ Invite the children to make up motions to go with the rhyme. For example, they could walk in place for the first line of the rhyme, pretend to hit their heads for the second line, and "tumble" down as Jill might have fallen. Use the motions children suggest to show respect for their ideas.

◆ Show children the empty pail and ask them why Jack and Jill were going up the hill to get water. Explain to them that a long time ago, when the rhyme was written, people did not have running water, so they had to get water from a well.

◆ Place the pail in the Water Table for them to play with during Center Time.

Modifications/Accommodations

Autism: Use pictures to present key concepts. Write the poem on chart paper with small drawings above the following key concepts: *Jack and Jill*, *hill*, *pail*, *water*, *fell*, *crown*, and *tumbling*.

Speech or Language Impairments: Recite the poem several times before assessing. Then have the child complete the line as you recite it line by line, omitting the last word. Review the poem several times a day for the first week; later review it weekly.

Hearing Impairments: Use gestures, drawings, and pictures as you present the concepts found in the poem. Have the child recite the poem with you slowly, one line at a time.

- **Music:** Tell the children that they might already know a song about Jack and Jill, "Two Little Blackbirds." Sing the song at the end of the day before children leave the classroom and ask them if this song is about the Jack and Jill characters in the nursery rhyme.

Two Little Blackbirds

Two little blackbirds
Sitting on a hill.
One named Jack.
One named Jill.
Fly away, Jack.
Fly away, Jill.
Come back, Jack.
Come back, Jill.

Review
Ask children to tell the story of "Jack and Jill" in their own words.

Assessment Strategy
Request individual children to recite "Jack and Jill," or as much of it as they can.

Visual Impairments: Describe each picture as you present it. When discussing key concepts, show concrete objects or movements related to the following: *crown, tumbling.*

Cognitive and/or Developmental Disabilities: Use simple language, vocabulary, and short sentences in your explanations. The key concepts that you should focus on are *hill, pail, water, fell down, broke, crown,* and *tumbling.* Have the child point to pictures to demonstrate key concepts. Review the poem several times a day for the first week; later review it weekly.

Emotional Disturbance: Seat the child next to you. Have her give you materials and pictures during the lesson. Remind the child to keep the water in the water table before playing with the pail at the water table during Center Time. Supervise the child closely.

Other Health Impairments/Attention Deficit Hyperactivity Disorder: Make sure that you have the child's attention before speaking. Use motions as you recite the poem. Motions are enjoyable for all children, but are especially important to include for this child who has an increased need for movement. Some possible motions include:

Jack and Jill went up the hill (hands moving back and forth as in going up hill)
To fetch a pail of water. (hands grab the pail by bending over, hands rounded)
Jack fell down (fall to floor gently)
And broke his crown, (hold head, pained expression on face)
And Jill came tumbling after. (roll over)

Orthopedic Impairments: This child will need physical assistance with a pail at the water table. Otherwise no accommodations should be needed.

Curriculum Connections

- **Language and Literacy:** Talk with individual children or small groups about names that begin with the letter "J." Ask children to identify names of classmates, friends, and other people or places that begin with "J." Add some of these names to the classroom Word Wall.
- **More Language and Literacy:** Focus on rhyming words, such as words that rhyme with Jack (back, sack, and so on) or Jill.

"Hickory, Dickory, Dock"

Time
20 minutes

Materials
picture of a mouse running up a clock (illustration from a Mother Goose book)

two or more clocks, one digital and one large analog

picture of a grandfather clock

paper clock face

triangle (instrument)

Objectives

Children will:
1. Retell the story of "Hickory, Dickory, Dock."
2. Recite or sing at least one line from "Hickory, Dickory, Dock."

Lesson

◆ As children gather for Circle or Group Time, begin singing the musical version of "Hickory, Dickory, Dock." Because this is a familiar song, the children will probably join you as you sing. Show the children a picture of the mouse as you sing the song.

Hickory, Dickory, Dock (traditional)
Hickory, dickory, dock,
The mouse ran up the clock.
The clock struck one, the mouse ran down,
Hickory, dickory dock.

◆ Ask children several questions about the story in the rhyme, such as:
  ◆ Have you ever seen a mouse run up a clock?
  ◆ Why do you think the mouse was running up the clock?
  ◆ Why did the mouse run back down?
  ◆ What does it mean to say "the clock struck one"?
◆ Show the children the clocks. Say, "These are clocks; they tell us what time it is." Point to the digital clock and ask if anyone can "read" the time. If no one responds, tell them what time it is. Ask children why it is important to know the time during our daily lives.
◆ Show the picture of a grandfather clock. Explain that it is like the clock in the nursery rhyme. Explain that these large clocks chime the time at the start of each hour and sometimes more often. Point out that this type of clock is called a grandfather clock because of its size. They usually make deep sounds when they chime.
◆ Use the clock face to show the "1" and explain that on a grandfather clock, the clock will chime one time to indicate the hour.
◆ Demonstrate chiming "one" with the triangle.
◆ Sing "Hickory, Dickory, Dock" several more times, giving individual children a chance to strike the triangle at the appropriate time during the verse.
◆ If time permits, use the triangle to strike other times, such as 4:00 or 7:00, asking children to count the number of times the clock is chiming.

Modifications/Accommodations

Autism: Use pictures to present key concepts. Write the poem on a chart paper with small drawings above the following key concepts: *mouse, ran, up, clock, strike, one,* and *down.* Direct who, what, when, and where questions to this child instead of why questions.

✦ **More Science:** Place other measures of time (hour glass, sun dial, stopwatch, wrist watches, time clock, speedometer, and so on) in the Science Center for children to explore.

Review
Sing the song once again before asking children to summarize the main points of the rhyme.

Assessment Strategy
Individually, give children an opportunity to strike the triangle one time and retell as much of the mouse's story as they can remember.

Speech or Language Impairments: Review the poem several times a day for the first week; later review it weekly.

Hearing Impairments: Use gestures, drawings, and pictures as you present the concepts found in the poem. Have the child recite the poem with you slowly, one line at a time.

Visual Impairments: Describe each picture as you present it. Discuss key concepts: *running up*, *striking the time*, and *running down*.

Cognitive and/or Developmental Disabilities: Use simple language, vocabulary, and short sentences in your explanations. The key concepts that you should focus on are *mouse*, *clock*, *one*, and *down*. Have the child point to pictures to demonstrate the key concepts *mouse* and *clock*. Have the child show one finger, and have her point to show the concept *down*.

Emotional Disturbance: Seat the child next to you. Have her give you materials and pictures during the lesson. Affirm her for participating appropriately in the lesson.

Other Health Impairments/Attention Deficit Hyperactivity Disorder: Make sure that you have the child's attention before speaking. Use the following motions as you sing these words, and then invite the children to sing and do the motions along with you.
Hickory, dickory, dock (clap once as you say hickory, dickory, and dock)
mouse (finger on tip of nose to wiggle it)
clock (point to wrist)
one (hold up one finger)
mouse (finger on tip of nose to wiggle it)
down (point down to the floor)
Hickory, dickory, dock (clap once as you say hickory, dickory, and dock)

Orthopedic Impairments: Help the child strike the triangle.

Curriculum Connections

✦ **Math:** Place the paper clock face, or any of the clocks you used in this lesson, in the Manipulatives Center. Concepts about time are difficult for young children to comprehend, so whatever experiences children have with the clock face should be exploratory in nature. If they want to know more information about telling time, be as concrete as possible with your responses. For example, say, "It is 10:00. Ten o'clock is when we have snack." Or, "Your parent will pick you up at 3:30."

✦ **Science:** If possible, locate a wind-up clock to place in the Science Center and remove its back so that children can observe the spring, gears, and oscillating wheel inside. Answer the questions children might ask with straightforward responses.

"Humpty Dumpty"

Time
20 minutes

Materials
picture of Humpty Dumpty sitting on a wall (use an illustration from a Mother Goose book)
egg
small painter's drop cloth (or newspapers)
CD of Thomas Moore's "Humpty Dumpty Dumpty" song (available in a recording titled *I Am Special*) (**Note:** If this CD is not available, consider using Thomas Moore's book by the same name)

Objectives

Children will:
1. Describe the dilemma or problem that occurs in the "Humpty Dumpty" rhyme.
2. Recite at least one line from the "Humpty Dumpty" rhyme.

Lesson

◆ Show the children the picture of Humpty Dumpty and ask if they know who it is.
◆ Say the nursery rhyme and ask what Humpty Dumpty's problem is.

Humpty Dumpty
Humpty Dumpty sat on a wall.
Humpty Dumpty had a great fall.
All the king's horses and all the king's men
Couldn't put Humpty Dumpty together again.

◆ Show children an egg. Demonstrate what happens when eggs fall by dropping the egg onto a protected surface, such as a painter's drop cloth or a stack of newspapers.
◆ Be prepared to explain that some problems occur that we cannot fix, for example, a broken egg cannot be put back together.
◆ Tell the children that all they can do now is clean up the mess!
Note: Wash hands after touching raw eggs. Also wash or dispose of any material that had raw egg on it.
◆ Share Thomas Moore's musical version of "Humpty Dumpty Dumpty," introducing the motions that accompany the song.
◆ Play the recording several times until children appear to tire of it.

Modifications/Accommodations

Autism: Use pictures to present key concepts. Write the poem on chart paper with small drawings above the following key words: *Humpty Dumpty*, *sat*, *wall*, *fall*, *horses*, *men*, and *put together*.
Speech or Language Impairments: Recite the poem several times before assessing. Then have the child complete the line as you recite it line by line, omitting the last word. Review the poem several times a day for the first week; later review it weekly.
Hearing Impairments: Use gestures, drawings, and pictures as you present the concepts found in the poem. Have the child recite the poem with you slowly, one line at a time.
Visual Impairments: Describe each picture as you present it. Discuss key concepts: *Humpty Dumpty is an egg, eggs break easily, a broken egg is hard to fix, what happens when something breaks that cannot be fixed.*

- **Social Studies:** Talk with individual children about problems they encounter that they cannot solve (death of a loved one, death of a pet, divorce, a natural disaster such as a tornado or hurricane, and so on). Be prepared to listen and express sympathy for the child's plight. Consider making referrals for professional assistance when children and their families are dealing with extreme crises.

Review
Ask the children to tell the story of Humpty Dumpty in their own words.

Assessment Strategy
Ask individual children to recite the "Humpty Dumpty" nursery rhyme (or any portion of it they remember).

Cognitive and/or Developmental Disabilities: Use simple language, vocabulary, and short sentences in your explanations. The key concepts that you should focus on are *sitting*, *wall*, *fall*, *horses*, *men*, *putting together* (fixing). Have the child point to pictures to demonstrate the key concepts of sitting, wall, fall, horses, and men. Review the poem several times a day for the first week; later review it weekly.

Emotional Disturbance: Seat the child next to you during the lesson. Make sure that the child is watching as you drop the egg. Provide extra explanations for this child about the problem with fixing a broken egg. Attempt to fix the egg, and explain that there are things that cannot be fixed. Talk about what can be done at home or school to solve a problem that is hard to fix.

Other Health Impairments/Attention Deficit Hyperactivity Disorder: Make sure that you have the child's attention before speaking. Use the following motions as you sing the song:

Humpty, Dumpty (hands for egg)
Sat on the wall. (sign for *sit* with index finger and long finger of right hand striking the top of the index finger and long finger of the left hand twice)
Humpty, Dumpty (hands for egg)
Had a great fall. (sign for *fall* with index finger and long finger of right hand standing on the top of the index finger and long finger of your left hand and falling off)
All the king's horses (sign for *horse*, making the horses ear with your right index finger and long finger, then flopping forward) *And all the king's men* (arms to your sides showing muscles)
Couldn't put Humpty together again. (shake head)

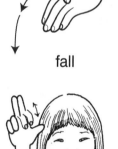

sit

fall

horse

A simplified alternative to the motions above is to clap to the rhythm of the poem or use rhythm sticks to tap the beats.

Orthopedic Impairments: The child will likely need help making the motions for the song. No other accommodations are anticipated.

Curriculum Connections

- **Art:** Provide commercial or teacher-made playdough for children to form Humpty Dumpty creatures.
- **Dramatic Play:** Add a crown, stick horses, and other props (capes, teacher-made soldier helmets made from gallon-sized ice cream container, and cardboard breastplates) to the Dramatic Play Center for children to use to reenact the Humpty Dumpty nursery rhyme.

"Little Jack Horner"

Time
20 minutes

Materials
plum
picture of Little Jack Horner
  (optional)

Objectives

Children will:
1. Recite at least one line from the "Little Jack Horner" nursery rhyme.
2. Describe one activity they do that makes them feel good about themselves.

Lesson

✦ Place the plum in front of the children as they gather for Circle or Group Time and ask them what it is.
✦ Say, "Today's nursery rhyme is about a boy and a plum. Listen to the rhyme to learn where he found his plum."
✦ Recite the nursery rhyme and ask children to tell what Jack was doing, where he found his plum, and what his reaction was.

Little Jack Horner
Little Jack Horner sat in a corner
Eating his Christmas pie.
He put in his thumb and pulled out a plum,
And said, "What a good boy am I!"

✦ Ask children to explain how they think Jack felt about finding the plum. Show them a picture of Little Jack Horner, if available.
✦ Ask, "Have you ever felt good about something you accomplished like Jack did when he found his plum?" Make suggestions, if needed, such as finishing a task, getting dressed by themselves, helping a parent cook or make something, and so on. Keep in mind that some children will respond to this question easily, while others will not. Encourage shy children to contribute; for example, say, "Jacque, I know you like to paint at the easel. Is easel painting something you feel good doing?"
✦ Tell them that you are going to prepare a "What I Feel Good About" book for the class. Request that during Center Time, each child spends some time with you dictating a sentence or two about their proudest accomplishments. Invite the children to illustrate their sentence. Add the pages to the book.
✦ Say the rhyme again, asking children to recite it with you.
✦ Ask children to supply appropriate motions as they recite the rhyme.

Modifications/Accommodations

Autism: Write the words to the poem on chart paper. Make small drawings above the following words to represent the meaning of the words: *Little Jack Horner*, *corner*, *Christmas*, *pie*, *thumb*, *plum*, and *good boy*.

- **More Language and Literacy:** Ask children to dictate at least another sentence to you for the "What I Feel Good About" class book. Invite parent volunteers to help with this, if you want. Encourage children to draw a picture to accompany their sentence dictations. Taking photographs of children participating in their "What I Feel Good About" activities is also another approach to organizing the book. Attach the photographs and/or the pictures they draw to their sentence dictations. Share the book with the class one day and at an Open House for families.
- **Snack:** On the day you present this lesson, prepare plums for snack.

Review

Ask children to review the story line of the "Little Jack Horner" nursery rhyme.

Assessment Strategy

Individually ask children to recite the "Little Jack Horner" nursery rhyme or retell the story line in their own words.

Speech or Language Impairments: Say the poem several times before assessing the children's ability to recite the rhyme or retell the story line of the poem. Then say the poem one line at a time, with the child repeating after you. Say the poem, omitting the last word and having the child supply the last word. Finally, slowly say the poem chorally with the child.

Hearing Impairments: Use objects, gestures, and movement as you present the lesson. Make sure that the child can see your face and mouth when you speak.

Visual Impairments: Let the child feel the plum and other props that you use. Describe any pictures that you present during the lesson.

Cognitive and/or Developmental Disabilities: Emphasize key concepts such as *corner*, *pie*, *plum*, and *thumb*. Have the child identify these items in pictures. Review the poem several times each day for a week; then review it weekly.

Emotional Disturbance: Have the child sit next to you during the lesson. When making the "What I Feel Good About" book for the class, you may need to remind the child of some of the things that he does well.

Other Health Impairments/Attention Deficit Hyperactivity Disorder: Make sure that you have the child's attention before speaking. Have the children stand to recite the poem together. Use the motions that the children make up along with the poem.

Orthopedic Impairments: Assist the child in making the motions to the poem if you use them. No other accommodations are anticipated.

Curriculum Connections

- **Art:** Encourage children to make pies with commercial or teacher-made playdough. Then they can stick in their thumbs just like Jack did.
- **Language and Literacy:** Play a small group game called Jack in the Corner. Put one child ("Jack" or "It") in a corner of the room while the other members of the group sit at a nearby table with you. Call a word and ask "Jack" to say a rhyming word. If the word "Jack" responds with a rhyming word, then he gets to come out of the corner and choose one of the remaining children to replace him. Select words to rhyme from some of the nursery rhymes that have been discussed during the nursery rhyme study, such as:

Word Called	Possible Response
Humpty	Dumpty
Hubbard	cupboard
Muffet	tuffet
dock	clock
Jill	hill
crown	down

"Little Boy Blue"

Time
20 minutes

Materials
small doll
toy cow and sheep figures
picture of Little Boy Blue

Objectives

Children will:
1. Describe the dilemma or problem that occurs in the "Little Boy Blue" rhyme.
2. Recite at least one line from the "Little Boy Blue" rhyme.

Lesson

+   Begin by telling the children that today's nursery rhyme is about a shepherd named Little Boy Blue. Ask if anyone knows what a shepherd is.
+   Explain that shepherds look after cows and sheep, making sure they do not wander away from the pasture.
+   Recite the nursery rhyme and ask children if Little Boy Blue is doing his job.

Little Boy Blue
Little Boy Blue, come blow your horn;
The sheep's in the meadow, the cow's in the corn;
Where's the little boy who looks after the sheep?
He's under the haystack, fast asleep.

+   Ask, "Is it a problem for Little Boy Blue to be asleep? Why? Why might he be sleeping? Why would he need to blow his horn?"
+   Encourage children to tell what can be done to solve the problem.
+   Repeat the poem and use the doll and animal figurines to demonstrate the story. Tell the children that you will be placing these items in the Dramatic Play Center so they can use them to retell the rhyme at a later time.
+   Choose one child to be Little Boy Blue and assign the rest of the children roles as cows or sheep. Ask the cows and sheep to move around the classroom pretending to graze on green grass while Boy Blue sleeps.
+   Wake up Boy Blue and ask him to do his job as shepherd and bring all of the animals back to Circle or Group Time.
+   Then re-enact the rhyme with another person serving as Little Boy Blue.

Modifications/Accommodations

Autism: Use pictures to present key concepts. Write the poem on chart paper with small drawings above the following key concepts: *boy, horn, sheep, meadow, cow, corn, haystack,* and *sleep.* Recite the poem several times and point to the words as you recite it. Have the child recite it aloud with you as you say it slowly.

Review

Ask the children to tell why the shepherd in the rhyme was named Little Boy Blue. Then repeat the rhyme with children once more time before moving to other classroom activities.

Assessment Strategy

Ask individual children to recite at least one line from the "Little Boy Blue" rhyme (or retell the rhyme in their own words).

Speech or Language Impairments: Say the poem one line at a time and have the child repeat each line after you say it. Then say the poem, omitting the last word of each line. Ask the child to complete the line. Then have the child say the poem with you.

Hearing Impairments: Use pictures and gestures as you present the poem and the concepts.

Visual Impairments: Let the child touch and feel the doll and animal figurines.

Cognitive and/or Developmental Disabilities: Use simple language, vocabulary, and short sentences in your explanations. The key concepts that you should focus on are *boy*, *horn*, *sheep*, *meadow*, *cow*, *corn*, *haystack*, and *sleep*. Have the child point to pictures to identify these concepts. Review the poem several times a day for the first week; later review it weekly.

Emotional Disturbance: Seat the child next to you. Have her give you materials and pictures during the lesson. Affirm her for participating. Talk about why the sheep were in the meadow and why the cows got into the corn. Talk about what can happen when we are not doing our jobs. Ask why the child thinks that Little Boy Blue is sleeping during the daytime. If the child does not know here are a few suggestions: he went to bed late, or maybe he did not take a nap.

Other Health Impairments/Attention Deficit Hyperactivity Disorder: Make sure that you have the child's attention before speaking. Ask the child to make up motions to accompany the poem, or clap the rhythm of the poem to give the child the opportunity for movement.

Orthopedic Impairments: Physically assist the child to act out the roles in Little Boy Blue.

Curriculum Connections

+ **Art:** Place scissor, glue or a stapler, blue fabric swatches, and any other material so the children can make clothes for dolls in the classroom. Invite them to use the dolls to reenact the nursery rhyme.
+ **More Art:** Host a Blue Day event. Place blue construction paper or blue butcher paper in the Art Center for children to fashion clothing items to wear (hats, sashes, pull-over shirts, bracelets, banners, and so on). At a designated time during the day, ask children to put on their blue "clothing" and parade around the classroom (or even down the hall, if possible). Call the boys "Little Boy Blue" and the girls "Little Girl Blue."
+ **Science:** Obtain blue paint color cards from a local paint store and put them on the Science Table. Encourage children to put them order them from lightest to darkest. Ask individual children which one of the blue chips Little Boy Blue might have worn.

"Little Bo Peep"

Time
15 minutes

Materials
toy sheep figures
sunbonnet
picture of Little Bo Peep

Preparation
Hide the sheep figurines around the room before the children arrive.

Objectives

Children will:
1. Tell that Little Bo Peep is a shepherd.
2. Recite at least one line from the "Little Bo Peep" rhyme.

Lesson

- ✦ Wear the sunbonnet to Circle or Group Time to attract children's attention.
- ✦ Tell the children that they will be learning about another shepherd in the following nursery rhyme:

Little Bo Peep
Little Bo Peep has lost her sheep
And can't tell where to find them.
Leave them alone, and they'll come home,
Wagging their tails behind them.

- ✦ Ask these questions, acknowledging that young children may have creative and unique responses to your queries:
  - ✦ Who is the shepherd?
  - ✦ What problem did she have?
  - ✦ Why did she have this problem?
  - ✦ What did she need to do to solve her problem?
  - ✦ Why would you think the sheep would come home on their own?
  - ✦ How is Bo Peep's job different from Little Boy Blue's job?
  - ✦ Why would Bo Peep wear a sunbonnet?
- ✦ Repeat the rhyme and tell children what "wagging their tails" means. Let them "wag their tails" like the sheep might have done. Ask them what sound sheep might make when they come home.
- ✦ Invite the children to look for the hidden sheep. Be prepared to give clues if children have difficulty finding some of the sheep.
- ✦ Put the sheep figurines and the sunbonnet in the Dramatic Play Center.

Modifications/Accommodations

Autism: Write the poem on chart paper with small drawings above the following words: *Little Bo Peep*, *sheep*, *home*, and *tails*. Recite the poem several times and point to the words as you recite it. Have the child recite it aloud with you as you say it slowly.

Speech or Language Impairments: Say the poem one line at a time and have the child repeat each line after you say it. Then say the poem omitting the last word of each line. Ask the child to complete each line. Then have the child say the poem with you.

✦ **Language and Literacy:** Spend time with small groups of children reviewing some of the nursery rhymes they have learned thus far in the study. Make some comparisons among "Little Miss Muffet," "Little Jack Horner," "Little Boy Blue" and "Little Bo Beep." For example, the rhymes show the characters outdoors; some deal with animals, they are dealing with problems, and they are all described as being little.

Review

Ask the group to tell the story of Little Bo Peep in their own words.

Assessment Strategy

Show individual children pictures of various Mother Goose characters and ask each child to identify Little Bo Peep.

Hearing Impairments: Use pictures and gestures as you present the poem and the concepts.

Visual Impairments: Describe the pictures as you show them. Let the child feel and hold the sunbonnet and sheep figures. Help the child to find the sheep during the hiding game by providing clues such as "You're getting warmer (colder)," "It is somewhere to your right (left)," and "It is higher (lower)."

Cognitive and/or Developmental Disabilities: Emphasize key concepts such as *sheep, lost, find, home*, and *tails*. Have the child identify pictures of Little Bo Peep, sheep, home, and tails.

Emotional Disturbance: Seat the child near you during the lesson. Supervise the child closely during the activity where you find the sheep.

Other Health Impairments/Attention Deficit Hyperactivity Disorder: Make sure that you have the child's attention before speaking. Use the following motions with the poem:

Little Bo Peep (hold shepherd's crook)

lost (hands out, palms up)

sheep (use the sign for sheep, with the right hand making a V with the tall finger and index finger; then stroke upward from the wrist to the crook of your left arm on the inner side of your arm)

doesn't (shake head)

find (hand above eyes, turning head)

leave them alone (nod head)

home (hands point together make roof of house)

wagging their tails (shake tails)

sheep

This poem also will help children with speech or language disorders, autism, and cognitive disabilities.

Orthopedic Impairments: Assist the child physically to find the sheep when they are hidden.

Curriculum Connections

✦ **Books:** Add gender-positive literature to the Library Center, such as *White Dynamite and Curly Kidd* by Bill Martin, Jr. and John Archambault, and *The Queen Who Couldn't Bake Gingerbread* by Dorthy Van Woerkom. Remind children that both Little Boy Blue and Little Bo Peep were able to do the same jobs.

"Mary Had a Little Lamb"

Note: "Mary Had a Little Lamb" is not technically a nursery rhyme because it was written by Sarah Joseph Hale of Boston in 1830. However, most teachers recognize it as a nursery rhyme-type song.

Time
20 minutes

Materials
picture of Mary and her little lamb at school

Objectives

Children will:
1. Describe the dilemma or problem that occurs in "Mary Had a Little Lamb."
2. Recite at least one line from the "Mary Had a Little Lamb" rhyme.

Lesson

✦ Show the picture of Mary and her lamb and say, "I'm sure you already know the nursery rhyme we're going to talk about today." Allow time for children to respond to the picture.
✦ Say, "I'm going to teach you some new verses to the song." Sing as many of the verses that you believe your children are interested in hearing.

Mary Had a Little Lamb
Mary had a little lamb,
Little lamb, little lamb.
Mary had a little lamb,
Its fleece was white as snow

And everywhere that Mary went,
Mary went, Mary went,
Everywhere that Mary went
The lamb was sure to go

It followed her to school one day
School one day, school one day.
It followed her to school one day,
Which was against the rules.

It made the children laugh and play,
Laugh and play, laugh and play.
It made the children laugh and play
To see a lamb at school.

✦ Ask the children some or all of these questions:
   ✦ Does Mary have a problem?
   ✦ Why do you think the lamb made the children laugh?
   ✦ What would you do if a lamb were to come to school?
✦ Remind the children that a lamb is a baby sheep. Ask if they can remember any other nursery rhymes about sheep. Repeat the rhymes as they are mentioned.
✦ Tell the children to pretend that you are Mary and they are lambs. Sing the song again and move around the classroom as the children follow you wherever you go.

Review

Ask the children to tell what they remember about the rhyme. Allow individual children who want to repeat the rhyme to do so.

Assessment Strategy

Ask individual children to repeat as much of the "Mary Had Little Lamb" nursery rhyme as they can remember. Children may choose to sing the rhyme because doing so will be easier for them.

✦ Return to the circle area to sing the song one last time. Ask children to tell how they would feel if an animal (or pet) followed them everywhere they went.

Modifications/Accommodations

Autism: Write the words to the poem on chart paper with drawings above the following words: *Mary*, *lamb*, *fleece*, *snow*, *school*, *rules*, and *laugh*. Point to the drawings as you sing the song.

Speech or Language Impairments: Recite the poem several times before assessing the child. Then have the child complete each line as you recite the poem line by line, omitting the last word. Review the poem several times a day for the first week; later, review it weekly.

Hearing Impairments: Use gestures, drawings, and pictures as you present the concepts in the poem. Have the child recite the poem slowly with you, one line at a time.

Visual Impairments: Describe the picture that you show of Mary and her lamb.

Cognitive and/or Developmental Disabilities: Use simple language, vocabulary, and short sentences in your explanations. The key concepts that you should focus on are *little, lamb, fleece, white, snow, school, rules, laugh,* and *play*. Review the poem several times a day for the first week; later review it weekly.

Emotional Disturbance: Seat the child next to you. Have her give you materials and pictures during the lesson. Talk about why rules are important at school. Affirm her for participating.

Other Health Impairments/Attention Deficit Hyperactivity Disorder: Make sure that you have the child's attention before speaking. Clap the rhythm you recite the poem or sing the song.

Orthopedic Impairments: No accommodations are anticipated for this lesson.

Curriculum Connections

✦ **Art:** Place small Styrofoam balls, cotton balls, and other art materials in the Art Center. Invite the children to make lambs.

✦ **Listening:** Use a cassette recorder to tape all of the verses to "Mary Had a Little Lamb" and place the tape in the Listening Center. Include a copy of "Mary Had a Little Lamb" by Sarah Josepha Hale so children can "read" along as they listen to the recording.

✦ **Music:** Just for fun, sing "Mary Had a Little Lamb" substituting the word "baa" for words. Ask for children's suggestions for other animal sounds that might be used instead ("moo," for example or "woof," "neigh," and "cheep").

"Jack Be Nimble"

Time
15 minutes

Materials
candle and a short
   candlestick
picture of Jack

Objectives

Children will:
1. Demonstrate how to jump.
2. Repeat at least one line of the rhyme.

Lesson

✦ Place the candle and candlestick in the center of the
   Circle Time rug. As children arrive for Circle or
   Group Time, show the children the candlestick,
   and ask them what it is.
✦ Ask, "Have you ever jumped over
   a candlestick?"
✦ Show a picture of Jack jumping over the
   candlestick. Recite the following rhyme:

   Jack Be Nimble
   Jack, be nimble; Jack, be quick.
   Jack, jump over the candlestick.

✦ Ask children why Jack might have wanted to jump over
   the candle and candlestick.
✦ Remind children that they have heard other nursery rhymes about boys
   named Jack. Ask if this is the same Jack. Accept whatever answers they
   give, though pictures in a nursery rhyme book might sway their responses.
✦ Position the candle in the middle of the circle and ask children to jump over
   it. **Note:** Do not light the candle!

Modifications/Accommodations

Autism: Clap the rhythm of the poem several times as you say it. Encourage
   the child to clap with you, and then to say the poem with you as you both
   clap the rhythm. Have other children jump over the candlestick before
   asking this child to do so.
Speech or Language Impairments: Recite the poem several times before
   assessing. Then have the child complete the line as you recite it line by line,
   omitting the last word. Review the poem several times a day for the first
   week; later review it weekly.

Review

Ask children to recite the poem in unison and demonstrate how to jump over the candlestick.

Assessment Strategy

Ask each child to repeat as much of the rhyme as he can.

Hearing Impairments: Make sure that the child is positioned so that he can see your face and mouth. Have the child recite the poem with you slowly, one line at a time.

Visual Impairments: Describe the picture of Jack and the candlestick. Help the child to jump over the candlestick.

Cognitive and/or Developmental Disabilities: Use simple language, vocabulary, and short sentences in your explanations. The key concepts that you should focus on are *quick*, *jump*, *candlestick*, and over. Have the child point to pictures to demonstrate the key concepts of jump and candlestick. Physically demonstrate the concepts *quick* and *over*; then have the child show you how to move quickly and to place something over the candle. Review the poem several times a day for the first week; later, review it weekly.

Emotional Disturbance: Seat the child near you during the lesson. Before asking the child to jump over the candlestick, remind him to be careful as he jumps.

Other Health Impairments/Attention Deficit Hyperactivity Disorder: Make sure that you have the child's attention before speaking. Before jumping over the candlestick, remind him that you will jump one time, and that someone else will have a turn. Ask him how many times he will jump. Remind him to be careful as he jumps.

Orthopedic Impairments: Assist the child in jumping over the candlestick. No other accommodations are anticipated.

Curriculum Connections

+ **Dramatic Play:** Place the candle and candlestick in the Dramatic Play Center for children to reenact the nursery rhyme.
+ **Math:** Provide various sizes of candles for children to put in order from largest to smallest. Or have them use circumference as a way to seriate the candles (thinnest to thickest).
+ **Music:** Teach children the rhyme using the tune, "Mary Had a Little Lamb."

Jack, be nimble; Jack, be quick,
Jack, be quick; Jack, be quick.
Jack be nimble; Jack, be quick,
Jack, jump over the candlestick.

"Old King Cole"

Time
20 minutes

Materials
picture of Old King Cole
pictures of a pipe, a bowl,
    and the three fiddlers
    (if available)
crown
king's cape

Objectives

Children will:
1. Identify a picture of Old King Cole.
2. Name one thing Old King Cole wanted.

Lesson

✦ As children gather, put on the crown and the royal cape and tell the children that they are going to learn a rhyme about a king today.
✦ Show the children a picture of Old King Cole and ask why he might be called "old."
✦ Ask them to listen to the rhyme to find out what the king wants.

Old King Cole
Old King Cole was a merry old soul,
And a merry old soul was he;
He called for his pipe, he called for his bowl,
And he called for his fiddlers three.

✦ Repeat the rhyme, showing the pictures as you recite the nursery rhyme.
✦ Ask them again what items the king wants. Tell the children everyone wants things, but unlike King Cole, we don't always get what we want.
✦ Develop a discussion about items children might want but not always get.
✦ Repeat the rhyme, and tell children that King Cole could issue a command and it would be followed (because he is king). Ask, "Is this true of us when we want something?"
✦ Remind children that when we want things, we should ask in a pleasant way, saying "please."
✦ Provide an opportunity for a few children to act out the rhyme for the rest of the class. Then let the players choose children to take their places and act out the rhyme a second time. Continue dramatizing the rhyme until children tire of the activity.
✦ Add the props to the Dramatic Play Center for use at Center Time.

Modifications/Accommodations

Autism: Write the poem on chart paper, with small drawings above the following words: *king*, *merry*, *call*, *pipe*, *bowl*, *fiddlers*, and *three*. Recite the poem several time and point to the words as you say them. Have the child recite it aloud with you as you say it slowly.

Review

Hold up pictures representing the rhyme and ask children to identify them (Old King Cole, the pipe, the bowl, and the fiddlers).

Assessment Strategy

Ask each child to repeat as much of the nursery rhyme as she can remember.

Speech or Language Impairments: Say the poem one line at a time and have the child repeat it after you say it. Then say the poem, omitting the last word of each line. Ask the child to complete each line. Then have the child say the poem with you.

Hearing Impairments: Use pictures and gestures as you present the poem and the concepts.

Visual Impairments: Describe the picture of Old King Cole as you present the lesson.

Cognitive and/or Developmental Disabilities: Use simple language, vocabulary, and short sentences in your explanations. The key concepts that you should focus on are *king*, *merry*, *pipe*, *bowl*, *fiddlers*, and *three*. Have the child point to pictures to demonstrate the key concepts of *king*, *merry*, *pipe*, *bowl*, and *fiddlers*. Have the child show the concept of three by counting to three and showing you three fingers. Review the poem several times a day for the first week; later, review it weekly.

Emotional Disturbance: Seat the child near you. Have her give you materials and pictures during the lesson. Affirm her for participating. Ask about how Old King Cole would have asked politely for the things that he wanted.

Other Health Impairments/Attention Deficit Hyperactivity Disorder: Be sure that the child has an opportunity to act out the part of Old King Cole. Talk about the fact that Old King Cole may need to learn to wait.

Orthopedic Impairments: Physically help the child to act out the part of Old King Cole.

Curriculum Connections

✦ **Art:** Provide materials (construction paper, glue, glitter, markers, and so on) for children to make individual crowns to wear in the classroom.
✦ **Language and Literacy:** Add a CD of violin music to the Listening Center for children's enjoyment.
✦ **Special Visitor:** Invite someone (a parent or a high school symphony performer) who can play a violin to come to the classroom for a very short demonstration of "fiddle" music.

Introduction to Music: What Is Sound?

Time
25 minutes

Materials
noisemakers (triangle, drum, rattles, clappers, or whatever else is available in the classroom)

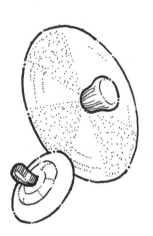

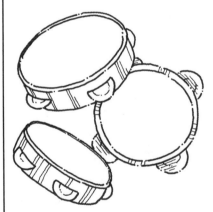

Objectives

Children will:
1. Identify sounds they hear in the environment.
2. Identify a song when they hear one.

Lesson

✦ Begin the lesson by asking children to close their eyes and listen carefully to what they hear.
✦ After about 15 seconds, call on individual children to describe what they heard.
✦ Show the children a variety of noisemakers. Ask them to close their eyes again while you use one of the noisemakers to make a sound.
✦ Call on one child to identify the noisemaker that you used.
✦ Tell the children that what they heard was sound. Point out to them that sound is anything they hear.
✦ Then start singing a familiar song, such as "Skip to My Lou" (they will probably join in as you sing).
✦ Tell the children that music is a specific type of sound, which is pleasant to hear. Ask them to name other songs they enjoy; refer to them as "music" as you sing a few of their suggestions.
✦ Explain that sounds (and music) can be loud or soft (or you may prefer to use the terms loud and quiet). Demonstrate by playing the noisemakers loud or softly.
✦ Ask the children to sing "Skip to My Lou" in a quiet voice (instead of a loud voice). Use a well-known chant, too, such as this one:

Bernie Bee, Bernie Bee (Traditional)
Bernie Bee, Bernie Bee,
Tell me when your wedding be.
If it be tomorrow day,
Take your wings and fly away.

Modifications/Accommodations

Autism: Offer the child a choice during the assessment part of the activity. For example, shake the noisemaker and ask, "Is this sound or music?"
Speech or Language Impairments: During the assessment, provide the definition to the child and have him respond with the word sound or music: A specific type of sound, one that uses a singing voice is called _____. (music)

Review

As children leave the circle, ask them to name a sound they heard in the classroom at Circle or Group Time.

Assessment Strategy

With individual children, ask each to define the words sound and music in their own words. (Sound can be defined as anything that human ears can detect. This includes pleasing sounds and noise, which is often unpleasant. Music is a series of sounds that have rhythm, melody, and harmony.)

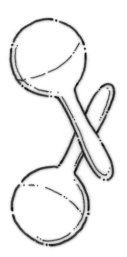

Hearing Impairments: Hearing the various sounds may be difficult for a child with a hearing impairment. Allow the child to place his hands on the noisemaker as it is played. In doing this, the child will be able to differentiate between when the sound produced is loud or soft.

Visual Impairments: Let the child touch and feel the noisemaker and other items used during the lesson.

Cognitive and/or Developmental Disabilities: Use simple language and vocabulary, repeating phrases frequently. During the review, allow the child to listen to the noisemaker and then ask the child if what he heard was sound or music?

Emotional Disturbance: If requested, allow the child to keep his eyes open during the lesson, if he does not want to close them. Praise the child for his participation in the activity.

Other Health Impairments/Attention Deficit Hyperactivity Disorder: Use visual cues to help the child monitor his voice and activity level.

Orthopedic Impairments: Position the child to be activity engaged throughout the lesson.

Curriculum Connections

+ **Language and Literacy:** With small groups of children, experiment with words that are onomatopoeia (*swish*, *pop*, *bang*, *splat*, *crackle*, *crunch*, *swoosh*, *whee*, *meow*, *woof*, *moo*, *neigh*, *quack*, *cheep*, *tweet*, *plop*, *drip*, and so on). Make a recording of children using these sound words to place in the Listening Center for later enjoyment.
+ **Music:** Place instruments that are new to the children in the Music Center. You might prefer to limit the number of instruments in the Music Center to cut down on the noise. Provide musical instruments the children may not have seen before, such as a xylophone. Set aside specific times during the day to work with small groups of children, teaching them about rhythm or keeping a steady beat.
+ **Science:** Provide several jars with varying amounts of water in them. Encourage the children to experiment with the sounds the jars make when tapped. If possible, prepare eight jars that represent the notes in an octave from "do" to "do." Demonstrate how to sing "do, re, mi, fa, sol, la, ti do."
+ **Writing:** Begin a collection of words that represent various noises the children hear throughout the duration of the study. Ask them to identify sounds they hear in their homes, on the way to school, on the playground, and so on. Record the collection of sounds on a chart or in individual class books that the children keep.

What Is Music?

Time
25 minutes

Materials
rhythm sticks or a drum
    (optional)

Objectives

Children will:
1. Sing songs in group settings.
2. Name a favorite song.

Lesson

+ Begin the lesson by singing a familiar song that the children enjoy.
+ Ask the children if they like the song. Ask them to name other songs they enjoy singing.
+ As songs are suggested, ask the group to sing them with you (or you may ask individual children to lead their favorite songs if they wish).
+ Remind children that music is enjoyable because it provides us with various feelings. Name one of your favorite songs and say, "I like _____, because it makes me feel like dancing."
+ Ask children to tell how their favorite songs make them feel. Write their replies on a chart or on a chalkboard.
+ End the lesson by asking children to stand and march in place as you sing "Yankee Doodle" or another song with a strong marching rhythm.

Modifications/Accommodations

Autism: Use picture feeling cards when asking children to tell how songs make them feel. Children can point to the appropriate pictorial representation of their feelings. For example, a photograph of a child with a frown on her face would represent the feeling of sadness.

Speech or Language Impairments: Use rhythm sticks to tap the beat of each song. This will allow participation in a child with limited speech abilities. Provide two choices when asking the child how her favorite song makes her feel. For example, "Does your favorite song make you feel happy or sad?"

Hearing Impairments: Place the child near you so she can clearly hear directions and songs. This is especially important for a child who reads lips. When singing, add movement that supports the beat of the song. Many children with hearing impairments have a difficult time keeping the beat to a song unless there is physical movement, such as tapping or bouncing, involved.

Review

Ask the group to remember and tell the difference between sound and music. (Sound is any noise that can be spoken or heard. Music is enjoyable to hear, because of its melody and rhythm.)

Assessment Strategy

Ask individuals to name and sing their favorite song during Center Time. Some children may not want to sing the song they name, but they can say what it is. Write the names of these songs in a prominent place in the classroom.

Visual Impairments: No modifications are necessary.

Cognitive and/or Developmental Disabilities: During the assessment phase, offer a close-ended question to the child. For example, "Are music and sound the same thing?"

Emotional Disturbance: Remain close to the child to monitor her behaviors. it may be necessary to designate the area in which the child can march to "Yankee Doodle."

Other Health Impairments/Attention Deficit Hyperactivity Disorder: Use proximity control to help the child remain on task when marching to "Yankee Doodle."

Orthopedic Impairments: If the child's specific impairments prohibits her from marching in place, allow her to move her body or help her move her wheelchair to the music.

Curriculum Connections

◆ **Connecting with Home:** Allow individual children to bring the class recording of favorite songs to take home overnight or for a weekend to share with their parents (see Listening below). Provide a sign out/sign in sheet for the class recording to keep track of which child's family has it.

◆ **Listening:** Make a recording of the children singing their favorite songs (either as a group or individually). Add the recording to the Listening Center for children's listening enjoyment.

◆ **Music:** If possible, add an old guitar to the Music Center. Invite the children to play with the guitar as they sing their favorite songs.

◆ **Special Visitor:** If parents have musical abilities, such as playing a musical instrument or singing, invite them for a brief performance for the children at the end of the day. Extend these invitations at any time of the year, but they are more pertinent during the music unit.

Time
25 minutes

Materials
recording of someone singing (or a choral group)
copy of the poem "Singing Time" by Rose Fyleman in *The Arbuthnot Anthology*
picture of human vocal cords

Objectives

Children will:
1. Identify singing when they hear it.
2. Tell that singing is accomplished with human voices.

Lesson

✦ Begin the lesson by singing another one of the children's favorite songs ("This Old Man" would be a good choice).
✦ Tell them that singing is what we do when we follow melodies with our voices. Explain that air has to pass from the lungs across our vocal cords to produce sounds, whether they are spoken are sung.
✦ Show a picture of human vocal cords, and tell children these are in our throats.
✦ Sing another verse from "This Old Man," and ask children to place their hands on their throats to feel their vocal cords vibrate as they sing.
✦ You might explain, too, that the vocal cords are a type of musical instrument, because they help people make melodies when they sing. Ask children to place their hands on their noses and cheeks and sing another verse of "This Old Man" to feel their heads resonate.
✦ Play a short choral or solo selection for the children and see if they can identify the song and that someone is singing it.
✦ Read "Singing Time" by Rose Fyleman or another selection that defines the joy in singing. Ask children to talk about their enjoyment of singing.
✦ Explain to the children that they can use the "do-re-mi" information they learned in the previous lesson to sing any song (see the science curriculum connection in Introduction to Music: What Is Sound? on page 338). Demonstrate by singing "Mary Had a Little Lamb" using only syllables. For example:

Mi-Re-Do
Tune: "Mary Had a Little Lamb"
Mi-re-do-re-mi-mi-mi, re-re-re-, mi-sol-sol;
Mi-re-do-re-mi-mi-mi, re-re-mi-re-do.

Modifications/Accommodations

Autism: During the lesson, use pictures, objects, and gestures to provide visual support for the child.
Speech or Language Impairments: During the assessment phase allow the child to point to his vocal chords instead of "telling" where they are located.

Review

Ask children to tell point to where their vocal cords are located and how they think singing happens.

Assessment Strategy

On an individual basis, ask children when they like to sing.

Hearing Impairments: Seat the child across from you where he can see your lips and face. Strategically place the child close to the tape or CD player. Repeat key concepts and check for understanding periodically. Refer to pictures and objects throughout the lesson.

Visual Impairments: As you present the picture of the vocal chords and read the selected book, describe pictures verbally. If possible, use a three-dimensional model of vocal chords.

Cognitive and/or Developmental Disabilities: Use short sentences and simple vocabulary throughout the lesson. Substitute terminology such as resonate and melodious for more simplistic words. Repeat key concepts and review them daily after completing the lesson. If possible, use a three-dimensional model of the human lungs and vocal chords to show children how the air moves through the vocal chords. A verbal description may not be comprehended.

Emotional Disturbance: Seat the child near you during the lesson. Affirm him for participating in the lesson.

Other Health Impairments/Attention Deficit Hyperactivity Disorder: Make sure to secure the child's attention before moving from one activity to another. Allow the child to assist in turning the pages of the book and affirm him for his help in the activity.

Orthopedic Impairments: Be sure that the child is positioned so that he can see the models and pictures used in the lesson.

Curriculum Connections

- ✦ **Language and Literacy:** In small groups, ask children to explain the differences between: solo singing and choral singing; children's voices and adult voices; women's voices and men's voices; and singing and instrumental performances.
- ✦ **More Language and Literacy:** The word sing is such great for phonemic awareness experiences. Work with small groups of children to brainstorm as many words as possible that rhyme with sing, and add them to the classroom Word Wall. For example: *wing*, *king*, *ding*, *fling*, *ring*, and *sting*.
- ✦ **Music:** Prepare a few songs that children can sing to another class (or to their parents, director, or principal) at some point during the study of music.

MUSIC

The Orchestra

Time
20 minutes

Materials
recording of an orchestral
performance
The Maestro Plays by Bill
Martin, Jr. and Vladimir
Radunsky
picture of an orchestra
pictures of individual musical
instruments

conductor

orchestra

Objectives

Children will:
1. Identify that an orchestra is a group of musicians who perform using musical instruments.
2. Pretend to conduct an orchestra like a conductor.

Lesson

✦ Remind children that they have been learning about music and ask them what they have learned so far (sound, music, and singing).
✦ Tell them they will be talking about an orchestra in this lesson.
✦ Share a few minutes of an orchestral performance; then ask the children to describe what they heard.
✦ Point out to the children that what they heard was not like singing. This recording is an orchestra, and the musicians who play in an orchestra play various instruments.
✦ Show children pictures of an orchestra and musical instruments. Tell them that the person who directs their performance is called a conductor or a maestro.
✦ Introduce the book *The Maestro Plays* to the children.
✦ Share the orchestra recording again and request that the children stand and pretend they are conductors and "direct" the orchestra.

Modifications/Accommodations

Autism: Use pictures and objects throughout the lesson to provide a visual reference.

Speech or Language Impairments: Provide a carrier phrase if the child does not respond to questions, For example, when you ask who directs the orchestra, provide the carrier phrase, "A conductor directs the _____." If she does not respond, hold up a picture and have her complete the sentence.

Hearing Impairments: Refer to pictures and objects throughout the lesson. Repeat phrases frequently and check for understanding. Seat the child across from you so she can see your face and mouth. Integrate signs for words such conductor or orchestra.

Visual Impairments: Describe pictures as you present them. When reading The Maestro Plays, vividly describe what is occurring in the pictures.

Cognitive and/or Developmental Disabilities: Use simple vocabulary and language as you present concepts. Check for understanding frequently. The terms conductor and orchestra may need to be pre-taught.

Review

Ask children to tell what they learned about the orchestra and the conductor.

Assessment Strategy

Individually, ask each child to identify what an orchestra is and who directs the orchestra.

Emotional Disturbance: Seat the child near you and provide close supervision during the lesson.

Other Health Impairments/Attention Deficit Hyperactivity Disorder: increase opportunities for movement within the lesson. This can be achieved by allowing a child with ADHD to help gather materials or to push the button on the recorder when playing orchestra music.

Orthopedic Impairments: If a specific orthopedic impairment prohibits a child from standing, allow her to role play the "conductor" from a seated position.

Curriculum Connections

✦ **Bulletin Board:** Begin developing a bulletin board showing musical instruments in preparation for the specific lessons that will follow. You can find posters of musical instruments in teacher supply stores. On occasion, public libraries have poster collections that can be checked out for a few weeks. Encourage children to draw pictures of various instruments to add to the bulletin board collection.

✦ **Field Trip:** Some symphony orchestras prepare special programs for children. Make arrangements for a field trip to hear an orchestra perform. If this is not possible, encourage parents to take their children to concerts that are developed specifically for young children.

✦ **Music:** Add a conductor's wand or baton (or more, if available) to the Music Center. Observe children using it in their play.

✦ **Special Visitor:** Invite a musician to come to class to demonstrate what he or she does in a performance. Some high schools will send small ensembles to schools or child-care centers if arrangements are made in a timely manner. Remind the musicians to limit the amount of time they ask children to sit and listen. Request that their sessions with children be as interactive as possible.

The Marching Band

Time
20 minutes

Materials
recording of marching band
  performance (a collection
  of Sousa marches is
  excellent)
instruments used in a
  marching band (drums
  are best to use)
band uniform
baton
picture of a band in action

marching band

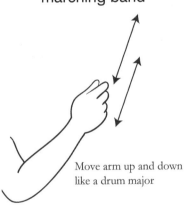

Move arm up and down
like a drum major

baton

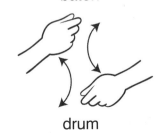

drum

Objectives

Children will:
1. Describe how marching music makes them feel.
2. Demonstrate how to march in place.

Lesson

✦ Tell the children that this lesson is about another group of musicians who play together, called a marching band.
✦ Play a recording of marching music and ask children to describe how the music makes them feel.
✦ Ask the children to stand and march in place as you continue to play the recording. You may want to use the drum to demonstrate the steady beat as the children march in place. Individual children could also play the drum, especially if you have several to share. Ask them to tell how they felt as they marched in place.
✦ Continue the lesson by showing the band uniform and director's baton. Help them recall that an orchestra leader is called a conductor, and tell them that the bandleader is called a director.
✦ Add the picture of the marching band to the class bulletin board started in a previous lesson, and ask children to distinguish between bands and orchestras by looking carefully at the pictures.
✦ Ask children to tell about marching bands they may have seen in local parades or at sports events in their community.

Modifications/Accommodations

Autism: Provide various pictures of places where marching bands play and places that marching bands would not play. Have the child point to those cards depicting proper locations of placed you would see marching bands.
Speech or Language Impairments: Allow other children to begin the review of the lesson and then use a lead-in sentence to guide the child in responding to places he has seen a marching band. For example, I have seen a marching band at _____."
Hearing Impairments: Allow the child to place his hands over the CD player to distinguish the changes of tone and pitch in the music being played. Move the child closer to you or to the area where the music is coming from. Pair key vocabulary, such as *marching band*, *baton*, and *drums*, with simple ASL signs.

Review

Ask children to name places where they may have seen a marching band.

Assessment Strategy

With small groups of children, play recordings of an orchestra performance and a marching band performance and ask the children to differentiate between the two.

Visual Impairments: Allow the child the opportunity to manipulate the various objects that are being used in the lesson, such as the baton, hat, uniform, and so on.

Cognitive and/or Developmental Disabilities: During the assessment phase provide a close-ended question. For example, "Is the sound you hear a marching band?" Many new vocabulary words are introduced in the lesson. It may be necessary to break the lesson into two smaller lessons, one emphasizing the instruments and the other the conductor/director.

Emotional Disturbance: Place children into smaller groups when marching. Designate a specific area in which marching can occur.

Other Health Impairments/Attention Deficit Hyperactivity Disorder: Provide opportunities for movement, such as allowing the child to pass out the drums being used in the lessons.

Orthopedic Impairments: Provide hand-over-hand assistance to children who cannot play the drums. Children do not need to use drumsticks; they can use their hands to beat on the drum.

Curriculum Connections

✦ **Dramatic Play:** Place the band uniform and director's baton in the Dramatic Play Center. Encourage the children to pretend to have a marching band.

✦ **Music:** Invite a band ensemble from the local high school to come and perform for the class. Ask the ensemble to make their presentation short (approximately 15–20 minutes) to accommodate children's innate need to be active. They should also consider allowing children to march around the classroom while they are performing.

✦ **Outdoors:** Have a number of twirler's batons available for interested children to experiment with twirling a baton. Answer their questions about baton twirling and demonstrate how to twirl if they ask.

Introduction to Instruments

Note: Many of the activities suggested in this lesson and the ones that follow require pictures or photographs of musical instruments. Consider contacting a music store for catalogs and brochures of various musical instruments. You can also approach a music teacher or band director and ask that person to share any outdated catalogs, so you will have the number of images you need for children to create posters and to post on bulletin boards.

Time
20 minutes

Materials
collection of musical instruments (percussion instruments are better for children to use; for hygienic reasons, the teacher should be the only one who uses a wind or brass instrument in the classroom), or use rhythm instruments, if these are easier to provide pictures of musical instruments (if possible, have samples of wind, string, brass and percussion instruments)
Note: A classroom poster set of musical instruments is available from Oceanna Music Teachers Resources (www.oceannamusic.com; 1-877-296-9079).
instrumental recording (one used in one of the previous lessons would be appropriate)

Objectives

Children will:
1. Name at least two musical instruments.
2. Demonstrate how to keep a steady beat.

Lesson

- Begin the lesson by asking children what they have learned about music so far.
- Tell the children that they are going to learn more about musical instruments in this lesson.
- Show children the collection of musical instruments and tell them that these instruments make music. Demonstrate how each instrument is played and, if possible, let children try to make music on percussion or string instruments (doing this depends on the condition of the instruments and whether your children will be able to use them without being destructive).
- Tell children that there are four basic types of instruments: wind, string, brass, and percussion instruments. Show examples of each as you name the types.
- Remind the children that musical instruments are used in orchestras and marching bands.
- Play an instrumental recording and ask children to pretend to play one of the four types of instruments as a movement activity to accompany the recording.

Modifications/Accommodations

Autism: Allow a child with auditory sensitivity to wear headphones or step away when instruments are played.

Speech or Language Impairments: When asking the child to identify the basic types of instruments, provide a choice. For example, "Is a violin a string or a percussion instrument?"

Hearing Impairments: Let the child feel the differences in the strength and intensity of the vibrations that come from the instruments as they are played.

Visual Impairments: Provide opportunities to hold the instruments. When showing pictures, describe the feel, texture, and colors of the instruments.

Cognitive and/or Developmental Disabilities: Review the meaning of each type of instrument several times. Then have the child repeat or rephrase your statements. Provide several opportunities for review of key vocabulary.

Review

Show children the musical instruments again and ask them to identify the four basic types of musical instruments.

Assessment Strategy

Ask individual children to identify a specific instrument type (wind, string, brass or percussion). Doing this assessment might be difficult for some children, so be prepared to prompt them or allow them to choose a buddy to help them identify instruments.

Emotional Disturbance: Seat the child near you during the lesson. Let her help by holding the photographs of the instruments. Affirm the child for helping and participating.

Other Health Impairments/Attention Deficit Hyperactivity Disorder: Establish a consistent signal, such as a raised finger, to get the child's attention. Make sure that you have the child's attention before giving her instructions.

Orthopedic Impairments: Assist a child with grasping difficulties to hold and manipulate the instruments. Be sure the child is positioned to fully participate in the lesson.

Curriculum Connections

✦ **Bulletin Board:** Add the Music Bulletin Board begun in a previous lesson by marking sections and labeling them with the four types of instruments (wind, string, brass, and percussion). As the next four lessons emerge, add pictures to each section to help children identify the four types.

✦ **Language and Literacy:** Add a collection of books about musical instruments to the Library Center. Some suggested titles are:

> *The Story of the Incredible Orchestra: An Introduction to Musical Instruments and the Symphony Orchestra* by Bruce Koscielniak
> *Meet the Orchestra* by Ann Hayes
> *Zin! Zin! Zin! A Violin* by Lloyd Moss
> *Our Marching Band* by Lloyd Moss
> *The Maestro Plays* by Bill Martin, Jr. and Vladimir Radunsky

✦ **Science:** Begin a collection of found materials that make noises (pots and pans, pan lids, empty jars and mugs, empty tin cans; empty Pringle containers, and so on.) and invite children to bring other items to add to the collection.

String Instruments

Note: This lesson builds on the content that was presented in the lesson titled "Introduction to Instruments." If you began the bulletin board display about musical instruments, each of the following lessons will add to it. Ask parents to send in magazines that contain pictures of musical instruments.

Time

15 minutes

Materials

pictures of string instruments
violin or an example of
     another string instrument
recording of string instrument
     performances (classical
     examples are abundant,
     but consider bluegrass
     options, too)

Objectives

Children will:
1. Name at least one string instrument.
2. Say that instruments with strings on them are *string instruments*.

Lesson

◆ Remind the children that they have talked about the four main types of musical instruments.
◆ Tell them that today's lesson will emphasize the string instrument category, and show them the sample string instrument and pictures.
◆ Show them how sound is made on a string instrument by plucking the strings or using a bow to make sounds.
◆ Tell the children that sometimes a violin is called a fiddle, and play a short musical piece played with a violin (or other strings).
◆ If possible, show children the strings that are inside a piano.
◆ Tell the children that throughout the next few days, we will be making class posters showing the various types of musical instruments. Say, "We will be making a set of posters over the next few days to put up in our classroom. This special project will help others know what we're learning. Today we are beginning with the string instrument poster."

Modifications/Accommodations

Autism: Use pictures, objects, and gestures as a visual reference throughout the lesson. During the assessment show the child two string instruments and ask him to point to a specific one. For example, say, "Which one of these instruments is a violin?"

Speech or Language Impairments: During the review provide a forced-choice question. Hold up a selected instrument or photograph of the instrument. For example, show a violin and ask him to name it. If the child does not respond, say "This violin is a string instrument because it is played by plucking the _____."

Hearing Impairments: Seat the child across from you so he can see your lips and face. Repeat words as needed, checking for understanding periodically during the lesson. Allow the child to touch and feel the various instruments that are played: a violin, for example.

Visual Impairments: Replace photos of instruments with real string instruments. Allow the child to feel each instrument during the lesson, review, and assessment. If instruments are not available, describe each photograph in detail.

Review

Ask children to name as many examples of string instruments as they can (use pictures as prompts for them).

Assessment Strategy

Ask individuals to name one example of a string instrument.

Cognitive and/or Developmental Disabilities: Review the meaning of string instruments several times, periodically checking to be sure the child understands.

Emotional Disturbance: Provide consistent levels of reinforcement to the child for participating throughout the lesson.

Other Health Impairments/Attention Deficit Hyperactivity Disorder: Establish a consistent signal, such as a raised finger, to get the child's attention. Make sure that you have the child's attention before giving instructions.

Orthopedic Impairments: Assist the child as needed to participate in creating the string instrument poster.

Curriculum Connections

✦ **Art:** Provide a large piece of poster board or butcher paper and encourage children to tear examples from magazines to glue onto the display (or they may cut with scissors, if they have begun this skill). When the poster is complete, put it on the classroom bulletin board about musical instruments. This activity should continue until children are satisfied that they have included all the pictures they can find.

✦ **Music:** Invite guest artist to come and play a banjo or a mandolin. Make sure he or she understands that children will be curious about the instrument and request that he or she keep the performance brief to accommodate children's physical needs.

✦ **More Music:** During Center Time, play examples of string instrument recordings for children to enjoy as they do other activities in the classroom.

Wind Instruments

Note: This lesson builds on the content that was presented in the lesson titled "Introduction to Instruments."

Time
15 minutes

Materials
pictures of wind instruments
clarinet or an example of
   another wind instrument
recording of wind instrument
   performances (classical
   examples are abundant)

Objectives

Children will:
1. Name at least one wind instrument.
2. Say that instruments that people play by blowing into them are called *wind instruments.*

Lesson

✦ Remind that children that they have talked about the four main types of musical instruments.
✦ Tell them that today's lesson will emphasize the wind instrument category, and show them the sample clarinet and pictures of other wind instruments.
✦ Show them how sound is made on a wind instrument by blowing into the clarinet to make sounds.

Modifications/Accommodations

Autism: Use pictures, objects, and gestures as a visual reference throughout the lesson. During the assessment, show the child two wind instruments and ask the child to point to a specific one. For example, ask, "Which one of these instruments is a clarinet?"

Speech or Language Impairments: During the review provide a forced-choice question. For example, show the child a clarinet or a picture of a clarinet and ask her if it is a clarinet or a recorder.

Hearing Impairments: Seat the child across from you so she can see your lips and face. Repeat words as needed, checking for understanding periodically during the lesson. Allow the child to touch and feel the various wind instruments that are played.

Visual Impairments: Replace photos with real wind instruments. Allow the child to feel each instrument during the lesson, review, and assessment. If instruments are not available, describe each photograph in detail.

Cognitive and/or Developmental Disabilities: Review the meaning of *wind instruments* several times, periodically checking to be sure the child understands.

Emotional Disturbance: Provide consistent levels of reinforcement to the child for participating throughout the lesson.

Other Health Impairments/Attention Deficit Hyperactivity Disorder: Establish a consistent signal, such as a raised finger, to get the child's attention. Make sure that you have the child's attention before giving instructions.

Orthopedic Impairments: Assist the child as needed to participate in creating the wind instrument poster.

Review

Ask children to name as many examples of wind instruments as they can (use pictures as prompts for them).

Assessment Strategy

Ask individual to name one example of a wind instrument.

Curriculum Connections

✦ **Art:** Provide a large piece of poster board or butcher paper and encourage children to tear examples from magazines to glue onto the display (or they may cut with scissors, if they have begun this skill). When the poster is complete, put it on the classroom bulletin board about musical instruments. This activity should continue until children are satisfied that they have included all the pictures they can find to represent the wind instrument category.

✦ **Music:** Invite in a guest artist who can play a wind instrument, such as flute or piccolo. Ensure that this individual understands that children will be curious about the instrument and request that he or she keeps the performance brief to accommodate children's physical needs.

✦ **More Music:** During Center Time, play examples of wind instrument recordings for children to enjoy as they do other activities in the classroom.

✦ **More Music:** Show small groups of children how to make kazoos by placing paper over the teeth of small combs and blowing on them with tunes they know. You do not necessary have to have enough combs for every child in your classroom to have one, because you can change to paper with each new child using the comb teeth kazoos. However, if you want every child to take home an example of these simple kazoos, purchase enough combs for each child to have one (these are rather inexpensive items).

Horns

Note: This lesson builds on the content that was presented in the lesson titled "Introduction to Instruments."

Time
15 minutes

Materials
pictures of brass instruments or horns

trumpet or an example of another horns

recording of horn instrument performances

recording of "76 Trombones" from *The Music Man* (optional)

Objectives

Children will:
1. Name at least one brass instrument.
2. Say that instruments made of brass are called *brass instruments*.

Lesson

✦ Remind that children that they have talked about the four main types of musical instruments.

✦ Tell them that today's lesson will emphasize the brass instrument category, and show them the trumpet and pictures of other horns.

✦ Show them how sound is made on the horn by blowing into it. Explain that horns are often called brass instruments because they are made of brass. Call attention to the fact that they are shiny because of their metal. This is the reason they are brass instruments.

✦ Tell children that marching bands are composed of many brass instruments.

✦ Because conductors frequently include brass instruments in marching band music, you might want to play a recording so children can march as they listen to horns ("76 Trombones" is a great selection).

Modifications/Accommodations

Autism: Some children with autism are sensitive towards sound. Before blowing into the horn, give the child a signal to prepare him for the sound. If the noise is too much for the child to handle, provide headphones or ask the child to retrieve something from the other side of the room during this time (increasing distance from the direct sound of the horn).

Speech or Language Impairments: No specific modifications needed.

Hearing Impairments: Allow the child to place his hands on the instrument when you play it. This will provide tactile vibrations when it makes a sound.

Visual Impairments: Allow the child the opportunity to handle "real instruments" instead of looking at photos of the instruments. Check with local high schools to see if they might be willing to lend out instruments for the day.

Cognitive and/or Developmental Delays: During the assessment part of activity, ask the child identify one brass instrument by pointing to a picture of it when you name the instrument.

Emotional Disturbance: If you think the child might be disruptive, use proximity control.

Other Health Impairments/Attention Deficit Hyperactivity Disorder: Use verbal cues as a means to remind the child to remain focused on the task.

Review

Ask children to name as many examples of brass instruments as they can (use pictures as prompts for them).

Assessment Strategy

Ask individual to name one example of a brass instrument.

Orthopedic Impairments: Be sure the child is positioned to see and participate in the activities. When adding to the instrument posters, offer assistance with cutting and gluing if a child's specific disability interferes with the activity.

Curriculum Connections

✦ **Discovery:** Make a collection of items that are made of brass (such as pitchers, urns, plant containers, and so on) and place them in a prominent place in the classroom.

✦ **Group Art:** Provide a large piece of poster board or butcher paper and encourage children to tear examples from magazines to glue onto the display (or they may cut with scissors, if they have begun this skill). When the poster is complete, put it on the classroom bulletin board about musical instruments. This activity should continue until children are satisfied that they have included all the pictures they can find. If you are using this approach during your Music Unit, your bulletin board is almost complete.

✦ **Music:** Invite a guest artist who can play a brass instrument to come to the classroom. Ensure that this individual understands that children will be curious about the instrument and request that he or she keeps the performance brief to accommodate children's need to move.

✦ **More Music:** During Center Time, play examples of brass instrument recordings for children to enjoy as they do other activities in the classroom.

Percussion Instruments

Note: This lesson builds on the content that was presented in the lesson titled "Introduction to Instruments."

Time
15 minutes

Materials
pictures of percussion instruments
drum (your classroom rhythm instruments are a good choice for this lesson)
percussion or rhythm instruments (enough so that children will be able to play them all at the same time)
recording of percussion instrument performances

Objectives

Children will:
1. Name at least one percussion instrument.
2. Say that instruments that musicians hit to keep a steady beat are called *percussion instruments*.

Lesson

✦ Remind the children that they have talked about the four main types of musical instruments.
✦ Tell the children that today's lesson will emphasize the percussion instrument category, and show them the drum.
✦ Hit or tap the drum. Explain that drums are often called percussion instruments because they make sound when they are hit or tapped.
✦ Explain that marching bands are composed of many percussion instruments.
✦ Introduce the concept of steady beat, and tell the children the percussion instruments (especially bass drums) keep the steady beat to the music.
✦ Play any recording and ask children to use rhythm instruments to keep the steady beat with the music they are hearing.

Modifications/Accommodations

Autism: Use rubber mats on the drums if the child is hypersensitive to sound.
Speech or Language Impairments: During the assessment part of the lesson, provide numerous pictures of instruments and allow the child to select those that are percussion instruments.
Hearing Impairments: Allow the child to feel the vibrations of the drums as they are hit. Count aloud the specific beat of the drum. Seat the child across from you where she can see your face and mouth. Repeat words and phrases often, checking for understanding.
Visual Impairments: During the assessment phase, use real objects instead of pictures as the child selects those instruments that are percussion instruments.
Cognitive and/or Developmental Disabilities: Use simple vocabulary and short sentences in your explanations and during the lesson. Repeat key vocabulary. After the lesson, review this activity daily to reinforce vocabulary concepts.
Emotional Disturbance: Seat the child near you during the lesson.
Other Health Impairments/Attention Deficit Hyperactivity Disorder: For the child with ADHD, make sure that you have her attention before you speak.
Orthopedic Impairments: It may be necessary to help the child with an orthopedic impairment prepare the poster.

Review

Ask children to name as many examples of percussion instruments as they can (use pictures as prompts for them).

Assessment Strategy

Ask individuals to name one example of a percussion instrument.

Curriculum Connections

✦ **Art:** Provide a large piece of poster board or butcher paper and encourage the children to tear or cut out examples of musical instruments from musical trade magazines to glue onto the poster. When the poster is complete, put it on the Musical Instruments bulletin board.

✦ **Music and Movement:** With small groups of children, experiment with all the ways one's body can be used as a percussion instrument (clapping; stomping; patting one's thighs, chest, head, and other body parts; moving one's hands back and forth to make swishing sounds; clucking one's tongue inside their mouths; and so on). Record the children's efforts and place the recording in the Listening Center.

✦ **Special Visitor:** Invite a guest artist who can play a percussion instrument to play for the class. A timpani or adult-sized xylophone will attract children's attention. Ask the visitor to keep his or her performance short to accommodate children's shorter attention spans and their need for movement. Also make sure the visitor knows that the children will be curious about the instrument.

Accommodations—Changing instruction to provide an appropriate way for children with disabilities to access information and demonstrate mastery of skills.

Adaptive Holder/Gripping Devise—Any devise used to assist a child in gripping or holding a specific object. An example of a gripping devise would be the use of Velcro taped to an object and also attached to a child's glove to help the child pick the object up.

ASL—American Sign Language

Bolsters and Wedges—Devices (similar to pillows and pads) used to support a child in a specific position.

Bubble Wrap Gloves—A technique often used to assist children who are tactile defensive towards specific objects (often those objects that are sticky or gooey). Bubble wrap is cut into two hand shapes that are slightly larger than the child's hands. The two pieces of bubble wrap are taped together on the outer edge creating loosely fitting mittens to be placed on the child's hands while he is exploring the object. Use caution with bubble wrap gloves as many children who are tactile defensive may also resist any object over their hands.

Developmentally Appropriate Practices (DAP)—Teaching children in a manner that considers their age, individual abilities, needs and interests, and culture when determining what classroom activities should be used with them (often referred to as "best practices").

FM System—An amplification system worn around the neck of child with a hearing impairment. The teacher wears a microphone that broadcasts to the child's FM receiver.

Forced-Choice Questions—Questions with answers such as true/false or yes/no, or questions in which the teacher offers two or three possible answers, allowing the child to select from a reduced range of options.

Hand-Over-Hand Assistance—The placement of the teacher's hands directly over a child's hands as he or she assists the child with a specific task.

Inclusion Classrooms—Classrooms that include all children, both with and without disabilities.

Impulsive Behaviors—Specific behaviors that occur without direct intention or thought from the child and are often difficult for a child to control.

Lap Pad—Term used to define a weighted pad, such as a bean-filled stocking, that is placed on a child's lap to remind him or her to remain seated.

Modifications—Necessary changes to expected criteria on assessment activities for children with disabilities.

Object Cues—An object, such as a toy or household material, identified by the child and teacher, that is used as a prompt to elicit a response from a child.

Peer Assistant—Assigning one child to help another child, as needed, to complete a specified task or activity.

Peer Modeling—Asking a child or a group or children to demonstrate acceptable or appropriate behaviors to other children in the room.

Phonemic Awareness Activities—Classroom activities designed to facilitate children's understanding that letters make sounds.

Picture Communication Symbols—An alternative communication system composed of icons or pictures to assist a child in communicating his or her wants or needs.

Picture Cues—Photograph or picture representations that elicit responses from a child.

Picture Schedule—A representation of the daily schedule through pictures, such as icons or photographs displayed in the classroom.

Preteach—Teaching a specific skill or concept to a child prior to the time when the skill or concept is formally introduced to the class.

Proximity Control—Placing the child within a certain distance from the teacher so the teacher is close enough to intervene as necessary. This distance serves as a reminder to the child of the teacher's presence to help the child maintain appropriate behaviors.

Reinforcement—Use of extrinsic or intrinsic means, such as verbal praise or stickers, to encourage a positive behavior to occur again.

Self-Stimulation—Repetitive behavior that causes sensory gratification (sometimes called "stimming").

Scaffold—Method in which someone with more knowledge helps a person with limited knowledge understand a given concept or response by providing a series of cues in order to ensure a correct response.

Sequence Activities—Instruction that helps a child to understand the concept of putting objects or events in order.

Tactile Defensiveness—Children with an inability to tolerate touch either due to over- or under-reactivity to sensations.

Transition Cues—Any form of cuing (verbal, object, or visual) to prepare a child to move from one activity to another.

Verbal Cue—A spoken prompt that elicits a response from a child.

Visual Cue—An easily identified symbol or physical object that visually prompts a child to respond.

Visual Proximity—Keeping a child within the visual range of the teacher.

Wait Time—The amount of time given to a child for a response. Ample wait time would be based on the child's cognitive ability to plan and make a response.

"Wikki Sticks"—Long pipe cleaner-like manipulatives that have a sticky wax outer coating.

Resources

Additional Children's Books

Anno, M. 1997. *Anno's Counting Book.* New York: HarperCollins.

Burton, V. 1967. *Mike Mulligan and His Steam Shovel.* New York: Houghton Mifflin.

Clifford, R. 2005. *Rodeo Ron and His Milkshake Cows.* New York: Random House.

Crews. D. 1978. *Freight Train.* New York: HarperCollins.

Crews. D. 1997. *Truck Board Book.* New York: HarperCollins.

Darling, K. 1998. *ABC Cats.* New York: Walker & Company.

Darling, K. 1997. *ABC Dogs.* New York: Walker & Company.

Day, A. 1989. *Carl Goes Shopping.* New York: Farrar, Straus, and Giroux.

Day. A. 1991. *Carl's Afternoon in the Park.* New York: Farrar, Straus, and Giroux.

Day. A. 1992. *Carl's Masquerade.* New York: Farrar, Straus, and Giroux.

Degen, B. 1994. *Jamberry.* New York: HarperCollins.

Downs, M. 2005. *The Noisy Airplane Ride.* Berkeley, CA: Ten Speed Press.

Duke, K. 1998. *One Guinea Pig Is Not Enough.* New York: Dutton Books.

Duvall, J.D. 1997. *Ms. Moja Makes Beautiful Clothes.* New York: Children's Press.

Galdone, P. 1981. *The Three Billy Goats Gruff.* New York: Clarion Books.

Grover, M. 1997. *Max's Wacky Taxi Day.* New York: Harcourt.

Hoban, T. 2000. *Let's Count.* New York: Greenwillow.

Hort, L. 2003. *The Seals on the Bus.* New York: Holtzbrinck.

Lionni, L. 1992. *A Busy Year.* New York: Scholastic Inc.

Maloney, P. 2003. *Bronto Eats Meat.* New York: Dial.

Maxley, S. 2001. *ABCD: An Alphabet Book of Cats and Dogs.* Boston: Little, Brown & Company.

Mayer, M. 1993. *A Boy, A Dog, A Frog, A Friend.* New York: Puffin.

McMullan, K. 1998. *If You Were My Bunny.* New York: Cartwheel.

Miller, V. 2002. *Ten Red Apples.* Cambridge, MA: Candlewick.

Murdock, H. 1990. *There Was an Old Woman Who Swallowed a Fly.* New York: Penguin.

Potter, B. 1991. *Tale of Peter Rabbit.* New York: Penguin.

Priceman, M. 1996. *How to Make an Apple Pie and See the World.* New York: Bantam Doubleday Dell.

Raffi. 2003. *The Wheels on the Bus.* New York: Random House.

Shefelbine, J. 1998. *A Lot of Hats.* New York: Scholastic, Inc.

Stevens, J. 2005. *My Big Dog.* New York: Random House.

Strickland, P. 1990. *Digging Up the Road.* New York: Orchard Books.

Strickland, P. 1993. *Working Wheels.* New York: Dutton.

Tyson, L. 2003. *An Interview with Harry the Tarantula.* New York: National Geographic Society.

Walsh, E. 2000. *Mouse Magic.* New York: Harcourt.

Walsh, E. 1995. *Mouse Count.* New York: Voyager Books.

Walsh, E. 1989. *Mouse Paint.* New York: Orchard Books.

Walton, R. 2001. *One More Bunny: Adding from One to Ten.* New York: HarperCollins.

Walton, R. 2004. *Bunny Christmas: A Family Celebration.* New York: HarperCollins.

Willems, M. 2003. *Don't Let the Pigeon Drive the Bus!* New York: Hyperion.

Zekauskas, F. 2004. *Just Schoolin' Around: The Red Sweater.* New York: Scholastic, Inc.

Zion, G. 1956. *Harry the Dirty Dog.* New York: HarperCollins.

Teacher Resources

Arbuthnot, M., R. Bennett & Z. Sutherland. 1976. *The Arbuthnot Anthology of Children's Literature, Fourth Edition.* New York: William Morrow & Company.

Behrend, K. 1991. *Guinea Pigs: A Complete Pet Owner's Manual*. New York: Barrons Educational Series, Inc.

"Foods and Festivals," in *The Scholastic Early Childhood, Theme Builders for Kindergarten*. 1996. New York: Scholastic, Inc.

Quinn, C. & C. Luetje. 1982. *Hooray for Holidays: A Book of Celebrations*. Redding, CA: Judy/Instructo.

Schiller, P. 2006. *Fabulous Food*. Beltsville, MD: Gryphon House, Inc.

Schiller, P. 2006. *The Infant/Toddler Photo Activity Library.* Beltsville, MD: Gryphon House, Inc.

Schiller, P. 2007. *Preschool Photo Activity Library.* Beltsville, MD: Gryphon House, Inc.

Strong, T. & D. Lefevre. 1995. *Parachute Games*. Champaign, IL: Human Kinetics Publishers.

Warner, L. & K. Craycraft. 1987. *Fun with Familiar Tunes*. Carthage, IL: Good Apple Publishing, Inc.

Index of Children's Books

Index

X

Y

Z